Reflections in a Paper Moon
Book One
Chased by the Dragon
L. A. Espriux

Book One titled *Chased by the Dragon* is first of a series describing the traumatic beginning of a life mingled in turmoil, overcoming obstacles, and eventually leading to the Vietnam jungles of Southeast Asia. But this story is not just about ambivalence of one's nature, about violence of war, or even about beating the odds. It is memoir left from one generation to another, exposing the roots buried within genealogical myth of mortal expectation and meaning of the term duty. This narrative beginning of an extraordinary journey that promises to take the reader into darkest valleys of what defines humanity, ultimately leading to a crossroad of extraordinary potential or eternal consequence. *Chased by the Dragon* is a chimera born of more than shadow or dream: all things subliminal Reflections in a Paper Moon.

Reflections in a Paper Moon Book One

Printed in the United States of America

Softcover ISBN: 979-8-9867838-5-7

eBook ISBN: 979-8-9867838-6-4

Published by L. A. Espriux
Publication Date 09/20/2024

Special dedication to Rudy and Jean

Acknowledgement to the Artist of this Book

Front Cover Original Artwork by *Cendi Baugus*
Part One Illustration **First Ellipse** by *Jean Hamby Baugus*
Part Two Illustration **Dark in a Tiger's Eye** by *Bonnie Blackmon Guirguis*
Part Three Illustration **Dragons of Air** by *Cendi Baugus*
Part Four Illustration **China Moon Rising** by *Cendi Baugus*

CONTENTS

Part 1: First Ellipse..4

Poem: Travelled Distance..5

Chapter 1: Valleys in Early Reflection.............................6

Chapter 2: Ghosts of Liberty Town................................15

Chapter 3: Family Chronicles..30

Chapter 4: Revelations..42

Part 2: Dark in a Tiger's Eyes.......................................61

Poem: Dreamer...62

Chapter 5: The Awakening..63

Chapter 6: Someone Else in the Mirror.........................79

Chapter 7: Confessions..104

Part 3: Dragons of Air...126

Poem: Remembrance Day..127

Chapter 8: The Island of Paradise Lost.........................128

Chapter 9: Becoming a Marine.....................................143

Chapter 10: FMF Westpac Vietnam..............................167

Chapter 11: Vision of Shangri-La..................................186

Chapter: 12: Making of a Sergeant................................205

Chapter 13: Finding Excalibur......................................217

Chapter 14: Slaying the Dragon....................................229

Chapter 15: Revival of Past Sins...................................240

Chapter 16: Taking of Hill 34..257

Chapter 17: Operation Elysian Fields............................273

Chapter 18: The Rain of Hanoi Hannah.........................282

Chapter 19: Wind Called Mariah...................................298

Part 4: Signs from the East...311

Poem: China Eyes..312

Chapter 20: Hong Kong Queen of the Orient.................313

Chapter 21: Star of Providence.....................................336

Chapter 22: Sins of Wander Lust...................................352

Chapter 23: Beacon in the Night...................................375

Chapter 24: The Color of Marine Green........................384

Chapter25: Messengers Sent from Beyond...................392

First Ellipse

Traveled Distance

Hearts broken yet to mend
Rich and beautiful places already been
Where sunsets golden splash a striated sky
Where dreams and shadows twined together lie
And I in ocean deep wish to sleep
Among the souls of noble men
To know no more the world of air and fire
To be free of love and all desire
And pass through the center to see the end
Atoms and constellations before time began
Where galaxies adorn a celestial queen
From inside black holes chorus of angels sing
Where particles inferno of sun and wind
A spark in new heaven all born again
Made of greater stuff than flesh and bone
A new star ignited bright spreading in night
A crystal light to see or to blind the sight
Distant travelers this world made to walk
To know as once I was known

L. A. Espriux

Chapter 1

Valleys in Early Reflection

*M*ountains and valleys of the moon appear discernable in *the full symmetry of a bright lunar day. Nearly I can reach out and touch the contour of this alien   landscape: a presence taken for granted by curriculum of predictability lighting way to sojourners through errant time. Almost I see reflection of what was, what might be now. Almost I see eclipse of another future shining naked through window of my soul long before this constellation traveler traversed immutable course through heavenly passage. Almost I glimpse face of another face painted upon crumpled canvas of faces erased by hand of steady time. And wonder if I might see their many faces again.*

Basque people hold a tradition that w*hen spring Doves return over peaks of the Pyrenees and gather into the budding branches, this sign of the "Gernikako Arbola," a fabled oak tree in Gernika, where the early Basque and the Castile establish a peace treaty remembered as the Biscayan* **First**

Laws. This is the Basque heart, the Basque soul, testament to all future generations first sired at the ancient feet of the European continental divide. According to the dictionary of names, my surname means *Mighty in Battle*; my family name originating from old Euskera, a lost derivative of the feminine connotation that translates *"a spirit beautiful"*. It is unclear if this is a measure of affirmation or inflection of characteristic, only that the root meaning very old in Basque genealogy. It is through this genesis that children inherit the inscribed values of their father's father, from blood to blood, in acts of war and deeds of conquest. Written in this blood the hope of worldly kingdoms etched into concentric patterns left behind in time. After my generation no more the promise reflected through these eyes; no more will the call of the Pyrenees echo my soul, except by a will greater than flesh and bone: a faith more abiding than this passage of spirit only. Even as I write this testament, I am aware that memory, like history, subjective, and laced with myth. Nor always records the whole truth. Nevertheless, I will endeavor to provide clear reflection with some license of trusted witness.

Born under the constellation of Pisces in the Chinese year of the Dragon, I survive by a miracle. It is in the lamb of winter, one of those cold dark mornings when the wind blows from the north-east, as remembered by my mother. It is a difficult birth that nearly kills us both. In those days, I suppose medical knowledge less rehearsed than it is today; or maybe because in military facilities there are fewer live deliveries. Whatever the reason, the doctor forced to make a difficult decision. Better to sacrifice the infant, than lose the mother. Using a pair of forceps, he pushes into the canal, clamps firmly, and mightily yanks. The prevailing acceptance is that the head will separate. My skull misshapen, bruised black and blue, I cry my first breath. Maybe I knew even then the world of men, reluctant to be born.

Poor Jean, a young girl of nineteen, must massage behind my ears daily to release the delicate appendages pinned into deep depressions

left by the metal forceps. I suppose I must have been a frightful sight-
- a bit alien-- a bit horrifying to a new mother, who has known only
rejection in life. I am her first born--or at least the one that survives-- and
she loves me, nurses me into the human race. If the doctors told her
anything else about the anomaly of my birth, she does not remember.
She is still too young to accept the responsibility of a new child alone,
too traumatized to comprehend the meaning. In her mind, I am the
miracle of a man-child issued from her own body. Also, I am the first
heir apparent to her dashing young husband, a man nurtured upon
the Ventura foothills of Southern California on opposite side of the
grand North American divide.

My father, the prodigal of my namesake, fulfills in measure the
romantic dreams of a young girl in love. He is every bit a Smiling Jack,
handsome and dashing in his Air Force uniform. At least this is how I
remember him from one faded photo my mother chooses not to burn.

He and my mother divorce before I turn two. Packing her bags
one night, and me like a papoose, she catches a train headed east. We
live in Oxnard California at the time. This promised land of my
father'snativity becomes a prison of despair. Intended to be a transfer
so thatmy mother might be close to a family she felt never to have. In
reality itis a purgatory, trapping her in a dusty impoverished town of
Spanish America nestled between the vast expanse of open sea and a
barrier of dry desolate lands stretching endlessly into a blanket of smog.
The worst part, she has evidence that her husband-- yes, my father--
seeing anotherwoman! This isjust another betrayal in her life. Just another
history of pain,she wishes not to remember.

I have only a vague recollection of the night we depart. I play in the
center of a bed with four wooden posts and roll the red wheels of a blue
toy motorcycle on the taunt bedcover. My mother enters the room
crying and begins dressing me. I witness fear for the first time, fear in her
eyes of an angry dark shadow snarling from the hallway. Then I begin to

cry. A horn blast from outside, she sweeps me up in her arms and carries me into the night. In the receding distance I hear voices of confusion; my mother weeping, as she climbs into a waiting taxi. I will later remember that blue motorcycle slipped from consciousness on this terrible night, never to be handled again. Also lost presence of peaceful serenity and of something innocent; something absent and left in the shadows. It will be a lifetime before I see my father again.

Existence proves to be not easy for a young woman alone in the post-World War days of economic revival. True that Korea has raised its head and that America struggles against the ever-expanding serpent of Communism. Nevertheless, the conflict distant; and except for those directly involved, it seems only vaguely real. Reality to my mother is daily survival and her new baby to care for. She lands a job with Southern Bell as an assistance operator: a beautiful voice, my mother, a sweet southern bell herself, dripping with the pleasantry of magnolia. Perhaps Southern Bell shared my bias when they hire her. However, she suffers from bad health and consequence of a poor diet. I believe that at least once she may have died were it not for me.

I am perhaps three, the recollection of the event much in a haze. There is a large stuffed pink elephant; and I believe a companion monkey. My mother lay in bed all day and is very sick. Evening shadows creep sinister, a fist of darkness closing around the one-room apartment. In a sudden fit of lucid panic, my mother weakly pleads for me to go next door for help and then succumbs into feverish delirium. I cannot say exactly what triggered in my mind. The door handle reach too high for my small arms, so I use the pink stuffed elephant as a pedestal. I often consider that maybe the proverbial angels on a pinhead present this moment. All I know is that somehow I reason to open the access, find my way down the stairs, and to the door of a neighbor. Those large stuffed animals have altogether faded away into oblivion along with the event. However, their essence exists always like some piece of eternity inside of me.

My mother dates a few men, but no one very seriously. I remember fat Earl with the large powder blue convertible (*maybe a Buick or a Cadillac*). He seems good-natured, but just not for her. There is an older man, who smells a bit like my great grandfather Poindexter. He comes once or twice, forgets his tie, and never returns. Then there is the good looking tall blond Merchant Marine. He will prove to be her Waterloo; and she surely his. I must say, looking at early pictures of them together, they make a handsome couple then. My mother remains in my mind exceptionally lovely further verified by old black and white photos: nice smile, perfect teeth, and a strong shapely body. In fact, she matures into womanhood perfect, except for the blemish of an unsightly dark purple-red birthmark slashed across her left temple. As Oscar Wild puts it, she blossoms one of those 'dappled things in nature': the very defining essence of true beauty. Despite this unseemly physical mar, my mother proves a Siren of mythic proportion; and has already snared poor Rudy, the young sailor man, who hoped to escape to the sea, condemning him to a landlubber's existence.

Now Rudy aspires to be a man of the world, an artist, well read, self-educated, brilliant by any standards. He should have gone on to college; or at the least remained in the Merchant Marines and become a sea captain. I think that deep down he always hated himself for failing to pursue his greater dreams. Maybe this is why a bitter place exists always inside him, a place distant and silent, seething poison especially when he drinks. Despite his failings, Rudy surrenders to the better man of his nature, a part of him too good, perplexingly complex with lofty moral standards, even he has difficulty to reach. I think these ideals of perfect aspiration also the fires that flame his greatest torment here on earth.

Those early first years remain the best. They are the simple good times. The only time I remember when Rudy and Jean really seem in love with each other. After Rudy junior and Penny born, less than a year apart, my parents buy a simple two-story mill village house in a small town near Rudy's family. Together they make it the *"best looking house"* in the whole neighborhood. With some paint and dedicated effort, Rudy is a wizard raising Camelot for his Queen. Jean, on the other hand, has a distinct hatred of bugs, rodents, and germs. She becomes a terminator exterminator with Joan of Arc zeal on a crusade that promises no rest to the unclean.

At this time, we have no television. However, Rudy blessed with a clear baritone voice that carries between the two upstairs bedrooms, each night reads aloud Kipling's collections of stories. During these cherished nights, I fall asleep in the adventure of exotic wars: frightening imagery of creatures and unspeakable action. It terrifies me and soothes me at the same time, creating a place of imagination in my mind, a place thatI like to retreat to even after all these years. This Rudy is the one I love and respect. The Rudy I will always remember with certain awe, as one might revere the words of wisdom from the lips of an ancient king.

It is while living in this house that I become aware of time, and a sense of what it means to be timeless. The summer night hot and humid, Rudy and Jean sitting in homemade wooden chairs beneath the pale slivery shadow of a China Berry Tree that leans beside our house. I lay nearby propped against a hill that slopes into an adjacent forest at the perimeter of our backyard, a bivouac of shadows stretching into darkness beneath magnitude of twinkling stars. Then a stranger approaches out of night and begins talking, as though he knows us all since a long time. He speaks about heaven, and of things in the earth, that wait to be reborn. He speaks about faith, and of things in life still to come. As he leaves, he speaks specifically to me.

"Child, do you see that star just yonder?" He raises his arm toward a distant point of light. "That is called Alpha Centauries. The light you see now left that system millions of years ago. Many of those stars in the sky are already dead and only their light remains. Time is in the imagination.

We are precious little compared to the glory of the universe."

He departs as apparitional as when he arrived. I remain transfixed beneath that wondrous canopy, my mind reaching into the vastness of time and space. My whole life-- the lives of entire civilizations-- all wisps of shadow between the twinkle of a star-- all that is, but a dream fleetingly remembered.

My sense of mortal reason expands incomprehensibly this night. No longer that boy on a hill looking up at a magnitude of stars, I feel a sense of being everywhere-- part of everything that ever was and will ever be. I see beyond the mountains of the moon, beyond the gaze of fixed constellations. I witness great distant suns dying, others born again, the universe merely a thought in the mind of some great being. I will never perceive time the same after this.

Many years later, Rudy and I sit in the backyard of another house in another town, another time. The crest of a full moon appears on the mountain horizon, Rudy's shadow surrounded in a magnitude of stars etched in the night sky. Once, his shadow frightened me, being the shadow of something else. Once there was a monster in his eyes, a restless tormented creature reflected in the contours of the distant moon that haunted my childhood nightmares. Now, this orb of night different in my mind, more near, it has become a comforting spirit to show me many new ways.

"Do you still remember that China Berry that grew beside the old house in Liberty?" He asks reminiscently.

"That was the first tree I ever climbed," I reply proudly. "The first time I ever felt near the stars."

"It's funny how you remember some things and other things not at all. I practically rebuilt that house, but the tree I recall clearer than anything. I used to climb trees, but that was a long time ago."

"The thing I remember most is you reading Kipling's, *The Man Who Would Be King*."

"Oh yes, Peachy. He was a character all right." Rudy's eyes wander into the branches of a nearby Sweet Gum, then to the azure hump of the Blue Ridge Mountains, the molten moon climbing ever higher above the eastern summits. "No man can remain free, or even make himself a king forever. Sooner or later, all must pay the price."

I think that deep down Rudy a simple man. Always he longs for something in the past, something once he knew, but lost at sea. He has no desire to be a king of the world. Life at sea, all men equal to their task. Only the Captain Lord, his rule by knowledge and by experience. During his navy years, Rudy had taken part in a post war nuclear testing project named Operation Sandstone at a group of islands in the South Pacific known as *Enewetak Atoll*. His ship, the USS Pasig, a World War One refit that still served a relevant purpose, is assigned to re-supply water to the larger vessels. All lambs sent to the slaughter. They swam daily in the hot contaminated waters, ate the radiated fish, worked and played in the fallout of nuclear rain.

Many years later Rudy will grow bitter as he thinks back on those warm tropical days, only a teenager then. In time, he realizes the truth. A fact that he and all the others only guinea pigs left within lethal range to test the effects of a new weapon. Those effects remain with him all of his life, manifesting into gout, painful fissures, and eventually a deadly inoperable cancer that takes him within six months. Perhaps it is this early exposure to radiation that makes him feel bad most of the time. Or, as Jean often curses with bitter conviction: *"It was the alcohol!"*

I actually do not remember many days when Rudy truly happy, as though an infection of lingering sorrow in the past that still remains, which permeated his bones, and contaminated his soul. We also talk about other things this night, as twilight creeps into deeper valleys of night, his face changed to ashes.

He likes often to recall his time spent in the Merchant Marines serving as a boatman pilot bringing one of the big cargo haulers into port. But this particular night he speaks about an event that happened in the past, many years earlier, while home on leave. Rudy confesses he the one driving a car that crashed, killing a boy he knew well. Rudy's strong young body shattered, leaving him with a broken back. A miracle that anyone survived, but five out of six do survive. They all had been drinking; Rudy too young to realize the night treachery of a mountain road. Together they agree to a conspiracy of silence about who really behind the wheel, a silence lasting over fifty years. I do not know why, but this night he tells me the truth, as though the burden of his friend's corpse too heavy to continue carrying alone.

"Do you think God will forgive me?" He enquires to no one, staring up at the stars fading into a somber night sky.

"Yes," I reply after a long silence. "I believe God can forgive all things, being greater than everything."

"Good," he whispers, a dying hiss that continues to echo in my mind to this day.

Chapter 2
Ghosts of Liberty Town

*L*iberty town remains a place with dark legends, born from even darker mysteries. In my young imagination, it is a place from the pages of Grimm's Fairy Tales. It is a place possessed by fire-breathing dragons, haunted houses, headless demons, wood nymphs, and witches. Especially dangerous are angry trolls that live in the shadows beneath small wooden bridges. Other creatures too terrible to describe that inhabit upper branches of ancient knotted trees, whose principal diet being young boys that stay out after dark. There are strangely beautiful things as well.

For example, the lovely old woman that occupies the grand white plantation style house on the corner of our street with an array of colorful flowers sprouting from her faded head. I often watch her kneel tenderly over her tulips planted among flourishing hedges of Rose

Bushes, as a new blossom reaching skyward from beneath the brim of a yellow sunhat reminiscent of mad Ophelia in one of Shakespeare's plays. There exists something immortal in her eyes when she smiles, as though ghost of a sad reflection remains chained in the depth of her soul. The light in her eyes reflecting timeless and capturing somehow the nostalgia of a bygone era soon erased. She is as an element survived beyond all tomorrows, only glimpsed in the present, altogether erased from existence. There also lives the old man with stinging red eyes, sometimes seen wandering twilight streets just before sunrise, a disenfranchised ghost, all seeing and ever-present, but remaining always enigmatic in most everyone's mind. By many accounts, he sleeps in the ruins of a decaying smoke stack of the old abandoned cotton mill site built before the Great Depression. I am not sure if this story true, only that it seems likely. Then, there is my stepfather's dear mother, Bessie Baugus, a gnomish little creature, who makes the best biscuits I have ever eaten, and who buzzes around like a dizzy June Bug every time we stop in for a visit.

"You all are just strangers," she often remarks when we arrive; "Lord knows I pray for every one of my children." Then with a wayward glance aimed toward me: "I pray for you too, Sunny, how I pray for you the most."

I never knew if this to be a proclamation of protection, or her personal battle against some apocalyptic vision of the future. But Grandmother Bessie is a sweet little lady, who becomes old before her time, refusing to change until the day she dies. She will in fact reach well over a hundred years before the reaper of time calls on her again. Even then, she will wane slowly, like a lunar eclipse that will outlast nearly all of her six children.

Liberty possesses worldly landmarks of mystery great as any wonder of the world. The gorge of Devil's Canyon, the geographic anomaly to the north of town, is a gaping hole of bright red clay scooped from the base of a low-lying hill. According to local legend, when the moon is full, and while men sleep, the devil crawls out from a deep crevice and wanders about until sunrise. To the east creeps the Liberty basin swamp that curdles south and then north, forming a kind of inland peninsula, trapping the inhabitants that live there, while leaving only one solid route of escape. In this nether region of shadow and mist slithers every unnamed phenomenon known to man. Amphibious monsters that crawled from the Devonian mud grew legs and arms to become anthropomorphic horrors of the imagination. Other creatures formed from once vital things, now soulless demons with devoted purpose to haunt the living.

Many foundations of old-south estates that once embellished the region, now skeletal remains protruding from overgrown meadows, laced with ragweed and rabbit tobacco. Large prehistoric stumps jut out of fallow ground like medusa heads with roots slithering into the air. Once upon a time were groves of Weeping Willows, Black Walnuts, and Pecan trees planted around edifices of magnificent cotton plantations, hewn down and ripped out of the earth in protest to their existence. Yet, the spirits of these despotic ruins manage somehow to remain regal, refusing to dissolve completely into shades of time.

I remember one particular place discovered by me and my younger brother, Rudy Junior, while hiking through a little-known area in search of Polk-Salad springs. Little Rudy is Rudy Senior's first born, blonde, blue eyes, and a seriousness beyond his years. I liked little Rudy even then, not just because we are brothers born of the same mother, but also because he is someone I can talk to and who understands. True that we have our moments of sibling rivalry; nevertheless, my only little brother remains in my mind a complicit companion of youthful adventure. And even though we will eventually grow into separate ways, I continue to love him as only a brother can. Whatever else might become of us, this bond of blood connection will never change.

It is little Rudy, who discovers first the artifact of a crumbling chimney, like a headstone marking center of the perimeter. An old baking oven encrusted with dark blue ceramic appears among the remains depicting the daily life of pioneer Europeans that once settled and prospered here. Our first reaction is determination to break it open by force. Using a rusted piece of metal tubing, I begin hammering at the exterior, shattering the ceramic to pieces. Then little Rudy discovers something I have missed. A small latch, once released, reveals a blackened interior with moldering ashes petrified by time. We then turn our attention to the scythe of a rust-red cotton gin dissolving to powder with a claw reaching threateningly out of a tangle of sharp thistles. A blood offering from a quick nick makes us decide to leave this apparatus alone. Only one wall partition remains intact, rising chest-high from the rest buried beneath a sea of overgrowth.

"I bet this is where General Lee used to live!" Little Rudy exclaims, climbing upon an undefined perch center of a fallen foundation.

"I can see him now doing battle!" I acclaim, boldly assuming the stubborn stance of the fallen Confederate General standing in Liberty town square.

This solitary statue represents one of the few monuments we have ever seen, being reminder of a history, we know little about. This day, we believe ourselves discoverers of a lost piece from the past never witnessed by human eyes. We will continue to guard this secret discreetly, returning on occasions to keep us in remembrance to the importance of the find. Then we just never go back. This fabled home of Robert E. Lee vanishes into the encroaching foliage lost in time and imagination.

The true beating heart of Liberty is the red brick Cotton Mill marked by two blackened smoke stacks belching a dark shadow that towers over the little town as an unrelenting task master of necessity. This solitary demon provides the main source of employment to the generations that sweat away their lives through changing shifts in lower bowels of a raging beast that never sleeps and never grows old. In this restless belly of industrial innovation toil the working class, whose children destined through provisions of inequity to follow in the steps of their fathers to serve the insatiable needs of a monster created out of the ruins of many divisions.

Grandfather Hugh, Rudy's father, has spent several decades of his life on the graveyard shift. Over time, the pallor of his skin fades so gray that no amount of sun can change. He loves night fishing and owns a red and white fiberglass boat equipped with a thirty horsepower Johnson motor that always needs some tinkering.

"We're going to go out and catch a whole mess of Brim and Crappy with this Johnson," he proclaims proudly to his son, Rudy, after bringing the new rig home. "They'll be jumping into the boat--just you wait and see!"

At the time, I believe Johnson to be a technology that catches fish somehow. I imagine the motor discriminately sucking up schools of Brim and Crappy and pouring them into the belly of the boat. Grandfather Hugh then proudly produces a new rod and reel bought from Sears.

"But this is for them Big Mouthed Bass." He adds with a wise wink. "There's a monster down there somewhere, and I aim to catch it."

Grandfather Hugh remains almost mythical in my young mind. I can still see him standing there beside his beloved boat and new Johnson motor carefully covered by a red tarpaulin, the shiny new rod and reel in hand, and wearing his green waders. To this day, Grandfather Hugh still inspires me with the awe of an old Germanic king survived from a bygone era. He will later retire from his mill position and become nearly blind by cataracts. But this does not stop him from driving. Once, with the whole family packed into his proud 1956 Oldsmobile 88, Hugh shoots through a narrow one-way underpass, barely missing a truck at the other end.

"Damn Papa, are you crazy?" Rudy curses truly shaken. "You are supposed to pay attention to the signal light!"

"Don't worry son, they seen me coming." Rudy just sighs and shakes his head.

The site of Liberty Mill is not without its darker history. Originally built on the bones of an Indian cemetery in the 1920s, rumor persists that six men mysteriously lost their lives during the construction. After the mill goes into production, work accidents among the employees commonly occur, making many superstitious that it might be cursed. In the early years of the Second World War, decision made that time has come for a bigger and newer mill located on the opposite side of town in an attempt to escape geographically as far away from the original site as possible. This new edifice constructed without incident, made of bright red newly kindled bricks, two large shiny steel smoke stacks shipped by rail all the way down from Detroit, and furnished with electric generators large enough to swallow ten men at a time. Several cast iron dye vats, gigantic steaming ladles of different colored soup simmer constantly, each with enough capacity to feed the entire community if converted to the purpose. The new Liberty Mill is without question a marvel of modern engineering and practical innovations, one of many early prototypes destined to eventually revolutionize the textile industry throughout the south.

I remember particularly well a black slug-filled cesspool behind the mill property enclosed by a chain link fence. It proves too high to climb, even though I try to scale the barrier more than once. I often fling rocks and bottles into it on my way back from school. It torments me to consider the many treasures trapped in the stygian mire. My youthful intrepidness searches those depths profoundly, dredging up all manner of horrors. Once I find a dead cat in a gully, stiff as cardboard, and infested with insects. Picking it up by the tail, I lob the mummified remains over the barrier. It lands almost dead center. Instead of sinking right away, the carcass makes a splash on the surface, slowly absorbed into the inky liquid.

"There be death in that pool sure enough," sounds a voice behind me. Mr. Bones, who lives just across the street, looms threateningly over me like an emaciated scarecrow. He is retired now, after working a life-time on graveyard. With eyes dark sunken pools peering out of deep cavities, a face void of human emotion, shriveled and cracked like worn-out leather. He seems to me as dry and hollow as the dead animal I have just dispatched.

"I seen things in the night, especially when the moon be full," he continues. "A boy like you ought not to stir up what he don't know."

He then turns and disappears back into his house. I decide to avoid the place after this encounter. Many years later, the mill decides to drain the cesspool, releasing the many secrets at the bottom. A rusted revolver with two spent cartridges, a live pineapple grenade, and two human skeletons wrapped in what appears to be rotted burlap, like the kind used at the mill to bundle rags. Liberty's sheriff contacts the forensics department in nearby Anderson County. For more than a week, they sift through the mud, finding only a brass locket engraved with the name Gracie Bones, the name of Mr. Bones' wife. Rumor is that she had left him for a piano player twenty years earlier. By now old man Bones dead, too, his past sins, like his life, all but forgotten. His common mill village home of three decades now occupied by new tenants. No one ever suspected him capable of such a gruesome act of murder.

The identity of the second skeleton continues to remain a mystery to this day, but many of the hardworking mill hands believe the piano player got his just dues. After all the excitement ends, the empty cavity of the drained pool refilled, along with an added barrier of bobbed wire strung along top of the fence for extra security.

Not much exciting happens in Liberty. The small mill village town a trap designed to snare those that remain from generation to generation, providing the human grease of much-needed manpower. A place of despotic rule appointed to a few descended from the mill gentry, who live up on the hill in new brick houses. It is a place barely on the map, with few visitors from the outside, except when an occasional passer-through finds it by mistake on the way to other places. Those residents occupying the mill houses on the street where Hugh and Bessie live exist as ghost in my childhood memory, their eyes vacant, the pallor of their skin matching worn-out clothes rarely changed. From one shift to another, they come and they go; a stream of humanity filing in and out of the monstrous belly of a wailing machine that never sleeps, neither at peace. They are as appendages of that machine, no longer aware of the natural beauty in the surrounding terrain of their privileged and unprivileged lives.

The greatest pleasure for most is to drink and to frighten small children with stories of knotted tree monsters that devour all but the hands and feet of their victims; or the joy of slipping a red-hot chili pepper to an innocent presented as a piece of candy. How hollow their laughter now, echoes of demons resounding in my mind to this day, faceless and bred from the mechanical clank of metal against metal spawned from within a restless beast. Bessie wisely determines that none of her six children will ever work a mill shift. And none ever did. Only her two daughters will remain in Liberty, and both will marry men in occupations far removed from mill village life.

Because of the geography surrounding the Liberty basin, a tranquil pleasantry persists defining the picturesque legend of the old south. Trees of Black Pecan and ancient towering Oaks line the narrow two lane streets, hovering protectively over a few more ancient estates. On at least one of these premises rests the skeletal remains of a stone barrier once a fishpond, a pool now dead and stagnant, teaming with hordes of tadpoles hatched in spring. The pond altogether dry by midsummer shows no life at all. Groves of Weeping Willow flow into grassy green valleys, changed light brown in winter, until the replenishing deluge of April rains return. Flowering Dogwood and Chrysanthemums bloom for half the year, filling the air with rich aromatic odors. Even the necropolis of the town cemetery not without a certain chivalrous charm, the entrance guarded by two belly canons poised on either side of a bronze statue of Lafayette. Within are unkempt avenues of a wandering maze, cutting between cracked monuments and crumbling sarcophagi that marks the oldest part of Liberty Cemetery. The later additions little more than sections of cheap hand-made wood crosses or simple pots containing dead withered flowers. In all appearance, the contemporary wealthy now choose burial elsewhere.

I meet Terry, my first friend, in the second grade. Terry is like me, energetic and quick; except Terry quicker, an asset, which will prove fatal. One day after school, he and I, along with my older cousin Tony, play football in Terry's front yard. Suddenly, a strange vampire-like creature swoops over our heads from a nearby tree. We begin instinctively to pounce on the thing. Tony and I miss, but not Terry. He catches the nimble animal by the tail, extending it out toward us. Whipping around, the sharp teeth sink into Terry's hand. Nevertheless, he refuses to release his hold, and clasps the creature by the scruff of its neck using his free hand.

"I never saw a squirrel like that before," Cousin Tony remarks.

We lock the vicious little animal into a rabbit cage, watch it scurry viciously along the chicken wire walls, sometimes clinging upside down to the top, until our youthful imaginations lose interest. We later learn that Tony only partially right. It is indeed a squirrel. But not just any squirrel, rather a flying squirrel from the jungles of South America escaped from a local zoo. We will later learn something else as well. The animal infected with Rabies. Only we know nothing about Rabies or its seriousness. I hear that Terry has fallen ill and unable to attend school.

Then I hear that he is dead. I doubt that I fully understood the concept of death at that time. Only my friend gone and I would never see him again.

The memory of Liberty is not immune to events of even greater tragedy. One summer afternoon while playing on the front porch of our house, I witness an apocalypse in the sky. Rudy has just finished changing some of the wooden planks and added a railing I think designed especially for me to climb. He began the project on the weekend by pulling out all of the rotten boards, leveling the structure by raising the support beams, and finishes the night before with a coat of fresh clean wintergreen paint. He has already repainted the house a flawless blizzard white, adding New England style green shutters, and refreshed the exposed large water meter pipes on the east side with some left-over marine grey primer. As I have already mentioned, Rudy possesses the instincts of an artist, along with ingenious skill to make his home the nicest house on the mill circle.

As I swing upside-down from his finished handiwork, I hear a loud rumbling noise approaching from the Piedmont hills behind our dwelling, accompanied by a rush of hot air. Leaping from the banister, I run to the far side of our house to see what it is. My feet step into a mush of over-ripe persimmons, the sticky goop squeezing between my toes. Then the sky darkens, the belly of an enormous commercial aircraft slices overhead with one of two propeller-driven engines on fire. It appears to be at the height of the persimmon tree trailing burning flak. I watch in frightened amazement as the large commercial airplane continues its descent, coughing and swaying like a dying bumblebee at summer's end. A few seconds later, an explosive blast booms from the direction of the Cotton Mill, followed by an eerie silence. All quiet, except for an unearthly static crackling in the air.

When Rudy gets home from work, we pack into the family Buick and drive to the disaster site less than two miles away. The doomed craft has met its end at the Liberty High School, trailing heaps of scattered debris ploughed into the varsity football field. The crater, still burning, measures hundreds of feet long. The loss of human life and property damage recorded horrific. Predictably no one in the local area knows anyone who flies, but everyone will remember this night with tales of the dead, as though the bodies their own. I think it is the first time in history that the Liberty Tigers missed an entire football season. This is the real tragedy that strikes Liberty's residents the hardest: the destruction of their local team's practice field just before playoffs, and with nowhere else to go. A chunk of titanium-silver plating that landed only a few feet from where I stood that day remains in our yard for several weeks. Being too heavy to lift, this exciting piece of air debris becomes to my parents an eye sore in their front yard for several weeks, until Piedmont Air comes and hauls it away. Rudy and Jean did not wish to have junk cluttering the efforts of their labors, forced to call several times before finally it is removed.

As if one disaster not enough, a second occurs closer to home in the coming autumn. Our nearest neighbors live in a house built identical to ours. Except, this structure so dilapidated that it sags to one side at the foundation, lacking even the most essential upkeep. Three generations continue to live here. And I am certain that it would have served to shelter another three generations were it not for the carelessness of an old man with a lighted cigarette. Awakened early one morning by a bright reflection of orange and red shadows licking my bedroom walls, I pull back the curtains to see a rush of flames licking the night sky like a great blazing Christmas tree. I can feel the melting heat even from here, the house altogether consumed by the time the local fire department arrives. Considering the quick intensity, I doubt there much they might have done anyway. Fortunately, two certain fatalities spared because someone in the house got up to use the toilet: the grandfather, who started the fire by falling asleep in his favorite chair while smoking, and his youngest granddaughter snuggled in his arms. I only vaguely remember this little girl, a playful little nymph always wearing the same dirty white dress, as she played on the collapsing front porch or ran through the unkempt backyard like, as Grandmother Bessie would say, *'a lovely unwashed little savage in need of Christian values.'*

I once saw the interior of this house the night a black tornado tore across the Piedmont area. An evening in late summer, I am playing in the backyard with a ten-cent wooden airplane. An abrupt gust of wind sucks my prized toy straight up and out of sight. Dark clouds boil suddenly over the Piedmont hills and begin to coalesce, instantly changing into a funnel. As the tip tears across the terrain, trees uproot like sticks of splintered wood, chewed and spit out by a chimera monster devouring everything in its path.

"Quickly-- come inside Sunny!" Jean shouts shrilly above howl of the wind and then pulls me into the house.

Rudy is working on a job out of town. Jean, frightened to be alone, goes to these neighbors and pleas protection for her and her children. Not that this house could have withstood the storm better than the one she lives in, but perhaps because of an innate instinct that there is safety in numbers. These folks are more than happy to receive us all. The electricity goes out for perhaps fifteen minutes, and then shudders back on. A tall oak tree towering in this neighbor's front lawn provides a false sense of abiding security. During worse of the storm this giant sways erratically, whipping across the roof and sending defiant shudders through the weakened structure. I remember seeing my wooden airplane stuck in an upper branch. One of the men tries to retrieve it for me using a ladder and two long bamboo fishing poles tied end to end; but alas it is too high, the wind making the climb too precarious. We kids spend most of the storm watching The Wizard of Oz on a black and white TV set. The tornado changes direction and swoops into the lower-lying Spartanburg district, where it inflicts incalculable damage to the local Air Force training base.

I never knew what happened to these hospitable people after their terrible personal loss. The morning after the fire, the family packs into an old pick up and leave with nothing but the clothes on their backs.

"Been nice being your neighbor," one of the young men says politely to Jean before they go.

Like tumble weeds after a storm, they just disappear never to be seen again. My own family will eventually also move, migrating further north toward the mountains of Appalachia. In time, Liberty with all its history and local legends will fade into vague memories of nostalgic childhood. But not before I leave my own mark of destruction.

The house we live in is at the very bottom of the village horseshoe street cut around the circumference of the new mill. Beyond this perimeter stretches miles of virgin, mostly uninhabited forest-covered elevations laced with patches of swampland. These are the last days of August. A field of swirled brown grass rolls from the border of our backyard toward an adjacent forest, creating waves of an amber sea mixed with stalks of Rabbit Tobacco and deceptively deep. Burning trash billows smoke from the open mouth of a rusted oil drum used by Rudy earlier in the day before going to work.

I decide to ignite a stick and begin dancing in circles through the turf of dry grass, pretending I am an Indian, oblivious to the imminent danger. At least twice I fall, my flaming torch slipping invisibly beneath the fluffed dry turfs. Momentarily surprised by a rodent jumping into the air, followed by another, and still another leaping frantically out of the surrounding brush. In shocked horror I realize the terrible reason why! The crackling of burning fire is now everywhere! It spreads uncontrollably through the dry underbrush, flanking me on three sides. I try desperately to put it out, beating the flames with my burning stick, which only makes things worse. I see Mr. James, an old local farmer clothed in smelly worn-out overalls and a gray sweat-stained hat, standing at the edge of the field. He appears apathetic, like a hoary autumn scarecrow placed there to watch the watchers.

"Please help me, Mr. James," I implore this implacable stoic.

"There ain't nothing to be done, boy. That'll teach you not to play with fire."

Now the blaze has grown out of control, racing in all directions, consuming the chafe left over from a dry hot summer. Fortunately, the prevailing wind carries the flames away from the community and over the mostly uninhabited piedmont foothills. It decimates the forest floor, scorching trees in its path, a flash of inferno apocalyptic in proportion.

By mid-morning, state firefighters bring the timber fire under control. How far it has burned, my young mind cannot even begin to grasp. A count in the hundreds of acres and would most likely have reached north Georgia were it not for the moist barrier of the denser marsh. My mother says that Rudy spent nearly the whole night fighting the monstrous blaze with other capable bodies from the community, and then went to work the next morning. I can only imagine the thoughts in his mind.

A police officer and the Fire Marshal come to our house the next evening. They talk for a long time. Rudy and Jean only hang their heads in shame. However, the law, like everything else of that era, was old-south economic chivalry, a point that saved my family from certain financial disaster, considering there are no actual credible witnesses, no loss of life, or real taxable property damage. Also, considering the judicial dilemma that Rudy never legally adopted me, it is pointless for the state to prosecute. Besides, everyone knows that the occasional bush fire an overall good thing. In the end, the unusual dryness of nature shoulders the blame. I often think about the smaller creatures; how they might have fared. To this day, I feel a burden of guilt when I imagine the carnage that was; but even more about what might have been.

The next year, the conception of my youngest sister Cendi; and Kennedy elected to the presidency. It is the year Rudy and Jean find a most wonderful house in the suburbs of Greenville City. The mortgage increases from twenty-nine dollars to sixty-five dollars a month, a sizable difference during those times. However, Rudy is smart and a good worker. The man from the sea becomes a true landsman at last; his past but a distant dream slipping ever farther away in a tide of what might have been.

Chapter 3
Family Chronicles

$\mathcal{T}$ he Baugus family can trace their linage in American history

back to one of the early immigration vessels sent across the seas from Western Europe at turn of the Twentieth Century. Grandfather Hugh, a man, tall and stout, with chiseled Germanic features is husband to a small gnomish woman descended from Black Dutch. As a matter of observation, all their four children are more Germanic in appearance, than Dutch.

Nevertheless, Bessie insists the opposite, especially in light of Germany's disgrace after the Second World War. Hugh rarely says much, often preferring escape into the den after supper to sit in his favorite chair and puff on a briar pipe, while reading evening edition of the news.

"Lord, if it wasn't for the Dutch side no one in this family would ever amount to anything!" Bessie complains each time. "I'm just so thankful to be here. The good Lord knows I am thankful."

Bessie berates Hugh often because she says he has a history of setting a bad example by coming home drunk and not taking good aim for the toilet. In retrospect, I think there some merit to her disdain, considering that for the exception of her two youngest, Larry and Joyce, all the Baugus children struggle with bouts of alcohol addictions. Uncle Junior, a Chief in the Navy, grows to become the spitting image of Hugh. The only thing he likes better than drinking is fighting. And when Junior comes home, sooner or later the sparks begin to fly during the course of a Baugus reunion. Rudy, on the other hand, being next to the eldest, most resembles Bessie. For reasons no one fully understands, Rudy and Uncle Junior react together like oil and water. Almost always they end the evening cursing each other belligerently, making threatening jesters that neither man sober enough to execute, with the exception of once when they nearly kill each other.

This happened soon after moving into our new Greenville home, Uncle Junior pays us a visit driving a sporty new British-Red MGB. He brings gifts for everyone. For me, a toy airplane, a submarine for my brother, and delicate oriental parasols for my two sisters. To my mother he gives two intricately painted Japanese porcelain dolls that bring tears to her eyes. I cannot remember the present to his brother, only that through course of the evening Rudy and Junior get more and more drunk, begin bantering insults, and inexplicably strip down to their boxer underwear. Finally, an all-out brawl explodes between them.

We children are already in bed and come running out of our rooms all at once to witness Rudy and Junior wrestling half-naked on the floor. Rudy ends triumphant on top, his penis dangling in Uncle Junior's face, until he cries for mercy.

I suppose this is when they realize an audience present. They both

31

get sheepishly to their feet, as Jean tearfully orders us back to bed. Junior packs his belongings and leaves never to return. To this day, only the two brothers know what really happened. According to Rudy, the escalated violence began with an inappropriate remark made by Uncle Junior about Jean, forcing chivalrous response.

Later, while lying in bed, I hear my mother and Rudy talk through the most of the remaining night; their voices rising and falling like troubled wind.

"He is your brother, Rudy," my mother's voice carries softly. "You shouldn't have done your brother that way."

"But I beat that son of a bitch this time. You saw it. Just because he looks like daddy and is a Navy Chief, he thinks he can come into my house impressing everyone with his gifts. But you saw tonight who's the better man!"

Then only silence prevails, a silence lasting into the sting of morning light.

Aunt Betty is a suffering angel, and kind to a fault. She always makes me feel special, a doting second mother I embrace affectionately. She gives me all of her eldest son's toys as he outgrows them, and even his clothes. She does this humbly, without expectation of return.

My favorite Aunt has grown complacent in her marriage of nearly thirteen years to a dark burly man named Bruce, who works hard for my Uncle Charles as a sewing machine salesman. Beneath the varnished veneer of Betty's smiling face seethes the poison of many disappointments. Maybe Bruce is not such a good salesman, because it seems he never makes much money. And what little he does make over expenses, Betty squanders on toys for her two children, Tony and Pam, or on jars of creams and makeup.

Betty was once very pretty, like a painted doll, eyes and mouth perfectly symmetrical, as though she came out of a box from one of those large department stores, complete and needing nothing extra. A dominating picture hangs over the living room sofa taken when she and

Bruce got married, depicting them as a Prince and Princess of Camelot. However, as the years pass, both change, but Aunt Betty changes most. Only she is the one person that does not notice. The smooth veneer of her makeup grows cracked with deep lines of despair; her eyes sinking darker and sadder through the years of disillusionment. She wears painful red lipstick, which over-exaggerates the contour of her mouth; and in time, her hair changes from summer blond to a dry flaxen color damaged through many seasons of home-bleaching. Yet, with all this, Aunt Betty remains somehow still regal and somehow reminiscent of the younger version of herself, like a Dorian Grey portrait that refuses to grow old. My Aunt Betty will always remain in my mind a lovely doll trapped in web of her own imagination.

My earliest recollection of my Cousin Tony is that of a quiet boy, secretive, and with a singular pleasure killing small animals. However, I wish it clearly understood that Tony not sadistic, but a true huntsman in every sense of the definition. He communicates with his prey, like a priest executing last rights to the condemned. Tony always has the odor of the dead creatures he often brings home, an acrid sweet animal sweat mixed with fresh blood. Years older, he towers over me, as proud Orion with his bow and pellet gun slung over his shoulder. I sometimes follow him into the woods. This only angers him. He often turns and grabs me by the scruff of my neck, demanding that I return to his mother'shouse. Once, however, Tony decides to take me with him.

"So, you want to know what it's like to go hunting," he says when we are deep in the woods. "I'll show you what they see when they see me. You got to see in their eyes to know what I mean."

Tony positions me beneath a Black Walnut tree, and then produces an empty soup can from his knapsack. Carefully placing the container on my head, he instructs me not to move. Measuring twelve paces, he turns, aims, and fires his pellet gun. The can pops loudly over my head, and still rattling, falls to the ground.

"That was fun!" I laugh. "Let me try."

Tony insists that only he shoots his pellet gun. He repositions me against the tree, takes aim, and shoots. It is another bull's eye shot. The third time something goes wrong. Perhaps, an insect passes in front of the hunter's aim; perhaps a slight breeze as his finger squeezes the trigger. The next thing I know I am on my cousin's back crying, as he carries me through the woods.

"You say that you fell and hit your head on a rock," he demands, once I stop wailing. "Don't mention anything about the can or the gun."

Uncle Bruce is standing in the back yard spraying his tomatoes with a garden hose as we break through the foliage.

"What in the world!" He exclaims, dropping the hose and begins intently to examine the bleeding wound etched into my temple just above the right eye.

I doubt Uncle Bruce believes the story about the rocks. Aunt Betty comes running out of the house, a furious seraph with black streaks streaming from her eyes.

"You poor boy, what has happened to you now?"

Uncle Bruce confiscates the pellet gun anyway and locks it into the tool shed. Many months later, the pellet works its way through the skin. Altogether forgetting the experience, I later think the knot on my brow just a huge pimple.

"When did you get this, Sunny?" My mother demands upon examining the small piece of lead; "Never mind-- thanks to God! And all this time I thought you might have early stages of Elephant-man disease. It relieves me to know that you were only shot."

Bruce and Betty later conceive another child and name him Barry. I will never really know Barry, only I am sure he received a lot of love from two people, always kind to one another; and always they were kind to me.

They say that Uncle Larry turned gay after his divorce. Bessie never stops condemning his ex-wife, and later condemns Larry's only daughter, Jill, as though the guilt of responsibility somehow migrated to her. When Uncle Larry comes home for a visit with his boyfriend partner Gene many years later, all Bessie can talk about is Jill's shamefulness by never writing or calling her father. As long as I can remember, Uncle Larry remains a stranger to me, a frail looking man, tall and lanky, with a feminine character. He might have been considered pretty, except for deep acne scars that mare his high cheekbones. Even as a teenager, Larry keeps mostly to himself, often locking himself in his room when there are guest,allowing only his sister Joyce to come in.

Aunt Joyce is the best of the Baugus clan, beautiful as an angel, possessed with a natural kindness that emanates through the clear blue passage of her eyes. She flutters lovingly to the needs of all, never complaining and always without expectation. If anyone mortal worthy of a greater kingdom not of this earth, it is Joyce. At present she sacrifices her youth and happiness to sooth the selfish needs of others. Joyce wipes away the tears of her brother, cleans up after the parties over, and fills the emptiness of her mother for the rest of her life. It seems Joyce destined to remain forever an old maid, when she meets a divorced preacher named Leroy. Leroy, a kind soft-spoken man, loves food, or any other good thing the Lord might bring his way. He lost his pastor-ship because of a failed marriage, something at the time unthinkable among Southern Baptist. To Bessie, being a good church-going soul, this represents an unpardonable sin. Nevertheless, Joyce loves Leroy. She loves him not as a brother, not as a friend, and not because of duty. And she loves him with all his mortal faults. But mostly she loves him because Leroy makes her feel complete as a woman should feel.

"Leroy stays, Mama, or I go."

Bessie knows for the first time that Joyce has made up her mind. There is nothing more to say: nothing she can do. Despite her moral conviction, Bessie accepts the divorced preacher as her new son in law.

In time, I think she even grows fond of Leroy. At least she stops referring to him as the prodigal son.

"You're worth a million dollars," Leroy often says to Bessie when she gets into one of her obstinate moods.

She only turns her head and smilesas only Bessie Baugus can. As for Leroy, his greatest passion is to feed the world. After marrying, he and Joyce purchase a parcel of land near Lake Greenwood. Many months of hard work they restore a dilapidated water paddlemill built along the path of a dammed creek. Together they will fulfill Leroy's lifelong vision to produce his own packaged grits and cornmeal. Leroy's dream will last for as long as dreams do. Less than a decade later, he sadly sells his family christened *Steward's Stone Wheel Mill* to a northern couple of and submits to a retirement of failing health, eventually leading to convalescence. Poor Joyce remains steadfast at hisside, being both grace and the curse of her good nature.

Aunt Ruth looks the spitting image of Rudy. She can consume as much alcohol as Rudy and Junior together and still walk a straight line. Being a certified nurse, a fact she never lets anyone forget, makes her aware of many secrets about getting high without anyone knowing. Unfortunately, Ruth will later suffer from Type One Diabetes that eventually cripples her with a series of progressive amputations, as well as damage to her retinas. She is married to a salesman named Charles, a half-Jewish fellow on his father's side, who has a knack for wheeling business. They team together and produce two boys named Ike and Kit

Ike is the eldest, born with an anomaly of fiery red hair and a defectin one ear requiring several surgeries. Kit, on the other hand, arrives in the world with an angelic countenance, disarming to anyone who does not know him. Ike and Kit turn into angels all right, but not the kind from heaven. This terrible twosome run around the house naked in the presence of visitors, rarely bathe, except when the babysitter able to catch them; and whosetoilet training learned from the family pet. Once, while we are visiting, Ike clothed only in an Indian bonnet, walks boldly to the edge of the roaring fireplace and proudly releases a stream of pee. Not Rudy or Jean, neither Charles, nor Ruth say anything, but continue to sip their beverages as though nothing has happened. Once finished relieving himself, the red-headed savage proudly smiles and runs into another part of the house hooting and howling.

You may think that I judge my favorite cousins harshly, but in reality, I envy their free spirit, the untamed harness of their natures defiant of all social restraints. Perhaps, had Ruth and Charles had exercised greater attentiveness as parents, these two boys may have achieved even truer greatness. Instead, they find comfort in shadowy reflection of that greatness. Ike joins the Shriners, aspires to become one of Greenville's more successful businessmen, gets married, sires two sons, and builds a home in the wealthier section of Paris Mountain. Kit, on the other hand, marries and divorces more than once. Alcohol becomes Kit's greatest demon, women the nemesis of his torment.

For many years, he and Ike share a business cleaning carpets and upholstery, but eventually have a falling out. Kit moves to Myrtle Beach, South Carolina, and lives many years a life he hates; married to a woman he could never really know. Later he returns to Greenville and opens a successful antique store. Just as the two brothers are getting to know each other again, Kit suffers a tragic end, murdered by a fatal shot to the head inside his shop. It seems his ex-girlfriend and business partner arranged to have him silenced before he can testify at her fraud trial. The boyfriend that pulled the trigger arrested and sent to prison. He should have gotten the death penalty, but spared by a life imprisonment law. Because of a conspiracy of silence, not enough evidence to convict the girlfriend. Ike will never completely get over the loss of his brother. Nor will I ever forget.

It is a documented fact that the Money family first came to Americaa few years prior to the Great Depression. Cynthia Jane Money is the last of several children born to an honest hard-working family prior to the Great Depression. Her father one of America's last Black Smiths still considered a trade of substance during those early years of the twentieth century. His profession doomed to die in the wake of the automobile. Cynthia gets married young to a handsome tall Englishman named Herman William Poindexter, an uncommon stone embedded in a cluster of common society. According to family legend, my great grandfather's father and his half-Jewish wife flee England to escape the wrath of the local monarchy. Their offense is anyone's guess, only that the couple abandons family and wealth to begin a new life on shores of the distant North American continent. They buy a piece of property on 34th street in the greater metropolitan district of New York. In later years, they bear a son and name him Herman after his father. When Herman Poindexter turns sixteen years old, he strikes-off on his own, following tracks of the railroad.

Herman and Cynthia meet in *Shorterville*, Alabama and are eventually married. They will produce four lovely daughters: May, Lee (my grandmother), Mildred, who I never met, and Anne Mari, the sweetest woman you will ever want to know. My great grandmother insists until the day she dies that somewhere a land deed exist proving that Herman's widower father still owned the land on 34th street before dying mysteriously in 1929. She further insists that her father-in-law murdered and the land stolen by those in high places to make room for the Empire State Building project. On two separate occasions, detectives hired to make investigation at the New York land claims office, never to be heard from again.

"Somewhere is a wooden trunk," my great grandmother swears; "and hidden in that trunk a will and original deed with Herman's father's signature. Once we find it, we'll all be richer than with beans!"

Of course, the fabled trunk never surfaces, with the family legend remaining an unsolved mystery to this day. But like all legends, it is the very substance of plots and sub-plots, leading upon a questto find hidden secrets of promised riches.

My Great Grandfather Poindexter remains in my child's mind a great Wizard. He stands tall and wirily, a bit like a wise old grasshopper with sparkling blue eyes. He rarely says much, but when he does say something, it is less likely to be what one might expect an adult to say. He communicates with animals, as though they are people: some his friends; others vehement enemies. He always keeps a loaded .22 by his side when sitting in his favorite chair on the front lawn, taking a discriminate shot at any Blue Jay that strays onto the boundaries of his property. All other birds welcomed with generosity to the bounty of his feeder, which also provides sanctuary to squirrels, or any other small wild animal that arrives on occasion. However, he particularly dislikes domestic strays-- especially cats! Maybe, because felines are often caught stalking his feeder, the creatures become his mortal enemy. He might have shot them as well were it not for his wife, Cynthia Jane, who swears if he ever kills a cat then he will eat it for supper. Nevertheless, I think that deep down Herman Poindexter a gentle soul, who keeps the disappointments of his life buried and who always loved me as the son he never had.

One early summer just before I turn four, this Merlin of nature shows me how to catch and personally navigate a June Bug. The air thick with the dizzying swarm of emerald-green insects, he reaches out and snares one in his hand. Gently tying a piece of string around one leg, he hands the other end of twine to me, releasing it back into the air. For a time it is like flying an airplane. Inevitably, this restrained scarab collides with one of its fellows, separating the limb, limping away like a damaged B-52, becoming lost in the frenzy.

My Great Grandfather Herman represents to my creative muse a presence profoundly wise. He often shares with me the most wonderful stories about the bird families that congregate at his feeder. He has names for all of them, complete with genealogies and personal histories. They are in my mind distinct tribes segregated by the sounds they make and by the richness of their colors. I imagine these feathery creatures spanning the continents with elves and fairy princesses riding upon their backs. I wish to be small as these, soaring toward adventure with my Great Grandfather holding tightly the reigns. He only smiles at my impetuousness, his clear blue eyes promising that one day we will ride the winds together.

Most fascinating of all his possessions is the red and white 1955 Plymouth sedan parked in a garage behind his home, which he affectionately calls 'Baby Jane'. Of course, I never knew why he called his car this, only it seems somehow suitable to the smooth contours and comfortable matching interior. My Great Grandfather promises that one day he will allow me to drive this wonderful chariot alone. He even buys me a toy replica from a local five and ten cent store that looks just like the original Plymouth.

"This is your very own 'Baby Jane'," he says pressing the magnificent metal cast toy into my small hands, "at least, until you are old enough to have her for real."

I continue to dream about this old car for many years, as though it a fabled chalice of some future coronation foretold by an ancient prophet. I never knew what happened to that 'Baby Jane' after Great Grandfather's death. Only that the memory remains rich in my imagination to this day, a legendary epitaph enshrined to benevolent memory of one I loved.

As in all family chronicles, there are plots and sub-plots, distant Aunts and Uncles, stories told and retold, over and over again like folklore. Sometimes a funny tale about someone's brother returned safely from the war, only to lose his false teeth while fishing and never has enough money to get new ones. Or the tragedy of a sister lost as a child, disappearing mysteriously in a swamp, and cries of lamentation still heard every anniversary of that night. These are just some of the rich metaphors of my family, each with their own beginning and their own ending, and each a part of me.

Chapter 4
Revelations

*E*arly morning one awakes to slight chill of a blue mist that
has crept overnight along the Blue Ridge Mountains and curled along
the foothills of the mighty Appalachians. The sun climbs over the eastern
ridge, the mist drawn serpentine away and vanishes into a clear azure sky.
This is North Greenville of South Carolina. The Greenville I remember.
We live on the Blue Ridge slopes at the bottom of these mountains on
the tail-end of the great Eastern Continental Divide. It is rare that one
appreciates the natural wonder of where they happen to be. It is like the
proverbial greener pastures on the other side of the fence or sweeter
waters in another valley. Here the defining essence of my home, only
I do not perceive it at the time. And once this place of earthly utopia
gone, it is forever lost. Here the beginning of confederation to maintain
slavery fueled by selfish plantation owners; and here this cause justifiably

defeated. It seems odd now to remember growing up in this rural urban community of folks-- some able to trace their not so proud heritage back to battles of the Civil War. Tales of chivalry and slaughter intoxicates my youthful imagination with images of oppression and anger. Not my anger, but an anger of prejudice and defiance passed down from one generation to another. Through these descendants legends and myths of that period continues to remain darkly alive. They are the bitter, falsely self-edified children of a defeated cause, instructed to cling to the insult of that defeat only, blind to the evil that it represents. Physical prowess becomes standard of right and wrong, the facade of outward beauty the only defined good—all fixed in the eye of one who writes as a measure to enshrine history.

I am a shy child growing up. I know even then I do not belong and think myself the problem. Therefore, I spend much of my youth alone, introspective to my social environment. My favorite escape is to climb to the very top of a cluster of Sweet Gum trees in our backyard. I sway back and forth to the currents of summer wind. In autumn I can almost touch the stars, feeling at one with the Harvest Moon. Here I am suspended free, fixed between heaven and earth, neither mortal, nor immortal. Here, only the moment real, the world of men small and insignificant, all elements frozen in course. From this perch in the day time, I can see rich green ivy valleys flowing into the zenith of a striated sky billowed toward the azimuth of a distant ocean cascading into eternity. The only law that applies to these moments, is the eventuality that in the course of time I must return to earth. There is a point in childhood where fantasy and reality blend intricately.

Shadows sometime become real; some shadows of things that were, others things that will be. I think a monster lives under the house, and a ghost in the attic that sometimes hangs garishly from a piece of rope at the foot of my bed. My youngest sister Cendi shares with me many years later that personal research reveals our childhood home occupies the site of an Indian hunting ground. She claims also to have seen and felt things not there... but are. According to urban legend, the original owner of the house went mad, or became evilly possessed. He takes a machete and drives up Paris Mountain to the home of his estranged father in-law. First hacking this relative to pieces, he then murders his own wife and two young children. After this terrible deed, the man returns home and hangs himself. I am not certain as to the validity of this version, considering that southerners love story telling over a good meal. Nor am I certain it is not true. According to some accounts, the police arrest the man at the scene of the crime, and that no one ever died in our house. I prefer to believe this to be a truer version. Still I will never forget the evil torment on that hanged face in the corner at the foot of my bed, as I struggle in twilight between sleep and awake.

My younger brother, Rudy Junior, and sister, Penny, born only a year apart, are two peas in pod, and are both native-born to Greenville, while we lived in an apartment on Rutherford Street. This before we move to Liberty; before I became aware of many things. Recollections of this period vague, only that we lived on the second floor of a building constructed of red brick and with a covered arched balcony above two large box shrubs. This is also the place I soar into heavenly bliss; and also glimpse into the pit of deepest hell.

The day I fly proves an event of memorable consequence to Jean as well. She stands on the balcony feeding our caged canary at the time. I have just finished watching an impressionable episode of Superman starring Rex Reed. Finding a bath towel and securing the cape around my neck, I run and leap over the balcony into expanse of open sky.

"Up—up and away," I shout, sailing effortlessly past my pregnant mother.

Jean collapses on the spot. I am flying in my mind, free to explore the limitless possibilities of the world beyond. For some reason, I think that to fly an innate ability given to everyone. Not until the large box shrubs below our balcony snags me do I realize the terrible deception about things seen on television, along with the profound truth about gravity. Fortunately, I survive with only a few scrapes and bruises after a man on a ladder lifts me screaming from the snare. By evening meal, I have forgotten all about the adventure. However, it will take poor Jean much longer to recover.

The only other vivid recollection of that time remains to this day obscure, dark, and frightening. From the beginning, the blond-haired man from the sea and I do not get along. He sees in me the undeniable evidence of the first man Jean ever loved. I see in him an antagonist, who wants to steal away the affections of my mother. Then one day he grows tired of being nice, and decides on a showdown. I think it began with a toy Southern Bell telephone truck I kept pushing down the stairs. Twice he retrieves it with threatening warnings. The third time he roughly grabs my arm and escorts me into the cellar. Here is a shadowy place, a place I have never visited. He perches me up on a wall beside a cave filled with moldering gray ash, a depository for the wood-burning furnace. Rudy then takes a large leather strap and hangs it on a rusted hook beside my head. He next produces a straight edge razor from his pocket and begins passing it slowly back and forth on the leather strap.

"You know what lives in there?" His eyes glare mean and evil.

Speechless, I dumbly shake my head no.

"They found a little boy's shoe with the foot still inside," he replies, making a final swipe of the razor. "That's what happens to little boys when they don't listen."

He then pockets the razor and removes the strap from the hook. Folding the thick leather strip in half, he unexpectedly lashes me across the legs.

"Boy, you are going to listen to me when I tell you something?" He then grabs my shoulder. "Because if you don't, I'll put you in there and you'll fall straight down into Hell."

I am paralyzed, too frightened to say anything, trapped on that narrow ledge between two devils. Nevertheless, I guess the strategy effective. After that, even Rudy's shadow fills me with a dread unthinkable. Growing up I never experience much of a loving father role model.
Rudy fulfills the greater expectation of manhood, as defined in his generation, representing a solid pillar of strength and unquestioned authority. This also makes him overbearing and unreachable. His favorite pass-time is to sit in the backyard and sip on a can of beer, while gazing longingly into the eastern sky with regret stamped in his eyes. Often he does this alone, preferring the quiet of his solitary thoughts. I sometimes watch him secretly, as darkness descends, transforming him into a shadowy creature marked by the demonic glowing red eye of a burning cigarette, a legendary presence neither man nor beast. Sometimes he will sit there for hours, moving only to get a fresh beer, the restless torment of a disillusioned fallen angel made bitter by earthbound existence.

Many years later, I will meet my biological father. Perhaps, I always thought that with my real father it might have been different. However, he turns out to be a wanton womanizer, pretentious, and a coveter of wealth. Like Rudy, he, too, will one day fall to earth. I will reserve the essence of this meeting for later.

My only true friend and companion remains my mother. We bond in a special way during those early years before she meets Rudy. She protects me and continuously defends me from injustice, even when I err. She is the one to teach me how to play baseball and basketball, a tough coach with a soft heart. She explains the difference between right and wrong, and encourages me to be more than my failings or achievements. Most importantly, I learn from her the strength of compassion, over the destructive might of anger. Jean also bears the stigma of being from a broken home. Her father now lives on a farm in Alabama. Her mother the sole proprietor of a seamstress shop in a small Florida town named Zephyrhills.

Grandmother Lee, as she prefers to be called, remains elegantly beautiful, worldly smart, and strong-willed to a fault. She and Jean just never got along, a continuing tragedy that overshadows all of our lives. Jean's father's name is Oliver Hamby Senior on record as the son of a poor Scott Irish farmer. He will one day become a farmer himself after his failed marriage. A gruff portly man with a bizarre sense of humor, Oliver never had a chance. It is unfortunate to say, but Oliver Hamby fades as a common stone in the brilliant sophisticated presence of Grandmother Lee. It is hard to imagine them once married and that they conceived four children together. According to my mother, it broke Grandfather Hamby's heart when Lee left him, a disappointment he never completely gets over. Yet, I truly marvel at the personal accomplishments of my grandmother. Because of a desperate shortage of men during World War II, it became necessary for women to occupy positions at shipyards and factories. Prominently displayed in my Grandmother's sewing shop is a picture of her in work britches standing beside a newly minted B-29 Flying Fortress, a welding torch in one hand, and a bottle of Coca Cola in the other. She seems happier in that photo than ever I knew her. This enigmatic woman's life continues to impress me with admiration, as I imagine all the places she has been and things she has done.

In reality, Lee emanates a presence iconic and untouchable, altogether lacking in natural affections. Oliver, on the other hand, altogether too human, flawed with natural vices, making him charmingly volatile and unpredictable. He laughs when he ought to cry, or makes a bad joke when he should remain somber. Something dark and frightening about Oliver Hamby only felt, something hidden beneath the facade of his alligator smile, like topsoil covering hiding a trove of dark secrets buried below. I spend one hot Alabama summer on my grandfather's farm and his new family, an adventure of terror and revelation that I have never forgotten.

I just turned ten years old. Grandfather Hamby drove up to Greenville for a visit along with his second wife, Ellie May, and his cute youngest daughter, Linda, Linda, a couple of years younger, adorned with a brilliant southern smile and a nature of simplistic charm making me feel warm and happy inside. My connection to her is immediate, a feeling of intimate friendship never felt before. We hold hands, talk, and share silences filled with complicit communications. As they prepared to go back to their farm, Grandfather Hamby asks if I might go back with them for the summer.

After much pleading by Linda and me, I cram into the backseat of the old Edsel sedan beside my favorite sweet-smelling cousin and arrive six hours later in the delta farmlands of Tuscaloosa, Alabama. Grandfather Hamby has a magnificent spread with fenced green pastures, a corralled barnyard, and all manner of farm animals. However, the animals on this farm will prove not to be the variety found in the story of Charlotte's Web. These more on the order of Orville's allegorical novel Animal Farm, cunningly hypocritical, and possessed with mean spirits. Somehow, they know from the beginning that I am ignorant of farm life.

My first morning-- a morning that starts at 5:00 A.M-- Aunt May tells me to go out and feed the chickens. She first straps a bag of crushed dried corn kernels around my neck and orders me to go out and throw it on the ground with a spreading motion. I can barely contain my excitement. I am a farmer now, just as seen on T.V. At first, everything goes well. The chickens come running up to me, and then into the direction I fling the corn. Then something in the shadows begins goggling loudly. I sling some corn into that direction, but instead of being content, out plops the biggest chicken I have ever seen, with a long slithering neck and nearly my size. I throw another handful of kernels at it. This only enrages the creature further. Suddenly its wings shoot out like an umbrella, as it runs toward me. I attempt to escape, but in one great swoop it launches on my back sending me face down into the dry manure splattered earth. The Goliath creature then begins striking me on the head with its sharp beak. I try to rise up, but the thing too heavy, intent on pecking me to the death. Aunt May appears running out in response to my cries and shoos the monster away.

"You have to watch them turkeys!" She exclaims, raising me up. "Maybe its best we let Linda feed them critters for now on."

However, I will have my revenge before returning home. My grandfather decides to kill the bird and serve it as a kind of last supper before I leave. This remains a most memorable meal served hot and accentuated with Aunt May's special gravy.

This turkey is not the only antagonistic creature in the barnyard community. The pigs rude and altogether threatening, the cows nonchalant moving away when I approach, their bulging pink utters sagging nearly to the ground, choosing to cud grass elsewhere. The first time milking a cow is an event particularly traumatizing. Linda only laughs and taunts because I was not born a girl I lack the right touch. Aunt May has names for all the larger animals. The pigs she calls Ma and Pa, little Oscar, Willie, and so on. The three cows named Mabel, Sally, and Stubborn May. However, my greatest nemesis is Billy Boy, a two-ton bull, partially blind, and with one of its horns broken off. Billy Boy always pretends to ignore me. He will take a position alone at one end of the pasture or another. When approached, he charges like a freight train to the other end. I learn quickly to move aside and let him pass. In time, I give up trying to befriend this reclusive Minotaur. It becomes clear from the beginning that Billy Boy, in his animal reasoning, has it out for me. All that summer, I observe him to stop whatever he is doing when I climb over the fence into the pasture, steadfastly watching my every move with those unblinking cold animal eyes. Inexplicably, he will decide to charge in the direction I just happen to be standing.

"I don't think Billy Boy likes me much," I complain to Aunt May.

"Nonsense," she replies, "that old bull don't see you for nothing. He's blind as a bat and only good for studding. Critters don't think the same way as people."

I take her word for this. Then one afternoon I enter a discreet portion of the pasture, a place Billy Boy never goes to. Finding the pleasant shade of a tree, I lie down and drift off into a lazy summer nap. I awake to a terrible noise, the earth violently shaking beneath me. Looking up, I see the waggling head of a bull with one horn, its eyes rolling around in their sockets. I just manage to turn on one side as the enormous hooves splatter the earth inches from my head, sending a wave grass mixed with mud into my face and mouth. By now, Billy Boy is standing some distance away, staring at me the way always he did. I avoid playing in the pasture after this.

Farm animals are not the only creatures that inhabit my grandfather Hamby's farm. Nor do all things dead remain dead. There is a large room with a walnut dining table in my grandfather's house reserved exclusively for guest. Taking up an entire wall, looms a grandiose painting depicting infamous massacre of Custer's last stand. The ill-fated general positioned nearest the front, his two hands holding smoking revolvers, surrounded by encroaching Indian warriors on a battlefield strewn with the butchered remains of his fallen cavalry. In the background of this darkly macabre scene an Indian kneels on the back of a screaming soldier in performance of removing the living man's scalp, another Indian preparing to throw a hatchet.

This gruesome portray so shocking that I avoid going alone into this room even in the daytime. As I have already stated, my grandfather has a sometime bizarre sense of humor. He simply cannot resist the opportunity to have some sport with the naivety of a child placed in his care. One afternoon he shows me something that continues to give me shivers. This robust man just loves telling stories, and especially to the naivety of a captive audience, the colorful narratives often laced with connotations of vulgar adjectives.

Fortunately, these deeper meanings escaped my youthful comprehension. Through an archway adjacent to the dining room opens a drably furnished area where the family gathers nightly an hour before bedtime in front of a flickering black and white television. In those early days of rabbit-eared antennas, it is able to pick up only a couple of TV channels--even those less than clear, continuously fading in and out into intermittent snow followed by a loud hissing noise. The rabbit-ears, decorated with streams of aluminum paper, preoccupy Aunt May's attentiveness, as she is continuously adjusting the aluminum strips in an attempt to clarify the image. At the far corner of this chamber occupies a leather mahogany brown reclining armchair reserved exclusively for the comfort of my grandfather. The evening ritual gathering in the is room serves as a refuge daily drudgery, a place and time where all equal. The first few days I run here after evening dinner and plant myself into that chair.

"You better not let Oliver see you in his chair," scolds Aunt May each time, as each time my grandfather lumbers in, removing me with a painful groan without saying a word.

One afternoon after lunch, he says that he wants to show me something. He fills an empty canning jar with water, takes a tablespoon and tops it from the pouring sprout atop a box of Carolina Salt. He next takes me into that room of Indian slaughter.

With lightning-fast reflex, he catches a fly out of the air and forces it into mouth of the jar, until it is completely submerged. The fly struggles, bobbing to the surface. He uses the spoon to force it down again keeping it pinned at the bottom. It causes me agony to see even this insect suffer. Though it is just a common housefly, at this moment I share a kinship of one living thing to another.

"Let it go!" I plea clemency, each time the struggling insect surfaces, only to bepushed back down.

Then it becomes still, a corpse at the bottom of a watery grave.

"When Linda was about your age, I brought her home two rats in a cage. They were no bigger than her little hands. One was black as a crow, the other white as snow," Oliver begins reminiscently. "The white one she named Powder, the black, Soot. But them rats soon escaped, and started wandering around the house just like any other pet. Soon they grew big as cats. But we didn't care so long as they stayed off the kitchen table." He chuckles. "But Powder turned bad somehow, maybe because it was made too beautiful. The beautiful things are the worst for evil."

A glimmer of sadness flashes in my grandfather's eyes.

"We found Soot under Linda's bed with its throat torn out. I knew it was Powder that done it. That night as I went to sit down in my chair, I heared a hiss— but it was already too late. I sat square down on that rat's head. There was aloud snap that May heard clear in the kitchen. I jumped up. Powder's head twisted upside down, and those bloody red eyes kept watching me as it scurried off somewhere to die. But that rat didn't die and was changed plum evil. Neither was it so beautiful anymore. In pitch black you can sometimes see those demon red eyes watching, and its head stayed forever cocked to one side like this."

He turns, gawks at me, his tongue hanging out, and his eyes bulging. This moment, my grandfather changes into a frightening apparition, the haunting image of one undead not soon forgotten.

"Old Powder still haunts around this house like a ghost." He continues, looking at me seriously. "Sunny you better to watch out when you sit in my chair. Sometimes that old rat likes to nestle between the cushions, and got teeth sharp as razors."

My Grandfather Hamby then performs an amazing miracle. He fishes out the dead fly and covers the corpse with table salt poured from the spoon, cautioning me to remain silent and to watch. After a few minutes, the mound of salt begins to move. Then out crawls the housefly, shakes its wings, and flies away. I remain speechless. I knew little about death, but even less about resurrection.

"Now don't you be sitting in my chair tonight," he calmly warns, rising stiffly to his feet, and then ambles away.

I stopped sitting in my grandfather's chair after this, and in future make a point to avoid that chamber of death and resurrection. I never actually saw Powder, but I felt its evil presence on more than one occasion. However, I suppose it gave me some comfort then to know that my grandfather can raise the dead just in case. I will learn more about death, and the ways of farm-life before the end of that summer. Two weeks later Aunt May decides to have chicken for supper. She grabs two hens by the neck from the barnyard, hangs their heads from a wire noose, and then lopes-off the bodies with a large sharp butcher knife. One falls dead immediately, the other strikes the earth running and vanishes under the house foundation.

"Sunny, you crawl under there and get me that chicken!" She demands.

"No, Aunt May!" I cry-out horrified.

"You go under there right now or I'll take a hickory switch to you."

Aunt May, a no-nonsense woman descended from the prairies, lacks even a hint of levity or any other emotion that might evidence a sense of humor. Her countenance severe, as a Whistler painting purposely subdued of vibrancy, yet possessed with a depth of meaning like dangerous currents below the dark surface of a swift river. She will later become legal guardian to Linda's only child, who unfortunately comes into this world cursed with a bi-polar disorder. They say that the infant born with demon eyes and that he later took pleasure in being cruel to small animals. Linda later tells me that this aggression provoked by others, because her only son Rick, a kind, sweet boy, who she continues to visit in a prison for the criminally insane. It is my understanding that after going off his medication for a time, Rick murdered Aunt May in a violent fit of anger. This senseless execution marking the tragic end to a life portrayed

by so little expressed happiness.

This day Aunt May is very much alive and wants that escaped chicken. I crawl warily into darkness, as though entering the dreaded gate of Dante's Inferno. Here the earth grey dead powder devoid of life or light, a place alien haunted by a mythical white creature with fangs and demonic red eyes. I find the headless chicken carcass approximately below the position of my grandfather's armchair. It has struck a column, truly deceased in this labyrinth of the undead. Quickly grabbing the wing, I scramble back the way I came. Aunt May takes the fowl without saying a word and disappears into the kitchen to perform the gruesome task that farmwomen know all too well.

"That's the best fried chicken I ever ate," Grandfather Hamby exclaims with pure content after the evening dinner.

Aunt May just stares coldly across the table at me. I think I can see a hint of pride in her eyes. However, the most horrific and barbaric event of gruesome murder will be the slaughter of Willie one bright Sunday morning.

Oscar, my mother's oldest brother, lives not far away, arriving early before church service with an ax slung over his shoulder. He and my grandfather talk for some time, the tone of their voices serious. After their conversation ends, I follow them out to the pig stall. Willie, already segregated since the night before, sways back and forth in a narrow wooden stall. I think the animal knows what is coming. It pokes its flat moist nose through the fencing and begins sniffing my leg obsequiously. It looks frightened and seems to be pleading for mercy. My grandfather appears from an adjacent shed holding a single barrel shotgun.

"Let him go, Oscar," he says reverently.

Uncle Oscar opens the gate and herds Willie out into the apple orchard. He then takes a position several yards in front of the pig with ax in hand.

"You was a good hog, Willie." My grandfather says, aims his shotgun atthe back of the animal's head, and squeezes the trigger.

A terrifying bang shatters the reverent solitude of the Alabama morning followed by a haze of gray smoke heavy with the stench of gunpowder. Willie just stands there for a moment, swaying slowly back and forth, a large bloody gash ripped across the right side of its head where once had been a pink ear. It suddenly charges at Uncle Oscar, squealing madly. At the last moment, my uncle steps to one side, firmly burying the axe blade into the center of the creature's head. Willie continues to run with the axe handle bobbing up and down, and slams into the trunk of an apple tree. It lies shaking for several minutes, followed by slowing spasms, and eventually stiffens with all four legs spaded into the air.

"We'll make a farm boy out of you yet," Uncle Oscar laughs, slinging me up on his large shoulders.

It never occurs to him that my silence the traumatic shock of a ten-year-old, who has just witnessed a most brutal slaying. Later that day I hide under my bed and begin crying for no reason. I never thought about Willie again, not until just now.

Linda remains my first true intimate relationship outside of my immediate family, even more complex than shared with my two sisters. We play and pretend together in ways never experienced with anyone before. We are nearly the same size so she allows me put on her dresses and we have tea parties accompanied by delicious mud cakes. Linda is particularly lonely since her older sister, Shirley, matured enough to have a boyfriend. I see Shirley only a few times that summer, as she seems always to be coming back or going out on a date. At least the rest of that summer, Linda is less lonely with me around.

One day in August during a solar eclipse, we receive strict instruction to hide under our beds and not look at the sun for fear of going blind. I ask Linda if I can stay with her. We remain together nearly all afternoon playing with her dolls, pretending to be other people. We imagine the wonders of what life must be beyond the farm and beyond the foothills of the Carolina Mountains. The last evening, we make a pact that we will always be friends no matter where life takes us.

As planned, Rudy and my mother arrive the following afternoon with my brother and two sisters, after making a hundred-mile detour to pick me up on the way back home from Charleston. They stagger in exhausted from a three day family vacation to the Carolina coast. Grandfather Hamby insists they stay over for a night or two before rushing off.

After a little convincing, Rudy makes the decision to remain at least the night. That evening we all sit out on the front porch shelling Butter Beans for Aunt May to cook up the next day. As dusk settles around us, Linda and I start running around playing tag, until a swarm of bats descend, shadowy wraiths darting back and forth invisible through twilight sky. My mother has brought me a black ship captain's hat as a souvenir that Linda has been wanting all evening.

"Give me your hat and I'll show you a trick how to catch bats." Linda coaxes with covetous appreciation for my recent gift.

I trustingly pass her my new hat. Tossing it high into the night air, once, twice, and on the third throw, a bat flies into the brim and falls to the ground. We pounce on the bobbing cap at the same time to insure capture of the flying rodent. Just luck we escape rabies infection from a bite. My Grandfather arrives just in time, releasing the ugly creature before it can do harm. The bat's claws have badly shredded my new hat, prompting Jean to immediately throw it away for fear of disease.

"Bats eat mosquitoes," Grandfather Hamby says in a pained tone and holding his side. "You kids leave them be, and they'll leave you be. Now get into the house and be off to bed."

By now, I have gotten use to farm routine. Linda and I talk through the wall that separates our rooms for nearly an hour, before finally drifting into night slumber. I awake to the terrible wailing of my Grandfather Hamby. Aunt May stands over the kitchen stove heating up bags of corn meal and placing them around the distraught man's kidneys.

"Don't worry any. Oliver is just passing a stone." I overhear her say to my mother. "It happens once or twice in a year. He'll be okay tomorrow… or the day after."

My mother and Rudy decide it is time to leave and want to get an early start. Break of day just beginning over the rich harvest of Alabama farmland, a place in the sun I will always remember fondly. I feel apprehensive that Grandfather Hamby might be on his deathbed, as I hug him goodbye that morning. If farm life has taught me nothing else, then it is that nothing lives forever. Then, I remember the fly at the bottom of the glass, and am convinced he will not stay dead. Linda and I embrace each other tenderly, promising to see each other soon, and promising to never forget. But we do forget. There will be many traveled distances before we see each other again.

It is good to return back home where chores linked less to daily necessity. Because my mother and I share a unique complicity by being forced early to survive only with each other, we do not always need language to communicate. Jean is not the perfect mother, nor I a blameless child. I think there are times we disappointed each other over the years, but we never really dislike each other, managing always to forgive. I recall many summer evenings sitting on a grassy hill beneath the Sweet Gum Trees that grow beside our home and just talk as evening dew settles around us. Had I been aware at the time of how fleeting time, I would have cherished those moments more, captured that dew in a jar to preserve forever. Often we speak about the past, and how different things might have been; and sometimes about futures of things yet to come, about stars and time without end. One such evening my mother wishes to sharesomething special with me.

"You can see the man in the moon tonight," she remarks, pointing up at the larger than usual planetoid, an intense reddish yellow sphere floating just above the treetops.

I look, but see nothing, except the bright disk of a full moon. "Sunny, look harder, it's right there if you just try to see!" My mother flusters.

No matter how hard I try, I see nothing that even resembles a man.

"Oh, just forget it!" Jean says at last, disappointment in her voice, because her eldest child unable to perceive something so elemental to the structure of the universe.

She then rises and departs into the house. I remain there for what seems like a very long time. I look at the moon to the left, to the right, and even try standing on my head to see how it might appear upside down. Still, I can make out nothing that even resembles the visage of a man, or any other anthropomorphic body. I do not know rather to cry or be complacent. Why can I not see what is so apparent to the rest of the world?

Just as I prepare to give up and go inside--I see the thing! Cold terror creeps into my stomach, changing into a convulsion of real fear, as a shadowy chimera slowly fades into semblance. There, hovering in the night sky, the image of a creature that has lurked in the depths of my subconscious mind since earliest memory. The dreaded thing now fixed in heaven to watch-- not just me-- but myopic curriculum of the entire world! It is the same image tattooed on Rudy's right bicep: an ugly gargoyle creature resembling a horned beast with many evil eyes.

My mother later reveals that the marking actually the tattoo of a tropical dancing girl gotten when Rudy drunk and in the Navy. He tries to conceal it after getting married, a botched attempt by the tattoo artist that results in something indiscernible. To all, that is, except to me. Then, during the fall of the Berlin Wall many years later, I perceive an identical insignia on the forehead of the then Prime Minister of Russia, Michel Gorbachev, a birthmark splashed across his forehead all too familiar; a prophet of Anti-Christ stamped with the sign of the coming beast to run a precipitous course of future determination. This night I go inside and say to my mother that I have finally seenthe man in the moon.

"Good," she replies proudly. "I knew you would as soon as you put your mind to it. Now you run off to bed before your daddy comes home." That night I sleep with my head under the covers and pray never again to look into that dragon shadow hovering over the earth. I will continue to see it for many years to come, until an eclipse of new meaning opens my heart anew.

A lifetime later, my mother and I huddle together on this same hill against the chill of another Carolina autumn. By now my mind scarred by greater fears and inspired with even greater hope. Now the platform of a balcony where the Sweet Gums once stood, the memories of my childhood almost unrecognizable. However, I will have learned many better things through the years, things I wish to share with my greatest friend. This particular night it is time to reveal to my mother vision of another night when once my eyes opened to something new.

While visiting one of the flat top mountains of Grand Mesa Colorado, I see clearly the true visage in the moon through the eyes of a woman I know for only a short time. We walk together a night in early spring along an alpine trail of melting snow; my heart drawn to another destiny, not here. This place found by accident, a place between the stars and void of time. I see poised naked in this Colorado night the moon as never seen before. This woman named Candace tells me to look with my heart and not with my mind. Then I behold her clear and beautiful, a face I will never forget even after so many changes. I see for the first time a nurturing presence looking down upon the earth. It is face of the woman in the moon.

"Can you see the woman in the moon?" I ask my mother these many years later.

She looks for a moment puzzled, blinks her eyes.

"You are right, Sunny. It is face of a woman. How did you know--and to think that all these years I thought it was a man up there!"

Placing her head on my shoulder, she exhales a sigh of relief, as peace of the Blue Ridge settles in our souls, as dew of seasons past.

Dark in a Tiger's Eyes

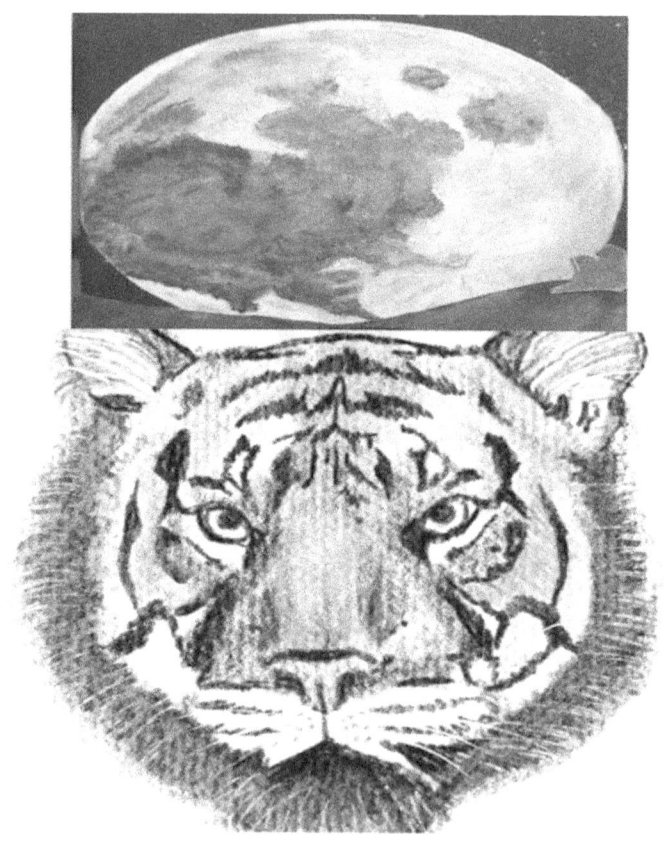

Dreamer

The tiger Dreams of wings

Fleecy white his heart sings

Broken claws changed ivory things

The tiger born on a silver stream

The dove Dreams in jungle fuse

Shadow stripped amid leafy green

Golden eyes in a vision seen

Darkness his step bearing silent dew

The tiger rising from his dream

Reborn new

Chapter 5
The Awakening

*T*o see in the tiger's eye is a reflection confusing. Those early years growing up in Greenville swirl into a mixture of poor self-esteem and confused identity. I become too much familiar with girls in school. I prefer their company. I prefer to play their games; but most of all I feel kindred belonging that I just do not experience with other boys. Even then I do not like confrontation, wishing always to avoid it whenever possible. Unfortunately, the boys also know this. They sense it through animal instinct that warns I am something different. I often intentionally violate the teacher's rules just so that I might stay after school, hoping that all the other students might be gone by the time I go home. Sometimes this ploy works; but sometimes one of the bullies catch me walking home and beat me up just for the fun of it. In time I learn that the best thing to do is curl into a fetal position and cry. This seems to appease my assailant for a while, but after a week or two, the cycle starts again.

My mother expresses increased agitation because always my new jeans stained with grass or my shirt torn. Rudy does what he can to teach me how to fight. He makes me put up my hands defensively and boxes my ears until I cry. Nevertheless, I fail to apply any of these basic techniques in actual battle. I suppose that in time we all begin to share the same revelation of hopelessness. I am not the warrior, nor destined to seize the staff of empowerment. I rather to escape into the world of literature, only paradoxically I am also a poor reader, therefore attending special speech therapy training in the third grade in attempt to correct a speech impediment instructing me on how to form '*L*' and '*TH*' sounds. This helped in my speech, but not my reading. I theorize that I may have been dyslectic, later confirmed by a girlfriend, who taught children with special learning disorders. I fail the second grade and may have forever been silenced by my inability to comprehend written sentences were it not for Aunt Betty.

That summer she gives me a stack of my Cousin Tony's old Superman and Super Girl comics. I think the colorful pictures the hook that most captures my interest. After a while, I begin to recognize words and sentences associated with the vibrant cartoons. Yes--in time I begin to read and to comprehend! After this epiphany I discover identities written in biographies about past lives such as Abe Lincoln, Thomas Edison, and George Washington Carver, discoverer of wondrous uses of the humble peanut. These, just to name a few, allowing me escape into the intricate minds of these other lives. I most appreciate stories by Herman Melville, Jack London's Call of the Wild stories, and especially books written by James Fennimore Cooper. My truly favorite author at the time was Cooper, whose stories inspire me to strip away my clothes and disappear naked into the nearby mountains to live free as one of his Indian characters. This ideal of liberty and social abandonment appeals most to my introvert character, only I am more spoiled to urban comfort.

Alas, I can only experience these moments of liberation between cover to cover. In the real world I feel less bold, forced to hide in the school library during lunch or in the bathroom at recess. I want no part of present society, my truest desire to be left alone and altogether forgotten. However, in time I do make one friend, someone who thinks similar to me. His name is Franklin, a science prodigy, the third and last child born to an extremely poor family. Franklin has made his own reflecting telescope from an empty milk carton, a pair of discarded eyeglasses, and a car side mirror he finds while walking home from school. With a few strips of black electrical tape removed from wire insulation and a piece of copper tubing for an eyepiece, we can actually discern the borders of the Sea of Tranquility through this homemade device. Later Franklin will inspire me with the novel idea of creating a moonscape inside a grocery box complete with phosphorescent stars painted stars splashed into a night sky, ignited by a black-light sun, and a model NASA lunar landing craft. My mother spends many hours helping me make papier-mâché craters and cutting out cardboard lunar mountains. Rudy provides a jar of gloss white paint at the end to add a touch of realism to the scene. After the project complete, I spend hours at night just looking at this grand achievement. Even Franklin expresses wonder at all the detail.

"I think that you are the right stuff that NASA is looking for," he tells me one night, as we peer into the night sky through his homemade telescope. Then pointing to the moon," I know that's where I'm going someday."

Franklin will never go to the moon, but he will end up getting an important job with NASA. On the other hand, I am destined to take a different course. However, I think in the end we both achieve our dream of escape fixed in the vast frontier of distant space. In the third year, Rudy's job takes him to Raleigh North Carolina. Hired as Head

Foreman for a large construction company, he must go where they send him. The projected contract is for two, maybe three years, so the company relocates the families of its staff and pay for temporary house rentals in the surrounding area. In September, we board-up our Greenville residence and move to *Cooleemee North Carolina*, a small farming community less than twenty minute drive to the construction site. Our new home, architecturally inferior to the Greenville dwelling, sags in deplorable condition.

"Only two years," my mother says repeatedly, "only two years!"

The *Cooleemee* Elementary is like all schools everywhere. And like all schools, it also has packs of bullies. How they manage to find me so quickly, I will never know. By the end of the first class day, enemies are afoot, sniffing out the new arrival. The faces different, but the onslaught of harassment follows the same pattern. At least that day I make it home without incident, my spirit devastated. One of these boys stands a giant like none I have ever seen outside of fairytale. He should have been in High School, stuck in the fifth grade since three years. The school will eventually pass him; not because of grades, but because of the threatening enormity of his size. This farm boy will make a fine addition to the Vietnam effort.

It all properly begins on the third morning as I hang up my coat behind a walled partition at the end of the classroom. This morning the beginning of a change that will change everything. I have just placed my coat on a one of many hooks, when another boy removes it and disrespectfully drops my property to the floor. He then proceeds to hang his own jacket in place of mine. Indignant, I pick up my coat, remove his, and replace mine on the hook. Without saying a word, this unknown nemesis strikes the back of the head.

What happens next shocks me as much as it does my assailant. All that I remember is seeing a flash of light and feeling a surge of incredible force. My fist animated into a blur of mechanical destruction. I must have missed more than once in the narrow space, because cracks appear in the wall showing fresh splinters. By the time the teacher rushes in, my attacker huddles into a fetal position on the floor bleeding profusely from the nose and mouth. I receive punishment, of course; but I do not care. This day I have discovered a switch. A switch once turned on, unleashes boundless carnage, somehow making me a little less fearful. The next day in Gym, the events of the previous morning have gossiped throughout *Cooleemee Elementary.*

One of the top dogs decides it time to put me in my place. Leaning over a water fountain and taking a drink, this new attacker shoves me from behind, rupturing my mouth against the metal fountainhead. I cry--I always cry--the difference being that now my tears mean something frighteningly terrible. Once again, I animate into a frenzy of decisive victory. I can still see the shock on his face, as my relentless fist propels him backward. No one bothers me after this. However, I will still face one last opponent. Somewhere always a giant walks the earth.

"I got to do it," he says intercepting me on the front lawn of the school.

He speaks as though this just a job to perform, a job he hates, but a duty reluctantly obligated. I nod my head in acceptance and remove my coat. I have little desire to fight this Goliath. He rises to a height nearly tall as Rudy, thick tree trunks for legs, and with powerful arms to match. And what is the point to this anyway? A slight nudge with only one consuming hand, I am lifted bodily into the air, and sprawl backwards on the ground. Leaping back to my feet, I charge mightily, striking the granite of his body like a doll thrown against a wall. I think here he gives me a few light body jabs, but never once touches my face, nor deploys even a little of the force he might have. With a swiftness that defies his stature, he reaches down, grabs one heel, and lifts me at arm's length. I flail helplessly against the air, twisting and clawing just out of effective reach.

"Do you give?" He inquires calmly.

What else can I do? I bow my head in surrender. He gently lowers me to earth, cocks his head to one side, and eyes the crowd of students that have gathered around to watch the slaughter.

"This is my brave friend," he proclaims. "Don't none of you bother him ever again."

He then lumbers off like some kind of mythical creature. I am embellished with a new kind of respect that day. No one dares challenge me after this public fight. At last, I have found the peace sought for since so long.

I begin to like *Cooleemee*, feeling free to explore the small community with my bicycle unafraid for the first time. I discovered a recreational area with an outdoor basketball court and a practice field designated part of the *Cooleemee High School*. At times, there are a few boys and girls close to my age at the basketball court. I know the basics of the game from my mother, who once played on her school team. Although on the short side, I soon am able to compete with the best. One evening on my way back home, I take a different street hoping to save time. I stumble upon an old Baptist Church, the door standing open, but no one inside. The sun has just begun its final descent, the last golden embers reflecting through the stained glass windows. There reverences an unearthly silence about this place, a silence as one might imagine an exhumed grave.

My exploration brings me eventually to the pulpit. During my youth, I have little comprehension of religion. While living in Liberty, Rudy's pious mother tries once to enroll me into The Liberty Baptist Sunday school. This ends in disaster with me expelled because of an altercation started by yet another bully. They seem to be everywhere. Except for the occasional Easter Egg hunt at Aunt Joyce's church or Sunday morning T.V. sermons, I have little congregational experience. Rudy is a self-declared agnostic. Jean will become a Jehovah Witness for a while, a religion steeped in guilt and apocalyptic visions of God's fiery judgment. Unfortunately, I do not find any particular presence in this sanctuary. What I do discover surprising and altogether without precedence. In a small chamber behind the Pew hang several robes belonging to choir members.

Something about the odor, about the ambiance, the smooth touch of the royal purple and ruby red garments. I am instantly overwhelmed by an erotic urge. I put on one of the purple robes and masturbate. You can only imagine the guilt I feel later as I race home.

To be honest, this is not the only time I have used a garment to achieve orgasm. The first experience happens the summer prior to leaving our Greenville home for *Cooleemee*. My mother sits on the grass while Rudy Junior and I run around her playing tag. Then I trip and fall against my mother's bosom. I remember feeling strangely elated, a feeling of warmth and security spreading through my body.

At this same moment, Rudy arrives with a fresh beer in hand. He suddenly flies into a rage, roughly grabs my arm and orders me to go to my bed without supper. How could I have possibly understood? At the time I do not think either Rudy or Jean possessed much comprehension of puberty. No doubt they went through it, but repressed the associated guilt. Both grew up in repressive strict environments and I am the first child either of them raises.

That night I cry myself to sleep. Aroused by sensation of a pleasant dream, I open my eyes to darkness. The nature of this dream I can only surmise. I lay on my stomach, rubbing against something smooth and soft--something that feels good. Then I realize why I am feeling this way. Today my mother has folded her laundry in my room and inadvertently left behind a silky black slip. This undergarment the reason for my physical excitement, the touch sending pleasurable shivers through my whole body. The more vigorously I rub against it, greater the sensation. Suddenly, I think I have wet my bed. A rush like nothing ever experienced before resulting in a damp stickiness-- not urine, rather something I have never seen before. Something disgusting that has issued from my own body.

In time, I will get over this initial revulsion. I keep this garment remnant for many months hidden secret at the bottom of my closet. It provides me a sense of wellbeing and comfort. Often I put it on in order to fall asleep. This slippery garment--the odor and texture-- embody expression of emotion I must keep secret and within. This dark pattern of pleasant association continues to haunt me to this day. In times of isolation, it becomes a retreat from pain of loneliness and absence through rejection. After this, I learn to exercise carefulness not to show outward affection toward my mother when Rudy present.

It is this very evening my time in *Cooleemee* will crash to an abrupt end. For Jean the move to *Cooleemee* like stepping back in time, representing the poverty she wishes to forget. The dread of importunity she will be once again trapped in a small town, reminding her of the unhappy days in her youth-- and always the fear of remaining too long. The confirmation of Jean's seething unrest boils to the surface when the neighbor's dog, a motley gray Bull Terrier, is found with its throat torn out in the sump-well beside the carcasses of two dead rats. The saga of meaning only too clear, confirming everything my mother hates and fears. The two dead rodents measure half the size of the dog. The killer rat must have been enormous--and rats this big are indeed dangerous--especially to young children! The same night Rudy makes the mistake of his career. He arrives home after work drunk and passes-out on the living room floor. By time I arrive home, my mother has already packed our 1959 station wagon with clothes and essentials. Little Rudy and Penny are crying hysterically, because of something big Rudy has said, and baby Cindy already asleep, secured in her travel chair on the car back seat.

An hour later, we navigate toward the freeway, and then head south to Florida. My poor mother drives all night, which is perhaps not a good thing, considering she has an eye stigma with an etymology label 20/20 minus 1, which translates as poor night vision. I suppose she just had to escape somehow. She appoints me her designated navigator. As the headlights of approaching traffic get near, she moves to the right close to the shoulder. It is my job to tell her if she ventures too near the edge. At least twice, the tires sink into the soft earth at the edge of the pavement, which my mother manages to recover.

"Sunny, you are supposed to make sure that doesn't happen," she scolds on each occasion. "Put your head out the window so that you can see when I get close."

It is a night of adventure, a night I learn purpose and responsibility. Also a night I consume many varieties of insects. A few hours before sunrise, she takes refuge at a motel somewhere off the main route, where we all pass out into oblivious sleep. The bright morning sun fills the chamber of the small motel room like a burning chariot of summer.

We awaken to a park of fantastic creatures: giant green dinosaurs, pink Tyrannosaurus, and purple flying reptiles. We are in the land of Florida. By dinnertime we pull into the driveway of mother's grandparents. Sheis like a younger daughter to them, and I am as the son GrandfatherPoindexter never sired. On many occasions, he urges my mother to let him adopt me, but she refuses, preferring to keep her family together.

We will spend two magical weeks in Florida. These are days of summer vacation, while others are still attending class. The first day Rudy Junior and I play vigorously, burying each other in mounds of silver Spanish moss and climbing the prehistoric trees. We are transported into fairyland populated by the several species of colorful birds that gather on my Great grandfather's front lawn. Each morning, we get up early to explore sandy lanes of rural Zephyrhills, thinking this is our new home from now own.

Then one Saturday morning Rudy arrives on a Greyhound bus, ending the magic of our new found independence. By now Jean realizes the tragic reality of being solely responsible for the mouths of four hungry children and nowhere to call home. Better the presence of an ogre with work ethics, than the uncertainty of trying to make it alone.

The very next morning we unceremoniously load up the Plymouth and head north with Rudy at the helm. We first return to *Cooleemee* and pack all our belongings inside an old rented moving truck with worn-out tires. Less than two weeks later we are back in our rural Greenville home, resting at the foothills of the Blue Ridge Mountains. To Rudy it means a second chance to have his wife and family again, even at the sacrifice of the best paying job he ever had. To Jean it is a compromised reprieve from hosts of unpleasant memories and restoration of a better dream. To me it is like returning to a land of the not yet vanquished, except now I might know a way to defeat them.

After tendering his Foreman position, Rudy takes another job that pays less. Better a reduction in salary than to lose everything. In retrospect, I respect him for this. As for Jean, her natural instincts will prove justified. One of Rudy's co-workers from the Raleigh project calls him a year later and reports that people in *Cooleemee* are getting sick because of contaminated well water. Jean just sits at the kitchen table with a knowing grimace on her face.

Greenville has changed ever so slightly during the year of our absence. The house and the neighborhood remain the same. My toy plastic B52 Bomber crashed in a bramble of weeds in the backyard still where I left it. The disembodied black slip, hidden safely in the bottom corner of my bedroom closet, possesses less appeal now, so I return it to the laundry hamper. Jean seems not to have noticed. Two of my neighborhood friends, Tommy and Nelson, have grown nearly a foot taller; whereas, I remain roughly the same height. This is particularly unsettling when we play sports. At every competition, they are able to out-reach me, out-stride me, and out-jump me. However, I possess speed, my body compact and solidly made. In time, I get past their gloating. They, too, soon realize that size less meaningful within context of team effort. Together we make a good team, especially in football.

My old enemies are once again afoot by the end of my first school day, their familiar taunting oppressive and depressing. Chuck, also known as Hawkeye, and his brother Steve, both clean-cut boys, but mean. The eldest brother, Chuck, enjoys most to bully me, possessed with a personal grievance that I will never fully understand. He catches me just as I am leaving the school grounds. First, he pushes me hard against a tree, and then begins threatening how he plans to "whip" me good.

"Just don't hit me in the face," I plea, tears welling in my eyes.

Chuck cannot resist the bait. He hits me squarely in the mouth. I remember particularly well the almost pleasant taste of copper, followed by a force of blind rage. I am not exactly certain of the events that follow next. By the time I become conscious again, Hawkeye lies curled in a fetal position on the ground bleeding and crying for mercy.

The next day Donnie, 'Bulldog', Hawkeye's neighbor and best friend intercepts me a block from my home. Donnie, being bigger and taller than Chuck, probably figures I had just gotten lucky; but I dispatch him in pretty much the same way. A few days later, the turn of Gerald 'Casey', the official school bully that everyone fears. Casey, a Colossus compared to me, larger than most boys our age, must have thought that what he heard just has to be wrong. He does not fall like the others.

Casey just stands there swaying back and forth, a dazed look in his eyes. He stops being a bully after this. In time we will even become acquaintances.

This is when I realize that *Cooleemee* not just a place on the map, but also a place inside of me. I know I will never fear defeat again, never again the victim. I might lose, but not defeated! I do not become a bully—that is not my way-- content just to be liberated from the fear.

That same Christmas, Rudy gives my brother and me each a ten-speed English racing Raleigh bicycle. Rudy knows quality, quality deprived to him and his older brother, and determines his children will have the best he can provide. Riding free on this precision foreign glider gives me wings, allowing me to soar in ways never imagined. It, also, makes me the envy of our neighborhood. My greatest passion is to ride this three-speed chariot to the ends of undiscovered countries and beyond where heaven and earth meet. To feel the power of speed, as I change through the gears, pedaling as fast as humanly possible, the rush of wind in face--for an instant lighter than air–this represents the nearest to real freedom that one might attain here on earth. At times like these, it seems only a thread keeping me bound, a thread so easily separated; yet I know even then that I must remain. I do not believe in astral projection in the incarnate sense. Nor do I believe us altogether carnally fixed. I do believe there are places dangerous to the soul between enclaves of light and shadow, where the essence of life might project, and sometimes not return.

My first experience of this place glimpsed on a fiery autumn day, when rays of the setting sun ignite the south into flame. Mounted on my swift red English bicycle, believing myself invincible and with freedom to go anywhere I choose. Von Holland Drive, a steep incline almost vertical, requires conservative vigilance even by the most experienced navigator. Usually I apply my brakes, descending cautiously. Today I am intoxicated by a daredevil spirit of irrational challenge. Those first few seconds consume my reason. A most exhilarating awareness, a feeling of being timeless and unrestrained by the laws of nature--no longer grounded to this earth! Halfway down, a car unexpectedly pulls out of a driveway. I reflexively swerve right, leaping over a narrow drainage ditch and into someone's backyard. Just when I think myself safe, an invisible clothesline wire strung between two trees hangs me by the neck.

I distinctively remember seeing from a distance my bicycle continuing without me, as I am lifted bodily into the azure of a cobalt evening sky, fading darkly and pierced with the occasional ember of an evening star. An acute sensation of not being able to breathe; my bodily existence memory only of a distant element melted irresistibly into the cool moist clay of eternity. Next, I pass through a thin veil of atmosphere into a void of gigantic burning spheres laced with beads of smaller spheres strung together like shimmering pearls. I reach out to touch one of these bright souls of light.

My eyes open; it is twilight. Coughing and gasping for breath, the taste of fresh hot blood in my mouth, I rise from the earth alive. My bicycle rests in the next yard, crumpled beside the black trunk of a Pecan Tree. The front wheel warped, dangling with wires of broken spokes; with no chance of riding it home. Carefully, I sneak into the backyard of my family home, hoping no one will see me. That evening, Jean thinking I have a case of laryngitis, Jean pours tablespoons of foul tasting cough medicine into my mouth. Because my little brother so much younger, he is not yet able to appreciate the future elation promised by his English Raleigh stored safely in the garage. Secretly I cannibalize the front wheel from the bicycle of Rudy Junior. It will be more than a year before anyone discovers the deception, and by then it will no longer matter. At the age of thirteen, my little brother will inherit my own bike, as I move on to other challenges.

This near-death experience the first time that my soul completely disconnects from my physical being, but will not be the last. My second recollection of an Astral body experience happens on graduation day of my fifth grade. This being the last day of the school year, I have all my gym equipment to take home for the summer. Included are my running sneakers tied together by the shoelaces and draped around my neck. I decide to loiter for a while and talk to three acquaintances in back of the gym building. One of these fellows is a seventh grader, soon to begin

Parker High, his days at San Souci Junior High at an end.

"You little boys take care of yourselves the next two years," he jokes.

"I'm not so little," I reply stubbornly. "I'm almost as old as you."

This is true, since I had failed the second grade, a setback that my mother never lets me forget. This boy, neither a bully nor typically rough, acts almost playful, making light of most everything. He swings behind me, grabs the two sneakers, and pulls them together, tightening the string around my neck.

"I'll bet it won't be long before you cry uncle," he laughs, pulling the shoes slowly apart, applying ever more pressure.

I do not resist as the string tightens, but rather feel at peace, almost euphoric, determined not to give in, not to allow this bragger the pleasure of victory. I remember staring intently into the clear deep blue of the afternoon sky and thinking to myself that I am there, not in my body. At one point, I recall a sensation of suffocating, a pain distant and somehow irrelevant.

I am walking along a smooth black road lined with gnarled trees spreading on either side, an array of colorful flowers flowing between these watchful guardians. Beyond a most extraordinary yellow sun slices into the horizon, dripping into a golden lake melted at the end of the road. What I remember most is a sense of wellbeing, a sensation of passage toward a world without end. Then all fades darkly into total blackness.

The first thing I see upon opening my eyes, the shining face of a girl looking down at me, her distrait voice rising out of a distinctive ringing in my ears. The three boys have run away, probably believing me dead.

"You shouldn't have let him do that," this angel says, helping me up, unraveling the taunt shoelaces from around my throat.

"Do what?" I query confused, that familiar taste of copper in my mouth again.

"Let him chock you like that. I saw everything. You just stood there until you fell down. Didn't your mother ever tell you not to tie your shoes around your neck? It's a wonder you are still alive."

She introduces herself as Carolyn and walks away. I remain seated on the grass truly shaken. Carolyn is right. My mother has warned me often about placing things around my neck-- and also of many other dangers yet to come. If only I had listened more attentively. However, this experience like many others reminds me that the concept of being more than just physical presence. Knowledge I will retain and ponder secretly in present time.

There is more than one kind of death: death of the flesh, but the soul remains. The slower death of the soul, when the flesh becomes only a shell of existence, and time becomes a meaningless prison. To know this kind of dying is the unmasking of all hope and all pretenses. This is the true knowledge of human mortality.

My brother, little Rudy and I, play one evening beside a large drainage pipe at the bottom of *McMakin Drive*, listening to the echo of our own voices inside this manmade cave. Without warning, a woman appears over the edge.

"Could you boys please do me a favor?" She vacantly inquires. Her eyes red and teary, her face drawn and haggardly tired, like someone deprived of sleep since a long time.

She asks if we will come into her house located at the other end of the drainage pipe and meet her son. Apparently, he has heard the echo of our laughter and wishes to meet us.

"This is Perry, my son," his mother's voice crackles. "He has Leukemia and must remain in bed."

My brother and I introduce ourselves, sit on the edge of the boy's bed, and just talk for a while. I have never heard the word Leukemia before now, only hope not to catch it. At a point Perry desires to play a game of Parcheesi, but after only a few moves is too weak to continue.

"Perry is tired now," the mother intervenes. "You boys should really go and come back another time."

We say goodbye to Perry, who by now has become despondent, little aware of our presence. Next evening I decide to drop by and again say hello to this new friend. His mother answers, looking somehow different from the night before, somehow more at peace.

"I'm sorry, my son is dead," she says crying and closes the door.

She continues to cry from behind the barrier, a wailing sound piercing to the soul every time I think about it. I have often wondered what it like for young Perry to wait through those final hours alone in his bed, not to know the warm sun on his face or the joy of other children to share his imaginings. Looking back at these years, I suppose they really are the most innocent.

Already my childhood passing imperceptibly, like the waning of a full moon, only I failed to comprehend the meaning. The tiger has begun to stir from his dream, soon to walk camouflaged among the shades of mortality. There will come a day I wish he had never awakened.

Chapter 6

Someone Else in the Mirror

$\mathcal{T}$he early nineteen sixties America remains still innocent to true nature of the world. At least it imagines itself innocent and instructs its children accordingly. Our greater concerns at the time are routine drills hiding under schooldesks in the event of a Russian nuclear strike, beginning with threat of the Cuban Missile Crisis. We gradually become a society made enlightened through information provided every night in black and white on the six o'clock news hour. Told that in places like China and India children go to bed every night starving, still we manage to sleep peacefully in this knowledge. By now all aware that America has become entangled in another war somewhere far away and soldiers brought home daily in body bags, with prime-time TV ratings off the chart.

However, a few changes noticeable, creating more than a few waves of division in the small Southern town signs on buses and above drinking fountains, as well as indicators removed with the designation "*Niger Town.*" Even though I grow up in a segregated neighborhood, I manage to believe racism a thing of the past and no longer relevant. Maybe because deep down aware that I little to the pure breeding of this land, I secretly consider myself crossed somewhere in the middle between the downtrodden and the elite.

After the brutal murder of a beloved President of the people, America really begins to show obvious signs of fracture. John F. Kennedy, a rightful heir to Camelot, gunned down like a dog in the streets of a North Texas town-- or at least this is how Jean and Rudy remember him. The French have already pulled out of Vietnam after the massacre of *Dien Bien Phu.* It is the Kennedy administration that started the political machine of military engagement by sending US advisers to help train the South Vietnamese resistance army. Following Kennedy's assassination, Lyndon B. Johnson consummates the war by deploying U.S. troops to the region as a defensive measure after the first group of advisers massacred. There are many theories why the United States went there, and why the escalation allowed to continue. We are there all the same, and will remain there for many years to come. The only time I saw Rudy really cry is the day Kennedy assassinated in Dallas Texas.

That Friday after school, my brother and I go sliding down a steep hill off Poinsett Highway on sleds of collapsed cardboard boxes that serve to transport our family groceries from the local *Kash & Karry.* This dangerous thrill ends onto a sidewalk at the bottom of the hill. Beyond it a narrow curb marking the beginning of the busy Poinsett Highway. We always manage to escape by rolling off our platforms at the last moment, the flattened box continuing alone into the throughway squashed further by the heavy flow of rush hour traffic. However, Little Rudy decides to ride down in a box not flattened. He climbs in and shoots off like a bullet. To my shock, the spinning box slides beyond the sidewalk and into the busy four-lane, narrowly missed by two oncoming cars. Nose of a Tractor-trailer truck stops just in time on the opposite side, my baby brother crawling dizzily out of his would-be coffin. The driver scolds the boy to tears, and then safely escorts him back across the highway. I remain at the top, paralyzed and ashamed.

"You ought to take better care of your little brother," the man shouts up at me from the bottom of the incline. "If something happened to him today you would feel it the rest of your life."

A lot of truth and wisdom in this stranger's reprimand; at least this day my brother and I are lucky. Rudy Senior has already arrived home from work. We walk into an environment more somber than I have ever known. Supper not even begun, Rudy and Jean glued tearfully to the live television tragedy unfolding.

"He was a good man, killed like a dog in a south-Texas street," Rudy repeats, over, and over again, his face moist. "This day the world has changed for the worse."

I little realize the prophetic meaning in his words at the time. The world did change that day, moving closer to the brink of even greater change yet to come. My little brother and I stop sliding down hills in empty boxes after this.

On my fourteenth birthday, I receive a high-fidelity record player. Jean bought it on layaway, paying five dollars a week for six months. This is my best gift since the bicycle. The same week I obtain employment delivering newspapers for Greenville News in my neighborhood. With my second weeks earnings I purchase my premier record 'Swan Lake and Sleeping Beauty' by Tchaikovsky; and then two weeks later it is Peer Gynt by Grieg, and The Planets by *Gustav Holst*. These classics transport me into a wonderful dimension of poetic meaning and imagery, an escape from the physical world of violence and the often feelings of rejection. This instrument of man's better ingenuity becomes as a close companion, consoling my battered emotions, an entertainment escape unlocking the Pandora Box of my imagination. On the fourth week I discover something new at the Seven Eleven quick market where I purchase my records. An innovative collection series of audio plays by a recording company named Bell Camp: Jules Verne's 'Twenty Thousand Leagues under the Sea', 'Journey to the Center of the Earth' and 'Around the World in Eighty Days'. My next paycheck went to the purchase of H.G. Wells classic 'First Men in the Moon' and 'The Time Machine'. In the following weeks and months arrive several other productions, including The 'Invisible Man', 'New Adventures of Superman', and strange tales narrated by Alfred Hitchcock. Within less than a year, I collect them all, listening to them over, and over again. Even to this day I still occasionally seek nostalgic comfort through the worn-out vinyl of these wonderfully created recordings.

Now there exist dividing lines of protected segregation in our home. My brother and I share a room, and my two sisters, Penny and Cendi, have their room. In conditions like these a phenomenon occurs. Two distinct and separate tribes evolve, each with their own tactics, strengths, and weaknesses. The words boys and girls become a battle cry of assault and counter assault. In reality, I have mixed feelings about this, but being the eldest, a responsibility of despotic command settles on my shoulders. When territorial disputes arise, it is up to me to make the peace by any conceivable tactic. Little Rudy and Penny become the worse adversaries. Born only eighteen months apart, physically very similar, and with personalities to match, they morph into natural enemies. Once Penny kidnaps Little Rudy's GI Joe and buries him alive beneath a sandpile in our backyard. It takes my brother three days to finally discover the fate of his beloved effigy. In retaliation, he violates Penny's Barbie dolls in a most horrific way, stripping them naked of their fashion wardrobes; hangs the exposed bodies in my sister's closet by the neck along with a Ken doll displayed upside down beside Barbie.   Both dolls mutilated with marks of slow torture. My brother will eventually grow up to become a collector of knives, swords, and guns. He mostly keeps to himself today, and no one knows what is really in Little Rudy's mind.

From the beginning, Cendi runs free a true child of nature. Born with a streak of autumn red hair searing along the center of her head and large hazel blue eyes, she shines mystical even then. At five years old, she sprints around naked in the snow, until I catch the laughing child and usher her back inside. Cendi, unbothered by the cold, only stares unblinkingly into my face with eyes so deep that I imagine not of this world, more a wood nymph trying to escape back into nature, as a spirit contained in a bottle of the present wishing to return to the wild. The greatest fault of my little sister is that she never tells a lie, even when strategically advantageous. This makes Cendi an unreliable agent when it comes to conspiracies of subterfuge. I, therefore, make it a point to tell this little sister only those things I want everyone else to know. Cindy will be an adult before I get to know her again, a beautiful woman, but still not altogether of this world. Lured into witchcraft for a while with her cousin Pam, both influenced by the popular TV series Bewitched, she is lured into the world of the unseen. Until those shadows of reflected light begin to turn against her. She tells me many years later while home on a visit, that these powers assaulting her. By then I have power of a greater spirit and dispel the darkness in the name of one I now know, those lesser lights consumed by greater magnitude. I realize then how much alike we are, how similar our demons. She has a daughter now from her first marriage, and has since divorced and remarried again. I like to think that we remain kindred souls, always connected regardless of time or geography.

My sister, Penny, is perhaps the most practical us all. Even as a child she exhibits a natural intelligence that enables her to see clearly most situations and to know the appropriate action. She marries a man named Tony at a young age and buys a house in the higher elevation of Traveler's

Rest to raise their two boys. They are the first in our family to own a satellite home entertainment system capable of receiving international broadcasts and to build a deck with swimming pool only steps from the kitchen. Although Tony and Penny will live the American dream by accumulating debt, they never stop wanting more, representing the true backbone of the credit system. Perhaps, because Tony grew-up in poverty bred to mountain life, he desires better in his life and for his family no matter the cost. Penny and Tony have always been the greatest example to me of southern hospitality. They shelter and feed me on numerous occasions through the years, and I know I can knock on Penny's door anytime and be well received. As brother and sister, we have our differences, but Penny remains loyal and good through all hardships. Penny is now head of an editorial staff for a local news network. Unfortunately, she and her husband do not always choose to eat wisely, my concern for my sister's health counter-weighed by pride in her personal achievements.

"If God wanted me thin and always stereotypically beautiful, then he would make me less hungry." She affirms in so many words after a discussion about her weight.

Maybe Penny is right, maybe it is much about vanity. How long we live is not so important as how we live. Tony finds a good paying job early in life working as a mechanic at one of the local mills. Despite many failings unimportant to mention here, Tony proves a man smart and with a natural friendly way to convince other people to at least let him try. Tony can talk a frog out of a pond--or say those that know him well. He and two of his brothers will later create an unregistered company doing house renovations for the more wealthy residents of *Paris Mountain*, preferring the often undeclared profit of living on the crumbs that falls from those plentiful tables. This simple man with little formal education and an enterprising spirit will do surprisingly well for himself and his family. But sadly Tony will die suddenly from a heart attack before turning sixty.

But I get ahead of myself. In the course of time brother and sisters will go our separate ways, but in this presence my siblings are still small children with so little knowledge of the greater world beyond the wonderful green elevations of our nativity. Like every generation, we grow-up oblivious to rare enchanting mornings of winter after a rainstorm changing to snow, the sun shining bright through still naked trees encased in an armor of sparkling crystal. We take for granted the peaceful evenings of early spring, as blue mist slithers around the mountain slopes in our view, curling catlike, and then gone before early twilight. These mountain foothills releases a cool refreshing breeze during the hottest evenings of mosquito infested summers that help us sleep. Rich autumn ascents ignite with blazing colors of fantastic fire that dances over the horizon during the months of Halloween and Thanksgiving, before changing into winter dark and skeletal. All these images lost in a rite of passage that all must pass through waning innocence.

Those last years living in the home of Rudy and Jean are the most illuminating, as well as blinding to my fading youth. The new paper rout carries me into a territory labeled the lower Von Holland valley, mostly rented homes belonging to the cotton mill district. Like many southern towns, a third of Greenville's economy thrives on textile. Not all those living here work shifts at the mill. Nevertheless, the district is reputed to being the cheapest place to find a house or apartment, attractive to poorer folks. As in all economically depressed urban neighborhoods, the houses sag neglected, the lawns over-grown with weeds, especially during summer months; and most of the kids wearing unwashed hand-me-downs. Lower Von Holland represents a condition shared by most poor mill hands that have never known another life, a condition that goes back several generations. It is not the same kind of physical poverty you might find in the ghettos of larger cities, but more a poverty of the soul. Often both parents work fulltime jobs just to keep food in the refrigerator. After a long shift, one or both too drunk by suppertime to prepare a decent meal, often passing-out in front of the TV with the children left to fend for themselves. Fortunately they remember to leave my weekly due for the daily paper inside a sealed envelope stashed in the mailbox or under the pot of a dead plant on the front porch. Even these people possess values of commerce.

The first couple of weeks pass without incident; however, on the last day of the third week, a gang of five boys corner me determined to make their territorial position clear. I attempt to reason with them, explaining that my presence only transitory. Stating that beyond my duty to deliver papers, I have no wish to remain. Then the largest of the five challenges me to a fight. I can feel the emotions welling up inside, the familiar sickness of fear. I back away only to trip over my heavy canvass paper bag. As I right myself, this boy strikes me in the face. The rest is history. I do not think this assailant ever expected the rain of unleashed fury. When the episode over, the five move off with only a few distant taunts. The following Monday, these five boys return accompanied by another three led by a brave new champion. This one also falls, as did his predecessor. On Friday, the last day of the week, my nemeses ambush me again. This time they have brought the biggest boy in the neighborhood with them. I will later learn that this Goliath a second year high school student, and also the older brother to the first boy I dispatched.

"My name is Joe and this is our neighborhood," he says as a *matter-of-fact*; "we can't have someone coming down here beating up everyone. We deserve the same respect as you people up on the hill."

Joe, less formidable than the titan farm boy in *Cooleemee*, stands a good foot taller, stoutly built with rough mechanic's hands probably from working on his car. In that moment I am inspired with a revelation. All these boys really want is that I lose. They do not care to whom, only that my defeat will guarantee continued dominance in their own neighborhood. The moment Joe and I engage I realize he really does not wish to hurt me. He is here on a mission, a representative commissioned to ensure neighborhood pride. Maybe, also, a little hesitant that if I should defeat him-- then who else left? I move deceptively strong and fast, plus what he has already heard makes him think twice. After taking a couple of quick body jabs, I purposely lose my footing and roll down an embankment into the trickle of a nearly dry creek bed. To my surprise, Joe appears over the edge and shouts down.

"Do you give?"

I am neither hurt nor tired, only wishing this ritual of violent engagement to end.

"Yes, I give." I shout clearly from the bottom of the creek bed.

Without another word, Joe and the gang go away. I suppose there must be a certain unspoken code of honor, after all, because no one in lower Von Holland ever challenges me after that. They are as ghost, vanished into the same ether from which they appear. I will meet Joe once more under very different circumstances. I hear that he got drafted into the army the following year and shipped-off to Nam. What happened to him after this is anyone's guess, vanishing from history as do all legends in course.

A month later, I meet a new friend while riding my bicycle, a slightly older boy whose family has emigrated from Mexico. He introduces himself as Roberto and at first glance looks a little intimidating. Then expression on his face changes into a friendly grin and this first perception evaporates. We become friends almost immediately. He has a custom bicycle made with cannibalized parts he openly admits to stealing from other kid's bikes: slick tires, raised handlebars, and a banana seat. My moral values are a little vague at this time, not fully comprehending that every crime has a victim. I, therefore, accept Roberto's free-market style without further interrogation. Maybe he is a thief, but an honest one, and with a puss-in-boots swagger that makes everything he does seem justified. Nevertheless, there is always a price for thievery. My personal lesson will come a few months later while shopping at a K-Mart store with another friend named Tommy Belk. Tommy shoplifts a Tachometer for his older brother, but the poorly conceived caper goes all wrong. A sympathetic security guard apprehends us at the door before actually leaving the store and only calls our parents, instead of the police. In my case, that will be punishment enough.

I guess that I think Roberto cool to build his own bicycle regardless of how it accomplished. One day he tells me he knows a way to the top of the dominant green water tank on the side of Paris Mountain. Intrigued, I ask he show me. I have ventured only as near as the chain-link fence that surrounds the base, without it ever occurring to me there might actually be a way of reaching the top. I follow Roberto up a well-defined winding path up a steep grade. We pass a gated side entrance to the tank continuing up toward the summit. My friend then swings around and follows a fainter footpath into surrounding brush. My English glider, although excellent for speed, no match for the smaller, more agile banana bike able to leap over rocks and root tentacles with ease. At one point, I am forced to get off and walk. By the time I catch up with Roberto, he is stopped and waiting at the edge of a narrow chasm at the top of the towering green water tank. A skeleton lattice of scalpels consisting of two-by-fours laced along the backside of the tank for maintenance purposes. At the end of the scalpel boards a negotiable space of less than three feet to the top of the water tower. Roberto leaps easily over on his bicycle; but I decide to abandon my ride for the moment and jump over on foot.

The view of a panorama I call home stunning from this unobstructed elevation, clearly visible Jack's Auto Garage, belonging to our neighbor, Jack Rogers, a local NASCAR racing legend located on the corner of Poinsett Highway and Mc Makin Drive. Obscured behind a ridge of pine trees above the garage, I barely make out a slither of the new white roof Rudy paid to have redone just s few months earlier. Roberto points to a position to the left saying this direction where he and his family live. The water tank stands at least thirty feet high and a third that volume in circumference. Instead of being smooth, the surface composed of large metal plates riveted and then spot-welded together. Near the center, a shallow pool of rainwater collected in an enclave designed for a purpose unknown, reflecting brightly the afternoon sun. Although the view magnificent, my attention quickly returns to the fact that I am actually standing atop the prominent green monolith dominating the face of Paris Mountain. Roberto begins showing off the agility of his bicycle by doing wheelies and breaking in circles.

"Here, you try it," he says, handing his bike over to me.

Secretly, I envy the style of this little Frankenstein hybrid. It looks a bit like a chopper made popular by the recent release of the Hell's Angels movies. Tommy and I saw the first of these films together. Upon returning home, Tommy insists that I tattoo a skull across his bicep with the added words Hell's Angels. After fulfilling his request, he turns to me and says with tears in his eyes something unexpected.

"Now it is your turn."

I do not want a turn, nor do I wish to appear babyish in front of my competitive friend --boys and their pride! Fortunately, I have the good sense to choose he tattoo only the word "*Poet.*" Poet, the name of a minor character in the movie, also consistent with the fact I write poetry. Today this embarrassing tattoo on my left arm has faded small and blurred, prompting people to often ask what the word '*Post*' means. Thank God I did not ask to follow his creative design!

Roberto's bicycle inspires a less confident feeling, being much different than my Raleigh. Not use to the raised handlebars, it responds clumsy and poorly balanced, deceptive in the turns. After making a few circles, I decide to give it a good test. Starting from one end of the tank,I peddle fast as I can through the shallow pool, planning to stop before reaching the other extreme. Upon nearing the point of no return, I reach on the handlebars to apply the brakes. To my confusion, there are none. By the time I remember this not my bike and stomp on the back pedal, it is already too late. Now I understand the meaning of the word "slicks." In dry conditions, they are probably better than other tires, but lose all grip on wet surfaces. I do not remember thinking anything, continuing to slide toward the edge, all the while desperately attempting to separate from the accelerated mechanism. Only succeeding at the last moment, watching the splendid bike sail into air and disappear into a cluster of treetops.

My salvation based more on divine intervention than on skill, spared certain injury-- perhaps even death-- by the baggy brogan blue jeans that I always hate to wear. The crotch area has caught on a jagged rusty piece of sheet metal peeled back by time and neglect only inches from the edge. A miracle the denim did not rip, and even more that the sharp metal did not slice me open like one of Rudy's filleted fish. I hang there, my feet suspended over the rim, like a discarded rag doll, until Roberto's voice shocks me back into the moment.

"I'm okay!" I shout back. "But your bike…"

Roberto, truly shaken, helps me to my feet, realizing the nearness of tragedy. Nevertheless, I feel a little guilty for the certain loss of his transport.

"Don't worry about that," he says assuring. "I can always make another. Promise you won't tell anyone. I could get in a lot of trouble-- so promise me!"

What else can I do? My own bicycle safe; and except for a few cuts and scratches, I am unharmed. We search the brush for a long time, hoping to find at least some pieces, but never discover the resting place of Roberto's bike. It is probably stuck high up in a mountain Pine to this day.

That night I have a dream. I am flying at last, only I no longer believe that I have gained Superman powers. Instinctively, I reach out to grab the top of a passing tree, and then another, only my inertia too great. I see another tree approach, and attempt to seize it. But the dry sprigs tear-off in my hands. I continue to travel higher and higher. As I pass one of the taller sprawling firs, I see Roberto's bike at the top like a bright Christmas star. I awaken to the peaceful thought that my Mexican friend's unique contraption will remain untarnished and forever timeless.

Two weeks later, I see Roberto for the last time. He informs that his family has received deportation orders to return south of the border. I do not know what this means and envy the idea that Roberto so lucky to go away to some place more exotic than the Greenville foothills of Paris Mountain.

This year will be the last time I go out on Trick or Treat. A week before Halloween I discover a most beautiful blue dress in someone's garbage while on my delivery route. Perhaps the garment a discarded prom costume; or maybe just an elegant evening dress taking up space in some girl's closet; but to me it represents the most exquisite design I have ever seen. I love the texture, the smell, the delicate loveliness of the material. At my earliest opportunity, I try it on in the family garage. The dress fits perfectly. I am immediately transformed in a way that I cannot describe. I change from a shy defensive boy, into a dazzling princess. I like the way the dress contours my body; but even more than the look, I like the way I feel in it. It is like seeing me for the first time; to see and to feel myself as I truly am. For several days, I sneak out to the garage and try on my new dress. However, it is not satisfying to always hide this way. As Halloween approaches, I design a most ingenious plan. I inform my mother that I want to go out as a ghost. I spend almost half of my week's earnings on a black party-wig with a silver crown from a five and ten cent store. The night of Halloween, I put on my blue dress and wig, smear on some of my mother's lipstick, while concealing my real costume under a white sheet with eyes cut out. Penny almost exposes my deception as I depart into the night, but is distracted by little Cendi. Penny has always had a smart intuition. Finally, I escape into the shadows free at last. A few blocks from home, I hide behind a bush and discard the sheet. Althougha little nervous in the beginning that someone might recognize my other self, especially one of my former antagonist; but when no one notices, I begin boldly going from house to house collecting candy.

"What a lovely princess," mothers often say.

This is all the validation I need and all that I want. I stay out a little longer than I should have, standing under a streetlight at the bottom of Von Holland hill, like Cinderella before the strike of midnight reluctant for this transformation to end, reluctant to say goodbye to this lovely introduction-- only it must end! A car pulls up beside me, a black T-Bird driven by a young man smoking a cigarette.

"Hi sweetie, you want to take a ride?"

It is Joe. The same Joe I had fought several weeks earlier. I shake my head no, fearing the worse.

"Come on honey; let me give you a ride home. The driver says swinging open the passenger side door."

"Thank you, but I live here," I reply in the highest tone I can manage, turn, and begin walking straight to the front door of the nearest house

The interior light closes and the black T-Bird speeds away scratching rubber. I immediately rush up the hill and recover my ghost sheetstill stashed under the bush. I sadly strip off my dress, the wig, and the empowering crown, placing them reverently in a nearby garbagecontainer, where they continue to glitter beautifully in the pale light ofa full moon. It is time for the princess to sleep again. And it will be a hundred years and another lifetime before a kiss awakens her again to shimmering light.

Rudy and Jean engaged watching Perry Mason on T.V. when I arrive, barely noticing that I continue to hug the sheet around my exposed body clothed by only a pair of Fruit of the Loom underwear underneath. I rush straight to the bathroom, pull out a pair of pants and a dirty t-shirt from the laundry hamper to become a boy again. That night I dream of castles, of frogs, and of a dark knight in his black T-Bird.

It seems the whole world at war. Not a night passes that we do not tune-in to watch the black and white images of America's first live televised war. We sit glued to the action, only the movie real: soldiers running from house to house of burning villages, the crackle of gunfire in the background, and the name of a new enemy of democracy wearing black silk pajamas. The stories of daily conflict broadcast from an exotic country somewhere in South East Asia called Vietnam. I remember once watching a shaking unscripted report showing a young Marine carried into a bunker with an undetonated grenade lodged in his back. A field medic narrates the event, explaining how complicated and dangerous rare it is to extract an unexploded device.

I am usually already in bed by the eleven o'clock update, never knowing the outcome. The six o'clock news soars daily in ratings, just another action entertainment show adding serious commentary to a continuing saga better than any soap opera. After a while, it fades with interest, no more real to most viewers than the T.V. series Desert Fox or Mission Impossible-- the true human tragedy forgotten between commercial breaks. The reality sinks its deadly teeth in one day I am visiting my friend Greg and receive news his older brother killed in action. We are playing basketball under the carport of his house when Greg's mother comes running out crying,

"Jimmy –God, your brother Jimmy -my son –my son!"

Here the face of lamentation for a child lost somewhere in field of battle. It is nothing new in history. The same record of events repeated over and over again, like the ballad of a Greek tragedy, only these characters I know.

Jimmy was a clean-cut good-natured boy, rarely cross with anyone: someone that once took time from his pretty date to climb an oak tree and retrieve a toy wooden glider for Greg and me. He single handedly restored a 1948 Buick and painted it powder baby blue, another relic destined to remain parked in the backyard until Greg gets old enough to drive.

Days later, I observe a hearse parked in front of Greg's house with a black coffin inside draped by an American flag. Jimmy lay in the ground for more than a month by the time Greg and I speak again. He leans apathetically on the handlebars of his bicycle, looks different in a way that I cannot describe.

"How is everything?"

My question is superfluous in light of recent events, since my friend's only brother now dead and buried.

"Nothing will ever be the same. One more year –just one more year– I'll be able to go! They will pay for Jimmy— every one of them gooks is going to pay!"

Greg and I make a pack between us this day we will both go to Vietnam and revenge Jimmy's death. We are, after all, a nation of warriors, and one of our own has fallen. Thirteen months older, Greg makes good his promise and ships-off into the Army a few months before his eighteenth birthday. After the loss of their second son, the family sells their house and move out into the country. I guess they have grown fatigued of T.V. wars, meaningless commercials, and tired of burying their dead.

In the last year of Junior High, the fighting starts up again. Mostly the challenges came from other schools. How they know about me beyond comprehension; only not a month passes before someone comes to my school wanting to fight. After a while I feel like an old-west gunslinger. I do not remember how many there were. Some faces I can still see the agony of their defeat, but most just a blur. However, I remember the hate I feel each time my hand forced and how the hate grows stronger each time.

I meet Carolyn again, the raven-haired angel, who once saved me. I enjoy just sitting and talking with her whenever I have a chance. I take the school bus just so I can sit beside her and then walk nearly a mile to my home. Carolyn is the only daughter to a Presbyterian preacher, and every word that pours from her soft round lips, laced with the sweetest poison. I suppose I might have done anything for Carolyn. Then Mickey comes between us. Mickey still attends high school, but should have graduated two years earlier. Except that Mickey dances with the best in South Carolina, labeled the Regional Light-Weight Golden Glove Boxing Champion. I know nothing of this prizefighter's career the day he steps aboard the school bus and demands that I stop seeing Carolyn. I only continue to look into Carolyn's large absorbing eyes.

"She is my friend," I say.

I probably meant more than just a friend, only the words come out that way. I think Mickey understands the meaning even better. He challenges me to step out of the bus so we might settle things man to man. Reluctantly, I see no other choice. How can I not defend the right of this beautiful damsel to be friends with whomever she likes?

"This is for you." I say, touching the melting softness of her hand.

Carolyn only smiles back sweetly.

I wish to make something clear. I do not believe that there is any such thing as a fair fight. I never consider myself the aggressor; but I most hate being forced into a conflict. I do not believe in using weapons against a person unarmed; nor do I believe in cowardly attacks from behind, or the collective cowardice of two or more against one. I do believe in honor, but not in arbitrary rules of a match I do not wish to participate.

Mickey professionally spares off dancing around like a hummingbird, bragging that no one can beat him. He also makes the usual threats: how he is going to whip my ass so badly that no girl will look at me when he is finished. He is still talking when I give him a swift kick to the groin, and then a second, followed by a quick uppercut to the chin, knocking him down on the ground. I jump on my astonished opponent and begin pounding him mercilessly. The Junior High coach comes running out and pulls me off the dazed featherweight.

"Do you know what you've done? Do you know who this is? I'm calling the police!"

I leave before the police arrive-- if they came at all. It is my understanding Mickey transported to the Greenville Hospital, where he spends two days. I never witnessed anyone collapse so easily. Either he has the proverbial glass jaw, or else I am getting faster and stronger. It is as though something powerful inside of me awakening. After this day, I see a respect of fear in people's eyes, a fear of me. Even Carolyn stops sitting with me. She laments that Mickey did not deserve a beating like that. I try to explain that I did not mean to hurt him and that I never want to hurt anyone.

Carolyn refuses to listen-- no one ever listens! I am now a victim of my own reputation, a reputation I never wanted. A rumor begins to circulate that Mickey's four older brothers have sworn a pact to get me. I watch my back continuously, expecting these assailants to strike me down when least I expect it. But they never come   after me. A month later, I am sitting in the bleachers during gym class and see Mickey walk in with his head hung down. Our eyes make contact. He makes a beeline to my position and takes a seat beside me.

"You beat me real good," he half slurs and extends his hand.

I accept his handshake, more puzzled than relieved. Saying only he will see me around, Mickey stands up and walks away as though nothing happened between us. I often think about Mickey, think that maybe I inadvertently took away his chance. He comes from the poorest family in the West Parker Mill district. All of Mickey's brothers Poe Mill hands, as are his father and mother. Mickey had opportunity to be something else, something better. That something broken in him the day of his defeat, his only chance evaporated. So Mickey takes his place among the shades of a Hades on the other side of the tracks.

This brief peace, along with an even briefer innocence of my youth, slipping ever farther away: my past fears, now future dread. I no longer discoverpleasured escape in my books or records. No longer am I able to soar with the wind. I am changing into something I do not like, something in my nature, but not my nature. The only way to describe it is that a dark piece of the cosmos manifesting from darkness, predetermined to destroythe child I wish to remain. Junior High School ends, which means first year attendance at Parker High School at summer's end.

I wish here to confess a crime. Every day after Junior High lunch period, we line-up and are herded into the school music room. The next hour spent reading excerpts from an acquired classic, or listening to the performance of an audio play. This activity represents my favorite hour of the day. Iremember particularly well a black-skinned copy of Moby Dick with color page illustrations created by hand. In association with this elegant book, an audio narration of Melville's masterpiece; and on the opposite side of this record disk, a moving tale called The Snow Goose. My teacher and the school coach are more than professionally involved. Therefore, after my fight with Mickey, Mrs. Campbell exiles me from attending her class, forcing me to sit outside for the entire period.   With nothing else todo, my mind begins to assemble a 'Mission Impossible' scenario.

One day when no one else in the classroom, I place a chair on the teacher's desk and unlatch the skylight window. This is once when watching T.V. pays off. I wait until a night in June after the school year ends for summer break. In a way I hope the deception discovered and that I will find the skylight window locked. I easily swing over the chain link fence and shimmy up onto the roof. The window opens easily just as planned. I   drop to the floor, wait patiently for the night security patrol car to make its rounds, Stuffing several of these marvelous books and recordings into a pillowcase brought to the occasion, I next exit through the front door, making a stealthy retreat back home with my acquired booty.

Interestingly, none of these acquisitions give me any pleasure at all. What I have stolen in turn steals from me. Many years later after dying and being born again, I gather my ill-gotten gains and present them to the presiding school administrator along with a full confession to the crime. He sorts through the relics puzzled.

"That wing of the school has been closed for more than two years. Nor is there any record of anything ever being stolen. I can see you have learned something important. If these things were once school property, then it no longer matters. Son, it is better that you keep it as a reminder of things, and the illusion of things."

This will not be my last criminal act, but the only one I clearly remember based solely on greed and personal obsession. The only one I got away with completely.

My last summer, I save money and purchase a second-hand Cushman Motor Scooter. It little compares to my English three-speed for versatility, except equipped with a three horsepower engine and faster-- which makes me now the king of Greenville! My most memorable event happens three days after buying it. My mother is visiting the home of an acquaintance a few streets over. The two women stand in the yard talking, when I smoothly zip around the corner. There is a law of physics that one must lean into the turn while conducting any two-wheeled vehicle; except I am too busy waving and showing off my new toy to pay attention to physics. I hit the wooden sign post squarely center of my chest, instantly knocked off my ride and onto the ground. The Stop Sign lies diagonally across my prostrate body, my scooter continuing without me.

My first thought is my motor scooter! Pushing aside the heavy 4 x 4, I leap up and begin running after my unpiloted machine.

Fortunately it runs aground in a ditch unharmed. Cushman deserves its reputation for toughness. My poor mother, on the other hand, collapses immediately into a hysterical daze. The things that woman has endured on my behalf.

Now there is no place I dare not to venture. The first extended journey is a thirty-minute ride to see my two cousins, Ike and Kit, on Rutherford Road the opposite side of town. They are less interested in my scooter, both being veterans of motocross bikes, presently agitated by a recent incident involving a much older boy that lives in an apartment complex nearby.

"He just won't let us alone. He must be like almost 20 years old--but I bet you could take him!"

My younger cousin Kit knows how to manipulate my ego.

The gunslinger I imagine myself to be boldly walks up to the door of this young man's home to set him straight. This will prove to be one of the more stupid things I have done. Without enquiry I say I am here to protect my two cousins. A maddened animal leaps from the darkened interior, pens me against the front railing, and begins pounding my head and upper body. Hanging precariously over the edge with one hand clutching the upper metal rail, I strike my infuriated assailant in the temple with the back of my free fist. As he falls back, I kick him a few times, sending him crumpled on the deck. Out charges a haggard woman swinging a broom and chases me down the stairs, as any mother will in protection of her child. Then I learn the truth. This poor young fellow afflicted with severe retardation; my cousins the real persecutors. I grimly accept the accolades of my two cousins without saying much. What else is there to say, being hailed a hero in their hour of need? I depart feeling another hollow victory in my gut. I think what most bothers me is that neither of them once say anything about my motor scooter or my proven freedom to travel across town.

Only a few weeks after buying it, a problem develops in the

Cushman's engine magneto. I take it apart and attempt unsuccessfully to repair the defect. Putting it back together in one piece without a manual proves impossible. I end up with a scatter of seemingly unrelated engine parts, which I throw into a discarded grocery box. I eventually exchange the disassembled scooter for a hand-brushed white 1947 Ford pickup, plus fifty dollars. The flat six-cylinder engine runs as long as I pour quarts of cheap recycled oil into the crankcase every time I drive it. First gear shot, I never manage to get up the steep hill of our driveway, leaving it always parked at side of the road below. Less than a month later, a tow truck takes it away one night while I sleep. Just as well, since I neglect to legally license the vehicle.

Tommy's father, a Second World War veteran, who works as an executive at one of the local mill offices, dies unexpectedly. A large burly man with strong Nordic genes possessed with an irritatingly superior attitude that he passes on to his three sons. This self-willed arrogance will reach from the grave and claim the future lives of his heirs like last rites of a Viking monarch. His poor widow finds herself doomed to a death of loneliness diligently enforced by her children. I talk with her one afternoon while waiting for Tommy to come back from the market. She confesses how difficult life since the passing of her husband, and how the boys react badly every time she considers going out on a date. In retrospect, I suppose this pleasant lady just too frail to break from tradition, too fragile to live the rest of her existence alone. In life, Tommy's father well versed in just about everything pertaining to war and strategy. His closet full of souvenirs brought back after the great conflict of nations ended: a loaded Lugar, a bowling-pin shaped grenade, and a blood-stained German infantry helmet pierced with a jagged hole. He expresses particular proud in a German Officer's hat and coat, which he claims to have acquired in exchange for a cigarette. He especially likes conducting war games, appointing Tommy and his younger brother Russell as the Americans, while casting me as the enemy.

I am forced to wear that punctured smelly German helmet, which weighs heavy on my neck and blocks my vision. He next instructs me to walk into an ambush either shot or captured. Bang— bang— it always ends the same. Fortunately, he has the good sense to arm us with painted wooden sticks that only simulate real guns, or else I would have been dead many times over.

Norman, the elder son, proves a particular disappointment to this self-proclaimed combat veteran. Norman wants nothing to do with the god of war and his souvenirs. He has the soul of an artist, a butterfly trapped in a bottle of time and genetics. I think Norman as much ashamed of his father, as his father ashamed of him. It is apparent early that this sensitive soul will never be a man's man; nor do I think he ever envisioned himself in that way. Norman, the only one of the three to go on to college, will eventually aspire to the cultivated position as a museum curator. I might have liked Norman had I been older and gotten to know him better.

Summer now at an end, the green on the mountains beginning to fade ever so slightly, and Tommy's mother found dead in her bed from a self- inflicted gunshot wound to the head. I lament that this lovely soul could not escape the demons of her affliction. She is already gone the dayI drop by Tommy's house unannounced, only I am unaware. I can see the shadow of her body curled across the bed through the open screen window, but think her only deeply asleep. Two days later my mother tells me the tragic news of her suicide.

The evening of the funeral, I arrive late at the downtown mortuary. Only a few mourners remain clustered together near the exit, but no one familiar. A shock to see the human replica stretched out in the expensive mahogany casket. Not the woman I knew-- not that woman with sad vacant, who served us hamburgers and iced tea. Then I recognize an almost undetectable scar on her wedding ring fingermade by a cut she received from a butcher's knife while dicing onions only last week. Death wears its own face. I have written a poem for heron this day to say goodbye to my friend's mother and to a friend. A poem conceived before witnessing this mask not worn by the living: inscribed before I accept the passage real. I slip the penciled paper into folded cold manikin hands as comfort throughout eternity. At least now she is free from future judgment.

As for Tommy, he spins from biker to a want to be rock star, which eventually leads into a darker snare of drugs and alcohol. I last see Tommy just after his second marriage. By now he works at a corner garage as a mechanic, looking many years older than his years.

"How is the military treating you?" His voice sounds hollow, only vaguely familiar.

"Just like your father always said military life would be."

"Dad served in the Army –Army is the best!" He proclaims with his father's pride, and then adds sadly, "Russell died last year. They found him in his van up around Lake Greenwood. They think he crawled into his sleeping bag and never woke up."

I will hear from other sources that Tommy's younger brother intentionally left the engine running and died of affixation, the circle of tragedy complete. These boys scarred by a family dynamic aligned bydestiny to fulfill the sins of the father.

I remember particularly well the night everything begins to change irreversibly and forever. Returning from downtown after a movie, I exit the city bus in front of Stone's Manufacturing on the corner of Poinsett and Blue Ridge. I decide to go along Blue Ridge Drive and cut up a smaller street to go home. This route a little longer, also means a quieter walk and less exposed than going down Poinsett. Just as I near the intersection a black 1964 Plymouth four-door sedan crosses my path. Hand painted on the driver's door is a black number eight centered inside a white circle. The Eight Balls, a small gang from the Berea district, have gained more than a little reputation, mostly for being hoodlums.

"I know you," shouts the driver, jumping out of the sedan. "You're that kid who beat-up my brother last month. We'll see how tough you are now."

A total of five teenagers pile-out of the remaining three doors and quickly surround me. My mind goes completely blank, my fear changed to lead in my stomach. A shove from behind causes me to stumble head first into a shallow ditch. Striking the bottom, my hands fortuitously wrap around a smooth hard stick of wood approximately three feet in length shaped like as axe handle lying at the bottom of this trough. It is as though a force overshadows me; this instrument, prepared over time by the steady process of nature, stripped of bark, made solid by rain and sun; and has been waiting through the seasons for my strength to give it purpose. The only way to describe what happens next, found in the story about Samson when he takes the jawbone of an ass and slaughters the Philistines. I leap-up a gladiator wielding the stick in all directions. I hit one in the side of the head, another on the shoulder blade. The driver I remember well, striking him in the groin. It turns out that the Eight Balls not so tough after all. They gathered their wounded and speed away.

I take this Excalibur weapon home with me. I will keep it proudly in my closet alongside my BB gun and a faded black and white photo of my father taken when he was a young man in the Air Force. That night everything somehow different-- I am different. Now I understand power and the magnification of that power through weapons of war. I can still smell blood, the fear-- but mostly I sense the nature of things small and of things great. But even more disturbing, I am acutely aware of destiny for the first time and the snare prepared for all in the course of that time. The Tiger now truly awake; nor will he dream again the same.

Chapter 7

Confessions

*T*he Vietnam War has become a subject on everyone's mind in one way or another. This soap opera airing so long that there seems no end to the conflict, as ratings rapidly decline. I skip the first day of High School, preferring instead to go joyriding with some new friends named Mike and Ronnie. These young gladiators, impressed by the way I handled the Eight Balls, think me worthy to join them. News circulates that I single-handedly sent the whole gang running. It turns out that the Eight Balls stopped being the Eight Balls after one of the members let it slip how they were humiliated. Mike, the sociable of the two, tall and lanky, always joking, except his jokes usually deadly serious. He comes from a long line of thieves and looks a lot like the Hollywood actor that played the main character in the movie Ali Baba. Subtle and persuasive, and like all con men, sensed the weakness and desire of his chosen mark.

I first become acquainted with Mike through his younger brother

Bill. Bill, a year younger than me, a little slow-witted at the time, but has the good sense not to follow his older brother into a life of crime. Mike takes an immediate liking to me. I guess he senses my need for approval, so he offers just that. Mike is the first person to introduce me to alcohol and its consequences. He tells me he knows a dance club where he can get me in without being carded. We walk more than three miles, stopping briefly at a liquor store to buy a bottle of orange screwdriver wine with my money.

"This old cheap wino stuff will keep out the cold," he says passing the bottle to me.

Because the taste so sweet, this concoction goes down easily, making me deliriously drunk by time we arrive. He gets us both in just as promised. I vaguely remember dancing with a cute girl and her asking me to make a musical request to play Tequila Sunset. I gallantly jump up on stage and shout that I want the group to play this song. After several songs I still do not remember hearing the requested song. The third time I climb up on the stage, grab the lead singer and yell into the microphone.

"I want to hear Tequila Sunset-- now!"

"No son-- no-- you can't do that here!" I hear Mike's frantic voice.

Mike leaps onto the stage, pulls me outside through a back door, and lectures me to remain here until I sober up. The next thing I know is a flashlight shining into my face.

"Are you drunk, boy?"

"No," I lie. "Someone gave me something to smoke and I got sick."

"You been smoking Marijuana! Come with me, I'm calling the police!"

A strong hand grabs me by the shoulder and starts leading me toward a car parked in the front. I begin to be enough sober to realize my lie worse than the truth. This is the sixties, after all, and drugs of any kind conjure specters much worse than alcohol use. As we pass a parked

Impala, I kick the front bumper.

"Look what you made me do," I cry, kneel down, and begin caressing the cold chrome.

This security guard must have thought me stoned out of my head. He stands there scratching his head. Then I do something unexpected that even I cannot explain. With all my weight, I jump up and strike the over-weight man square in the face. He manages to grab my shirt sleeve, ripping it in the process, but enough remains attached to keep me running blindly in a circle. Regaining his balance the guard wields his Billy Club, hitting me squarely across the face. Momentarily dazed, blood streaming from a wound above my right eye, I just stand there. Then like a maddened animal, I charge, bounce off the blubber of his stomach, rise back up, and bolt across the busy highway, diving headfirst into a deep vine-covered ravine.

"I'll give anyone five dollars to go down there and get that little SOB," Curses the security guard.

Then, the familiar voice of Mike shouts, "I'll go officer!"

Mike rushes into the camouflaged pit like a soldier in combat. After searching the brush for several minutes, he discovers me prostrate in a bed of Ivy, bloodied, and only half-conscious. He lifts me on his shoulders and follows the ravine for nearly a mile before finally re-emerging on Highway 291. From here, he commands a taxi to take us the rest of the way, managing to negotiate a fare-price with the driver for the few dollars we have left in our pockets.

"Damn, son-- you should have seen the look on that security guard when you popped him in the mouth! By God I bet he'll be remembering us for a real long time." Mike says in admiration on the ride to his home.

Mike second eldest son to a hardworking Italian immigrant family from New York, pretends to be nothing more or less than his nature. He has a streak of decency loyal only to his family and closest friends, with particular affection toward his father, who wears a back brace, barely able to walk since a terrible construction accident. His mother, the true breadwinner of the family, works two jobs to support her four growing sons and one daughter. She always looks exhausted, looks as though she lacks the energy to continue for even one more day. However, when it comes time for her second shift, this woman rises happily out of bed prepared and ready. Now looking back on it, I often wonder if perhaps her job an escape and being home to care for the many needs of her family the true burden. This night I have become just one more burden for her to tend. She places a cold compact over the open wound on my head.

"I'm calling your mother," she says in her no-nonsense sort of way.

I plea for her not to, but she calls anyway, after demanding that Mike give her the number. Jean rushes over immediately and takes me to the hospital emergency room. I see the fear, the shame, and the disappointment on her face. Nor will this be the last time. I end up having five stitches and remain repulsed to this day by anything even resembling the orangey-sweet taste of a wine screwdriver.

Ronnie, the most dangerous of us all, rarely smiles, never jokes, and always calculates. He suffers the stigma of being an only child, raised by a single mom, a full Mohawk woman, who drinks too much and has a bad reputation at the local taverns. Perhaps he hates most his father for abandoning them while Ronnie still in diapers. I think the hate for his mother less, but he hates her just the same, because always she is absent when most he needed her. Now Ronnie needs no one. The only time this dark shade seems truly human is when the three of us languish in his recently purchased 1962 Ford Falcon sipping a beer each of us secretly pillage from Mike's older brother's Budweiser six-pack. At moments like these Ronnie will sometimes snicker at one of Mike's off color jokes, resembling something dark hunched over the steering wheel reflected coldly by the pale instrument lights. Only Ronnie is allowed to drive his car; only he and Mike understand the tragic true meaning in their often colorless puns.

"Now we Musketeers got ourselves liquid courage and some wheels!" Mike howls out an open window, as though scenting the air for fresh prey.

Ronnie says nothing back, in every sense of the definition a lone wolf. In truth, I do not think he likes, nor trusts anyone. He can spend hours tinkering under his car; and the only time his needs extend to others is when a job too big to handle alone. As a result of his youthful isolation, Ronnie has vowed never to be venerable again. Despite their obvious faults, Mike and Ronnie share a certain code of honor: an honor among thieves-- maybe-- but honor all the same. These two never fight for fun or for reputation. What they do, they do for personal reasons, or because of an agreed upon definition of justice. I suppose this is what attracts me most to them. They prove loyal to a cause, even if that cause their own.

We three attend the same High School and cut the same classes. Mike, a month older than Ronnie, has a birthday making him old enough to buy beer and whiskey. Now we drink up any money left over after putting gas in Ronnie's car, but none of us old enough to drink responsibly. After a while we just hang out getting drunk without purpose or direction. Mike is the first to drop out of school altogether.

"I just don't think my services are any longer needed here," he proclaims one afternoon as we all three sat in Ronnie's car in the school parking, his beady eyes darting back and forth like a sly young fox. "How about you two-- ready for some real adventure?"
Ronnie only snickers, nodding his head approvingly, reminding me of the cartoon character Hardy Har Har. I say nothing. The idea of officially dropping out of school is frightening somehow. One thing to miss a few unpleasant classes--but to stop attending altogether becomes in my mind equivalent to heresy? --Besides, Rudy would disown me! I pretend to go along with my new friends, but without any true intention. We leave school grounds, pool our lunch money to buy a bottle of

Bourbon, then park on a quiet residential street to drink ourselves unconscious. Darkness descends by the time I awaken. Ronnie navigates his Falcon in weaving motions, with Mike slouched in the passenger's seat bobbing in and out of sobriety. Ronnie pulls up to the bottom of my driveway and orders me to get out.

"Son, don't let your mother know you been drinking," Mike mumbles after me as I stumble up the steep driveway.

"You're drunk!" My mother wails upon opening the back door.

"No!" I swear, and I keep on swearing against all the evidence.

"Rudy, see what you've done! This is all your fault by setting a bad example for your family. I hate it! –I just hate it!"

Jean disappears into the house crying. Rudy comes out alone to face me.

"Look how you have upset your mother. Now just say it, say that you have been drinking."

"I never touched a drop!" I blubber, looking Rudy straight into his eyes.

I then stumble over a small wall barrier running along the walkway, passing-out in the back yard. These are words I heard Rudy say on so many occasions, just before he and Jean started arguing. Words of defiance, of obvious untruth, words spoken to spawn the violence of so many other words. This denial gives me a certain pleasure; and never once do I recant, even when my mother pleas with me the next morning to tell her the truth.

This represents the real beginning of many endings. In October, I get a minimum wage job at Burger King making more money than I ever saw at one time. Ronnie picks me up one evening after work in his faded-greed Falcon, with Mike seated importantly in the passenger seat. I volunteer to treat us all to steak and beer, after Ronnie states he knows of a place off Wade Hampton Boulevard where no one will ask for ID. This plan might have been good, except for what we do not know. As we pass the Clock Drive Inn at the intersection of Pleasantburg Drive and Wade Hampton Boulevard, the back window of Ronnie's car shatters, spraying glass everywhere. Several young men continue running behind us throwing rocks and soda cans.

"Someone's going to pay for that," Ronnie swears, and pulls the vehicle into a nearby gas station already closed for the night.

As many as ten assailants chase us, some scaling over a fence barrier behind the Clock Drive Inn, all headed in our direction. Ronnie opens the trunk and we each grab a weapon. Ronnie takes a bumper jack, Mike a length of chain used to pull engines, and I grab a four-way lug wrench. We cross the busy highway and meet our attackers in an empty field. Each of these young men wear a white t-shirt painted with a black circle, and most armed with weapons of chains, knives, and wooden bats. The mob quickly encircles us. One of the members leaps forward wielding a knife.

I do not remember if he said anything, only that I raise the lug wrench instinctively and bring the instrument down on the crown of his head. His eyes roll back until only the whites visible. He then spins around and collapses lifeless on the ground. I will later learn that this young man the only near fatality of the battle, a steel plate surgically placed in his head, a terrible tragedy that continues to haunt me to this day. This singular act of counter aggression ignites a combat melee. We three manage to successfully dispatch these first scout members; but unaware that these represent only a reconnaissance of the much larger force. We have been lured into a trap, unsuspecting victims of a turf war between two rival gangs: Wade Hampton High and Greenville High. Ronnie's recently purchased car has a Greenville High sticker in the back window, an oversight that proves nearly fatal. We attempt to navigate back to our vehicle, but quickly surrounded by this unrelenting army of white t-shirts.

Ronnie's car trunk still open, inviting some of the less armed opponents to scavenge a weapon of choice, which includes two heavy magnesium rims with tires. For the first time, I am in a battle for my life, which can only be described as a personal fight for survival; a fight I cannot afford to lose. I vaguely remember the   peripheral vision of a tire bouncing toward my position, then hitting like the swat of a dark hand that knocks me to the ground. Upon regaining my footing, I am momentarily blinded by a sudden shock, my head now heavy, weighted to one side. I have the strangest sensation of time slowing down, my physical body connected to the present by only a thread of consciousness. My attackers begin backing away, a look of horror on their faces. Then I perceive the reason for their reluctance, a protruding shadow envisioned through the brightness of a street lamp. In Ronnie's trunk, among other tools, had been a three-foot long broad-tooth screwdriver used as a jack handle. This terrifying instrument now pierces the left frontal lobe of my forehead. They must have thought me already dead, refusing to believe anyone able to survive with a javelin lodged in their brain.

But I do rise up, a raging wounded animal, refusing to die-- at least not yet! Reaching up I grasp the screwdriver handle and attempt to excavate it free, only the broad tip wedged too tightly into bone of my skull. Then the rage subsides, changing into total clarity of purpose.

"Damn you all– you killed me! You killed me!" I bellow vengefully. "I will not die alone!"

The bones in my forehead crack loudly, as I twist the handle. The deadly weapon flies away into the night, spinning through the blackness of eternity, followed by a thick spout of blood-- my blood! Next thing I remember are two police officers, one holding my right arm, the other my left.

"Drop it!" A voice commands.

Bodies of my adversaries surround me, some crying, others

unconscious. I allow the heavy weapon to drop out of my hand. Ronnie staggers over with a switchblade knife protruding through his right shoulder, while aiding Mike bloodied by a head wound. He helps Mike into the back seat and climbs into the driver's seat of his Falcon. The police give instructions that we go directly to the hospital. In this day Greenville has limited police and emergency services. Since we are able to walk, they decide to allow us to conduct ourselves. Besides, only these two Greenville city cops stand between us and an enraged gang of more than thirty, including many injured. I take a place in the passenger seat and must change the gear shifter because of Ronnie's knife wound. Then a revelation of portentous magnitude strikes me.

"Go to the police station, Ronnie," I command with an assertion atypical to my usual nature.

Perhaps because of his injuries, or perhaps because it just makes good sense to him, Ronnie obeys. Even Mike, who usually makes all the decisions, remains uncharacteristically quiet. Two squad cars race past us in the opposite lane with lights flashing and sirens wailing. We must have been a sight to the duty officer when we stagger into the precinct, Ronnie pierced through still with a knife lodged in his shoulder. Mike only a little coherent, he and I both covered in dried blood. A detective takes our report in as much detail as we are able to supply, and then provides us escort to the Greenville General.

The hospital emergency ward resembles the aftermath of a war zone: bandaged bodies everywhere, congested corridors echoing with moans and groans of pain. An intern examines my head and asks what happened. I explain a flying screwdriver stabbed me. Maybe I did not make myself very clear. The young doctor (or maybe it was a male nurse,I never really knew) decides that the injury superficial. He adds a few stitches and sends me home without even taking an x-ray. To this day I have a deep indention just below the hairline over half an inch long.

I think that Rudy and Jean are truly frightened this time. The next morning paper reports that three Greenville High students decimated the infamous Wade Hampton Circle Gang. The body count of the injured estimated to be more than twenty. The article further affirms no deaths a miracle, with only one in critical condition.

An element of unspoken loyalty bonds together comrades in arms. No longer just friends, we are now three brothers. We will stand victorious through other battles as well, but none as monumental as this one. If only Mike and Ronnie had not been criminals. In all honesty, I suppose that without knowing it I have begun going down the path of lawlessness, only too blind to realize it at the time, slipping slowly through the cracks of moral dilemma. In the beginning, we are just warriors on the prowl. In time, however, the truest nature of my friends begins to emerge. One evening out of money, out of beer, and almost out of gas, Mike has a brilliant idea. He possesses a natural instinct for casing-out every place he goes. Having seen Rudy's collection of power tools once when the garage doors open, Mike convinces me that we can borrow the sander and the circular saw and pawn them until the following week. He promises no one will ever know. The idea seems harmless enough, so I agree to take these tools belonging to my father. Stopping at a local pawnshop, we receive twenty dollars for tools worth well over a hundred.

The following week, and the week after, Rudy's tools remain in the pawnshop. A month passes before Rudy discovers the theft. His instincts are right to blame me. He goes to Mike's house and threatens to rip off his head if he does not give him the pawn ticket. Mike knows Rudy capable of such an act-- and even worse! So he complies, sheepishly spewing empty meaningless apologies. Anyone who knows my stepfather knows never to cross him-- especially if he is drinking whiskey! Rudy infuriated to have to pay to get his own tools back condemns me vehemently as a thief. And who can blame him? I think Rudy would have put me out of his house that night were it not for my mother's pleas. We both know it only a matter of time until I lost my home and my place in it forever.

Ronnie wants a new engine for his six-cylinder falcon. He and Mike reason that with a few modifications the new Ford 286 will fit perfectly. I must give these two some engineering credit. Collectively bold when it comes to getting something they badly want. I am unsure if this scheme a product of chance or of brilliant planning. A lone State Trooper named Ledbetter patrols Poinsett Highway. Mike and Ronnie on actual first name basis with this corpulent swaggering highway patrol officer, who takes pleasure in pulling cars over just to kill the boredom. One night Ronnie makes two high speed runs from the Parkway outdoor cinema to the Stones manufacturing company and back again. On the second pass, the familiar flashing blue bubble of Ledbetter's patrol car appears behind us. Ronnie intentionally pulls close to some shrubs planted at the edge of the road shoulder. As Ledbetter exits his car and approaches the driver's side, Mike slips clandestine out of the passenger side and into the thick brush.

"Boy, I warned you more than once not to go speeding," the overweight officer huffs. "Now I'm going to have to give you a ticket."

"I'm real sorry Mr. Ledbetter, I just wanted to wind her out a little," Ronnie lies.

Just then, the 402 Hemi-loaded patrol vehicle races past, screeching up the highway. I think Ledbetter more stunned, than anything. He tells Ronnie to move over and for me to crawl into the back seat. The patrol car already out of sight by the time Ledbetter slams the inadequate Falcon into first gear. He and Ronnie both know the six-cylinder no match for a Police Special. Ledbetter commandeers Ronnie's car as far as the local police station.

It never occurs to the authorities that maybe Ronnie somehow involved. Instead of going back the way we came, Ronnie takes the longer detour along Route 281 and pulls into the side entrance of the Ford dealership. Parked in the back hidden in a shadow is the Police

Special with Mike waiting beside a red Mustang.

"Wait here in the car," Ronnie instructs and walks over to Mike.

Speaking in low tones they come to an agreement. Mike jumps into the Mustang, starts the engine, and peels rubber heading north on the 281 with the headlamps off. Ronnie follows in fast pursuit, the Mustang already out of sight. We turn on Paris Road headed toward the mountains, continuing past the main entrance of the Paris Mountain State Park. Everything happening so fast that I barely have time to consider the gravity of the crime my two friends have just committed, further compounded by the silent realization that I am an unknowing participated in a grand theft auto.

Arriving at a fork and taking a smaller road to a fabled area known as Blackberry Hill, we traverse a steep dirt trail into the blackness of an overgrown hollow. On more than one occasion we have come this way, as I silently recount frightening story of this place.

According to local legend, an abandoned barn sagging on the road side haunted by the ghost of a black man hanged there just because he was too fond of white women. They say that when the upper loft door is open, then it means his restless spirit afoot. This night that barn door stands open, only adding to the guilt of   my anxiety, convicting me of the terrible knowledge of the recent act. I deserve the punishment I might find, or even worse, the judgment that might find me.

Mike has already driven the stolen vehicle down the tractor track that runs beside the barn leading into the secret hollow of a prearranged rendezvous point. He hands Ronnie and me a beer upon our arrival in celebration of a well-executed crime.

"O' dumb Ledbetter," Mike jokes disrespectfully. "Without his Police Special he ain't shit! Here's to Officer Ledbetter!"

I drink up without saying a word. Now I am aware really for the first time how precarious my position. Ronnie and Mike will return later alone, remove the engine and transmission, grafting them into the Falcon. They even install Magnesium rims with racing slicks by precision drilling an addition stud hole. This turns out badly and they end up having to steal a stronger rear-end and driveshaft from another compatible Ford model to support the extra torque. For the next few months, Ronnie has the fastest car in Greenville, if not in all of South Carolina. Then one afternoon he and Mike while drinking and taking turns piloting the bird of prey, nearly terminate their notorious careers.

According to Ronnie, it is Mike's turn at the helm, claiming the over-powered Falcon flew off the road at a hundred and twenty miles an hour, crashing into a vine covered valley. Ronnie prescribed a back brace for several weeks. As for Mike--well Mike is just full of providence. It is a miracle both survive, and even a greater miracle that I am not with them on this furious flight. Sadly, both my friends will spend the next several years in and out of prison for petty crimes; trapped in a web of their own making.

Ronnie trades the Mustang engine and transmission from the destroyed Falcon for a 1960 Pontiac Catalina convertible. This car, originally from New York, where salt used on the roads in winter, has rust cancer along the door panels and around the rear wheel wells. Reputed to have the most powerful engine Pontiac ever made, it comes also factory equipped with a custom four-speed transmission mounted on the floor. Ronnie will miss his green Falcon, but this plush new road-master in time sooths some of his disappointment.

By now I fear no one, not even the arm of the law. I surrender to a violence inside that I have struggled against for so long, heading into a snare without caring. The more I drink, the more my anger seethes to the surface. One night because of a dare, I once break the window of a liquor store and steal two quart-bottles of whiskey prominently displayed on a center pedestal. Amazingly, the alarm does not go off right away. As I make my exit with a heavy bottle in each hand, my foot touches the broken edge of a shard, setting off the screaming alarm. I cut through a private yard to rejoin my comrades on the next street. Suddenly the interior light of a car turns on just in front of me.

"Who's there?" A distinctive male voice demands.

Startled I momentarily freeze, dropping both bottles. I then sprint past the vehicle and up a steep hill in back of the house, reaching the rendezvous point empty handed. Ronnie, already in the process of leaving, makes a U-turn to pick me up. I dive into the back seat feeling a false sense of safety in the presence of my comrades. Then the hornets arrive, screaming sirens and familiar blue bubble reflections of police cruisers surround the liquor store below. Ronnie cuts his headlights and takes a discrete route back to our mountain hold.

"Damn, son, you just let them bottles slip through your fingers like gold," Mike says shaking his head disappointed. "We could all be drunker than skunks by now, and all you had to do was just hold on to them bottles a little tighter."

In November my life as a future career criminal begins to unravel. This the night I steal a portable T.V. set from a local barbershop on PoinsettHighway near where I live. It begins with a couple of swigs of T.W. Samuel's whiskey from Mike's back pocket and a challenging dare. Even then Mike a bartender by nature, a profession he will engage in later years. Mike drops by the Burger King where I work as my shift ends, accompanied by another boy with small squinting eyes named Beasley. I have met Beasley only once before, and for some reason I cannot explain, dis like him from the beginning. The three of us stroll down the sidewalk passing back and forth the bottle of warm whiskey, when Mike's eye catches the color T.V. set left on after closing.

"My old man sure would like to have that," he says, placing the nearly empty bottle firmly in my hand. "Only someone with real balls would break in there and take that for my poor half-crippled Daddy."

His eyes roll toward Beasley, who immediately backs away shaking his head. Mike then looks at me.

"Looks like Beasley got a case of chicken shit. Show him real balls; show this chicken shit that you aren't afraid of nothing."

This is when I commit one of the greatest errors of my young life. Picking up a piece of loose asphalt, I lob it through the storefront window, completely shattering the glass. Realizing no alarm, I boldly enter the premises, grab the television set, and hand it over to Mike waiting outside. We all three run down an incline beside a nearby overpass and rejoin on the train tracks below. Somehow, Beasley and I get into a drunken argument. He pulls a Hawk-Billed knife from his pocket and begins slashing threateningly at me. I kick him once or twice with my right foot, managing to knock the sinister weapon out of his hand. As he searches the brush for his knife, I kick him again, this time in the face. He curses me belligerently, as he runs away frightened into the night. After the incident, Mike and I continue to walk along the tracks, momentarily halting so that he can get a better grip on his new prize. I realize my right pants leg wet, and so stop to examine it under the light of a utility pole.

"Damn boy-- you better get on home!"

To the horror of us both a half-inch wide cut four inches long slashes across my calf. Beasley's sharp Hawk-Bill had found its flesh after all. Nor will this be the end of his vengeance. I can actually see the muscle beneath the thick precisely incised dermis. Surprisingly not as much blood as one might expect issues from the deep cup. Once again, Jean takes me to the hospital that night and waits anxiously for the doctor to sew me back up. It takes several inner stitches and fourteen outer to close the wound. My mother fears it only a matter of time before something worse should happen.

Everything has changed dark now. Christmas comes and goes, but the tree just a tree with lights, my gifts practical acquisitions. I am now an outsider and everyone in my family knows it. I feel like a tragic character once played by the actor James Cagney, destroying everything and everyone he touches; a criminal whose mind and destiny fixed in a cast with no escape. I want desperately to avoid this fate, to undo somehow my past sins, only the poison within me still has a course left to run, the end more near than I could have imagined.

The lowest point of my shame is when I steal from a boy, who only desires my friendship. Donnie lives on the other side of Poinsett highway at the edge of a small cemetery opposite the Methodist church, just recently moved into Greenville, with his father employed locally as some sort of engineer, and is originally from Poland. Because of his father profession, the family relocates, making it difficult for Donnie and his younger brother to make real connections. Donnie is a kind individual, well spoken, with an England accent, and sincerely seeks a friendship. Sadly, he might have made a good friend were it not for my jealousy and feelings of inferiority. One morning, Donnie, his younger brother, and I decide to cut classes while waiting for the school bus. This is as daring a thing Ronnie has ever done in his entire life. For me, cutting class far less of a stretch, since I rarely attend since hanging out with Mike and Ronnie. We go to Donnie's house, since his mother not home. I presumed at the time that she is at work, but will later learn that the woman died only a year earlier of cancer while the family still lived in London.

This unfettered freedom liberates something inside of Donnie, something repressed since a long time. He goes wild, jumping up and down on the furniture, pulling clothes out of his father's closet. We watch TV, play Ping Pong in the basement, and might have done some real damage had Donnie not accidentally broken a Chinese urn once particularly dear to his mother. Donnie's euphoria ends flat. He collapses on the floor and begins pathetically to try and piece the shattered relic back together again. He then begins to panic, insisting that I must leave immediately.

Feeling a little offended by this sudden change, I ascend back upstairs unescorted to gather my things. Then I see several business suits scattered on the floor belonging to Donnie's father. I cannot say why, really, only that I have a sudden impulse to scoop as many up as I can carry. I think it began in my mind as a bad prank, never really intending to keep any of the stuff. Cutting through the adjoining cemetery, I pause at a sunken grave somewhere in the middle of this necropolis and drop the ill-gotten clothing. This is when my eye fastens onto a light brown camel hair jacket, and another made of English tweed. Although I know nothing about men's fashion, I believe these two coats special, as only on two occasions can I remember Rudy ever wearing a dress suit. Once for an Easter photo of him and Jean together; another time when he attends the funeral of one of his uncles. Perhaps these two dress jackets remind me of the gentry deprived to my genesis, a world of sophistication and elegant presence seen only in the movies. Or maybe it is something I see in Donnie that I feel never to have. I decide to keep them, as though these rags belonging to a man I have never met might impart some greater dignity to my estate. I take the over-sized garments home and hang them in the private fortress of my clothes closet.

Just before suppertime Donnie's father rings at the front door. I know it is him even before he says anything. The man possesses an air of dignity that I find angering, therefore I pretend dumbness.

"You were at my home today," he accuses, looking steadfast into my eyes. "Neighbors saw you dump my suit clothes in the cemetery. Fortunately, I recovered them, all, except two sport coats. Where are they?"

I swear ignorance. To lie now so easy that even I almost convinced of the lies. My mother, being a good soul, believes me innocent. Jean always wants to see the best potential in people. She confidently escorts the man into my room, opens the closet door to see for himself. Here hang the two jackets, prominently displayed in all their shameful glory. This kind unassuming man identifies his belongings and promises my mother not to call the police since things worked out okay, adding at the end.

"Donnie is a good boy. He would not have stayed home from school if not for your son. It has been hard for him and his brother since their mother died. Donnie doesn't have too many friends, so it's too bad that it worked out this way."

"I know... I'm so sorry," my mother replies, more ashamed than ever I have seen her.

Even though I do not know much about the meaning of God at the time, for some reason, I suppose that deep down I hope there something meaningful to prayer. Prayer to me has always been a deep urging in my being (perhaps the soul), which communicates through some magnified presence far beyondmy comprehension. This mediation more than conscious positivity, rather is the manifest evidence of a supernatural condition, which I now know to be greater than all other potentials. I will later be convinced that the power of real prayer-- and particularly those prayers of my mother--proof positive of manifest destiny to change directional course.

Ronnie needs a new transmission for his Pontiac. There is a junkyard on Poinsett Highway near the city limits named *Slayman Salvage* protected by a pad-locked gate and the fabled junkyard dog. The plan to tranquilize the dog with a side of beef spiked with sleeping pills and a rented lock-cutter. Of course, the flaw in the plan is the lock-cutter, acquired from the one tool rental in all of North Greenville. It will not take the police long to figure this one out. Mike, a part-time employee, has already cased out the premises during work hours, knowing exactly where to find the three hundred dollar mechanism. By now my friend Tommy, along with my nemesis Beasley, all part of the gang. We collectively agree to execute the crime together, according to the instructions of our team leaders. I swear reluctant allegiance to this ill-conceived mission. Some alarm inside warns this no longer a game, and that I am about to participate in an act with terrible consequence. On the other hand, how can I disappoint those that I believe to be my friends? The die cast made. Nor can I see a way out of the web. Once my family asleep, I place a blanket and a pillow on the floor beside the radio console near the dining room window so that I might hear my summons. I lay listening to the low tones of a classical piece on the radio, whensuddenly an inspiration of prayer sweeps over me.

"Please let them change their minds!" I make plea with sweat of anguish on my brow.

The morning sun blazes intensely through the window pane, stinging me awake. My mother enquires why I slept on the floor and not in my bed. I respond that I could not sleep and thought the radio might relax me. My prayer has been answered, the dreaded cup passed from my lips.

I receive no word from any of my friends that day or the next. Three dayslater, I meet Tommy walking up the hill of the street he lives on. He claims they came by to pick me up as planned, but when I did not respond to the knocking on the window, they went without me. They are able to grab the transmission and some professional tools, but Ronnie has a flat tire on Poinsett just as Ledbetter passing. It is simple arithmetic even for old Ledbetter to add up, the yellow tagged transmission, tools, and the rented lock-cutter. Two hours later, all four confess at the station. Beasley, however, adds to his confession that I was supposed to be with them that night, adding that I am the one who broke the barbershop glass window and stole the T.V. set only a few weeks earlier. With this new information, the police eventually come knocking at our door demanding to interrogate me further. Just as they are about to make a report Rudy steps forward.

"He's going to be seventeen in just a few weeks, Officers, and plans to go into the military. I know the service straightened me out. I'll gladly pay for the TV; just give the boy one more chance."

The two police officers look at each other, then at me. They say the insurance has already taken care of the TV, and seeing that I come from a good family they will give me this one chance to avoid having a record.

"In a month we are going to pass by here again. If you are not serving your country by then, we are going to lay charges," one of the men in blue promises before they leave.

That night Rudy and Jean argue until late.

"There's no other way." I hear Rudy say.

Jean only crying repeatingthe same words over and over again

"No, no--" I hear Jean wail repeatedly. "He can't go!"

I will always be thankful for what Rudy did. He believed me worth saving after all. How easy it would have been to allow me to fulfill his worse prophesy. I have become the prodigal son; but at the eleventh hour a door opens to another possibility. Also, Rudy right; there is no other exit.

Ronnie, Mike, Beasley, and Tommy are all convicted of breaking and entering and possession of stolen property, with three receiving probation. Mike is sentenced to a year in prison because of prior convictions. Early onemorning a week before my seventeenth birthday, I take a bus to the recruiting office on Main Street located beside the Greenville City cemetery marking thegraves of those formerly wealthy. I think first to follow Rudy's footsteps and enter the office for the Department of the Navy. Unfortunately, I am too young, eighteen being the minimum age. My second choice is the Air Force, as my father before me, but again rejected for the lack of a high school diploma. Of the three services that I am aware, the Armyappeals least to me. Maybe this lack of enthusiasm stems from reading too many Sad Sack comics as a child or from the Sergeant Benny comic strips in the Sunday paper. Maybe because so many casualties listed serve in the Army, including some I have known. Or maybe, just fear that I might become like Tommy's father.

The Army recruiting office is just down the hall, but first a soda. I insert a quarter into the coke vending machine. Nothing happens. I begin banging on the eight-foot high bandit to no avail.

"That machine gets stuck all the time," rumbles a voice behind me.

This fabled giant stands no less than six feet tall with muscles bulging at the seams of a striking blue and white uniform. He has a head geometrically squared by a distinct Marine Corps haircut, steely blue eyes, and a voice of absolute command. I have heard about Marines, as one might hear about a Phoenix or the fabled Minotaur, but I never actually saw one in the flesh. A swift jab with the broad of his hand and the soda tumbles into the bottom bin.

"I usually wait until the civilian leaves and take the soda for myself. But I know a Marine when I see one, and Marines are *Simper Fidelis.*"

He looks down at me with greater scrutiny, realizing I have no idea what he is saying.

"That means: always faithful."

Inviting me into his office, he begins sharing with me so many wonderful advantages of becoming one of the elite. He shows me pictures of exotic beaches with white sand and beautiful women in skimpy swimsuits. Even before he turns to the last page, I am completely sold on the idea. The only question that remains, can I qualify? He hands me a single page test sheet with mostly true or false questions. I guess I passed, because he only glances quickly at the answers. He proficiently makes a check mark with his pen and places the form in a brown folder on his desk. Here the beginning of a different kind of acceptance. Immediately, I feel an affinity toward this uniquely legendary branch of the Navy, as never I felt for anything before. He types out an official document and instructs me to have one of my parents sign it, and then bring it back with a copy of my original birth certificate as soon as I turn seventeen.

Upon returning home, I run into the house excited, the prospect of a new life; a different future clutched in my hand. Jean busily prepares supper and in the process of removing something from the oven.

"The Marine Corps--" she exclaims horrified. "Sunny-- are you out of your mind! The Navy is one thing, but my child is not going to go off and die in some jungle!"

We are still arguing by the time Rudy arrives home from work.

"It's better than jail, Jean. Since Sunny is old enough to steal and to bring shame to this family, then he's old enough to make up his own mind. If the Marine Corp will have him, then I'll take him there myself."

In reality, my mother is the only one with the legal authority to sign the form. Even though it against her every instinct, Jean reluctantly, painfully seals the contract, making me the property of the United States government for the next six years of my life. She, too, in the course of time will appreciate the greater power of prayer.

At 0800 March 12, 1969, just ten days after my seventeenth birthday, I board a green military bus and head for Paris Island. Even the name exotic, a place of refuge and escape, a place branded with much history spanning decades of many wars. I wave goodbye to my childhood, Rudy and Jean dissolving away into the distance as ghosts past.

Dragons of Air

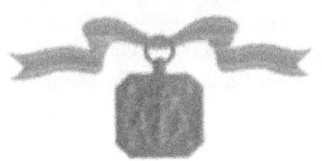

DEPARTMENT OF THE NAVY

THIS IS TO CERTIFY THAT

THE SECRETARY OF THE NAVY HAS AWARDED THE

NAVY ACHIEVEMENT MEDAL

Remembrance Day

I remember Shangri-La
deep emperor green of that country
Rich morning dipped with the silver dew of fishermen songs
their nets tangled in twilight-red between gray humped shoals
I remember the women black hair laced with flowers
exotic eyes deep fountains reflecting the myriad night
of an East Asian hemisphere
How soft their touch
Their lips as fresh fruit in a season golden with peace
Their laughter fading as a morning in Spring
as birds scattered by a hunter's gun
I remember the silence before thunder
as orange flames spread rich blistering the jungle fuse
Ghost of children wailing in smoky dawn mist
heavy with the dew of burnt flesh
And all that remains black twisted and scarred
A rain of smoldering white ash
that has lasted and lasted
in my mind to this day

Chapter 8
The Island of Paradise Lost

*P*arris Island does not live up to its name. It is actually just one of many coastal islands massed together off the South Carolina coast of mostly congested swampland. Beaufort Island, the largest, connected to the military base by the thread of a narrow bridge built over an area of dangerous quick sand. I immediately realize that Parris Island more aprison than the provoked imagery of its name. And like Devil's Island, only a few have ever escaped.

It is interesting to note that before 1913, when the Marine Corps designated it a Boot Camp training facility, Parris Island already had a long campaign history. It is first occupied by a small French colony in 1562 that comes to a disastrous end. Then later it is christened the Spanish settlement of Santa Elena, until ousted by the English in less than a decade. Disease bearing ticks and mosquitoes flourish in abundance, the terrain too dry or too moist; the temperature either too hot or too cold, making Paris Island the antipathy of earthly paradise.

The bus carrying new recruits comes to a stop in front of a simple whitewashed wooden building. The door opens and in steps a stout man, although not very tall, wearing a tan dress uniform and a broad-brimmed brown hat.

"Listen up ladies, from this point on you are maggots. For those of you who do not know what a maggot is, then look under a cow-turd and you will find a bunch of sickly white worms. Those, ladies, are maggots. From now own, you are what I say you are. Grab your useless gear and file out of the bus now!"

This introduction, designed for shock effect, rattles even the coolest of us. We look like a bunch of summer camp refugees, as different from each other as a herd of wild horses in spring: long hair, short hair, tall and short, fat and thin, pale and not so pale. We are maggots considered in Marine Corps language the lowest corporeal life form on the planet. Once outside, we are bombarded by screaming orders to stand straight, to stand at attention, and to make standing our new resting position. The commands ridiculous, since none of us understand the meaning. Nevertheless, we make a staggering attempt; our shoulders bowed forward, our stomachs weak and protruding. Someone makes the mistake of snickering, immediately walloped in the solar plexus and doubled over by our assigned nemesis from hell.

"Are you laughing at me, maggot?"

"No," manages a breathless reply.

This boy the tallest, strongest looking one of the group made to cry by a single jab. He will later become platoon leader designated to carry our training flag: an honor given only to a select few.

"That's No Sir! Is that understood?" Then turning to the rest of us: "You will address me as Sir in all contexts. You will not look at me, you will not look at the ground, you will not look at the sky-- your eyes will look forward at all times, and you will not breathe unless I give you permission. Isthis understood?"

We all mumble, "Yes sir."

"I cannot hear you!"

This time it is a clear sharp—"Yes Sir!"

This seems sufficient to please our disgruntled receptionist. We next form a single line and file into a barracks containing top and bottom sleeping bunks. It is only a little past six o'clock, but I think we are all exhausted by shock. We do not eat this first night. It must be around ten o'clock p.m. everything dark, everyone asleep. Suddenly the lights snap on and in steps two Bull Dog Drill Instructors no less intimidating than the one that greeted us a few hours earlier.

"Get your sorry maggot asses out of bed," bellows one of these new comers. "I want to see every eyeball looking straight ahead!"

By nature, I have always been a deep sleeper, believing I am able to sleep through most anything; but the sheer riot of screams, sticks banging against the metal bed frames causes me to leap up in panic. I find myself standing at attention along with everyone else, before my mind even comprehends. Half an hour later again lights out, allowed to go back to sleep. No sooner have I fallen asleep again, the disturbance repeats. This goes on all night, until rising and descending into sleep becomes an autonomic ritual.

At the crack of dawn our tormentors rout us for the last time. We stumble into the twilight of morning as zombies and are escorted to a building with a lineup of young civilians similar to ourselves. One by one, each enter a door on this side of the facility. At the other end is another door exited by a stream of recruits with shiny bald bowling-pin heads, dressed in baggy green fatigues, and looking like displaced refugees. Perhaps in denial, I do not equate the obvious meaning. Here I would like to point out that my hair has always been my greatest vanity. At nine years old, just before starting the fourth grade at North Greenville Elementary, Rudy determines that it time I receive a 'boy's haircut'. To my horror, he literally shaves my head. Crying and desperate, I attempt to reattach the severed locks; my vanity gone. It will be many years before allowed to grow my hair back to a decent length.

The first swipe of the buzzing electric razor makes a slick path across the right center of my head; the second pass screeches to a grinding halt, as edge of the blade gets stuck in the deep crater of my healed head wound. The barber huffs a rude comment and within seconds razors the balance of my beautiful covering. As a hairdresser will later tell me, hair is everything. Without our hair, who are we? This is probably the most degrading event of my military career. It provides little comfort to know the shearing happens to everyone. All that matters is my hair again taken away, and against my will.

Ordered to strip naked, we shower publicly, pumped with a battery of vaccinations, then issued military uniforms consisting of two sets of green fatigues, three skivvies and t-shirts, three pairs of socks, a rain poncho, and a pair of black leather boots with an extra pair of laces. A metal bucket stuffed with a piece of canvass, a knapsack, a haversack, buckles, straps, and poles termed our 782 gear. Finally, and most importantly, each assigned a M14 assault rifle for which we will learn profound respect-- and learn never to call it a gun. As for my wardrobe, even the smallest size twice too big for my body. I feel like an orphan child cast into a man's world, a world for which I am ill prepared.

The sun well above the horizon by the time we herd into the chow hall.I am starving. One thing I can say for the Marine Corps is that the food good and offers a broad variety of choice. Corn beef hash over toast orpotatoes affectionately called 'shit on a shingle' considered the staple ofevery meal, several meats and vegetables; always dessert and a fresh milk dispenser. My mother often refers to me as a bottomless pit because I am always hungry and even volunteer to clear the table after dinner just so I might scavenge the leftovers. Here I have all the food I could want, except for just one catch. After passing through the line and filling our trays with food, we are ordered to remain standing until every man in our platoon present at the table. Once everyone accounted for a fierce order to begin eating-- no talking, no looking to the left or to the right. Less than ten minutes later screams another terse order to stand at attention, gather our trays, form a single file, and dump the remaining food into a garbage pail. Once outside we must remain at attention until all the training platoons similarly pass through the same drill. This first breakfast a Tantalus nightmare-- after only two bites and still just as hungry-- I am forced to dump my heaping tray into a slop barrel. For the first time in my life I gain some idea what the term "starving children in China and India" means. From then on, I determine to make better use of the little time I have-- and from this point on it will be military time!

The bright morning rays contrast sharply against the narrow white building designated our barracks for next three months. No different in appearance from any other barracks, except this the barracks of Platoon 261. Ours to use, to maintain, and to call our own, which in time will be the only home I know.

Above all other statutes, there is a code that the inventory of each Marine Corps issue be maintained always in immaculate inspection order, which includes the person and property of every soldier from recruit up to the highest-ranking officer. Eleanor Roosevelt once remarked, *"Marines have the purest bodies and dirtiest minds of any men in military service."* I am not certain about the minds, but as for cleanliness, I can affirm this observation to be true. Every morning begins with a shower at 0500 hours, and every evening ends with a shower. Each recruit receives a scrub brush and a bucket. These two items with some water and bleach recognized as the backbone of all other training tools. First, the bathroom top to bottom, then on hands and knees to scrub every plank of the unfinished hardwood floor surrounding our bunks, through the middle, and out the door on either end of the barracks divided by starboard and port. By 06:00 hours we are dressed in clean pressed military fatigues, spit polished boots, and frozen at attention beside the foot of tightly military-style made beds awaiting inspection. If one of our Drill Instructors in a disgruntled mood (and always one of the three is), he willfully finds some fault with a bed because a quarter fails to bounce just right, or because a soldier's attire not up to protocol. This will send him into a rage, turning over racks, swearing, forcing all but the offender to do pushups. Every evening the ritual repeats in slightly different order until 20:00 hours and lights out. However, we do have our periods of quiet time often occupied by sitting on the edge of our racks reading the bible of our issued red training manual. The rest of the time we spend disassembling and reassembling our M14 rifle, until we are able to perform the procedure blindfolded. But most importantly we devote proper attention to polishing our brass buckles or spit-polishing our boots, with goal to see our own reflection. These hourly routines become the backbone center of our existence until the exact minute of lights out.

Our barracks becomes our temple to maintain in spic and span condition from port to starboard, including the common bath facility referred to as the Head. However, our designated personal space the most sacred of all. I occupy a bottom bunk and a black boy from Mississippi, about my age only a little smaller, assigned the top bunk. I do not know this boy really, except that he is soft spoken and somewhat withdrawn. His name is Samson, which I think ironic considering his stature. Occupying a neighboring bunk is a taller individual from somewhere in lower Georgia, maybe eighteen or older. He has a surly personality with an arrogant disposition that makes my skin crawl. I, therefore, go out of my way to avoid him; not because of fear, but because of a strong revulsion in my gut that might easily change to violence.

Then one morning a week after settling-in, this serpent raises its head. We are all on hands and knees performing our early routine scrub, when this southern bred elite stands and tosses his brush at Samson.

"Boy, while you are at it clean my area, too!" He snares belligerently.

Samson remains speechless. Perhaps he feels the intimidation of more than a century of oppression experienced by his race from ignorance such as this after the war to end slavery; or maybe Samson just wants to be a good Marine, saying nothing because there is nothing he can say that might change anything in the moment. But we are bunk-buddies. Nor will I allow this attempt at intimidation go without challenge. Jumping aggressively to my feet I tell this bully to clean his own side and that we will clean ours.

"So you are one of them?"

"Maybe yes, maybe no" I reply, not knowing what else to say, adding; "Only I am glad not to be like you!"

I have no memory of who threw the first punch, only that we are rolling across the barracks floor, when the verbally cruelest of the three Drill Instructors comes running in. He tears us apart like paper dolls and calls everyone to attention.

"So, you ladies like to fight." Then looking down at the taller boy, he demands: "Do you like him?"

Now less arrogant, he mumbles something about not having anything against me.

"Then are you queer for him?""No, Sir!"

"Then I want you to show me how much you are not queer. Hit this maggot so he will know how much you are not queer for him."

Instructed to face each other and look eyeball to eyeball, with me looking up. I cannot even begin to imagine what is going on in this fellow's mind. He strikes me forcefully, his fist glancing across my chest and neck. I do not feel pain, but I do feel the anger inside me growing. Then the Drill Instructor turns to me.

"Do you like this other maggot?"

"No Sir!" I shout clearly.

"Show me how much!"

I doubt that even this duty Sergeant expects what happens next. Like a loaded spring, my fist contacts the white Georgian cracker on the jaw, sending him dazed to the floor. He will never say anything to Samson or me after this.

My violent act sends the Drill Instructor into a rage. He hits me in the stomach so hard that my feet lift off the floor, joining my fellow Marine on the smooth unblemished surface. Without further ceremony, we are both ordered to help each other up and to return to our stations.

This morning will prove to be only the beginning of tribulation. A bulldog is not just an affectionate term for a Marine Corps Drill Instructor. Like the animal, only a certain breed of man can claim the title. Like all dog packs, there is one that rises above the rest. Our Senior Drill Instructor's name Gunnery Sergeant Garcia, a top-dog that hunches menacingly, with a square muscled body, an acne scared face scored like sandpaper, and matching vicious temperament. Being a Chicano from East Los Angeles, he has grown up tough, with an unsettling tendency to drool when he gets angry.

The two junior Assistant Drill Instructors are named Staff Sergeant McKinley and Sergeant Robinson, one tall and one short, like Mutt and Jeff, mischievously cruel, whose greatest pleasure is to assign unpleasant tasks to alleviate their boredom. These three Instructors serve as overlords of platoon 261-- my platoon-- forging a tenacious alliance of persecution, deciding collectively to break me or to make me according to the order of their charge. I think they think I will break; and want to see just how much it will take until I do break.

The first evening after my altercation, Staff Sergeant McKinley instructs me to make pushups in the middle of the barracks during quiet time, counting each one loudly, so I might be heard in the adjoining corridor. Beyond this corridor remains a mystery known only to our taskmasters. Ten minutes before lights out, a disembodied voice orders me to take a shower and make final preparations for the next day.

Marine Corps training instructors are not very creative when it comes to assigning new names to those they find difficult to pronounce, or names they consider not American enough. For a convenience known only to them, they generally choose from an abbreviated list. Anyone with a Slavic Eastern Europe name relabeled an Alphabet. There are alphabets one and two in our group, one Nip, of Japanese descent, one Beanpole from somewhere in South America, one Chief, of Navaho descent, a title which should be self-explanatory. Everyone else Hogs, unless otherwise solicited. Then there is the rare distinction of a name attributed to their particular focus of attention. For now own I am known as *PrivateEspi*. In reality, this not is so difficult of an adjustment, since my paternal assignment only recently resurrected. For as long as I can remember, I have gone by the first and last name given to me by my godmother. However, the legal name printed on my birth certificate, as alien to me   as to any stranger. From one day to the next, I become somebody else. And not a name I can easily pronounce, nor does it seem easy for other people. Roll call every morning and every night, each time my name mispronounced. I struggle constantly to remember my new identity. If the mispronunciation enough close, I shout: Here! I actually prefer *Espi*. This made-up acronym both easy to say and to understand, serving as an acceptable transition from the boy I once was to the man I am destined to become. In time, there will be no more of that boy at all.

"*Private Espi*-- front and center!"

I double-time to the squad bay center and snap to attention.

"*Private Espi* reporting as ordered, Sir!"

This morning, I face Sergeant Robinson, a cup of hot coffee in his hand, looking particularly agitated.

"Well private, you want to kick someone's ass today?"

"No Sir!"

"I haven't had any pussy for over a week, and when I don't get pussy then it makes me want to fight. I understand you are a bad ass. You want to fight me private?"

"No Sir!" I again report, already certain in my gut the rhetorical trap this conversation headed.

"So I'm not good enough for you to fight –is that right private?"

I reason that if I say yes he will tell me to hit him. If I hit him I will be court-martialed for striking a superior. If I say no, then it will confirm for all to hear that I consider him not worthy of combat. Therefore, I say nothing at all, each face to face, eye to eye, not flinching, not blinking.

He then takes his steaming beverage and pours it on my skinned head. The hot liquid runs down my face and along my body through the openneck of my Marine Corps issue t-shirt.

"Does that feel good, private?"

"No Sir." I growl through clenched teeth, my eyes locked into his eyes as if in death.

A silence passes between us, a silence that will determine a relationship of respect between us from this point on. He then orders me to drop on the floor and count out fifty pushups. Afterward exhausted, I continue my morning routine, being the last to join formation. This is the last time Sergeant Robinson confronts me alone.

Days and the weeks follow filled with physical training exercises, learning the use of military equipment and weaponry. Every free moment in between is spent studying the red indoctrination pocket manual about Marine Corps history and protocol. These are days of rage, of submission, and learning control: days that change into spring and then into a hot sweltering Carolina coast summer. At the end of these days, those that survive will take their place among the 'chosen few'. After a while, I become so familiar with my new name that I only vaguely remember the person from before. *Espi* do this-- *Espi* do that– *Espi* pushups, while others stand at attention. *Espi* run beside the truck with weapon presented, while everyone else rides to the firing range. During survival maneuvers at *Elliott's Beach*, I end up digging three foxholes before finally allowed to rest in one. Hand to hand contest and bayonet learning drills means me being matched against the biggest and meanest recruit my tormentors can enrage. I feel like a battered rag doll at the end of these sessions, sore with bruises and abrasions as real as any combat. However exhausted, however desperate, I determine not to satisfy my nemesis by crumbling. It is as though a core element of my being collapsing into a dense center, becoming more compacted, until only a hardness of will remains, forged with the steel of military discipline and tempered by a will greater than flesh and bone.

Week ten and platoon 260, the next barracks over, awakens to a gruesome discovery. One of the recruits has quietly hanged himself in the night from the end of the top rack by his rifle strap. Prior to this event, another young man lost his life trying to escape through the forbidden swamp. Out of more than a hundred young men that began training in our platoon alone, only seventy-one will graduate. Out of that number, only twelve distinguished to receive their first stripe of promotion to Private First Class. This honor granted according to the excellence of certain individuals exhibiting skills and achievements higher than the norm. The selection seemingly arbitrary by a few instructors, who themselves once were tested. To my surprise, my name– yes the name *Espi*-- clearly pronounced as the last of the chosen dozen. At first, I fear that it might be a mistake, or even a joke made in poor taste. Next morning, however, we twelve escorted to a designated area for a special parade practice. The next two days we twelve learn a separate set of drills to spearhead the upcoming graduation.

It is the last day before the big day: one of those hot mid-June days in the lower Carolinas, when everything seems to melt into everything else. It is a day of tedious drill repetitions. And next day I will be a true Marine. One of the Alphabets marches in formation behind me. Shaped like a bowling pin, tall and lanky, with a small head, his body tapering down to size twelve boots, he keeps stepping on my heels, causing me to trip and stagger. At one point Drill Instructor McKinley brings us to a halt, sheaths his flashing brass-handled marching saber, and rudely signals me out.

"Look down at your boots, Private. Are you one of those god forsaken individuals born with two right or two left feet?"

I attempt in vain to explain the situation.

"Damn it--You are almost a U.S. Marine! As a Marine, you will not give me any bullshit excuse! Fall in at the end of the squad."

He turns sharply and steps to the front of the column.

"Right-face-- Forward-- March--" he shouts at the top of his voice, like an enraged tiger.

Off they march without me. Instantly, a rage consumes me. I want to strike out; I want to cry! However, all I can do is just stand there. Then I commit the most unpardonable sin a Marine can possibly make. I throw my rifle and helmet on the tarmac. Another Drill Instructor from another platoon leaves his position and comes running over to me.

"What in the Hell is wrong with you, Private? Pickup that gear and join your formation! By God, your Senior DI is going to hear about this!"

Staff Sergeant McKinley, unaware of my transgression, continues to strut boldly along the tarmac swinging his saber. I slip back into the ranks unnoticed. Rendezvousing with the rest of our platoon, we then all march off for evening chow. By 18:00 hours still no indication of the crime or of the punishment. After showering, the rush begins in preparation for the next day-- the big day of graduation from Paris Island Boot Camp! Boots to be spit-shined, brass buckles to be brightened, and our new Dress Greens pressed to perfection. Two of the wealthier recruits have invested in Marine Corps Dress Blues, minus the "blood stripe", available as a special purchase only, and not standard Marine Corps issue. A more stunning uniform does not exist in all the military services put together; a distinctive attire glorious to those who earn it. Every aspect to this rich service outfit possesses an emblem of meaning. A midnight blue coat and navy blue pants, symbolic of the Department of the Navy; the white hat further reminder that Marines once part of a ship detachment, whereas the red and gold trim distinguishes the wearer as being also amphibious. The most striking feature is the red strip running along the side of the dark blue dress pants granted only to Officers and Non Commissioned Officers. It commemorates the blood of their brothers sacrificed at Chapultepec during the Mexican War. A history of meaning and distinctive pride thoroughly indoctrinated into our minds since the past twelve weeks. We are now the ones to carry a flag of noble victory and to fight the fight from the shores of Tripoli and into the halls of Montezuma. We are *"Semper Fidelis"* everyone!

These new recruits are allowed only to wear the coat and blue trousers. But for some a day will come when this magnificent uniform decorates them in all its intended glory, since it is also the traditional burial garment of   fallen soldiers. An hour before lights out Sergeant Robinson enters the barrack andshouts my name.

"Sir, yes sir!" I report, running to the bay center and snapping at attention.

"Gunnery Sergeant Garcia wants to see you on the double."

I sense an uncharacteristic softness in his voice, almost human, and that in this moment he feels human pity for me. I step through the bay doors and follow him down the hall to a sign labeled Gunnery Sergeant Garcia. I slap hard the door jamb, as instructed.

"Private reporting as ordered, sir!"

It is no man that greets me; rather a savage animal in such rage as I have never witnessed. He speaks words, but the meaning incomprehensible. His hot stinking breath wilts my very soul, reminding me of some hell demon out of a Bugs Bunny cartoon. Only this no cartoon; this demon real! With the sudden might of a gladiator executing a final blow, he punches me in the bowels, lifting my entire body physically against the wall. For several seconds I feel like a captured insect pinned by the powerful fist of this raging beast. I dare not breathe; dare not say anything, remaining at absolute attention. He then shouts for Sergeant Robinson waiting outside in the hall to come in.

I am unsure what this dungeon lord really commands; only that it sounds to me like "Feed him to the wolves!" Sergeant Robinson quietly escorts me back down the hall and orders that I remain at attention in a narrow broom closet. There is just enough room to stand, and here I will remain long after lights out, through the night, and into the next morning without sleeping. I am lost in a small corner of the universe alone and altogether forsaken.

At early dawn, I hear my fellow recruits rise to the junkyard dog yapping of Staff Sergeant McKinley and Sergeant Robinson. Then roll call, every name present and accounted; every name called, except my name. Clanking of gear, the clatter of boots, excited mumblings, as platoon 261 rush about in preparation for this most important day of their lives. Then I hear them file at attention and march as one heavy single body out the door into the light of their destiny, a destiny I am deprived because of a moment of unbridled anger. The minutes pass, as slow drips into eternity. Hours or days, time no longer with any meaning; only darkness, a darkness of my own making, surrounded by smelly mops, old rags, and buckets abandoned here. The door opens and there stands Staff Sergeant McKinley.

"What are you doing in here, Private? Get your gear and join the rest of your Platoon –double time!"

My bunk tightly made; my shoes and brass brilliantly shined; my dress greens pressed -- all in inspection order. I quickly shower and put on my uniform with a sharp new chevron sewn on the shoulder. Without saying a word, my Drill Instructor marches me to the parade deck to join my fellow graduates. I will never know for sure if the events of the preceding night part of another test; or simply forgotten until this eleventh hour. This moment I feel humility of profound respect for these three men. These men of the Corps trained me in strength, challenged me physically and mentally to be better than when first I arrived; and have in the end forgiven the weakness of my pride. I step out in the bright morning of my last day at Paris Island now a Private First Class, one of the proud, one of the few, a United States Marine.

Boot Camp is perhaps a bit misunderstood. Marine Corps training about much more than preparing one to fight and to kill and the effective use and deployment of military weaponry. It also teaches self-discipline and that the body and mind unified by will the most lethal weapon of all. It is not just about submitting to ideals, but mastery of potential. Yes, you learn humiliation measured against the obstacle of self-indulgence. Yes, you learn the meaning of weakness by discovering what it really means to be strong. By recognizing equal respect for others, you embrace the truest meaning of honor and loyalty. These are the most important twelve weeks of my life: days that turn into spring, then into hot summer, the summer I become a man at last.

Chapter 9
Becoming a Marine

*R*udy and Jean drive all the way from Greenville to witness my graduation. It is more than a five-hour drive from the Blue Ridge foothills to the coast along narrow country roads. It gladdens me to see them both. Exhausted from lack of sleep, I say little, escorting them to the once forbidden zone of the base cafeteria, where all the regular soldiers gather between duties. This is the closest to civilization I have been in three months. We talk for less than an hour and then they are gone.

"You have a shot at a future now, son," Rudy says just before they leave. "So don't fuck it up."

Rudy never was much for words. He speaks what he thinks and means what he says. For the first time, I finally begin to understand him a little better. The next morning every man in Platoon 261 packs his few belongings into a newly issued Marine Corps green duffle bag, turns in the heavy M14 rifles for the next generation of recruits to use, and boards a transport to a new training facility in North Carolina called Camp

Lejeune. Another exotic name for a place less exotic, named in honor of World War I Commandant, Major General Lejeune in 1942, and bears the distinction of being 'Home of Marine Expedition Forces in Ready'. Situated in southeastern North Carolina along the Atlantic Seaboard near middle of Onslow Bay, it is ideal for every kind of training exercise, from combat war game maneuvers through the sandy pine forest to large-scale amphibious operations.

The first two weeks consume us with taking written and dexterity test. Every Marine is classified in the beginning as a 0311, or Grunt, short for Combat Personnel, which means we all perform the same field training: keep proficient weapons practice, make Force Marches, and learn special field survival techniques. Some will receive an additional classification, a special operational skill based on aptitude and ability. My assigned description is MOS 3051, or General Warehouseman. Therefore, I begin participate in a special training program to learn clerical skills, inventory control method, and the operation of a variety of warehouse equipment. The most exciting piece of machinery on the inventory list towers an enormous oscillating all-terrain forklift. This monster vehicle, elevated by tires six feet in diameter, has positive traction four-wheel drive, front and rear suspension hydraulics, precision independently adjustable forks, and a powerful diesel engine positioned behind the seat of the cockpit.

In order to start this mechanical beast, one needs to insert a cartridge shaped much like a large bullet into a canister equipped with a firing pin. Each morning at daybreak, we start our assigned vehicles for practice-drills after shouting: *"Fire in the hole!"* The monster will shake and then roar to life like a disturbed Grisly, particularly frightening in the beginning. However, in time I get used to it, even grow fond of this magnificent mammoth. There will come a time when I realize that even this Goliath of man's determined achievement prone to a flaw of vulnerability.

As a new PFC I begin to comprehend meaning in the chain of command, as well as my position in this link. I swim a small fish in a smaller fishpond, finding myself suddenly bigger than many of my fellows with whom I graduated, and others I do not even know. When you pass someone in a corridor, with a stripe and you have none, then you move aside. If you have one and they have two, you give the right of way. If the person you pass is an officer of any rank, then you freeze at attention and salute. It takes some getting used to, but soon I learn always to remain diligent. Once I forgot to salute a Second Lieutenant, and get chewed-out mercilessly. I will never forget again.

Even though PFC is just one small step from the bottom, it did have certain advantages. For example, I manage to altogether avoid kitchen duty and shit detail (empting the Out-Houses). Authority is like a piece of dangling rope-- one must learn to hang on. My first real position of command is the assigned charge of our evening recreation hooch, an independent building furnished with two old couches and a chair positioned around a twenty inch TV set, two card tables, and a few board games. The armrest chair unofficially the throne of authority, considered off limits to all others who enter. Before being placed in charge, I had myself respected this rule, as did everyone else. At around 1900 hours, I need to make a head call. Upon returning I discover a large muscled Grunt Private occupying my chair.

"Up soldier," I order.

It never occurs to me that he might not obey. He just sits there with an arrogant smirk on his face. All eyes are on me waiting to see what I will do next. Again, I order him to vacate my chair, and again he ignores me. Without further ceremony, I grab him by the lapel and try to pull him up. He in turn grabs my neck and begins chocking me. I go wild, jump on his chest, and begin beating him on the head and face. He tenses up and attempts to stand, lifting me bodily into the air. I manage to wrap my legs around his middle in a scissor-hold, continuing to pound him. Then, he just collapses like a fallen great American Buffalo, remains unconscious for several minutes, slowly revives, and then leaves mumbling incoherently.

As I have already stated we are all classified 0311 at the core, but the true Grunt is a breed of a breed. It is not that they are inferior, only single minded in purpose. They think as a unit, not as part of a greater whole. Trained to take orders without question, to achieve an objective, and to secure a position; there is no commission of greater value than the dedicated Grunt. To think beyond their designated mandate is sacrilege to their assigned discipline. For the moment at least, we are all green ears of corn in a field, not yet fully formed. At the time, I thought we were all the same, all Marines; but the next morning as I exit the chow hall, I become cornered by another PFC from the newly formed Echo squadron. The conversation goes badly from the beginning, and we begin rolling around the sprawling roots of a sycamore tree locked in mortal combat. Who knows how far we might have gone if not broken apart by a Training NCO, demanding to know the reason for our conduct.

"Sir, this Marine violated one of my men –Sir!"

I suppose him to be the squad leader, taking upon himself the role of protector. Between hard breaths, I attempt to defend the events of the preceding night and that his man out of line.

"Your man refused a direct order. What would you do in my place?"

"It's just a chair--" stammers my opponent.

"I could give a rat's ass as to what happened," interrupts the NCO. "You PFCs are supposed to set an example for the rest of your men. I have half a mind to put you both on report and busted down to Privates. Since you are new, I will let it pass this time. By God you will get your turn to fight, but for now you stay apart."

Other than the occasional dirty look, the Grunts keep their distance after this altercation. The divisions have already begun, as each unit prepares for future duty.

Some of my childhood disturbances have begun to resurface. I catch myself sleep walking again. At least twice, I clearly remember waking up standing at attention beside my bed. One night I awaken to a cold squishy feeling between my toes, as something crushes beneath my foot. I leap back and quickly return to my bunk, convinced this all part of a dream. Next morning I discover the remains of an enormous mountain crab behind my rack. It resembles a large spider protected by a mossy brown armor insufficient against the weight of my body. As in all combat situations, better it than me.

At the finish of our four weeks of training, each unit as different from the other, as there are different shades of green. Without realizing it, we become segregated groups, each with a specialty, kind with kind. We are all green just the same, and part of a noble brotherhood. By the time I deploy to my first supply unit, I fully appreciate the chain of command and self-discipline that accompanies responsibility. I never fully understand the simplistic equation governing the Grunts way of thinking, but profoundly respect the purpose they serve.

Battalion Supply duty is actually not that bad compared to other operational units. The Grunts are humping hills from sunrise to sunset, Motor Transport always rebuilding engines and transmissions, the Mess Hall in continuous preparation of another meal at the end of another. The same goes for the amphibious fleet, tanks and helicopters, and even those in administration buried under mounds of bureaucracy. The big guns division seem to have it easiest; however, the price of their luxury often the cost of their hearing. Supply is the nearest to a civilian job as you can get. You rise every morning, lumber to chow, have a inspection, and stroll to your perspective warehouse. A duty roster is already prepared so you grab a coffee, take your worksheet, and go off in search of the designated isle and the roll. The Supply Sergeant and his Corporals divide us into teams of two; each team assigned a hand-pallet lift capable of moving a few hundred pounds by the effort of just one or two men. Every day the same: filling requisitions, updating inventory, receiving new inventory, and the dispatching of still more requisitions. After a while, it becomes mundane to the point of boredom.

My stationed assignment at Camp Lejeune does have one major personal benefit. At least once, sometimes twice in a month, I hitch a ride home with one of the Corporals that owns a car and from the general vicinity of Greenville. We call it swooping because sometimes as many as five cram into a car, pool together gas money, and fly as fast as conditions permit along two-lane country roads to take advantage of a weekend pass. It is about a six-hour drive, sometimes as little as five, at times the fog so thick that visibility reduced to only a few feet. This reenlisted Corporal proudly owns a new canary colored Swinger bought with the incentive money received to remain in the Corps for another six years. Stock off the showroom floor, this 340 Dart sold with a customized engine, matching wheels, and a four speed transmission that makes a sonic whine through every gear. This Nam veteran has nerves of steel, or maybe he just no longer cares, hugging the shoulders on every curve, sometimes leaving the road by leaping over hills on a straight way, and never obeys the speed limits. The greatest dangers along these narrow country lanes are posted signs indicating a deer crossing. We are lucky, except for one weekend, a weekend I miss because of guard duty. That Friday night, the Swinger crumpled to spare parts, totaled by crashing into a stag at a velocity of more than seventy miles an hour. Except for a few minor injuries, all occupants survive. You might think this would have been a deterrent. A month later, our determined navigator now has a beautiful new four-in-the-floor Super Bee with a lighting 383 Magnum engine paid for by the insurance company. The same weekend we fearlessly swoop again along those narrow roads, over hill and dale, and through blind patches of fog. I do not know if it because we were Marines or just plain young and thoughtless of consequence. As intrepid Argonauts, we make this perilous journey as often as we could, always in record time, departing our base on a Friday night, not to return until early Monday morning exhausted. Miracle that we make it almost every time; and even a greater miracle no one died.

In the beginning, I enjoy changing into civilian clothes and just relaxing in my room, sometimes listening to my records, sometimes volunteering to do familiar physical chores like cutting the grass, pulling up weeds, or organizing the garage. Obvious to all except me, I have too much energy and too much time. Jean encourages me to go out and do something, go to a movie, find a girl-- do anything, except hang around the house all weekend.

One Saturday night, I decide to take her up on the offer and jump a city bus downtown to see a late evening film. At seventeen, I am still growing, along with the physical training and all the protein I can eat, none of my own clothes any longer fit. Still, I prefer to go out as a civilian, than to be in military uniform, which requires a certain code of conduct. The only clean pair of socks I can find have been mistakenly washed with a red bed cover. The result being that my white socks now a hue of bright pink. At least they are clean, and time too short to care. Already half past eleven o'clock, civilian time, by time the film ends. I walk to a nearby corner and wait for the last bus to take me home.

A two-door sedan packed with college students pulls up to the light just as it changes green. A young man on the passenger side sticks out his head and yells "*faggot*", but before I can respond, the car speeds away. A few minutes later, the car passes again with someone shouting from the back passenger side "Queer –Queer", and again the car races away. Now, I begin to get angry, perplexed as to why they are doing this. Then I see them approach again from the opposite side and that the light changing to red. I bolt like a bull terrier across the intersection before the driver thinks to roll up his open window. He attempts to exit the vehicle. I shove him back and bash the side of his head with the back of my fist. The opposite side passenger also tries to exit on that side, but I manage to reach across and grab him by the neck simultaneously hitting him twice. The three in the back seat realizing they are pinned in the face of a monster freeze in petrified silence. No one speaks another word. Finally, the rage inside of me begins to subside. Comprehending that these youngmen have no real stomach to fight, I release my grip.

"You shouldn't make fun of people. You never know what could happen."

They remain sheepishly quiet until the light changes green again, and slowly drive away. Upon boarding the bus, I see my reflection in the overhead mirror. At first shock, and then I begin to laugh aloud. No wonder those college rednecks harassed me. For them I must have been something out of a bad Hollywood script. My slacks so tight that they bulge at every contour, the bottom cuff high above the ankles; and adding to this the pink socks and penny loafers. Even I conclude that either I look gay as a three dollar bill or a circus clown. Early the next morning I go to the local K-Mart and buy some new jeans and two pairs of socks. I think that my antagonist and I have learned an unforgettable lesson in fashion statement that night.

Six months after my first posting, I receive a promotion to Lance Corporal based on normal time and duty without any demerit points on my record. Usually, it takes between six months to a full year of service just to receive PFC, and another six to twelve months before being eligible for the next promotion. The grand leap to Non Commissioned Officer's status, or Corporal, usually takes between three to four years of professional service, and often granted with terms to sweeten a re-enlistment deal. It is rare for an off duty NCO to fraternize with men of lower rank, each having their own recreation centers. These segregated areas vigorously enforced. For an enlisted man to set foot in the NCO club uninvited a strict violation of military etiquette usually punishable with some unpleasant extra duty. According to an unwritten rule, only Corporals and up to Warrant Officers allowed gathering at the NCO Club. Of course, a Warrant Officer can go anywhere he pleases, being a unique highbred. Officers of every rank fraternize only in the Officer's Club, bearing the unofficial title of an elite "country club"; and only those few assigned to serve tables know for sure what it like inside there.

Everyone else gathers in the non-com recreation room to shoot pool,shoot the shit, and sometimes to fight. Not that it always like this, but sometimes men just need to release some of the poison. Being a Lance Corporal definitely has work advantages. It means being in charge of details, which also means I can decide when time   for a break or procedure for a particular assignment. However, this also makes me responsible for any errors. A mistake in the count, inventory misplaced or improperly stationed, I am the one to receive the brunt of displeasure that trickles down from the top. Two Corporals serve as watchdogs, following up my every move. When an error occurs-- and there were errors-- then, I receive reprimand in both ears. I make assurance that the same indiscretion never repeated a second time.

I buy another old Ford truck one weekend while visiting home. It has been in more than one accident, beat-up on one side, with a weak synchronizer for second gear that made an unsettling grinding noise from first to second; but at least it runs. I leave it parked under a towering Oak tree in back of a friend's house, using it only on weekends when I swoop into town. In those days, I never consider legally registering my vehicles. I suppose I figured I would wait until I buy a car that I intend to keep and that really interests me. Nevertheless, luck remains on my side, as I never get stopped even though the plates expired.

Mike still in jail and Ronnie resenting the fact that I have escaped into the military, an option he no longer has since his conviction. I help him once to replace a clutch in his Pontiac. He flies into a rage because I hand him the wrong tool. We get into a scuffle and I easily pin him down. I can see the surprise in his eyes, and cautiously let him go. He then grabsa bumper jack and threatens me, so I just leave. I will never again see Ronnie after this. Years later, I hear that his right leg ruined because of an accidental shooting and that he now walks with a gimp. From what I can gather, he had a 44-caliber revolver shoved in the belt waist of his pants that goes off accidently when he retrieves the weapon to threaten someone. Poor Ronnie never did have much luck.

Tommy is now a flower child, as are most of my former acquaintances. It is, after all, the last days of the sixties; and even though Greenville a little behind the times, the Hippie movement has finally arrived. Psychedelics drugs, marijuana, and hashes the exotic pleasures enjoyed mostly by music celebrities such as the Beatles and The Rolling Stones, now considered anti-establishment activities to pervert conservative values of the past. I must admit that secretly I rallied more on the narrow side of strict conservatism at the time. Being part of an elite corps, I embrace the patriotic idealism of a United America that shines as a clear beacon of liberty and justice to the world. The so called hippie movement represents in my mind a condition of rebellious anarchy. Although there will come an intersection, when these core statues tested by fire. But as a young Marine trained in discipline, I remain resolute to the principle of order, believing it my sworn duty to protect institutional stability against all potential threats-- even those shouted in the name of peace.

Every second weekend, I am assigned to Riot Duty, which means I remain on base in preparation to be sent to New York or Kent State, or anywhere else mob control might be necessary. Equipped with a silver colored helmet, a baton, and a faithful heavy M14 issued for the occasion, we resemble a science fiction battalion of star troopers. The strategy to form a single line with rifles extended and pointed at 45 degrees in front of us, as we stomp slowly toward the agitated crowd forming an impenetrable barrier. As an assailant steps within range, we are to scoop that individual down and in, using the rifle barrel as a lever, pulling the confused rioter behind, where a second wave waits ready to apprehend. I never actually have to go on one of these operations, but remain in ready, clearly convinced of being on the right side prepared to protect life and property.

It is an amazing transformation that someone you grew up with changed from being a redneck motorcycle junkie, to a child of peace almost overnight. At first, I want no part of this new kind of "tripping'. I hang around with my weekend companions simply because I have nothing better to do. One Friday night my resistance to this new wave about to change, when a blonde-haired woman with light blue eyes and a new matching blue *Z28 Camaro*, joins our group. Immediately seduced by her beauty, by the way her smooth corn silk hair moves when she turns her head in a certain way, I allow myself to experience new ways. She has recently turned twenty-one and feels hurt and abandonment at being dumped for another woman by her straight-laced fiancée. Her injury of rejection has changed to anger; her anger into rebellion of drug culture. That night I have my first hit of marijuana. I cannot even remember that girl's name now. I will see her this weekend and another weekend two weeks later. On our second rendezvous, the two of us decide to travel to Wood Stock, New York, together. We drive as far as Charlotte, North Carolina, where we both get cold feet, deciding to turn back. I often wonder what we might have become had we gone all the way. I later get news that she and her ex-fiancée got back together because she tested already pregnant, married, and moved to Charleston. Nevertheless, I will always remember that sleek blue *Camaro* and the way it glided on the open freeway nearly reaching speeds of more than a hundred miles per hour. Every weekend after this, I indulge in a few hits of marijuana, combined with an amphetamine speed pill, and occasionally some hashes. One Saturday Beasley– yes the same Beasley who ratted me out-- shows up with some mescaline he has brought up from Atlanta. Pedaled at the bargain price of five dollars a hit, we all purchase a tab and go to the Greenville city park in my old beat up pickup. Within the first half hour, awareness that this drug very different from everything else tried. Yes, I feel a physical sensation of being stoned, but also something

else, a condition more subtle, as if my mind were expanding beyond the boundaries of conscious thought and experience. I secure a pleasant spot beneath the shade of a walnut tree, lie on my back, and stare up into shattered pieces of an infinite blue summer sky etched into a tapestry of summer leaves. I am mesmerized by the revelation of a giant brain encompassing the universe, as though is a contained expanding bubble hermetically locked within an eternal loop of designed reason. Every soul that lives-- has ever lived or will ever live-- existing as a cell trapped within this matrix of synoptic activity, becoming the condition of an immense brain, with each cell living and re-living every moment, every experience of their lives, as repeating records playing and re-playing over, and over again. The duration of time and space in thought only, the concept of beginning and end only abstractions created relative to the choices exercised through individual experience. I hear the bedlam of all those souls as the roar of many oceans. I am only one among the many, trapped forever in a repeating scenario of a cycle without any means of mortal escape. This experience altogether elating, but also terrifyingly tragic in meaning, only I do not comprehend in the moment what really it means.

It takes several hours to find my proper moment back in time. None of my friends are very interested in the testimony of my vision; more influenced by the high. They warn me to make more effort to control my hallucinations-- a warning I should have taken more heed to.

Every weekend promises something different. I try several types of LSD distributed in colorful candy varieties, and even inject heroine twice. Heroine, the most seductive of all, she will pass among us as a lady of death sent to destroy. A young man from England named Jimmy comes into our fold like a character from some well-written mystery novel, dressed in a finely woven black suit, white shirt, and a tie. His father, a wealthy banker, spares no expense on his son's education. Therefore, Jimmy speaks with the loveliest, most sophisticated accent I have ever heard. The voice of a dark preacher sent to enlighten us to the deeper pleasures that only heroine might provide. We all chip-in and purchase a twenty-dollar bag of the soft white powder. Jimmy serves as our divine Sheppard to lead us to new pastors. He judiciously adds water to the powder and melts the solution in a large silver spoon using a cigarette lighter. Being a diabetic, he has a syringe and needle on hand. I am the first to receive an injection, since I have provided the lion's share of the money. Jimmy ties-off my arm using his finely crafted real snakeskin belt. With professional attention to raise the vein, he injects this concoction into my arm. Once the belt removed, a rush hits the back of my head and I collapse into euphoria. One by one, all allow themselves transported by this ferryman of darkness.

Heroine is a most unique drug in that it has two distinct levels of elevated highs. There is the physical part, when the body feels so heavy that it melts into everything else. Then there is a psychosis of experience called nodding, when one becomes part of another consciousness and a reality beyond imagination. The first couple of hours is a fascinating journey into a darkly beautiful landscape rich in color, an alien world populated by exotic alien creatures and a mesmerizing sky bright with moons and planets never imagined on earth— and this only in the beginning. Then everything begins to fade slowly into stark grey tones, the once beautiful landscapes dissolving into an oily black turbulent sea. A place where shadows change more defined, bat-like creatures circling a tunnel leading to the pockmarked garish face of a dead planet fading into an inky blackness, so dense no light can escape. I spend the final hours of that trip trying not to nod-off, afraid of that place and afraid of what those creatures might become.

Weeks later, I again become pressured into trying this evil drug. Only now I do not wish to trip, feeling an unconscious resistance even before my injection turn. Jimmy falls first under the influence, leaving the task of conductorship to Beasley. I have often wonder if maybe he altogether missed my vein because of inexperience; or maybe he just reasons my dose should be less this time around. I experience a small rush, but manage to recover. Each time I feel to nod, I fight with every fiber of my will, refusing to enter that world of beauty and darkness. By the end of this trip, I am exhausted, as though I have physically fought in some great battle. I determine never to try the stuff again; and I never do. Not because I do not like it, but because I sense this element stronger than my ability to defend against its subtlety of influence. I will later know men in Nam, who change overnight to skeletons under the influence of this insidious substance with power to suck out the soul. A month later, I receive information from a mutual acquaintance that Jimmy dead from an overdose. Beasley turns yellow with hepatitis, and altogether disappears. Fortunately, everyone else is too poor to continue using this Cadillac of drugs, and so return to other substances less expensive. At least they continue to survive through poverty; or at least this is what I think and hope.

I choose to swoop home less often and begin hanging out more at the USO club or playing pool on the base, even becoming fairly good at the game. But always there is someone better. One of the Privates from a neighboring warehouse named Jack befriends me. He is short in stature, built solidly square, and has a flame of Irish red hair. I saw him get angry only once and decide that he is possessed by the potential power of a Tasmanian devil. Jack confides in me that he has met a girl from his hometown Boston while on leave. Apparently, they met at a bus stop and he managed to get her name and address. Because Jack knows himself to be crude and not much for words, he asks me to help him compose a letter, making it clear that Jack's interest more than plutonic, adding at the end that when he sleeps *"he dreams the stars in her lovely eyes."* It turns out that she likes literature, poetry in particular, so I conspire to commit a transgression of deception. Using his basic description of how he feels for her, I embellish the raw imagery to compose a poem with elevated sensuality. I compare her skin to light graced from the moon, her eyes as pools born from the bottom of ocean deeps. I describe her hair as cascading down her shoulders and breast, and down to the softness of her elegant feet. Jack likes the poem, only little understands its meaning even though I try to explain it to him. His new girlfriend's letters become more intense after this, and Jack persistently demands fresh new ideas of expression. After a while I fully dictate the letters with Jack writing them down in his own handwriting. A week before Thanksgiving, Jack takes an extended leave back to Boston and returns ten days later with his new bride. She is every bit the quality of the many poems and love letters. Silently, I love her, only this lovely creature married to someone I call a friend. Together they rent a trailer off-base just a few blocks beyond the main front gate. This poor woman unhappy from the beginning, having no more in common with this brutish man, than a princess with a Minotaur. I want to tell her the truth that it is I-- not Jack-- who wrote her back so beautifully. But how can I without violating the sacred bond of friendship and faithfulness owed to a fellow Marine. Soon it becomes obvious that Jack hates something about her. Something he cannot express in words.

Maybe this is the problem. Since I can no longer be there to help him, he has nothing really to say. I begin to suspect he might be abusing her physically, a fact confirmed one night when invited to their trailer for dinner. Jack has drunk one too many beers before sitting down to eat. His wife and I are engaged in an interesting conversation about poetry, when suddenly he launches into a rage. In womanly fashion, his wife tries to console him by making light of his bad humor. He slaps her across the face with an order to shut up. Friend or no, I will not allow this. Maybe because I have seen my own mother with a blackened eye more than once, only too young to do anything about it, I have no choice but get involved.

"Don't you ever touch her again," I say, leaping from my chair.

"So, Lance, you think you can give orders here-- tell me how to treat my own wife, and in my own house!"

Now I would like to point out that a house trailer is no place to have a fight. It shakes, it sways, it vibrates. You hit one wall only to bounce off another. Jack and I altogether trash the dining area. During the altercation, his wife runs to a neighbor and calls the police. At first, they are going to arrest both Jack and I, but decide against it because of the pleading of his wife. After hearing the details, they order me leave and never to come back. I often think about Jack's wife. If she became trapped in a life of misery because of me; or if maybe she finally discovers a soul of poetry in the man that she married.

I receive a new assignment placing me in charge of a security section of the warehouse. This designated area in the southwest corner of the complex houses inventory of certain specialized equipment with a restrictive classification for inventory control. These specialty MOS classes are limited quantity and very valuable. Things like night vision Starlight Scopes, Sniper Scopes, hardened-steel K-Bar knives, special compasses, just to name a few of these supposedly inaccessible items. Other crates, stamped with a cryptic combination of numbers and letters, and bound by a security seal, for certain eyes only, without any nomenclature, meant to remain top secret, except by special requisition of cross-referenced paperwork. In the military, to be in charge of something means to be responsible for it. For the first time, I realize just how insecure this region of the warehouse. Anyone can walk in at any time and take anything they want. The Marine Corps enforces ethics against stealing; but in reality thievery did happen. Sometimes as small as a pack of cigarettes left unattended, sometimes money from an open locker-- the lesson being that every building has a share of rats. Once, I personally witnessed a First Lieutenant take a K-Bar knife to add to his personal collection. However, this possible scenario will end with my assignment to the unsecured area. I determine to devise a plan that will make my security area secure.

I spend the entire weekend moving and restacking empty crates so that the open side faces inward to serve as storage bins within the barricaded area. One of the hydraulics on the lift works loose and begins leaking fluid; but I manage to tighten it back before too much damage. I next devise a two-tiered gate, the top half opening toward the inside, the bottom half opening outward. As a final touch, I add wooden strips painted red to seam where the crates join, and use green netting at the top as an additional deterrent. My security cage now complete, I make a new inventory, everything dated and signed by me, with plans to have the sheets countersigned by one of my superiors the following Monday.

The part about Marine Corps appreciation for initiative is an over- embellishment, and only occasionally recognized. There is protocol and tradition; but more importantly there exist a chain of command. My interpretation of the situation is that a burden of responsibility has been assigned to my charge, and therefore my primary mandate to insure security protocol for the designated area. It never occurs to me that I am changing the traditional way of doing things, and without the approval of my direct superior.

"Lance Corporal by whose orders did you make this?" Lieutenant Taylor, the officer in charge demands upon seeing the goliath new structure adjoined to the rear of his office.

"No one's orders, sir—I felt the area not secure, and wanted to make it so, sir!"

"You are on report, Marine. I want you to spend the morning taking this monstrosity apart. After that you will be demoted to Private First Class–is that understood?"

Before I can say, 'yes sir' an officious Captain appears at the door to the front loading dock, and shouts.

"Attention!"

Surprise inspections, though not uncommon, usually leak some precedence of warning. This time it really is a previously unannounced surprise. A Major General-- who happens to be in the area-- has made the spontaneous decision to drop by our warehouse. Why he chose this particular warehouse out of a dozen or more, I will never know. Here an embodiment of the oldest person I have ever seen still in uniform. His face cracked and crumpled with scares and wrinkles made by countless battlefields. His large hands those of an embalmed corpse, pale and puffy; this living relic moving in slow motion. His steely cobalt eyes fix immediately on the red and green trimmed security cage. He takes several moments to examine it, and then demands in graveled voice.

"Who is responsible for this?"

"This man," gleefully volunteers Lieutenant Taylor pointing to me.

"So what do you call this, Marine?" The old soldier asks, staring steadfast down at me.

"A Security Cage, sir!"

"Captain," says the General to the officer who has called us all to attention. "See to it that plans are made of this 'Security Cage' and distributed to every Marine Corps warehouse division. Also, see to it that this man receives a promotion to Corporal."

He then turns to me again.

"Good job Marine," he pronounces proudly in a tone mixed with the grave.

Just like that, with less than fourteen months in service, I become one of the youngest Corporals in state-side history. Lieutenant Taylor is livid, his Adam's apple racing furiously up and down along his scrawny neck-- but what can he do? There now exists a new protocol, a new Marine Corps tradition born, solidly ratified by a Major General just passing through. Now I have real responsibility, a Marine Corporal in charge of a prototype Security Cage, inspired by a Lance Corporal, soon to be eighteen years old, and without a High School diploma. This template of design sent to every warehouse division for future implementation. At present, I am just relieved not to be demoted and never gave the event much real thought afterward.

By the time I swoop home again, I have a lot to celebrate. I stop first at Beasley's home and purchase four hits of LSD called Pink Flats. Beasley knows business opportunity and is now everyone's pusher. He tells me about a party that night, where several of my old and new friends will be. I pick up a six-pack of beer, and head there in my second gear grinder. I drop one of the pinks. Thirty minutes later and nothing happens. Deciding I have been burned, sold speed instead of LSD, I drop the remaining three tablets. A speed high better than to get no high at all!

At the party, I begin gulping down my beer, taking an occasional toke of hash as it passes my way, and forgetting all about the pinks. There is a rule in tripping that either you control the trip or the trip will control you. Drunk and hash stoned, the LSD strikes like an unsuspecting viper. Someone relays to me the event of a recent air disaster at the Charlotte Airport. I listen, but my mind has difficulty to comprehend the context or the meaning of what he describes. He then hit his hand hard on the floor and it explodes.

"What?" I ask, confused.

"The plane came down like this and flipped over."

Again, his hand explodes, as he hits the floor.

"What?" Again I ask, trying to understand.

My impatient narrator begins banging his hand on the floor, repeating something over and over again.

"It crashed– man, it crashed-- don't you hear what I am saying?"

Each time the explosion becomes more violent, and then my psyche collapses. I lie back on the floor in an attempt to recompose my reason. At this precise moment, someone rolls a watermelon in my direction. It grows larger and larger. Upon making contact, it changes into some kind of giant insect. I hear a loud snap in the back of my neck. What once was a conscious mind dissolves away into the churning web of a wakeless nightmare.

The next twenty-four hours I witness principalities and events as terrifying as any recorded descent into hell. Except here every analogy real, my mind no longer my own, my ability to reason severed, my soul trapped in a realm coexisting, yet invisible to the senses. I witness spirits in the air; horrible creatures exposed. I see face of true natures, entities not elemental to conventional reason, nor like anything to anything I have seen before. Great elephant-like creatures with wings floating on the ceiling, things of shadow crawling from cracks in the baseboards, and things too terrible to describe inhabiting places of greater light. Now aware of their presence-- but even more frightening-- they are now aware of me. These aliens now conscious of me enter by turn, becoming a kaleidoscope of different memories and personalities like flashes of awareness. I can still recall clearly a few, tormented screams in the background born of the music.

When I think back to this terrible experience, a song comes to mind by Three Dog Nights called 'Mama Told Me Not to Come'. Only flashes of conscious recognition, gone almost as quickly, like trying to hold onto chimeras of shadow. At some point, I clearly hear sounds of a baby crying. I look down to see my hands covered in blood, across from me a ghoulish looking young girl eating the flesh of a baby's arm.

"Monsters," I wail; "what have we done? –We are all monsters!"

Later told the crying baby safe in another room, and that it a watermelon we ate. However, it seems so real, so horribly real! In another event I am an ancient warrior king, armed with a battle-ax in one hand, a monster's throat in the other. I am later informed it was actually a hammer.

"You dare to challenge your Lord!" I threaten, lifting the fiend bodily against a wall with my free hand.

Fortunately, I pass out before inflicting any real harm. Through the course of these unsettling episodes I witness even bloodier battles in heaven, resulting in unspeakable carnage. Then the threshold of eternity swallowed in a void, taking with it those many worlds, and the many lost souls that inhabit those worlds, all fading away instantly into lights robbed of source.

Now in retrospect, I can only compare this experience to the madness of the Babylonian King Nebuchadnezzar, the greatest of all the kings chronicled in the ancient world. God removing his seat of reason for a season, making him as a wild beast because of mortal pride so that he might know the only true God of heaven and earth.

My friends have no experience of what to do. I have freaked-out in the very worst way. They lock me alone in a room and commune if they should call the hospital. After so many hours, I should be down. It is now the early dawn of another day, and still my mind gone.

We all have heard of people who never came back from a trip; but no one thinks it will happen to them or to someone they know. Nevertheless, it has happened to me. Worse than mad-- my mind and soul trapped in a region of existence where conscious and unconsciousness have fused together. In this darkness, I can see something shimmering in the distance. I keep concentrating on that one element of cognition, desperately trying to think-- to recover my very reason! Suddenly, there is a sharp decompression inside my head, like the whoosh inside a complete vacuum. Then I see something, something silver and almost familiar. Then another decompression and two more whooshes. I recognize the thing to be the florescent design on the tuner dial of a stereo system disembodied from everything else. Nevertheless, this solitary familiarity fixed in relation to a physical reality that I instinctively know must exist. This time three great swooshes, followed by a pop like an electrical shock, vibrating from the back of my neck and traveling down the spine. Now my senses begin to piece back the puzzle. I become aware of a stereo unit with a glowing green dial whole and solid. Then a couch appears and a chair with a small table beside, and to the left of this a window covered by drapes. Now I see the familiar outline of a door camouflaged on a wall. The reality of a world changes vaguely familiar. Almost I am back in present existence.

"Man, are you alright?" Beasley inquires truly concerned upon opening the door from the outside. "We thought you were cooked."

"Don't say anything," I warn, taking a wide birth. "Just don't say anything."

The exposed external stairway seems to move slightly, as I imagine a great serpent. I know it wants to change. It takes all my effort of will to insure it does not change. My truck engine growls alive, something dangerous; something I might not be able to control. I keep repeating to myself, only a few miles-- so many miles before sleep-- if ever I will sleep again. My only objective is to make it home. Pedestrians burst into fire as I pass, things not human lurking in every shadow. I kept reminding myself all this only a hallucination-- or things not of this world. I see undercover police at every intersection, narcotic agents in every car. I have inadvertently allowed demons into my mind, and they are looking for a way to pull me back into their world, a world of nightmare from which I will never escape again. I sense they are just beneath the thin veneer of this rediscovered consciousness. I need to concentrate and ignore the information of my physical senses. I manage to make it to my mother's house, a place of refuge and promised rest, and go straight to my room, ignoring everyone in my path. I lay prostrate on the bed of my childhood, hoping only to find rest. The walls keep trying to melt; so finally I give up, allowing them to melt and close my eyes.

It is Monday evening by the time I open my eyes again. I have slept for nearly eighteen hours and missed rendezvous of my return swoop. Now I am officially AWOL. No one in my family says a word, not even Rudy. I think this time they are all genuinely worried about me. They do not know exactly why, only that something very wrong. I get Rudy to give me a ride to the main highway and begin my long hitchhike. Luckily the first car that comes along driven by a Marine Captain returning from a two-week pass spent with his wife and two children. He has new orders sending him to Vietnam the following week, a tour of duty for which he has volunteered. I cannot help but wonder why he would choose to risk so much when he has so much here to live for. After a few minutes of disjointed conversation, he perceives my incoherent state of mind.

"Try to sleep it off, son."

I do not remember anything until being dropped off near my barracks. Fortunately, for me, Sergeant Mason, someone I know well, serves at the duty desk.

"You look like hell Corporal," he says, as I prepare to sign in. "Looks as if something bad took a bite in the wrong place. You are lucky it's me on duty tonight. I put you down for a ninety-six hour pass, so that makes you right on time. You best go get cleaned up."

I thank him and stumble off to my barracks. Mason and I had met several weeks earlier while playing pool. One Friday night we drive nearly three hours to Norfolk Virginia in an old Studebaker he bought for fifty dollars so that he might propose to a Navy Wave he has known for only one night. I serve as his moral comforter, which means I remain in the car parked near a docked Navy Frigate while he goes off in search of his love. A few hours later, Mason returns still holding a cheap ring he bought at a pawn shop.

"She isn't worth the bother," he proclaims and flings the ring into the dark oil-polluted bay.

Breaking out a bottle of whiskey and taking a gulp, he passes the poison over to me. After empting the bottle, we start the three-hour drive back only to discover that Mason's old Studebaker has a radiator hose leak. We try electrical tape, try our trusted utility belt, but nothing works for long. We pick-up cans and discarded bottles and fill them with water from the taps of unsuspecting residents while they sleep. Near the end of our journey, we actually piss directly into the steaming radiator. We get to within a mile of the main gate before the cylinder head gasket surrenders the ghost. Mason coasts to the shoulder, removes everything important to him from the vehicle. Together we walk the remaining distance never to look back again.

As faith would have it, on this night of personal terrible tribulation, my adventure with Sergeant Mason proves not to have been in vain. Had anyone else been at the desk, I would have been on report, and most likely demoted. I learn something important through this chance occurrence. By the letter of the law, Sergeant Mason should have reported me. However, we had shared something together of greater value, a bond of brother-hood that became a law unto itself. This does not mean us lawless by nature. We both share a profound respect for military code and ethical conduct. But sometimes there is an honor of higher principal, which a man must discern in the moment. There is yet more to honor I still have to learn.

It will be several weeks before I make the journey back home again. Home has become a den of devils in my mind, a place of shadows; a dark dominion I wish to escape. I no longer seek opportunity to take any more drugs, a wisdom I am thankful for to this day. However, there are still more passages to traverse also inhabited by those many demons of reflected light.

Chapter 10
FMF Westpac Vietnam

$\mathcal{D}$ifferent messages come daily from Shangri-La. Some believe the Vietnam conflict soon to end; others that it will never end. Everything about my military life has become boring and routine. My new security cage now changed into a prison. As a Non-Commissioned Officer, I find myself even more isolated. My former friends, all of lower rank, now less comfortable to horse-around in my presence; nor are we any longer permitted to socialize on base. Most of the other NCOs in their mid to late twenties, and with few exceptions, think me too young, lacking the time and grade earned by most of them after many years.

With justification, Corporals and Sergeants, considered the backbone of the Marine Corps, stand in the middle between the higher and the lower ranks. In other words, it is the responsibility of the NCO to get things done-- without prejudice and without excuse. From this standpoint, it is the worst and the best rank to be. My greatest personal barrier remains my youth and inexperience. In many ways, I still look like a kid in uniform. And in many ways, I am just that: a kid in uniform. I reconcile to spend my military career among the pine forests of Camp Lejeune, North Carolina, just six hours drive from where   I grew up. I cannot say the posting uncomfortable. I have achieved a comfortable rank, serving a unique position of military leisure, having perhaps one of the easiest jobs in the Marine Corps. Except, I wish for more adventure. This is not what I had signed up for. In a way, it feels too much like having an out-of-town job. I can go home when I wish, see friends and family, slowly being pulled into a trap of a mundane existence. Yes, the trap all too clear! I fear the comfort of becoming ordinary in an ordinary job with ordinary ambitions.

Announcement of elective requisitions appear monthly on the main bulletin board. Elective orders are voluntary transfers to other Marine Corps installations throughout the world. The eligibility of these transfers based on rank, MOS specialty, and duty record-- a guarantee of adventure to a young bored Marine. Then one morning the appearance of a requisition aspiring to the potential of my aspirations: demand for a Corporal with a Supply MOS assignment request to FMF WESPAC.

WESPAC can mean anywhere in the western hemisphere of the world, including California, Hawaii, Okinawa... and of course Vietnam. As I have already said, the Vietnam conflict already over in minds of many. By now I have grown indifferent to the idea of going there; no longer remembering the vows of my early youth. WESPAC represents possibility of change in my routine, possibility of adventure and travel to exotic lands. These orders are custom made just for me. I make a beeline to the Gunny's office and submit for a transfer. The

Master Gunnery Sergeant in charge of Supply, a good-hearted and a by-the-book man, more or less has taken me under his wing after my precarious promotion to Corporal. He never much liked Lieutenant Taylor, glad to see him taken down a peg or two by my meritorious rank assignment.

"So, you are off to see the world," he says, handing me the approval forms. "You be careful out there, Corporal. There are a lot of Taylors in the Corps. You will make a better Marine than he will ever be. Just watch your back."

This kind soldier further encourages me to take the GED (a High School Equivalency test) before I leave, after I confess that my greatest disappointment is not finishing high school.

"It would be my luck to get shipped to Nam and be killed. That would break my mother's heart. She wanted so badly that I finish high school. I thought I might take the next GED, but now I guess I will need to wait."

"You are smart, smarter than that jackass Captain Taylor. If you really want to take that test, I think I can get you in. If you study hard, I believe you can pass."

I am willing to try, even though the chances of me passing slight, considering my educational experience. The GED program is offered only once every six months, requiring advanced enrollment two months prior to the test date. As promised, Gunny arranges to have me accepted in the program with only two weeks to prepare. The mountain of study guides overwhelming. Nevertheless, I devote myself completely to the endeavor. Worst case scenario I will fail and need to reapply at some future date. Day of the exam I am presented with a written test lasting three hours, basically covering all the in class subjects I missed during the last years of formal education. It will seem irrelevant by the time I receive back the result. By then failure or success will no longer be a measure ofacademic theory.

I swoop home for the last time on a two-week leave. I tell my mother I am going to Camp Pendleton. This is no lie, since Pendleton my first waypoint of scheduled ITR training. For all I know I might end up there, so what was the point to worry her unnecessarily? In all this time, I have avoided the temptation to do any more hard drugs: an abstinence born partly of apprehension; but mostly because of a renewed sense of duty and future responsibility. However, every nemesis of experience has a Golden Spruce. That one fabled element more precious than all common variety; and so it is with LSD.

Since my earliest trip, I have heard from Beasley about the mythically rare Gold Microdot. Even the name sounds exotic and space age. The first Saturday of my last visit, Beasley, his girlfriend, and I drive a hundred and thirty miles to Atlanta, Georgia, to cop some Jamaican Weed and have a weekend party. The Main Street of downtown Atlanta has changed into a strip populated with hippies and dealers. Police Officers mingle among them, walking their beat, but helpless to do much more than keep the peace. No sooner do they pass than a transaction made. I have just negotiated a ten-cent bag of dope, when a voice behind me whispers the magic words.

"You want to buy a hit of Gold Microdot?"

Those spirits in the air have sought out my deepest desire and directed this courier to me. I know I should say no, allow this White Buffalo of opportunity to pass me by. Another part of me wants nothing more than to accept this unholy challenge and to go where never I have gone before. It sparkles beautifully in my hand, as a tiny bright gold nugget promising a   trip of rich experience. I join Beasley and his girlfriend at a motel just outside the city, and divide the Marijuana between us. I say nothingabout the Gold Microdot. I wish to take no chance of anyone playingwith my head. After talking for a while, I retire to a separate room. I determine to save the Marijuana for the next day, wishing to have a pure unadulterated trip that I can control. Now ready, the moment of truth arrived. Greedily swallowing the glittering tab, I stretch out on the motel room bed and wait. Twenty predictable minutes later, the first waves of the trip begin to ebb. A pleasant physical echelon of sensation spreads through my body, a feeling of floating-- my mind acutely aware of every micron of surrounding detail. I hear Beasley and his girlfriend making love in the next room with crystal clarity, their moans and the heightened excitement of their breathing. In the distance, a rumbling Doppler effect of a Harley, lumbering along the highway, terminated by a subtle click of the air-conditioning unit as the compressor kicks in. I watch a housefly bob in slow motion across my face, however, too fast for me to catch it. I begin having a wonderful time exploring new sensations and increased awareness when my eyes see what my mind ignores.

A spider has made her home in the north-west corner of the room just above my bed. No doubt it is a common variety, just the way of nature to help control the insect population; a friendly house spirit that has already captured in her stringent web the fly seen only moments earlier. Since earliest childhood, I retain a fear of all arachnids. Rudy has a cabin somewhere up in the mountains when he and Jean first get married. It has neither electricity, nor running water. I sleep that first night alone in a small room, not much larger than an oversize closet, on the top shelf
of a makeshift loft made into a bed. I awake terrified and screaming as things invisible swarm over my face and neck. Both my parents come running in with an extended lighted kerosene lantern.

"My lord—Rudy do something, there are spiders all over my child!" My mother cries in panic.

Rudy calmly lifts me up and brushes away the pests. An infestation of Baby Black Widows just hatched. I do not know if I received bites, or if the deadly venom too low to have any effect. All I know is that I escaped with a lingering terror that will haunt me the rest of my life. My final memory of Rudy's cabin in the mountains the rainy day we depart for the last time. That fall he sells the cabin for the price of a down payment on a family residence. The last image I have of that cabin in the woods is my red toy fire truck abandoned in the front yard beside a pile of fresh wood shavings. I always believed one day we would return to retrieve it. But we never do.

Here I am alone, under the influence of a powerful hallucinogenic, beneath the shadow of my greatest fear. I know exactly what is coming. I can feel my mind reaching up to touch this ever-watchful multi-eyed thing— my own mind now my enemy. I lay back on the bed to watch as it watches me. This creature grows enormous covering the ceiling, patient, waiting for my reason to collapse. There are other things writhing in the shadows, familiar things, also watching, also waiting. I determine not to move, not to think, and above all not to lose my fragile control. I use every bit of my concentration. It moves forward-- I stop it. Immediately it moves back again. The whole night I play this cat and mouse chess game. Except this no game I can afford to lose. I know only too well how high the stakes. Hours pass as the slow pulse of the universe, as an eternity collapsed into the singularity of this fragile moment, a space trapped within a space of finite terror.

The bright morning sun stings me awake. The great spider gone, and all that remains of that frightening night strands of a wispy web tucked discreetly into a corner held together by a tiny harmless insect. My universe safe—at least in the moment-- at least my reason still my own. This night I learn something about the nature of terror and the mind, something that will help me later. Having traversed this bright passage into psychedelics, now I am fully aware this angel of light is in reality darkness. I will not enter this principality again by the same way. But something of the darkness still remains, only I do not know it at the time. Nevertheless, I feel more free than felt since a long time. I will not see Beasley, or Tommy, or any of that crowd again in the context that I knew them then. I no longer wish to get stoned on acid or mescaline, now prepared to face even stronger demons.

The last week in my hometown, I meet a sweet young girl my own age named Linda walking along the train tracks that runs behind my old Junior High School. We sit together under a Dogwood tree near her home, drink a couple cans of beer, and kiss passionately. Linda manages a few nights to sneak out her bedroom window and make-out under the same tree. She claims to be a virgin, but for some reason I do not believe her, believing she only does it for the free beer and cigarettes. Nevertheless, this is the first girl with whom I ever had complete sex. I will later receive a letter from Linda while overseas. I think I wrote her back, but never receive a reply. I will see Linda more than a year later while home on another leave. Both her parents away, she invites me into her home and coaxes me to make love to her on the kitchen table. Then in the middle of the act, she begins moaning rape. Fortunately, I have not consummated the act, jump up, and quickly run out. I will never know if Linda serious or just play-acting. Nevertheless, I will see Linda again one last time many years later. Now married to an alcoholic car mechanic, she lives in a trailer park with her two boys just a block from where Linda grew up. Tired and overweight, this girl from the other side of the train tracks claims to remember nothing about me. It is just as well, since the person she once knew long dead by then.

I catch a military transport from Greenville to Atlanta, and then a commercial flight to San Diego. As the pilot makes his approach vector, he announces over the intercom to look out the starboard window. In the night patches of campfires blaze all along the California state. At the time, I do not fully comprehend the meaning of this enormous tragedy, a dramatic scene as might have been the burning of Rome. Years later, I will grow accustomed to this West Coast phenomenon, a combination of combustible summer dry canyons and thirsty Sierra forests ignited by errant lighting strikes or a careless camper. These sparks further fanned by a hot Santana wind in early autumn. California was burning, and allI can think at the time is how beautiful it looks from the air, as our plane circles toward the San Diego Airport.

While claiming my duffle bag, I meet a fellow Marine; an older Lance Corporal just arrived on a flight from New York. He introduces himself as Lance (really Lance Corporal Lance).

"So, Lance Corporal Lance is this your first time in California?" I ask jestingly, saying his name out loud.

"Nay, I was stationed in El Toro the first year out of training, then off to Quantico, and now I'm going back to El Toro as helicopter mechanic. I have an older sister living somewhere here in the San Diego suburbs. Hell Corporal-- we both have a few days to kill! What do you say we team up, find my sister's house, and do a little hell-raising?"

I am eager to join this career soldier on his quest. Lance is probably less than four years my senior, but possesses a mature swashbuckling style inviting to adventure. He had visited his sister a few times during his first tour at El Toro, knowing approximately the location and remembering only the street name. However, he cannot clearly recall the exact address number, which neither of us thinks all that important in the moment. SinceI still have a few days, including the weekend, before having to report for duty, I decide to join Lance on this promising odyssey. We have onlyforty dollars between us both, debating on rather or not to waste anypart of it on cab fare. As we consider our next move, a tall hooker with red hair walks-up and makes a proposition. Lance smooth-talks her alittle, but finally tells her that it is either her or cab fare. She departs, returning a few minutes later seated in a sagging Impala with her pimp at the wheel. She and Lance begin negotiating again. Then he squeezes into the front seat and motions for me to get into the back. We drive around for about an hour, up one street and down another. San Diego is a city laced with one-way streets that all look the same. The suburbs are not much different. Every street jogs Lance's memory, every house as familiar

as the next. At some point, we stop at a Seven-Eleven and buy some beer to help wash down a cheap bottle of whiskey the pimp has stashed in the glove compartment. Then Lance starts getting it on with the hooker. She moans and groans, the car interior sweating with lust. She reaches suddenly into the back and grabs me between the legs. I am shocked, as well as disgusted. First of all, I do not find her attractive; second, this not my idea of a romantic liaison. I push her hand away and say that I am okay. Fortunately, she contains her affections in the front seat after this, also involving the pimp navigator. Through the meandering maze of streets, the alcohol, and the sex, we somehow find the sister's house. At least I hope it is her house, since no one home. Lance gains entrance by prying-off a screen from an open bathroom window. He then lets us in by the front door. I had never participated in an orgy; the truth of the matter being that at this time I do not even know meaning of the word orgy. Now there are whores by choice, motivated by financial necessity; and whores that are whores because they like being whores. This woman fits every definition of a nymphomaniac. She has sex with Lance, then with her pimp; and if this not enough, she demands I join the fray of flesh. At first, I decline. Lance insists I participate because of my money contribution. I reluctantly shed my clothes and climb on top of the sweating sickly white flesh. It reminds me of being inside a slimy pickle jar, which actually sloshes upon penetration. I pretend immediately to have an organism, retract, and with draw to another room. Here I fall asleep upright in an armchair. By the time I awake, Lance lies passed-out naked and alone in his sister's heart-shaped bed. Our night visitors departed, as spirits fled from the light of my first California sunrise.

Lance's sister, Jill, arrives around noon, fitting completely the definition of a "beach chick" with peroxide bleached hair, a perfect

California beach tan, and tired dark circles under her eyes from lack of sleep. I suppose partying runs naturally in the family. Jill, a woman of maybe thirty-five, twice devoiced, and curses a lot in a squeaky voice that I find irritatingly cute. Had I been a few years older I may have had a chance with her; but as I have already said, I look even younger than my years, more of a boy in her mind. Still, I think Jill a refreshing change from the night before.

That afternoon the three of us go to the beach where I learn a little bit about body-surfing and how important it is to time a wave just right. Later in the day a friend of Lance's sister named Janet joins us, lighting-up a stick of Marijuana, which she freely passes around. Janet is a bookend to Jill in every aspect, except her hair raven black and cascades down to her ass. She and Lance hit it off immediately. That evening we are off to Mexico. After crossing into Tijuana, I have my first introduction to a Mexican dinner consisting of tacos and Margaritas.

As soon as one crosses the border from the U. S., there is a definite sense of being in another country. This border town changes alive with disorder after sunset, transforming from an improvised diver's habitation into a corrupt den peddling the bartered weight of every vise known to man. I will eventually see behind those many masks on different occasions, but this night I see only the lights and excitement of an exotic other land. After walking through the crowded streets for a while, we wander into a dirty smoke-filled tequila bar that Jill and Janet know all too well. There are no chairs, the tables low to the floor, necessitating that we sit cross-legged on small worn cushions spotted with vomit stains. Before we even order, a tray appears in the center of the table, serving several shot glasses filled with tequila, slices of lime, and a mound of salt. Janet first instructs Lance and me on how to combine these ingredients. She pours some salt in the palm of one hand, takes a slice of lime, and a glass of tequila in the other hand. In precise order she licks the salt, downs the glass of white elixir with one gulp, finishing by biting into the lime.

She glares across the table glassy-eyed and begins to laugh. Jill follows suit, performing the ritual in pro-fashion. Lance catches on right away. It takes me a couple of tries before I get the coordinated hang of it. The salt deadens the taste buds, the pure tequila alcohol more easily tolerated, and the lime destroys any after taste. It is a deceptive combination. Within minutes, we lay passed-out on the floor. I remember nothing, except grogginess upon regaining consciousness, feeling as though someone has hit me in the head with a hammer. As my senses begin to clear, I realize I have been robbed. Lance also robbed, including his expensive diver's watch. Instead of being upset, he just shrugs his shoulders and looks around the room glassy-eyed. We fortunately discover our wallets on the floor a few feet away with our military IDs intact, but all our remaining cash gone. The two girls have taken experienced precaution by hiding their money in their braziers. The thieves probably knew it there; but because of dominate Catholic upbringing, they dare not violate a woman's person for fear of divine retribution.

Not so innocently, we have stumbled into one of those clip-joints the military always warns soldiers to avoid when on leave. Jill and Janet and Jill just laugh it off like seasoned veteran California girls. They continue to pay for Lance and me the rest of the night, buying us drinks on our continued odyssey bar-hopping from club to club. They even have enough to pay for an early morning breakfast at a small Mexican cafe before crossing the border back into the USA. In this place crowds the souls of the day; those who actually work for a living and make the Mexican economy function. We order something that looks similar to an enchilada, but tastes and smells like dog breath. Mexican food is great in California, where all the ingredients wholesome U.S. certified. In Mexico you never know what you are getting. On a later visit outside of Loreto, located along the peninsula separating the Gulf of California and the Pacific, I ask a local police officer about a peculiar tasting taco purchased from a street vendor.

"Dog meat," he replies nonchalantly; "Not so fresh, but good."

I will learn this just the way it is in other countries. More often than not, it is better to eat meat offered by a host without questions.

The next day being Monday, I decide I have enough *R&R*. I promise Jill I will pay her back one day. Lance and I make plans to keep in touch once we report to our perspective bases and get settled in. Neither of these things ever happens, nor will I see Lance Corporal Lance or his sister again. This often the way of military life with men in uniform; men that rarely remember one day to the next when on leave. I am exhausted by the time I check into my new assignment, broke and in debt to a woman who thinks of me as a sweet kid with a funny accent. My first pay disbursement I attempt to locate Lance at El Toro, so that I might send him money to pay back his sister; only lack enough information to track him down. I doubt he would have given her the money anyway. Although Lance a fun drinking buddy, he would not have made a very responsible friend. I will always remember that first time in San Diego with Lance and the lollipop girls and the raging fires all around. My WESPAC adventure has begun.

ITR training is in fact every Marine's dreaded Grunt Day. Even the Grunts hate it. And when these guys hate something, it really is bad. A solid six weeks of physical drill designed to prepare every soldier for extreme combat conditions. From the hour I sign in, until the hour of deployment, I will not see or communicate with the outside world again. Our mornings begin at 0500, not 0530 hours. We force-march one mile before chow through desert terrain in the dark. It is still dawn by the time we return along the same route. Often we witness the black and white squashed remains of Tarantulas we have unknowingly stomped to death in the dark, oblivious to the migrating herd crossing our path. Many the size of a man's hand, reportedly a non-poisonous variety, and are similar in appearance to her deadly South American sister, identical in every way, except for a yellow and white banding. However, a painful bite from one of these creatures will make one deathly ill. I often wonder what the prognosis if one bitten by several of these creatures.

My rank automatically makes me one of several squad leaders. This means that I take a position on the outside. It is my responsibility to herd in any stragglers, insuring a semblance of formation during these terrain crossings. I am a yapping sheep dog running from one end of the squad to the other snapping out commands. Through the course of many rigorous days of training exercises, we will embark upon three thirty-mile force marches. The first with no gear, the second with half gear: rifles, helmets, and utility belt. The last fully loaded for combat, plus a thirty-five pound backpack and live ammunition. The only difference between me and my men, I am the one in command. In the Marine Corps, either you do or you do not. There are times when I desperately want to quit, but believe myself the backbone by which these men rely on for example and endurance. For me to abandon my resolve would mean to abandon the allied strength given to them through my example. Of course, it could also be that they think if a young kid like me can do it, then they surely can do it, too. It is times like these that a man becomes more than he is, when he becomes master over his body and his mind.

As is always the case, there happens the occasional rebellion. Once, two men spontaneously break out into a fight. Common knowledge is that these two have a history of animosity dating back to an alleged stud poker game, when one accused by the other of cheating. However, in the military no one gambles, so this persists as a rumor only. On a particularly hot day these two fall out of rank clawing at each other's throats. Without even thinking, I throw myself bodily between them splitting the two apart. Back on my feet, I grab the one closest to me, and shove him in the direction of our march with an order to catch up. The other protagonist quickly follows suit. I gain reputation of sincere respect after this event. I have handled a difficult situation alone and without hesitation. Men do not always recognize justice, but they do

179

respond to strength and leadership.

At times, it feels like boot camp all over again. We do everything on the run; everything we do with a designed purpose. We learn how to find water in the desert, which seems odd since the United States presently engaged in jungle warfare of steamy South East Asia. We discover the nutritional benefits of a variety of insects, including worms and a few non-poisonous reptiles. Just as a note, snakes do not taste like chicken, but worms definitely taste like worms. --And remember the Tarantula? Yes, we eat those as well after first removing the poison gland just under the fangs. In addition, we receive specific instruction on what to avoid. The whole idea of survival training is survival. It is to bring the body and the palate into subjection to what the mind knows to be necessary. If nothing else, I become acquainted with renewed respect for the human metabolism to convert all sorts of crawling and slithering things into consumable energy. I learn there are many things I will not eat by choice; but little I will not eat if necessity dictates. There is a Chinese proverb: consume the essence of an enemy and gain his strength. This proverb might as easily apply to passive things as well. I cannot remember in exact detail everything that happens during these weeks of extreme training, only that it all seemed vitally necessary at the time.

There are live ammunition drills, dry amphibious maneuvers, and deep-penetration war games. I remember particularly well the time my squad gets lost in the desert somewhere between San Diego and Oceanside. A transport has dropped us off at a blind position with only a compass and set of terrain maps. Our objective: to find our way back to base before morning by star triangulation and the use of a magnetic compass. Direction has never been my strong point; and in retrospect, I must have day-dreamed through the map reading class. I manage to locate what I think is the North Star just above the horizon at the tail of the Big Dipper. I remind the reader that this most luminescent object in the night sky is in fact Venus, a wanderer, and that location of the fainter *North Star* in the *Little Dipper* and not the *Big Dipper*. Venus just happens to be wandering near the tail of the *Big Dipper* this particular evening. Further adding to the confusion, the bright heavenly body appears fixed from my relative point of observation.

However, basic astronomy teaches that stars and planets have different definitions. Whereas, stars are stationary, and emit their own luminosity in the same way as our sun; planets have a fixed orbit, and are reflective, in the same way as our moon changing position constantly. If only my friend Franklin had been there to remind me that in the *Constellation of Ursa Minor* where I ought to point my compass. There is also a difference between true north and magnetic north.

Magnetic North is the direction the compass needle points; whereas, true north is the direction of the *North Star*. Using a map, one is able to calculate a formula to determine direction. Through course of the night, true north and magnetic north grow farther and farther apart, as the planetoids relative to earth's view drift across the horizon. Just as the sun begins to rise, I perceive the familiar outline of a military facility reflecting in the morning light. The wandering planet has inadvertently wandered us in a circle home. Only now do I further realize that all this time I have been reading the map upside down. Just another fortunate happenstance; else, we may have ended up in the true desert. Two hours later, we arrive with the undignified honor of being the last. Fortunately, my men remain ignorant of my navigation errors, no one else even aware of the secret bounty of blessing provided to the inexperience of their leader.

Ousted rudely from our sleep early one morning before reverie, we receive orders to pack our sea bags (a long sack with a shoulder strap made of thick green canvas). This is every Marine's travel kit designed to hold all personal belongings, provided it is properly packed. We assemble on the tarmac, surrounded by armed MPs. A burly Captain begins calling out names, and a Lieutenant beside him hands-out large manila envelopes printed with our military designation number and in large letters FMF WESPAC. Out of more than two hundred souls, less than half called, the rest dismissed for duty. We that are chosen then herded into waiting cattle cars (tractor-trailers constructed of wood grating and a single doorlocked from the outside.)

Two Military Police jeeps, one in front, the other rear, escort us far into the desert. Half an hour later, we arrive at a secret air base with a single runway, a control tower, and a couple of stray buildings. On a darkened runway hums an unmarked two-engine jet liner powered-up and ready for takeoff. Without ceremony, we file from the cattle cars directly to the loading ramp of the waiting jet. Here our orders collected by two officers asking each to confirm name, rank and serial number, before entering the cabin.

There is a distinct difference between this flight and the flight taken from Atlanta. For one thing, this jet smaller by comparison, and instead of pretty flight attendants, two sternly disciplined, never smiling, armed MPs watch over us. It bares more similarity to a prison flight. Less than three hours later, we make touchdown somewhere in Alaska. From the airport-terminal window, the Alaskan night appears as a barren gloomy terrain, the terminal gate a skeletal rib of passage into dismal ether. There are several indistinct shadows that loom in the distance, like unburied remains of dead carcasses, all obscured in this long Alaskan night. We lose five souls to this forsaken place; and even the prospect of Vietnam better than thought of committing a year of duty in this sunless region. Twelve hours later, I happily board another plane en route to the historic Marine facility, FMF WESPAC Okinawa.

Okinawa is a duty assignment made from the stuff of erotic dreams. It is a lush pacific island in the East China Sea off the southern coast of Japan. A rich garden planted with beautiful tropical trees, lush flowers, and the loveliest women that I have ever seen. Okinawa is more like R and R, than a duty assignment. Even the Officers laid back compared to stateside. This island truly the beauty of a sunrise in paradise, a place I could remain forever. It never occurs to me that the name Okinawa might mean something altogether different to those soldiers that fought terrible battles on these shores and in the jungles against Japanese kamikazes. In later years, I will meet one of these Second World War survivors. For him the place representing a graveyard of lost friends and terrifying memories. Even then his eyes still sees only the past. I will think of this man again many years later when I will look at pictures of a dangerous isolated military position I once occupied, now turned into a congested urban neighborhood visited by international tourist. My younger mind has difficulty to imagine the blood that ran like rivers down these lush green slopes and into an emerald East China Sea: all relative to context: each generation with its own memories to remember.

Our first stop an auxiliary airfield name *Le-jima* located on a sparsely populated smaller island off the east coast of the main Okinawa extension. For many this only a staging area; not everyone will remain in paradise. Since we arrive on a Friday, we receive Day Passes limited to a small village just outside the main gate composed mostly of a few bars and one or two restaurants. There are also girls, beautiful exotic oriental ladies, whose aspiring interest our pleasure and our paychecks. The first night of a weekend pass, I find myself in the company of some older baroness' languishing seductively within a dimly lit den. Painted like porcelain dolls and adorned in silk Kimonos, too perfect to touch for fear they might crack, they laugh between themselves, calling me 'cherry boy'. At first, I do not understand the meaning; but in time will comprehend it means a virgin. At first, I take offense, wishing to set the record straight. However, a buddy of mine whispers that I will have better chance at scoring free because Okinawa women (particularly the Prostitute variety) like to be the first experience in a young man's sexual exploration. Therefore, I accept to be called "cherry boy", a labelof special status, hoping that eventually one of these painted tigresses or one of their friends might devour me in passion. However, this was not to be.

The following weekend, our base commander revokes all passes,and we become confined to barracks under constant supervision. In the middle of the second night, lights snap on and once again the familiar order to pack all our gear. Judging by the tension, something big is up. Again, armed MPs escort us to a lighted tarmac, where a waiting jet prepares for take-off. The dispatch officer, a Captain, and an enlisted ranked Adjutant are waiting with a stack of brown envelopes. In a clear baritone voice, the Adjutant begins calling out names, reporting them to a position opposite side of a defined LZ. After calling more than fifty names, he promptly closes the roster and snaps at attention. This time, my name not on the list! I have escaped the final call of duty and this paradise island at last my next permanent duty assignment. However, my elation dashed to pieces when the captain orders the rest of us to pick-up our gear, to form a single line, and to board the wheezing airliner. Here we are issued new envelopes upon entering the cabin. Altogether, only thirty souls called. A remarkable reduction from when this journey around the world first began. We receive strict orders not to open our envelopes until fully air-born and granted permission to do so. As the airliner climbs into the sunless sky, suspense climaxes with the raspy report of a First Lieutenant in charge.

"Okay, gentlemen, you may now unseal your envelopes."

A quiet fills the cabin as we each tear open the sealed jackets and read our new assignments. The words like lead in my stomach read: FMF WESTPAC VIETNAM. I always knew this a possibility-- suddenly, the possibility a reality. I begin to truly comprehend the meaning and purpose of my many weeks of training. I am a United States Combat Marine about to embark on an undefined mission in an active war zone.You cannot get any more real than this.

Once the plane reaches cruisingaltitude, small complimentary bottles of alcohol, mostly Vodka and Seagram's whiskey, distributed. Perhaps, a bit unmilitary, but I guess they figure we might need a little extra courage. Being young Marines indoctrinated with the values of our nation, we down the available stock without reservation. The atmosphere within the cabin changes from seriousness to levity. You would think we are in route to a summer day camp, rather than a conflict zone. The empty bottles unceremoniously collected by an attendant, orders over the intercom to fasten our seatbelts. All return to reality of military discipline and protocol.

The jet begins a slow circular descent, shuddering against a thick wall of clouds. Emerging through a veil to the other side, the airliner lurches from side to side, now steady, flung back in time to a dangerous prehistoric epoch with sunless jungles and pin point flashes of firefights in progress.

No word spoken and barely a movement. The plane continues its calculated descent into this nether region of a lost world. The runway appears racing toward us, a slick diseased grey tongue extending out of a dark mouth and pulling our transport into the belly of a demon hungry for new flesh. The jet touches- down with a dead thump, growling to a halt; and then taxies quickly to a special area surrounded by walls. We have arrived in fabled Shangri-La. I am in Vietnam.

Chapter 11
Vision of Shangri-La

$\mathcal{T}$he French are the first to call this Asian destination Shangri-La. According to ancient legend, its genesis arose from the peaceful union of *Lac Long Quan*, which means King of the Sea, and Au Co, Princess of the Mountains. During the eighteenth century, this lushtropical paradise is considered a Mecca to the wealthy vacationers of the period. Then under the watchful scrutiny of a dragon rising over the east, the garden resort divided through unrest. By the end of the Second World War, the predominately Communist Viet Minh have successfully resisted the Japanese occupation. The party now turns its attention to the politics of declaring the country's independence, igniting the start of the French Indonesian War. An imaginary line drawn, separating north: those who wanted Communist rule; and the western sympathizers ofthe south preferring democracy. After the massacre of *Dien Bien Phu* in 1954, Shangri-La receives a more notorious reputation. The Frenchpull-out in total defeat; and the Americans, seen as true defenders of democracy in the world, slowly drawn into the tangled civil war.

But the real early history of this region is shrouded in myth and legends going back at least 4000 years, which reads like the chronicle of Middle Kingdom in J.R.R. Tolkien's 'Lord of the Ring'. An intricacy of eastern cosmology viewed through the concept of the five elements of metal, wood, water, fire, and earth. Or *Nghu Han*, a meaning that represents five regions of associated colors. The Center represents earth by the color yellow; the South symbolizes fire by the color red; the North water by the color black; the East wood by the color green; and the West metal by the color white. It is a history laced with fairy tales, good and bad spirits, extraordinary heroes, and powerful monsters.

What is known can be traced back to a time when the province first called Van Lang by the Hung or Lac. These being immigrants from greater China during the 5th century B.C., considered inventors of what is commonly called the *'wet rice'* cultivation technique. *Au*, or *Tay* Au follows these in secession. The two groups form the kingdom known as Au Lac, until the *Viet or Yue*, originating from the coastal provinces of ancient China come along with other ethnic groups that continues for over fifteen centuries, penetrating ever deeper into the Indochina peninsula.

The name Vietnam born somewhere near the beginning of the 19th century when the local Emperor, *Cia Long*, decides to rename the country to Nam Viet, as a way of unifying the old land of Au Nam and the new land of *Viet Thuong*. This royal request solicited directly to the authority presided over by the great Emperor of China. However, after consideration the request denied for reasons it might cause confusion with the already existing *Trieu Da* of the ancient kingdom Nam Viet Dong, and on the premise that it could lead to future territorial ambitions. Therefore, the Chinese Emperor purposes Vietnam instead, a name, defining the Viet of the south. This spelling will later be changed to The Republic of Vietnam as future symbol of Chinese authority.

Etymology and anthropology play a role in the shaping and reshaping of this distinct culture. Fragile tensions have always existed between the Viet of the north, choosing to identify with the policy claims of China; and the Viet of the south, who choose to resist immersion. The end of the Zhou dynasty in 249 B.C. makes mention of the Viet of the south. Marco Polo notes its presence in his 'Wonders of the World' as he passes along the wondrous coast of Vietnam in 1292 A.D. It has been witness to conquering dynasties, bloody battles and political betrayals mingled in the waters of two great rivers that flow through the region. The Red River in the north, joined by the greater Mekong in the south, precisely traces safe passages by early map-makers. Its southern delta, a termination point to the pre-Cambodian kingdom of *Funan*, or in Vietnamese, *Phu Nam*, visited by Romans and by Arab navigators. Even the famous Greek mathematician, Ptolemy, came here on his voyage to the Indies and Southeast Asia. Without doubt, this rich region once a principality of great influence and wealth, a former footstool of empires, which have long ago vanished into the diluvium mud of history, giving place to the genius of the cultivation techniques for growing rice, considered the world's greatest food source.

Of course, I know nothing of this history at the time. I am a young United States Marine, one of the chosen few, determined to fight my Nation's battles anywhere in the world, on land and sea, and if need be to die at the hands of my designated enemy as have other Marines before me. I doubt there is a single soldier arriving this day, who does not to some degree share these feelings. All patriotic in the beginning; all young, at the peak of our physical and mental training; and most importantly, all committed. At least this is the way I saw it then.

The first evening, we receive little information, other than the promise of being issued weapons and new assignments the next morning.

Already past chow time, packets of c-rations distributed, consisting of canned bread and everyone's cold favorite, corn beef hash. Lastly, four armed MPs usher us into the shelter of a barracks located a few meters   from the control tower. Off in the distance we can hear the sound of weapon discharge, exchange of an escalating firefight. No one speaks, but I think we are all feeling a little naked without a rifle. Our apprehensions prove valid as we settled in for the night. Suddenly our chamber sprayed with shattered glass, the emerald firefly of a stray bullet ricocheting through the oblong chamber.

"Mother of God--" someone shouts; "We're being over-run!"

Instantly, we drop to the floor dead men. I do not know if I slept any that first night in country, or if anyone else did. Nevertheless, we remain prostrate on the deck all night in anticipation of what might happen next. By morning, the assault successfully repelled, all quiet.

"Get your shit together, Marines," commands the seasoned voice of a combat-ready clad First Lieutenant bursting through the door. "You're in Nam, your new home for the next twelve months— and it's time to get you where you belong!"

First priority is to arm us with an M-16 assault rifle, two clips of ammunition, and an issue of combat gear. I feel relief, as though some essential part of me now restored. Even much later in life I will experience lucid moments, when I feel venerable not having a weapon at my side. A combat Marine with his rifle is the completion of a highly sophisticated arsenal. He becomes the effective tool to fulfill the mandate of all his training, a perfect killing machine if necessary. Our purpose not to think, or to have compassion, but to be and to do-- we were all Marines then!

After a decent breakfast, all ordered to line up near waiting transports to receive our new duty orders. Every new arrival subject to a requisition order, which determines his destination based on MOS. My original in-country requisition is to fill the position of a field Supply Corporal.

Yet, for some reason a confusion in the paperwork decides my original assignment no longer needed. After a few perplexing moments, the officer in charge crosses out my MOS and pencils in 0311 assigned to Fox Company infantry squad. A jeep transports me to a small muddy compound a few miles north, where I am assigned as one of twenty-six soldiers ordered to Field Reconnaissance duty. We divide into two units of thirteen men each. Mostly we conduct perimeter sweeps, checking for booby-traps, or tracking down snipers. Occasionally, we must go out on night patrols. These are the worst. There is nothing pleasant about being in the field. Exposed to the elements, continuously gnawed by mosquitoes, leeches, and jungle rot. The damp cold Atlantic terrain of Camp Lejeune remembered as paradise compared to this prehistoric South-East Asian hot-bed of dangerous insects, snakes, and stalking creatures. At least the enemies are men, except they have an advantage by knowing the environment. This first month is the worst I can remember, a month of torment, eating out of cans, gnawed constantly by mosquitoes, and plagued by continuous dysentery. I give special credit to those individuals, who endured an entire tour of duty out in this no-man's land. There is nothing romantic about it. Day or night, you creep around on patrol searching through a maze of jungle for anything irregular or that seems out of place. Once, I forgot an essential part of my training and reach down to pick up a pack of cigarettes I thought dropped by someone. A strong arm pulls me suddenly back and quickly away.

"I just saved your ass, Corporal!" A private snarls at me with a heavy Texas accent.

He then points out a thin spider thread running into the brush. Attached to the other end of the line is the release pin of an American made Claymore mine, this anti-personnel device designed at a sixty- degree arch loaded with seven hundred steel balls. How the Cong got it is anyone's guess. However, one thing for sure, were it not been for the experience of this watchful guardian, I would have been blown away, along with half of my platoon. That is the way it comes down in combatNam. The leader of the squad designated as the man with the most combat experience, not the pomp of a newly assigned brass. A Second Lieutenant that arrives about the same time as I do soon learns his rank counts little in the field. He quickly takes a back seat to the experience of this same Private, preferring not to take the lead for the better good; or at least until he becomes more seasoned. Not a single man disagrees with this decision. I do not remember that Private's name now. He proved, however, to be a good and wise leader, a guiding light of salvation to safeguard my life and the life of others during those early days in the field. We become somewhat close— at least as close as men under the pressure of combat allow themselves. One night, we are in the barracks cleaning our rifles, still trying to dry out after two soggy days in the deltas. I thank him again for saving my life. After a few moments of silence, I ask him a question I think on the minds of most here.

"Are you ever afraid?"

"No," he replies; "I eat fear before every mission, and shit it out on the way." He then breaks into a cowboy smile. "Hell yes, I'm afraid-- been scared shitless since the first day I arrived."

He then proceeds to tell me about his first duty with a company stationed in the north. They are on routine patrol, the day bright and sunny, the jungle like a tropical paradise in bloom. Suddenly, he finds himself on the ground, a peculiar silence ringing in his ear. He says he could feel his heart that moment, as the slow pulse of the universe, and dirt mixed with blood raining down on him. Slowly, he is aware of time again. He sits up, spits mud from his mouth, and sees a detached leg a few feet away. At first he thinks it might be his own, but soon realizes his body still whole. The man to whom the leg belonged also sits up and starts to laugh, saying that someone else wearing his boots. His eyes then roll back and he is dead.

"I'll never forget the almost sweet acrid smell, like a slaughterhouse, and we who survived like butchers covered in blood." Pausing, he smells his hands, as if the odor of death still clings to his flesh. "Fear is not what happens to you," he says, looking steadfast in the eyes. "Real fear is what you survive."

In those calm blue cowboy eyes, I can see the nightmare he saw, can smell vividly the death on his hands. We talk about other things, about girls, and about riding horses on his father's ranch. He plans returning to Texas one day, marrying a local sweetheart, and start up a stud ranch of his own. If nothing else, Nam makes us to dream.

My last night with Fox Company will prove to be an experience into Zen to mark me for the rest of my life. Earlier that evening, a volley of rounds pelts our position. We return fire, but there are no casualties on either side. HQ demands confirmation, unable to verify the event. Nevertheless, engagement is certain. The Second Lieutenant obtains permission to swing down into the lower delta and come up from behind in the hope of surprising the enemy platoon. Night has descended by the time we reach the extreme end of the flooded plain. The Second Lieutenant issues a command decision to cross the open expanse against the advice of the more experienced Private.

A monsoon night in Vietnam is a scene straight from the dark pages of every horror book ever written-- no stars or moon, a firmament above and below, wrapping the earth in a blanket of grey-black clouds that hug the ground with an everlasting embrace of shadow. The water tepid, an oily ooze, only a little thicker than the air, each step an effort against the suction of fertile soft mud that layers the leech-infested bottom. Occasionally, I nearly stumble over something resting below that reminds me of slick bones. Suddenly, the point man gives the sign that Charlie near.

We each freeze in mid-step, then the signal to go as low as possible. Slowly I descend, until the water an inch above my chin. I barely breathe, increasingly aware of each heavy drop of rain, tortured by an incessant horde of humming mosquitoes. These Erinyes slowly eating me alive! Helpless to move a muscle against their assault, the blood-sucking devils tormented me relentlessly. Moments pass as the slow wane of the universe slipping in and out of the surrounding darkness. The water as a great toothless worm gnawing my flesh numb, my body a rotting corpse hugged in its embrace. Charlie near, so near that almost I can reach-out and touch him-- so near that my fear resists the impulse to slaughter!

In reality, these Viet Cong just passing along a known land bridge less than a hundred yards south of our position. The keen animal instinct of our guide has evaded contact with an enemy engagement that would have been strategically to our disadvantage. Charlie will return home this morning and eat his rice silently for another day. At near dawn, we receive the all clear, make it to solid ground and setup a bivouac. We spend the next hour burning leeches off each other with lighted cigarettes. After this night Mosquitoes represent a pestilence of magnified   torment; and to this day, I am restless if I suspect even one of these Erinyes within my confined space.

Dead and exhausted, stumbling rag-tag into the security of our compound, I look forward to the dry comfort of a hard canvass military cot I call my bed. After time in the field, even the most rudimentary comfort a luxury. I have just taken off my soggy boots when the field Lieutenant steps into the hooch calling my name.

"Here, Sir!" I report, rising tiredly to my feet.

"So, you are a supply grunge," he says without much enthusiasm; "looks like they need you in the south. Pack your gear and report to a waiting jeep out front--ASAP Marine!"

He hands me an envelope containing my new orders and departs without even saying goodbye. This is the Marine Corps way. Every part has a function, until that function no longer needed, then repacked and shipped off for another issue. Working in supply has taught me a few things of importance. A multifunction device more applicable than one designed for single use only. I say my farewells to my comrades in arms. I particularly want to say goodbye to the private, who had guided us to safety on so many occasions, but this man not to be found. He will always remain an enigma in my mind, a small, but wiry cowboy with acute survival instincts. I consider myself fortunate that this individual raised up to guide me, as well as others through days and nights in no man's land. I can only grimly imagine what might have happened had he not been there. I hope he survives days in Hades and discovers his dreamat end of the monsoon rainbow.

The assigned jeep transports me through a maze of barely navigable jungle trails and across fragile suspension bridges newly erected by the Corps of Engineers. Too exhausted even to talk, I avoid conversation. The driver understands and allows me to nod off. There is always the risk of a booby trap, but neither of us cares to think about that much. We both have our assignments and this is all that really matters.

"Okay Corporal, you have a bird to catch," the driver says, nudging me awake.

The Huey touches down lightly in an open field, engines revving. Grabbing my gear, M-16 in hand, I board the restless dragonfly and am lifted into a veil of clouds. The UH-1C gunship is perhaps Bell Helicopter's finest design. Agile, practical, and with a heavy sheet of bottom armor, it can maneuver in any environment, manned with starboard and port gunners, mounted rocket projectiles and heavy front assault weaponry. A fleet can level a village in minutes, and can effectively crumble an enemy stronghold in less time than this. The only other combat vehicle more formidable is the sleek nimble Cobra mounted with two M-61 six-barreled Vulcan Cannons with firepower of 6000 rounds per minute capable of spraying every inch of a football field in seconds, or so they say. I can still remember dark nights watching two of these graceful ballerinas dance back and forth opposite each other spraying a red stream of death to the earth, every one hundredth round being a tracer bullet. Once while on patrol, we pass through an area after a Cobra barrage. The landscape eerie, not a living soul to be found; even the trees stripped of their branches, scarred and naked, as if a giant evil hand had decimated the area. Even the earth pummeled and ripped open. I still have nightmares of these relentless killing machines to this day, imagining what it must be like to be caught in their web of certain destruction.

At beginning of the flight, I feel exposed, an easy target for any guerrilla that might wish to take a pot shot. However, the crew of three assures me this unlikely, considering our speed and altitude. In time, I try to relax and enjoy the view. My journey begins somewhere north and west of *Da Nang* where a major tributary of the Great Mekong River flows from Laos in the west near the temple city of Hue on the coast of the China Sea. Hue, considered the former capitol of Emperors that ruled Vietnam in antiquity is a city with unique character. Before the war-- according to legend-- the Perfume River that flows through the metropolis acted as a border to separate the present city from the ancient city of the dead that contains the tombs of royalty and holy pagodas. *Hue* is precisely the midpoint between the Vietnam of north and south. From the Vietnamese capital of Hanoi, near the China border, to *Ho Chi Ming City*, where empties the lower Mekong Delta, is a Crow's flight of roughly a thousand miles, shaped like an elongated "*S*" not much greater than the width of Delaware at its narrowest point. Nevertheless, what Vietnam lacks in size, it more than makes up for in agricultural rice production. This small country blessed by unique climate and topography consisting of hundreds of miles of low coastal wetlands, has the capacity to feed a third of the world. It is not difficult to see why. There is not a waterway in Vietnam not fed by The Red River to the North, or the Mekong to the west, filtering through grids of rice paddies, acting as flood plains before leaching into the South China Sea.

As we sweep toward the coast and beyond the thick monsoon cloud cover, it amazes me the transformation from stinking mud rice paddies surrounded by camouflaged borders, into a framed symmetry of defined cultivation fields stretching into the horizon. From this perspective, all seems safe. Safe to admire the distinct regions laced with shadows and shafts of pure sunlight piercing through openings in the canopy. Safe to imagine the hand responsible for the sensual creation of soft white beaches and satin green jungles, safe even to dream without fear. In this moment, at least, Nam changed in my mind into the lovely paradise it meant to be: a land of ancient wisdom without war or violence.

Either for reasons of practical security, or because of his flight plan, the intrepid pilot makes the decision to swing inland choosing not to fly directly over Da Nang City. In the distance, I can see the ghostly skyline of what once must have been a modern metropolis, now only twisted skeletal remains on the horizon. Half an hour later, we pass through a region near the coast of extraordinary geology: islands of rock jutting starkly out of the flat delta plains hundreds of feet high. I count five in all, spread out like giant carved chess pieces of Samurai soldiers strategically placed to guard over a checkered board of rich cultivation fields.

"Gear up-- that's your new home at the foot of Marble Mountain," shouts the co-pilot above the roar of the helicopter engine.

In shadow of one of those geological monoliths appears the wispy sketch of a military compound near a white sandy beach consisting of several large aluminum metal structures, positioned around a waiting LZ stamped in the center. I have arrived at my new assignment.

"You're the new Supply Corporal?" A gruff Sergeant Major demands once the chopper touches down.

Before I can answer, he just wags his head apprehensively and tells me to follow him into the Command Post. I see in his eyes that this veteran soldier considers me a disappointment to what he expected. Like nearly everyone else, he probably thinks me too young to be an NCO, doubtful that I will last long in country. Nevertheless, he treats me in accordance to the courtesy of my rank, processes me into the 2nd Battalion 1st Marine Supply Division, and assigns escort to accompany me to the supply depot.

Gunnery Sergeant Corell, the Supply Gunny, is even less impressed, and makes it immediately known that I am expected to perform my duty with proficiency becoming of a Marine NCO.

"You are in charge of all warehouse functions and personnel, Corporal," he says with skepticism in his voice. "You are "Acting Sergeant" until a replacement comes in. I'll be honest, I would have liked a more seasoned man for the position, but we take what we get in this God forsaken hell hole."

I will in time realize that Gunny Corell has little faith in anything, is perpetually somber, a man never happy, never smiles. Nevertheless, I will grow to respect him in a reverent sort of way, as one might a distant father. And like my relationship with Rudy, I will always feel ambivalence when looking into his eyes, like starring into those of an almost-tamed animal guided more by hunger of instinct. Nor will I ever know much about this career soldier of untold sorrow, beyond a thin barrier of respect that will eventually bond us together: a condition less than friendly, yet more than veneer of military comradely.

I share NCO quarters with a Corporal Neider, the warehouse office administrator, who handles all the paperwork. Neider impresses me from the start as a pleasant fellow, intelligent, and always with a book pressed to his face when not on duty. He is the one to introduce me to the psychiatric theories proposed by Sigmund Freud's *"ID, Ego, and Super Ego."* Encourages me to read *"Last Flight of the Red Baron"*, and Tolkien's *"Lord of the Rings"*, among other books. He instructs me on how to play chess, but never shows me how to win. I truly respect the knowledge of this man. He has a baby face, shoulders that slump slightly forward, and easy going to the point of irritation to others. But everyone likes Neider and so leaves him alone.

Neider has less than a month tour of duty left when I arrive. The wall beside his bunk marred by a graffiti of three hundred and thirty-six marks clumped into groups of seven, adding a new one every morning as he counts down the days, until his release from purgatory. Neider only gets excited when conversation turns to when he gets back stateside to a waiting girlfriend and about eating a Michigan style hotdog, which I take to be an unusual delicacy from his hometown of Detroit. As I prepare my bunk the first night, he pulls out a foot long Bowie Knife from my assigned footlocker and hands it over to me. The wooden grip, black and charred, has the hewn appearance of being home-made or perhaps just badly repaired. Between the handle and the blade a hammered brass insert loosely joined, obviously not original. However, the broad steel blade alone appears authentic, dauntingly long, about a quarter of an inch thick at the ridge and over two inches wide. The back curved blade edge near the point equally dangerous to the razor-sharp front, making it a formidable weapon in trained hands.

"Here," he says giving the instrument reverently over to me, "it is tradition that this Bowie Knife be passed to each Warehouse Sergeant of 2nd Battalion. I hear it said that this compound over-run back in the early sixties, and that they found the warehouse sergeant dead surrounded by gook bodies with this knife gripped in his hand. Maybe it is true, I don't know. But I guess that it belongs to you until your Sergeant arrives."

I hold the blackened blade in my hand and imagine the blood-rage of hand-to-hand combat as a man of war, much like myself, stands against overwhelming odds; and how he must have fallen, going down and taking many with him. This battle scarred instrument remains the only surviving witness to a day of massacre. Little do I know in the moment, I will be the final possessor of this artifact of Marine Corps legend. An honor I bear proudly to this day. Although I have not yet read the tale of Beowulf and the sword of "*Hrunting*" given to him by *Unferth* to slay a monster, in time I discover appreciation of both its purpose and its meaning. I will eventually grow weary of the burden and give it to my brother, a collector of knives and swords, where it remains in company with the finest blades conceived, wielded by gladiators of every age. At this moment in time, however, I consider myself only the keeper of an honored relic from the past and dedicate myself to its safeguard until the arrival of my expected replacement.

As acting Warehouse Sergeant, my duty is mostly to coordinate supply liaisons to the field and to supervise LZ staging for helicopter deployment. I am in-charge of a crew of twelve men, mostly privates, and not a warehouseman among them. These are the declining days of U.S. occupation in Southeast Asia, only key personnel considered essential. The rest shuffled from any available source. Nearly all of these men are 0311, removed from the field because of psychological or disciplinary reasons, reassigned to compound duty in either the Mess Hall or Supply. As long as these men able to read and count; and still retain functioning legs and arms, they qualify. To most of these burnouts, warehouse assignment equivalent to an in-country R&R, with a lot of downtime between staging operations. Of course, it requires someone like me to make sure that the requisitions properly completed; one versed in the functions and protocols of inventory control and licensed to operate a three-ton rough terrain forklift. In truth, those first several weeks are just as boring as stateside duty, reminiscent of the television series MASH, everyone laid-back and casual until our services required. If not for the occasional crackle of gunfire echoing in the distance, indicating the exchange of an active fire fight, there might not be a war going on. Every day the same routine beginning with a leisurely walk to the chow hall for morning breakfast, followed by roll call, and the day begins as the day before.

Somewhere men are dying, but not here. The lush surrounding jungle green as the alluring eyes of a camouflaged cobra snake, disarmingly calm, hypnotic, an illusion that all the world at peace. The local farmers file into the surrounding rice fields at every sunrise and back to their villages before every sunset. Vietnamese women arrive daily into the compound commissioned to do tedious jobs in exchange for food, ushered out before the gate secured for the night. These women also transport drugs and black-market military currency to exchange for U.S. bills. No one seems to care as long as someone gets rich and the drugs continue to flow. I start using drugs again. This time marijuana laced with opium and a concoction called *Obesetol*, liquid speed used to keep us alert on nights of extra perimeter duty. I become too friendly with the men while on duty and think them my friends. First thing each morning, I swing by Neider's desk and pick-up the requisitions for that day. I pass along instructions with inventory sheets to my crew to palletize the needed rations and equipment; then using the RTF, transport the secured pallets to the LZ, or load them onto waiting trucks. Usually only boxes of C-Rations, but sometimes things more specialized like radio equipment and starlight scopes with separate power packs (each with a different MOS numbers). On occasion the requisition comes down for a command post field tent, which must be pulled out of storage and inspected for dry-rot. Then cross referenced with the correct support poles, stakes, and the right netting added. This requires my personal supervision. At times like these, 2nd Battalion Supply is a one-man operation from beginning to end. I am young, strong, naïve, tirelessly proficient, and mandated by tunnel vision obsession to protocol. Indoctrinated to believe the mission comes first, outweighing all other considerations.

I suppose I desperately want to be seen as one of the guys, and after only a short while begin to break a cardinal rule. I start fraternizing with these men after duty hours, accepting a turn from the bottle of their black market whiskey, sharing an occasional marijuana stick, and joining in laughter at their often off-color jokes. It seems innocent at the time. The whiskey sometimes makes me embarrassingly sick; the marijuana an opioid of escape incomparable to any other drug I have experienced. In Nam you can buy what they call a five cent or a ten cent bag (50 or 100 sticks) of pre-rolled joints laced with opium and sealed (or so they say) with water buffalo shit. Judging by the aroma, I believe this to be true. I only do it a few times, but each time floored after only the second or third pass. I also will learn the tragic consequence of certain decisions.

These are the early days of Haight-Ashbury, except for the absence of hippie chicks; and we are very far from the streets of San Francisco. Nevertheless, we have access to powerful drugs, the antiestablishment music of Hendrix's, The Beatles, Dylan, and many other icons of the period. Now that I think back on it, I do not remember any psychedelics. Perhaps these too high-tech for Charlie, or maybe there were; only I never knew about it. And maybe that is just lucky for me, considering my not so distant history with LSD. Each day we do what we must do, and each night party, oblivious to the fact that a war still rages around us.

The night of TET marks the end of the last lunar cycle, the Vietnamese equivalent of New Years at the end of January. Crammed inside a small   storage room located at the south end of a utility hut, I huddle with two privates squeezed between spare pieces of radio equipment. We have just begun passing around a second joint when a sudden unannounced rain of mortars rounds plummets the compound. My body numb, I struggle to stand up, but restrained by a tangle of flesh, arms and legs of dead men. Three times, I see myself rise and dive into the secure threshold of a foxhole. Each time I land in the bottom of the hole; only each time I am still inside the cramped space of that room unable to rise. Then hot white shrapnel tears through the thin walls in slow motion striking me in the chest. The pain excruciating, I pass-out.

Stabbed awake by morning light piercing through tattered holes, I am conscious that those death shadows of the night before have passed, leaving me and my two companions alive. The three of us still in the same position, not dead I imagined. We are all alive. The south end of the hooch ripped away, with only debris of splintered wood and twisted metal. How we escaped injury, I will never know. The shrapnel real, but my mind only invented the mortal wounds. It amazes me to this day how some region in the mind able to rearrange particle construction torecreate an alternate detail of events, just as real, just as much part of living memory. I will later be convinced this evidence of divine intervention acting outside of time. To this day I remember the pain of hot molten metal tearing into my body. Judging by the trajectory of those holes, I cannot see how it possible the three of us escaped without even a scratch. You perhaps know the saying about fools and the protection of angels. Sometimes I wonder if in some alternate universe, I was wounded, or perhaps even killed that night. However, in my universe I escape through an alteration of destiny just as real and for reasons unaware.

In fact, everything changes that night. Our only RTF, badly scraped by a mortar round, smolders outside the warehouse damaged beyond hope of repair. This means for now on everything accomplished manually. We fortunately have a good pallet lift inside the warehouse sufficient for transporting inventory to and from the landing dock. From here, we need to re-palletize to a truck or sometimes to a mule, and then unload again onto a supply net spread out on the LZ. It provides some satisfaction to witness the cargo hoisted away by a monster twin rotor *Ch-47 Chinook* helicopter. This is not the only change. The next morning Neider throws his packed sea-bag into back of a waiting jeep, anxious to catch his freedom bird. His time in purgatory ended at last. Neider is going home.

"Good luck Sgt," he says, giving me a playful salute and climbs into the passenger seat. "A little practice and you'll make a good chess player."

I bid farewell to the only encouraging person known since my in-country arrival, certain I will see him again in the future. Then he is gone. Later that day the Supply Captain calls me into his office and hands me a crisp envelope with new orders.

"Command has decided that Second Battalion First Marine Division will be the spearhead unit to re-deploy state-side. Inform your men that all rotations are hereby canceled." He pauses, looks at me as he might at a puppy assigned to be a guard dog. "You are Acting Sergeant. That means you will do the job of a Sergeant. –Do you understand? From this point on military protocol is in effect. As head of Supply, you will insure the inventory, packaging, and inspection of every piece of equipment. Are your orders clear, Marine?"

"Yes Sir!" I reply gun-ho, salute, and return to my barracks.

Of course, in truth I have only a vague idea what these new orders mean, or the true gravity of the situation. Nor do I yet comprehend my place in this new scheme of things. Just as I have received a change in orders, I will simply pass down the same official information. More than subordinates, more than comrades in arms, they are my buddies. They will understand, just as I understand.

Instead, I encounter vile mutinous reactions, as though the responsibility of this new directive mine alone. Among those most vocal, a man named Watson, who I particularly like and respect. Older than all the rest of us, perhaps in his early thirties, he exudes a confidant air of presence. Rumor circulates that Watson once held the seasoned rank of a Staff Sergeant, busted-down to a private for being discovered more than once drunk on duty. Indeed, he is a man to every season, a natural leader. Watson, once a good soldier, made bitter by his own mistakes, now a rallying presence of misguided influence to those young and inexperienced. This evening Watson obnoxiously drunk and in a particularly obstinate mood, rudely interrupts me in mid-sentence, laughing robustly before I even finish to explain conditions of our amended situation.

"You think we give a damn about orders," he snares vehemently, then spins around and faces the squad as though he the one in command. "Are you jarheads going to take orders from this pimply-faced kid? I say we all go inside and have a drink – and fuck this war!"

Just like that, they all turn their backs on me and return inside the barracks. I cannot even begin to describe what I feel in the moment. Humiliation, hurt, betrayal-- but most of all I am betrayed! I want to cry-- to tell someone-- but what is there to say and who might listen?

According to military protocol, this is not supposed to happen. A Sergeant, considered the backbone of the Corps, receives and gives orders according to a hierarchy of rank. He enforces those orders through the collective will of his Corporals. Together they stand between the powers, that be, and the unruly forces of harnessed youth and sometimes resentment constrained to comradely of the lower ranks. This moment I realize just how alone and ill-prepared I really am. Unknown to me at the time, I have just embarked on one of the greatest challenges of my life.

Later in the evening I receive tragic news by the radio dispatcher that Neider's jeep hit a mine planted on the road while in route to the airport, but unable to confirm if he lived or if he died. I linger in the rain until lights out. In the pitch dark, I feel demons crawling in the air and hear moans of torment from the shadowy keep of Marble Mountain. Things crouch in the dark like emissaries of the underworld sent to snatch us all away one by one. Now awake in a nightmare, I will not sleep the same again.

Chapter 12

Making of a Sergeant

J choose to no longer fraternize with my men— if I might even call them that. They belong to Watson now. In a way I feel a jealous lover, feel rage of hurt and rejection mingled with the fire of young Marine Corps pride. I am an NCO, which means I deserve the respect of my rank. Nevertheless, I express little outside emotion for the next several days. Part of the description of our revised mandate is to bring in every crate, every piece of equipment –some of which has been rotting in cratesstacked inside a fenced-in storage compound for the past ten years. To bring these containers, or at least their contents, into the warehouse for a proper inventory now added to the checklist of my normal routine. Each morning, I issue orders to fetch numbered crates to verify the integrityand condition of the contents. The objective to average seven a day, which means that in less than twelve weeks we will have unpacked and inventoried all the surplus gear going back a decade. Once this stage one of the operation accomplished, we must break open the crates and perform a detailed inventory. Not even the books clearly reveal the content of some of these banded rotting sealed boxes, conjunctive with many entry errors. For example, crate number 130 might show camouflage gear, but in reality contains magazine clips and bayonets. On one occasion cases of live ammunitions found in a case marked field equipment, an inventory belonging strictly to the domain of the armory. They are less than happy to come and pick it up. No one wants additional inventory to rectify.

From the very beginning, these men refuse even to look at the amended paperwork, doing only the necessary active field requisitions. I complain to Gunny Corell; his response to me blunt and unsympathetic.

"You are the Supply Sergeant-- Marine! It's your job to get it done."

I decide the only way to impress these men is by example. I will show them what has to be done. Each morning I gather the requisitions for that day, examine the available inventory sheets, and verify the staging. Then I begin the grueling task of breaking open the most accessible one starting with the top crate. The first enumerated box is crate number 485, which is the last stage here.

Of course, the RTF would have made this much easier. Instead, I use a RTV mule (a small flatbed Rough Terrain Vehicle), and begin the long task of transporting the stale, often mummified items to the warehouse loading dock. It takes me all afternoon just to empty the contents of just two crates, a far cry from the projected objective.

Once everything transferred to the dock, then begins tedious work of inspection, creation of a new re-inventory sheet, and itemizing each piece of equipment to stock into a temporary storage area. After this, a second inventory control sheet must be created, along with a voucher, testifying to those items verified as unusable, designated for supervisor-approved liquidation. I work tirelessly from morning 'til night, and not one man in the warehouse offers to help.

By end of the sixth day, the exhaustion catches up with me. So far I have encountered rats, snakes, and host of poisonous spiders and bugs. The incessant rain changes to sweltering heat, announcing the abrupt end of monsoon. I am a sight despairingly reflected in everyone's eyes, dripping with sweat and blood, like a dirty animal crawled out of a sewer. To make things worse, access to a bath happens only once a week because of a shortage of good water; and even the little we drink rust-colored with iodine. Better this than the alternative. Always the first to arrive at the warehouse, and the last to leave, often working late into the night, skipping chow, choosing to eat C-Rations instead. By now, I am aware my example of dedicated effort has become a source of humor to my men, as well as to Gunny Corell.

As for my men, they snicker to each other, without even an attempt to disguise their disdain. I see in their eyes they think me a fool, and the humiliation continues to build inside of me like a volcano nearing eruption. That   eruption comes one morning ten days later at around 0900 military time.

Gunny Corell shouts over a crackled intercom for me to report to his office. This is the beginning of one of the hottest months since arriving in country, the sweat mixing with humid steam trapped in the air. Nor have I eaten anything this morning. Gunny knows me near the breaking point.

"What in hell is going on, Corporal?" He demands across the void of his desk. "Why aren't your men out there helping you?"

I proceed to explain the situation. I tell him that they refuse to obey even the simplest command, confessing I no longer know what to do. He unceremoniously interrupts me in mid speech, his eyes narrowing to javelins of disgust.

"We have a deadline, Marine. HQ has scheduled Second Battalion to disembark on an LP10 less than mine months from now. We will be ready! I need every man to do his job. If you can't make these men work, then I will find someone who can! And you'll find yourself back out in the field –is that understood?"

In a fit of rage, I strip off the medal chevrons of my stripes, slam them down hard on his desk.

"That's damn fine with me!" I swear near to tears, and leave without being dismissed.

My humiliation now complete, I submit to the lowest position of human dignity. All day, I spend tearing open crates– two at a time, preferring to use my bare hands. A rage so primitive, I am numb to pain or exhaustion. Adding to the frustration, I am now a Private again, reduced in rank by choice, a feeling of utter defeat. Then the anger begins to change within me into something far more sinister and dangerous.

Why should my career be destroyed because of one man? I am certain Watson the source of this mutiny; only there is no way to reason with him. Nevertheless, he is the snake in the garden I need to pin under my boot-- kill if necessary. Certain this will be a duel to the death; I must be unwavering, absolute in my resolve. Even though I have been in battles
many, this one I can little afford to lose.

That evening I intercept Gunny Corell as he exits the adjoining Officer and Staff club. No, not even in Vietnam do the higher ranks suffer neglect. I think he was surprised, maybe even a little fearful as I step from behind a bush. He has learned through experience never to underestimate a man under extreme stress.

"I want another chance," I request, attempting to remain calm.

"Why? --What makes you think you can do now what you haven't been able to do all along?"

"I am a Marine NCO, Gunny. If I can't make them obey my orders, then I guess I should be a Private in the field. --But until I receive orders that say different, I am still acting Sergeant! I'm asking you to please give me one more chance."

Gunny Corell reaches in his pocket and pulls out the two black chevron stripes thrown on his desk earlier in the day.

"One week, Corporal," he admonishes, placing the insignias in my hand. "That's all the time I can give you. If I don't see those men in the field and jumping to orders in a week's time, then I will be forced to relieve you and find someone else."

I think I actually see a hint of compassion in the chiseled face of a man tired of war and who stopped long ago to dream miracle. Or maybe it is just a look pity and act of temporary reprieve. I doubt another man in his position would have given me that second chance. Gunny, a gambler at heart, a man that likes to bet on the long shots, losing more often than not. He realizes the Vietnam campaign near an end. That soon he will return state-side and become just another solitary drunkard military man kicked out of bars at closing time. Here Gunnery Sergeant Corell serves a greater purpose, Chief of Second Battalion Supply, a man made complete in the present by a lifetime of preparation. Deep down he is certain I cannot possibly beat the odds, more than likely just another lost cause. Vietnam has become a land of lost causes.

As bad luck would have it, next afternoon the Colonel of Command Post schedules supply for a battalion inspection. As a further fickle of faith, it lands on the same day I am on the duty roster for guard duty on the OP East Gate, a location nearest the rice paddies. It would just happen to fall on this day! Not the day before; not the day after; but on this day! Early next morning I issue detailed instructions, emphasizing this to be a stateside inspection, which means the barracks need to be clean, bunks made according to military protocol, and uniform dress code in affect. I single out the two senior Lance Corporals, placing them in charge; this like asking the mice to police themselves in the absence of the cat. It should have been no surprise, when at 1200 hundred hours-- a full two hours before my scheduled relief-- I spot the Colonel's jeep approaching my position along the dirt road running through the compound. Another Corporal from Motor Transport gets out with orders to relieve me. I experience a sickening feeling in the pit of my stomach that this not a good sign. The driver wordlessly transports me directly to the Battalion Commander's office.

"What in God's name kind of outfit are you in charge of?" This Colonel's rage surpasses even my own. "Shit paper from one end of the barracks to another, beds that look like they haven't been changed or made in a month of Sundays— did you lack information that there was going to be an inspection today?"

"It wasn't my fault, sir!" I manage.

"Not your fault! -By God, then whose fault is it—the Fairy Queen!"

I make futile attempt to explain, but I may as well have been attempting to reason with an enraged bear. This particular Colonel legendary, having a reputation to be one of the toughest S.O.B.'s in country. Rumor is that twice his own men shot down his helicopter, only no one able to prove it. Twice, he survives, and each time swears an oath of vengeance against those responsible. I will later suspect that the fictitious character of Colonel Kurtz in the film *Apocalypse Now* a composite of this individual and individuals like him. Such men are a breed unto themselves: men that long for war and military campaigns, only too happy to die in battle. Except, these men rarely do.

After nearly half an hour of berating me, I am dismissed with the promise of another inspection in one week's time. I suppose that considering this man's distemper I am lucky he did not bust me on the spot. My fate now sealed. No matter how I look at it, I have a Week-- and only a week-- to gain the respect and undying loyalty of men, who have shown obvious pleasure to see me destroyed. In reality they are collectively aware that someone else will come better armed and crush their rebellion. Someone they will have no choice but to respect, someone to lead them with an iron fist. Nevertheless, for the moment they have determined to take out their disgruntled frustration on at least one weak element—but only if I allow it to happen!

Before returning to the barracks, I must first report to the warehouse and sort paper work in preparation for the next day's work roster. Afterwards, I open a pack of C-Rations and eat my evening meal alone in the empty staging bay, as tasteless as the task I must do next. It is already dark by the time I trudge through the sandy expanse and storm into the barracks.

No one seems to care much, altogether ignoring my dramatic entrance. They gather as chattering buzzards around a make-shift poker table at the far end laughing and talking. Apparently, Watson has a strong hand-- like everything else, he proves a better than average poker player. Unbecoming of a Marine, I fling my M-16 rifle butt-first on the floor. It bounces like a plastic toy flipping against a wall and down the aisle of bunks that show still ravaged since this morning's failed inspection. No wonder the Colonel so upset. The entire barracks resembles the den of a flophouse. Without further ceremony, I step through the crowd and kick over the table sending money and cards flying. I think Watson most surprised of all. Arrogantly smiling, Watson shows his hand to the shocked spectators, a full-house, making him the uncontested winner, and then nonchalantly hands the cards to one of his shadows.

He then lunges forward bull-fashion, knocking me against a post, and bashing my jaw. I instantly explode into an animation of fist and hand-to-hand combat maneuvers. Watson matches my every move, proving a vicious and skilled opponent. Worse part of it, he is numb with alcohol, his flesh tough as animal hide. He just stands there and smiles as I pummel his head and torso with blow after blow. Once he gives me a kick square in the chest, knocking me clear through the thin wooden wall. I find myself stunned lying on my back in the sand, staring up at a stunning star-studded South East Asian heaven. Brushing away the debris, I leap to my feet again.

We fight non-stop for an hour, until both so greasy with blood and sweat that our fist just slips harmlessly on contact. At one point, both exhausted, sitting side by side on the wet wooden hooch floor mixed with whiskey and the slime of battle, we pause to glare at each other. Watson reaches over and slugs me again. I do not even feel it, vaguely aware of the deafening cheers from a tightening human circle around us.

"Go Watson--go! They shout in unison like yelping animals.

This is the moment I realize all these men I knew and once thought my friends in the beginning descended into a vicious pack, egging on my nemesis for the kill. I also realize I cannot win. I manage to find my rifle and march the quarter of a mile to the warehouse. This is where I will repose until morning, the only place I feel safe. That night I sleep the sleep of the dead, feeling nothing— and it will be a long time before I feel anything again.

Next morning I do not even bother going to chow. Except for a few cuts and bruises, my body less damaged than my pride. By 0730, the men start filtering into the warehouse as usual. By 0800, all accounted for, all except Watson.

"Where is Watson?" The Supply Captain demands.

"He's still in bed," reports one of the men.

"Acting Sergeant, that's your man," the Captain snaps at me. "Go down and get him, now!"

"I don't think I should, sir. I'll send one of the men—"

"I said, now, Marine!"

I do not remember that Captain's name. Only this man takes personal pleasure every morning to ensure the presence of every soul during each roll call. The rest of the day, he spends barricaded in his office unseen. I grit my teeth and heave a reply of acceptance.

"Yes sir--I will get him!"

The cast made, a choice not my own. As I trudge through the thick sand, I ponder what to do next. It is clear that I must kill Watson—certain he will leave me no other option. What other recourse is there? It is either him, or me. I feel suddenly calm, a confidence, as never I felt before. It all becomes so clear in my mind. What I will do and how I will do it. This duel is to the death.

I hand the barrack's watch my rifle, giving him strict orders to remain outside until I come out no matter what he hears. The hole in the wall patched with a poncho, dried blood still spotting the deck where we fought, along with several playing cards. Private Watson is just now getting out of bed.

"Private," I say coldly. "I want you dressed and in my warehouse five minutes ago!"

I am sure he thinks this particularly amusing. He grunts something that sounds between laughter and cursing, at the same time taking a swing. Of course, I have anticipated just such a move. Grabbing his arm and in the same motion bashing his face hard against a post, I knee him twice in the groin. Then swinging around to his side, I clutch the soft jugular of his throat with the fingers of my free hand. Next, I lift him bodily, slamming him to the floor, and pinning him in a scissor-lock. Pressing his neck against one of my thighs, I begin beating him in the face with the ball of my free fist. It all happens so quickly that Watson realizes only too late my purpose of coming. He struggles to break free, but the bonds of my rage too strong. I beat this man without mercy. Every now and then, I stop and ask him if he is prepared to follow my orders. Defiantly he spits blood, so I beat him more. Then I lean forward, look him in the eyes, and quietly whisper in his ear.

"I will kill you, Watson. I came here to kill you. Either you will follow my orders, or you will die. The choice is yours."

My resolve frightens even me; but must have been particularly terrifying to him.   I am now something I never knew I could be: an executioner with deadlydetermination-- ready for the kill! Suddenly the man's body deflates in my grip. A final gasp of air, his eyes roll back showing white. Watson is dead. Or so I thought.

"Please, don't hit me anymore. I will do anything you tell me, Sergeant. Please— please no more."

"Why should I believe you?" I am doubtful. "Because if I let you go now, then next   time I'll have to do it all over again-- and I swear I will kill you dead— do you understand what I am saying?"

"Please, Sergeant, don't kill me-- I promise. Just let me go."

I think Watson fears I might finish him off anyway; and part of me wants to. For several more minutes I continue to restrain him, coldly studying his swollen bloodied face for any hint of deception. I remember all those movies watched as a child, when the good guy has mercy on the bad guy, only to be betrayed. But who is the good guy here, and who the bad? Finally, I make my decision.

"I want you at the warehouse in ten minutes—am I clear?"

"Yes, Sergeant," he whimpers humbly.

"Are you sure you are not just saying what I want to hear?"

"No Sergeant--I swear!"

I instruct the barrack's watch to get Watson cleaned-up and see to it that he gets to the warehouse in the allotted time. I swing by my quarters and retrieve the Bowie Knife, slipping the monster blade through my belt. I will later make a sheath from a piece of tent canvass and carry it for the rest of my days in Nam. Now ready to take command, I must add to my arsenal every symbol of protection. I have won a major battle this day, altogether changed by the experience, prepared to fight every man of them if need be-- certain without any doubt that either I will win or I will die!

I return to the warehouse and call the men to a rally. Taking a position on top of a closed crate, I instruct everyone to wait. Gunny and the Captain watch through the window of the office, perplexed by the meaning of my actions. A few minutes later, Watson staggers into the assembly looking as though he has just escaped hell.

"Mr. Watson," I roar in a clear commanding voice; "report!"
Watson comes sheepishly to the foot of my perch and mumbles his presence.

"I can't here you, Private!" I shout ferociously.

"Private Watson reporting for duty, Sergeant!"

His sincerity unmistakable, the moment of truth arrived. I point to a crate overflowing with metal stakes ready for inventory. Usually, we assign these kinds of task to the Vietnamese women from the local village. Today, however, I wish to make a point.

"Mr. Watson, I want you to count tent pins today. I want you to bundle them into groups of five and stack them into stacks of twenty. Is that clear, Mr. Watson?"

He mumbles consent.

"I can't hear you!"

"Yes— Sergeant!"

"I want you on your knees, now; and count so I can hear you!"

Without saying another word, Watson knees down and begins counting aloud one through five, binding each bundle with packing tape. He then proceeds to count another five, and five after that, and so on.
I turn and face those men given under my charge, placing my hand naturally on the hilt of the protruding Bowie knife.

"Mr. Watson understands now, and if there is someone among you who does not understand, then he will meet me at the end of the loading dock, and I will make you understand! There will be no more bullshit! You are Marines, and I am presently your Sergeant. Until that condition changes or we accomplish our mission, you will do what I tell you todo. Is that clear?"

Only silence. Upon looking back, I suppose them too shocked at the time to respond. In my rage, I leap victorious to the ground, facing each one eye to eye. There are no challengers.

"Is that clear?" I shout again.

A resounding Marine Corps shout, "Yes Sergeant!"

"Then get to work! We have a supply chopper to load before noon. After that, we start bringing in boxes from the staging area by hand. Are your orders clear?"

"Yes Sergeant", again they roar.

Just like that they are military Marines under my charge again. I see in Gunny's eyes that he is impressed: at least his crisis over for now. He has his Sergeant; and I now hold the reins on my men. These trained soldiers, instinctively conditioned to respond to a certain kind of leadership, in that moment belong to me. I have learned a lesson of command that I will never forget. Perhaps this all seems a bit Machiavellian to the civilian way of thinking. But it must be remembered, we were not civilized. We were trained men of war within context of war operations.

There exists in such conditions a chain-of-command that must not be broken. If I had not released that monster inside of me, then I would have been defeated. Another would have taken my place empowered with force to achieve the specified objective. In the end, these men would follow the orders given by someone. This is just the way the operational machine works; the natural order of things when lives at stake.

I see fear in the eyes of these men that day— a fear of me. Not the fear of breaking military protocol— they are far beyond that. They have already witnessed the ugliness of combat, already soiled to the soul. Most of them just want to go home. Now they fear the insane rage of a man whose dominion over them irrevocable, believing through uncertainty that I will kill if necessary. This victory marks only the beginning, as many more challenges loom in the months to come. I have cut off the main head and subdued the dragon; but also I need it alive. None of them will look me in the eyes after this; yet I know what they are thinking. In time other heads will rear up. Other battles still to fight; and none can I afford to lose.

Chapter 13

Finding Excalibur

*a*n uneasy truce now exists between my men and me since the showdown. Watson has become quiet, inconspicuously fading into the ranks. He wishes only to go back to the states and receive a discharge, having gained the wisdom that there only one way this might happen now. They all follow my orders as they might any other Sergeant. Of course, they whisper behind my back. Nor does illusion of comradeship any longer exist between us. However, I have their attention, if not their full respect. Then something happens a week later that awakens me to the possibility of more imminent danger.

One evening while lounging in my segregated NCO quarters, the door separating me from crew quarters bursts open. I have just finished cleaning and oiling my M-16 and inserted an empty magazine. Hovering over me is a shadowy visage of a demon-eyed

American Indian. He clutches in one hand a seven-inch tempered steel K-Bar knife, inhaling and exhaling slow and methodic. Bad Warrior, the son of a Navajo tribal Chief from an Arizona reservation not far from the Grand Canyon, works alongside Watson. Rumor circulates that he wants to right a wrong; this sentiment shared by many in the beginning. His hot breath stinks of whiskey, the core of his eyes those of a wild beast, void of reason or mercy. At this particular moment, I have the mental impression of an angry black and white photo I once saw in a Time's Magazine taken of the infamous Apache named Geronimo, after his final capture. Now I comprehend the rage, the poison of bitterness able to infect a man's soul, sharing in the knowledge of what it means to stand resolute against overwhelming odds.

"I'll blow your head off, Badwarrior," I manage calmly; automatically raising my weapon, my finger poised on the trigger, and press the barrel tip into the soft flesh just below the man's Adam's apple.

Only I know the threat as empty as my magazine; yet what else can I do against blood lust for revenge? He continues to press forward, still determined, yet apprehensive of his next move, now questioning the resolve of his visitation. Then a figure appears behind him. It is another Indian named Sain, a Sioux from the Dakota Bad Lands.

"No—Badwarrior," he cries, racing forward and grabbing his friend gently from behind. "He'll kill you dead!"

Realizing that my weapon set on automatic fire, he looks imploringly at me, and begins to plea for his friend's life.

"He's just drunk Sgt., and doesn't know what he's doing. Don't kill him, please don't"

He then pulls Badwarrior away and back out the door. My bluff has worked, or at least I hope it has. The next morning I demand Badwarrior give account for his actions the previous night. Sheepishly, he swears to remember nothing at all of the said events and asks humbly for my forgiveness. I determine to keep my eyes on him from this point on,and Sain, too.

It is true what they say about Indians and whiskey. When sober, Badwarrior one of the kindest, most mild-tempered men I have ever known. However, that night I witness the face of another monster as bestial as my own. A monster freed by the fiery baptism of alcohol; unleashing an anger yoked through history of oppression waiting it's time to rise up in terrible fury.

I determine to sleep in the warehouse after this incident. At least I feel safer there. Sian's recollection of the events, as he perceived them, seals my reputation as a Marine Sergeant capable of anything. There might be the occasional minor skirmish of dissent, but no more open challenges. I am now an icon of respect, standing between the powers that be and the harnessed resource of these young able bodies. I stand alone, partly a legend, but more hated. Nevertheless, these men will do as ordered in the short term of a military operation, only ambivalently remembered in the end. Each day I await arrival of a Sergeant to relieve me of this burden; but he never comes. Dispatch rumors a Supply Sergeant sent- up from an installation near Saigon in the south, but killed en-route by sniper fire. Like most rumors, this remains officially unconfirmed. Another time, I hear that a Supply Sergeant requisitioned from statesidebusted at the Da Nang airport for drug possession. At any rate, threemonths and counting, I alone am the only NCO of Second BattalionField Supply.

By now, the big effort has begun. Often duty requires we   work twelve to fifteen hours a day. Battalion Supply is like a funnel: nearly everything must pass in and out with precision inventory. Motor Transport takes care of all the vehicles, including Tanks, Amphibious, and Special Terrain vehicles. The Armory is in charge of all the weapons and munitions, including the Big Guns. However, all the little things, those things used by everyone, only to be taken for granted— all these things belong to Supply: t-shirts, skivvies, socks, uniforms, canteens, field gear, flak jackets, knives and bayonets, C-rations, etc.— all part of daily responsibility. Had my men been trained supply personnel, then things would have gone easier— not less monumental, but easier. I must give these guys credit; but for a few exceptions, they work hard, learning procedures and techniques beyond their training. To exasperate matters even more, we must do everything by hand since the loss of our RTF. We are supposed to get another, but like everything else in Nam, the requisition lost somewhere in the cracks.

A Marine Corps Sergeant has no friends, except maybe other Marine Corps Sergeants. A Corporal might have friends, maybe even labeled the "good guy." A Sergeant is the motivation and the strength; therefore, the visible manifestation of oppression to those already discontent. Perhaps, had I looked like a Sergeant-- if I'd had the years of experience and the seasoned support of my peers-- then I might have been accepted and obeyed without resentment. In general, a Marine Corps Sergeant is the accumulation of many years of time and grade. I never met an NCO with less than four years of active duty, and Sergeants usually twice that. Here I am, a Corporal before my time, temporarily promoted (or so I believe) to the elevated position of Acting Sergeant in a combat operation. Forced to become something before my time-- both good cop and bad cop, both mother and father-- an inexperienced leader to a pack of disillusioned men, for whom the war over, and whose only desire is to go home. The reality is I lack the proper tools; and often wonder if these orphan children might have fared better in the reigns of a more experienced hand.

Every second week, in periods of regular rotation between Motor transport, 105's, and other base units, Supply conducts perimeter duty. Every unit, that is, except the Mess Hall. Marines need to eat, which takes all available hands to prepare each meal. The rest of us, however, must work for our hire. This means nightly rotating shifts to man strategic positions from inside the compound and checking the main gates for booby-traps. When field Grunt attachment of Echo Company away on maneuvers, it also becomes our responsibility to engage in operations outside the base perimeters.

One man from Motor Transport killed, another wounded by sniper fire while returning to their duty post after the mid-day meal. The shots originate from somewhere on Marble Mountain. The base CO becomes enraged and wants immediate retribution. It just so happens that Echo Company on a two-day mission to the south, and Supply next up on the duty roster.

"You find that gook-bastard, and bring me back his head on the tip of a bayonet!" The Colonel, not one to mince words, with no apparent recollection of our previous encounter; "Your orders, corporeal, are to avoid confrontation if possible;" Then looking straight into my eyes: "knock down every statue and alter if you have to! I want that sniper stopped!"

Intentionally, I assign Watson and Badwarrior to other duties, preferring that they not go along. I do not trust these men at my back with loaded weapons. The rest, including those of lower rank and nonessential in supply office administration, slap on full combat gear: flak jackets, helmets, and an extra magazine of ammo.

The base of Marble Mountain looms less than a few hundred meters from our location, being only one of five similar rock formations in the area, jutting out of the flat coastal plain. The geologic phenomenon that created these unusual monoliths is anyone's guess. This particular mountain is the largest, considered especially unique. A massive rock laced with a maze of caverns that makes it an ideal sanctuary as a Buddhist temple since many hundreds of years. Marble Mountain considered one of the most holy shrines in all of Vietnam, is also home of many spirits, particularly audibly present at night. I have often heard them when the wind passes through these hidden passages: a fluctuating pattern of moaning that sounds, like tormented demons in the air.

In straddled formation, we exit the compound by the front gate, walk several hundred meters down a dirt road, and take a well-traveled path along the facing side of the mountain. On this approach begins the arch of a passage leading to a narrow staircase hewn from the marbled stone, a series of narrow steps wrapping around the outer rim of a rocky incline. Each step tiny and closely spaced, designed for tinier feet of the local population. Steps made long ago by hands of mythical beings, an uneven stairway to heaven with lost significance in time. I estimate there to be more than a hundred, neat and precisely cut, an ascension chiseled out of the surrounding rock at least a thousand years before birth of the Roman Empire.

We ascend cautiously, in strides of several at a time, aligned in single file. I lead the way. I think my men truly glad to have me take the point. Seasoned in the field, they probably have decided that at least I will take the first sniper round. At the top of the stairs opens a narrow grotto that we must squeeze through because of our bulky gear. On the other side stands the jade statue of a beautiful woman pointing a finger peacefully upward, an expression of serenity on her stone face out of context to our purpose for being here. Beyond, opens a dry arid crater surrounded by a crown of dark rocks resembling dragon's teeth. By now, the sun blazes directly overhead, the enclosure as a burnt, almost symmetrical brown desert caldron, the air boiling into blistering waves of bottled heat. I will remember this place again later in life upon reading Dante's Inferno: the story of a man's passage through hell, then purgatory, and finally to paradise.

This my beginning passage into hell. Jabbed in the center, the sharp jagged spearhead of a clustered rock formation; and on the opposite side of this twenty-meter expanse gapes open another passage to receive us. The air changes immediately cool, upon entering the shade of a broad tunnel that slopes gradually downward. Light filters from somewhere above, casting shadows of grey hue eclipsed into even deeper shadows. It takes a few moments for our eyes to adjust, as shadows fade back into substance through the diminished light. Now we begin to discern the smooth contour of this well used interior.

"He's here—I feel it!" Sain whispers in true Indian fashion.

Descended from a bloodline of Indian scouts, it makes sense to utilize his natural intuitions. Even though Sain a close friend of Badwarrior, I trust him, confident in his loyalty. Not just a loyalty to me, but to the same Marine Corps principals I am loyal to. In many ways, this handsome young man reminds me of a character from one of Louie L'Amour's classic westerns. His features, those of a proud North American native, chiseled and unblemished, his eyes sharp and perceptive to the tiniest detail, Sain as incapable of betrayal as for a river to change trajectory of its course. He first arrived in country a grunt Private, assigned to a detachment in the north somewhere near Hanoi. According to entries in his permanent record, Sain's entire company nearly wiped-out, so as compensation they promote him to Lance Corporal and dispatched him here. Either that or to send him home; but no one leaves country before his time— this is just the way of Marine Corps protocol.

The passage opens suddenly into a grand cavern, the ceiling resembling a cracked eggshell seen from the inside. I determine this must be center of the mountain, the jutting dome appearing as spikes of a jagged crown seen from position of our compound below. To this day, I have never seen a cave as unique as this one, created out of churning magma reaching the surface through subterranean fissures and forming giant air pockets that cool into the pattern of these unusual tunnels. Once, in the distant post-diluvium past, this entire area lay submerged beneath fathoms of water, pushed up by geophysical forces beyond imagination.

Sitting against the wall of a grand cavern are two Buddha statues over thirty feet tall carved out of natural rock formations, positioned side by side in stoic repose, just as they have for unknown centuries. We are not alone. Children under the watchful eyes of young mothers run and play around the feet of these patient guardians as mothers and children everywhere, climbing the passive goliaths, participating in games alien to us, but familiar to them, unafraid in the shadows these giant protectorates. They altogether ignore our presence, jaded to the carnage of war, use to seeing soldiers in full combat gear, use to the killing, and the horrors since the violence began. They continue to play innocently, as children should under the watchful eyes of their mothers. Only it is also this innocence that we most fear.

We spend nearly half an hour here, exploring every nook and crevice where a sniper might try to hide. Satisfied the area secure, we continue our search through the upward incline of another passage. Here we discover a second chamber, less imposing than the last, a flight of perhaps twenty stone stairs leading down into a damp basin, guarded by two richly painted life-size oriental warrior statues midway down alertly standing upon two pedestals either side. This compartment barren, except for an alabaster altar attached to one wall, supporting another statue of a gilded sitting Buddha. In the center of this chamber, an oblong white stone table with three Buddhist priests hovered over a prostrate body wrapped in white linen. One of the priests holds a long thin knife made of pale wood, or perhaps ivory. Moving down to the ledge of one painted warrior, we hold position, fascinated by the ritual taking place. The priests ignore our presence, intently observing a phenomenon, which has special meaning to them.

Three shafts of light emanate through three symmetrically holes bored through the cavern roof. As the earth and sun align, these three beams begin to converge on the exposed throat of the dead body. Once the independent light sources meshed into one intense beam, the three priests begin chanting monotonously in deep low tones. Then the one holding the razor-sharp instrument begins slowly to slice open the dead person's throat. I will later reason that perhaps we had inadvertently stumbled into the middle of a secret ritual, witnessing release of the soul of the dead to the element of light for reincarnation.

It occurs to me that perhaps only certain dignitaries or men of special worldly attributes receive this particular kind of ceremony. Thinking the statues cemented firmly to the base, I thoughtlessly lean against the chest of one nearest me. To my surprise, it gives way, spins around, falls over, and begins rolling heavily down the remaining stairs. It comes to a sudden bone crunching halt face up, staring vengefully in my direction.

Fortunately, it does not break, but signs that the paint chipped in places. Instantly, the priests stop their ritual and begin moving toward us. Locked and loaded, safeties released, we begin to back out of the chamber the way we had come. Once clear of the entrance, the priests retreat to continue their service. In retrospect, I think them more annoyed by the interruption of their ritual, than the toppling of the guardian statue. In the heat of the moment, I fear we might have shot them all had they chosen to pursue us further.

No one verbally criticizes my clumsiness, but I see the judgment in their eyes, especially in the eyes of Sain. Worse, I know within myself that I could have been responsible for the loss of lives. One simple mistake, just one moment forgetting where you are, and what you are doing, chaos can strike at any time like a coiled snake. Reminded this day of something already I know-- something I will never again forget-- the enemy deadliest when one sleeps.

We continue to follow the passage upward, shortly reaching a bright portal opening onto a plateau with tended walls, pastel pagodas, and beautiful flowering gardens. Several Baddish monks with shaved heads move about in long robes altogether ignoring our presence. Near the canopy of an upper veranda walk three middle-age women dressed in white, surrounded by several young children. Suddenly, these children take us by surprise, dashing in our direction and holding tied handkerchief sacks in their small hands. Instinctively, we raise our weapons as a show of futile defense. We have all heard the stories about Viet Cong children and their candy bags rigged with explosives. They are upon us before we have any chance. At least this time, the bags empty, the children as children everywhere, so we give them candy and rations instead. This could have been a tragedy in the moment had we been more seasoned to combat, and therefore more proactive to what could have been.

One of my men, a hairy mountain of a man named Kong, looks down cruelly at one of the boys at his feet like an angry ogre ready to devour. His face breaks into a smile. He removes his helmet and flak jacket and sits down disarmingly on a stone bench, allowing swarms of playful laughing youngsters to surround him. They see past the menace of his appearance and begin immediately to pull on the strangeness of the wooly hair clumped on his hands and arms. This gentle man remains unflinching, allowing the youngsters to have their way. He will later receive a Dear John from his fiancée, and read the letter over, and over again. For weeks after this, he isolates himself in a corner of the warehouse during breaks listening to the lyrics *"black rooms with white curtains"* repeatedly, tears soaking the mat of his unshaved face. A large German fellow named Bush, assigned to distribute the mail, makes a mistake by saying something derogatory to him. Kong leaps up, lifts the two hundred-pounder like a GI Joe doll, and nearly tears-off the man's head. Nevertheless, Kong is a valuable asset, performing his work well, and always taking special interest in the details missed by others. I often wonder if this grisly fellow ever found his true love again.

We spend more than an hour exploring this plateau. It is Sain, who finds the scoped sniper rifle, along with a rice bag containing several rounds of ammunition tucked beneath a wooden altar on the porch of a brick temple façade. The weapon resembles a modified Carbine with

Chinese markings on a finally preserved wood stock. It is like finding a wondrous serpent in paradise. I take possession of the finely crafted gun, and sling it over my free shoulder. At least we will not return empty-handed. There is no way of knowing the owner of this deadly instrument, nor are there any voluntary witnesses. Since Private Bush also speaks a little Vietnamese, I ask him to interrogate the Monks. They only shake their heads and pull away. Of course, someone knows something. To many we are invaders, to some liberators— yet armed and dressed in full battle gear, we are soldiers of war, intimidating. To these simple monks, devoted to austerity, we are as storm troopers from another world wielding weapons of terrible destruction, no different from the VC. Especially frightening, Sain with his k-bar knife drawn, swiping the air dangerously in Indian fashion.

As in all true religions, they refuse to take sides, existing detached from the carnage and sufferings of the world around them. They live by the grace of whatever comes naturally to them, and by prayers. It is difficult to comprehend that one of these could be responsible for acts of violence. What they know, they keep to themselves. Had we been Chinese regulars, we probably would have slaughtered the lot of them; but we are United States Marines, restrained by a moral code of honor— or so I believe in the moment. I guess that in the end it comes down to personal choice and the situation. Had things happened differently, I suppose we could have committed murderer that day, an act as senseless and bloody, as happened at MeLie. However, this day, at least, no one needs to die.

It is nearly time for evening chow by the time we return to the security of our compound. The Colonel, although disappointed I have not brought him back a head, is delighted by the recovered souvenir.

"A *Mosin Nagant*," he says reverently, half under his breath; "good job Corporal…but next time I want the son-of-a-bitch who pulled the trigger!"

The snipping stopped after this. A Weapon, as precise as the *Mosin Nagant* type 53 Carbine, placed in the hands of a seasoned sharpshooter, is a weapon of choice. Russian in design and manufactured by the People's Republic of China since the 1940's, this beautifully crafted rifle has found its way into every border conflict between Communist and non-Communist factions. Predating the ever-reliable SKS, commonly known as the AK 47, by more than ten years in combat use, the *Mosin Nagant* is an antique worthy of any collection. This particular weapon a true relic: most likely, a family heirloom handed down from one generation to another. The Colonel, descended from a long history of men of war, knows a rare prize has fallen into his possession; but as all men of war, he will retain the exuberance of this discovery to himself.

As for me, I accept the satisfaction that no one else will die by this embellished handiwork. Yet, I must admit that I think the gun beautiful, like the mythical sword of Excalibur revived out of fabled time, and often wish to this day that I might have managed somehow to keep it for myself.

Chapter 14
Slaying the Dragon

$\mathcal{I}$ sleep every night in the warehouse alone, kept company by only the occasional sound of rats, as they flitter across the upper metal rafters, along with distant popping noise of firefights in progress. These soft sounds mix with the lull of an ocean breeze expanding the riveted metal interior plates ever so slightly. But mostly I hear the rats.

I learn to embrace this solitude; learn that there are solitudes within solitudes. I consider that madness not a condition, rather, a state of mind. Just beside the warehouse, less than one hundred meters from the loading dock, protrude barrels of the 105's Big Gun Division, lightweight, deadly accurate Howitzers with a confirm kill-range of more than ten miles as the crow flies. When these babies start talking, the entire galvanized steel edifice begins to rattle, capturing the noise of each blast and bouncing it violently against the shuttering walls of the nearly hollow structure. In time, I am able to sleep even through this intrusion.

By mid-February a shipment of un-constructed prefabricated boxes and special lining paper arrive along with instructions on how to sanitize gear before packing. As complicated a journal I have ever read, listing types of infestations and preventative procedures strict to FDA and other departmental regulations governing materials exposed to a foreign environment before being shipped to the continent of North America U. S. A.

However, in retrospect, I should have studied the material with greater attention. I spend nearly an entire night constructing alone the first prototype. The printed instructions almost useless, more confusing than helpful; and might just as easily have been a blueprint describing imaginary lines that frame the constellations. After three tries, I finally figure out the right formula. Now we are ready to begin the final stage of inventory. The next three weeks, we construct and seal more than seventy of these boxes, the contents cleaned, numbered, and sprayed with a variety of chemicals.

The men are actually beginning to see purpose in their work, as well as a sense of future in their accomplishments.   Still tensions remain high. I receive a new transfer from a Marine Reconnaissance group operating in the south near Ho Chi Ming City. It is rare to have a Recon transferred out, and like everything in respect to reconnaissance operations, the reason classified. His last name Rick-- or maybe it is his first name-- comes pre-labeled with the nickname "Ricky Recon." Soon everyone calls him this, even the base CO.

"You Recon's think you're hot shit— don't you Private?" The Colonel taunts during an inspection.

He takes special pride to inspect supply personally ever so often since the toilet paper incident.

"No sir!" Ricky shouts back in true Marine Corps fashion.

No doubt in all our minds he is every bit a marine, from the razorback sharpness of his haircut, to the chiseled appearance of his physique. Even the mirror spit-shine of his combat boots and the bright polish of his brass make all envy the package he comes from. Although he is soaking wet with humidity, Ricky somehow manages to keep his uniform immaculate and his shoulders squared.

"By God, Ricky Recon, you are a hell of an example for the rest of these men! --I don't give a rat's ass what they say! You still represent the finest in my book. Just remember, Private, here you follow orders. Is that clear?"

"Yes sir!" Ricky shouts back with overwhelming enthusiasm.

In all appearance Ricky Recon a good worker, follows orders to the letter without question, which also becomes a problem. For example, once I instruct him to remove all the compasses from one of the newly constructed containers to confirm the count. Two hours later, I find more than a hundred hand compasses piled on the floor with the ledger count confirmed exactly. As for Ricky Recon, he has altogether disappeared. Nor am I able to find him anywhere.

I later discover he has returned to the barracks and taken a nap. After this incident, I make certain my orders more specific. In all fairness to Ricky, part of the fault lies in his training. Reconnaissance operatives, although considered the best, are not necessarily the brightest. In fact, the main thrust of their thrust of their indoctrination is to learn to follow orders from a superior exactly without question and without conscience. However, Ricky Recon also has an obvious chip on his shoulder, making it clear from the beginning that he thinks himself better than the rest of us.

This reality difficult to dispute on the surface; but the fact remains that he has been reassigned for a reason, making him now my responsibility, as well as my problem. He never openly challenges me, but I feel his resentment. Feel that he resents the whole idea of being under my command, constantly doing little things to erode usurp my morale authority. However, I recognize early that he is mostly a facade, being mostly show. For instance, he often strips away his shirt, exposing the bulk of his pumped-up mussels, but exerts the least amount of effort during a collective project. So obviously present, sometimes I forget he is here; and manages to always slip away somewhere when most needed. It is just a matter of time before a showdown inevitable.

Since loss of our RTF, everything must be accomplished by will of Manpower. On several occasions, I examine the remains of the forklift for myself. Except for a mangled wheel and scorched hydraulic hoses, it appears superficially intact. Greater scrutiny, however, reveals a split in the engine casing and all the copper ignition wiring burned, fused into clumps of melted metal. I finally accept only a corpse left, a haunting relic to torment my mind with shades of what could have been, but not to be.

One evening just before sunset, a tractor-trailer pulls through the front gate with a load of forty-eight pallets of c-rations, each pallet holding sixty-four cases about thirty-five pounds per case. This day one of the toughest and hottest on record, all of our tensions at the boiling point, already exhausted. Nevertheless, dreading the knowledge of the impending necessity, we prepare for a long night beginning after evening chow.

Even Staff Sergeant Corell present, wearing his green t-shirt, ready to work and to supervise from below. Without hesitation, without even thinking that I might get tired, altogether ignoring the physical demands of the proposed project, I jump up on the truck bed. Cut away the bandings securing the first pallet and begin single-handedly passing the cases one at a time to the revolving line of men below. Using the hand- pallet-jack, someone rolls out an empty pallet to the edge of the loading dock, the cases re-palletized in reverse order.

A strange phenomenon happens to the body when controlled by

mind and by will. I become as an automated machine, neither aware of fatigue or pain. I empty one pallet, then another, and another after that. It is as though the creature of my being changed into a robot functioning at tremendous speed, my semi-conscious mind descended into a cognitive state, aware only of the shadowy appendages that step forward to receive the next case of rations. Three hours later, we near the end, with only two pallets left to unload. I have just heaved another case, when from the corner of my eye, I perceive the ghost of something coming toward me, instinctively knocking it aside with the back of my arm. The heavy case bounces away, striking the steel edge of the tractor-trailer bed.

"What are you doing?" I demand of the man, who has flung it back to me.

Ricky Recon mumbles something about me throwing the case badly, the corner striking him in the chest. I am in no mood for boy scout bantering.

"Don't do that again," I growl. "You catch it the way you catch it!"

I lob another case at him. Immediately, he tosses it back. I hit the case with my fist and dive down on what seems to me a shade only. Grabbing the man by the soft of his throat, I sling him back across the half-loaded pallet. I say nothing, but glare into the shadow of his face as he struggles in vain to escape. Strong arms try to pull me off, but for some reason cannot. His body goes limp, tears gathering in his eyes. I release my grip and raise him up.

"Get back to work, Private!" I command, and jump back up on the truck to finish the job at hand.

No one mentions this incident, not even Staff Sergeant Corell. As for Ricky Recon, he fades into total obscurity, always there, but not there, only vaguely remembered, as a ghost in my mind. I think I destroyed something of his pride that night, something already fragile, something that lurked hidden beneath the veneer of his outward presence. Some part of me now knows why Recon let him go; and why no one really likes or trusts Ricky Recon.

The news falls like a hammer. Seventy special shipping boxes packed and inventoried, ready to be sealed, just awaiting final approval. The sanitation inspectors arrive early Saturday morning armed with notepads and detectors to analyze humidity, bacteria, and only God knows what else. The first several pass with no problems, but then one of the inspectors detects a grouping of tiny holes in the wood of one box, then another.

"Do you see this, Corporal," demands the Second Lieutenant in charge, pointing out a seemingly insignificant pattern blighting the bottom corner of one questionable container.

I look closely. What I see are minuscule pinholes, barely visible; nevertheless, undoubtedly made by something. These prefabricated unconstructed boxes had arrived wrapped in special vinyl, stacked and delivered in a designated staging area in the warehouse. The wood supposedly pre-treated against fire and infestation, every precaution taken to ensure integrity. However, something has infiltrated, meaning a worst case scenario.

"It doesn't matter who's at fault," the Lieutenant continues. "They need to be incinerated— all of them." Then turning to his Aid, "Contact HQ and order a new batch, ASAP. I'm sorry Corporal; but you should have done a better job of inspection. You will have your new containers in a few days. We will be back a week after that. Be sure this time to visually check for all signs of compromise."

Before leaving, he hands me a small pamphlet with drawings depicting different possible blights and potential damage by improper construction. Next time I will be sure to note these conditions well. The more difficult task remains. I must inform my men that their many weeks of effort have been in vain. They grumble discouragingly amongst themselves; not more than this. In a way I feel guilty, as though I have somehow let them down.

"Would a real Sergeant have made this kind of error?" I ask myself often.

The question rhetorical, but one I ask just the same. However, I will survive to experience even greater regrets. As promised, several days later a new shipment of unassembled prefabricated shipping boxes arrives. It takes us all morning to unload the truck, totaling three hundred and eighty kits sealed in airtight vinyl. We do not destroy the others as ordered; rather, empty the contents of the ones already made, break them apart, and stack the wood slabs of the unused balance along the back side of the warehouse. No one seems to notice; and here they will remain even after we eventually pull out.

The next inspection goes smoothly and we seal the first fifty boxes with a special banding lock, impossible to violate, except by an executive order from someone with a special rating. Each fifty after this likewise inspected. I begin to appreciate the inspection team; and in time I think they begin to respect my manifest proficiency. Marine Corps discipline has begun to prevail. Personnel inspections now routine, meaning clean uniforms and clean rifles, an attribute based more on fear of reprisal, than the embrace of leading example. In later years, I will have opportunity to read Machiavelli, The Prince, and remember the line concerning the success of a ruler: *"it is better to be feared, than to be loved."*

In principle I agree with these words based on my personal experience. I know of no other way that I might have accomplished my goal at the time. However, there is a price to such abandonment of social and moral principle. I envision myself then, as a despotic warrior-king poised on a hill, striking down any that dare climb up in challenge. It becomes ground of a continuous battle, sapping the essence of my being, many dark spirits wrestled from shadow to light through all eternity. I learn to show no emotion, neither happy, nor sad; even my anger a bottled-up seething force beneath veneer of silent deadly rage. All know that it is there, a deadly serpent capable of lashing out at any moment. However, in the fifth month something happens that will make me and my Bowie knife legendary.

This event occurs on a Monday after noon chow, one of those sticky hot days when even time seems to move slower than usual, dripping with expectation that anything possible. Earlier a Huey-1 medevac helicopter crash-lands a few hundred yards from the warehouse just inside the perimeter. I have just finished gobbling down a c-ration breakfast of canned eggs, when the structure begins vibrating violently, as the erratic smoking flying machine nearly scraps the roof. Grabbing my Minolta camera, I jump on a flatbed mule and rush out to see it they are okay. Being the first to arrive, I find the two crew members unhurt and leaning against their crippled bird passing a joint between them. They hail me and offer a toke; but I refuse. The two are clean-cut, Ivy League in appearance, particularly jovial considering the nearness of disaster. The cause apparently a hydraulic oil line nicked by a stray round, or by normal wear. They agree to allow me to take some pictures, and even take turns posing with me. Looking at these photos developed more than a year later, I am uncertain that they were not making fun of me behind my back. I look such a rough kid compared to these college boys. Nevertheless, I experience several minutes of escape through this brief encounter, relieved to finally be able to laugh and talk with another human being. The copter will rest here for two days before a mechanic arrives with a refit from Helicopters Division located on the other side of Marble Mountain.

The day at hand promises nothing else special, other than the ever-present unknown. I assign my crew an important task of lining twenty newly constructed boxes, along with instructions to fabricate another twenty before the end of the day. I then return to the admin office to catch up on some paperwork. The inspection team, due back in two days, has predetermined that 2nd Battalion Supply should have an additional fifty crates packed and ready to be sealed according to the scheduled deadline. An irrevocable arbitrary calendar departure date made even tighter by the first batch of wasted containers.

An hour later, I return to find the warehouse empty. At first, I am stunned; then my surprise changes to anger, as I hear talking and laughter from the loading dock at the far end of the warehouse. My hand resting tensely on the handle of my Bowie knife, I race toward the source of all the commotion, my anger escalating into greater rage with each step.

"How dare them to disobey my orders this way –and with such open contempt!" I growl to myself, determined to nip this infraction in the bud in clear and certain terms.

Pushing through the barrier of men congregated on the loading dock, I break into an arena of not only my men, but personnel from neighboring 105's and all of Echo Company. I do not know the expectation in my mind really, as I leap angrily from the loading platform into center of this unauthorized social gathering.

"Look, Sgt, a snake," Badwarrior says pointing to something writhing at my feet.

Here slithers the largest reptile I have ever encountered. I have seen big river moccasins in Carolina and Georgia, some as long as four feet; but this monster almost twice that size, no less than seven feet long, with a diameter of a few inches in the middle. The beautiful greenish brown of its skin glistens brightly in the sunlight, pale yellow streaks running along the sides of its head and down the length of a splendidly scaled body. No doubt it has crawled from its den beneath the loading dock to absorb the midday heat. Only someone has detected its brilliant camouflage. Someone born on the high plains with eyes accustomed to discerning subtle shapes; and even the imperceptible slow breathing of a creature reposed in a state of half-life existence.

What I do next beyond comprehension, an act that remains in my mind ambiguous to this day. A primitive rage has built inside while crossing the length of the warehouse, primed and ready to explode. No longer rational, incapable of transcending the moment, I spontaneously reach down, firmly griping the serpent's tail, its head already buried in a hole hollowed beneath the concrete slab loading   dock. The reptilian creature desperately struggles to escape, so I give a hard yank. To my surprise, the snake's head plops out of the hole and lashes toward me mouth extended wide.

Instinctively, I begin whirling it around and around in an effort to keep the powerful head and body extended by force of gravity. The creature ripples and snaps, a live whip in my hand, being heavier than thought. The menacing jaw gaps open lined with deadly teeth, the broad sloped spear-shaped brow twisting and turning in an attempt to bite a captor so foolish to grab its tail.

Time slows down, becoming a pulse of motion racing through the reptilian body, through the elongated course of my arm, and grounding into the solid branch of my shoulder. In the foreground, I perceive, as in a dream, the horror-stricken faces of all those spectators watching on silently from distant shadows, expectant of what next I will do. Then time stops altogether, and I feel a peace not felt since a long time. I gaze deeply into those seductive black-green and golden yellow reptilian eyes, a calm impulse to allow the sting of those fangs to sink deep into my flesh. Then in one fluid motion, I slide the serpent to the earth, step hard on the slant of its narrowed head, pinning it under the heel of my jungle boot and slashing through the soft snake flesh using the sharp blackened blade of my Bowie knife. The detached body withers convulsively for a moment spewing blood and then goes limp. At least one head of the dragon in Shangri-La lays dead and bleeding at last.

"Get back to work!" I command, turning to my men, still holding the snake body in one hand and my dripping Bowie knife in the other.

I see true terror in their eyes that day; or perhaps this is what people see when they look into eyes of a mad man they know to be mad. A few waves of farewell to fellows across the way and Supply Company files quietly back into dungeon of the warehouse. The Captain from 105's, a corpulent man with curly red hair razed short, approaches me. Taking a bayonet, he pierces the snakehead through and holds it up for closer examination.

"Sergeant, you're crazy. But you already know that." He states simply, and returns to his side of the field carrying the severed dragon head with him.

Among the spectators are the two helicopter pilots that crash-landed earlier in the day. They look upon me as they might have at a monster, a sad revulsion in their eyes, upon seeing a creature beyond redemption. I do not wish to show it, but I am shaken to the very core of my being. Events happened so quickly that I had little time to think things through. The truth being I hate snakes, hate them with a primal fear of some ancient memory embedded into my collective unconscious.

Finally, I release my grip, allowing the dead headless body to plummet into the dry dust. My arms and knees weak from the experience; my pride and lack of repentance hardened to an element greater than present physical strength. Without further reflection, I raise myself up on the loading dock and return into the darkened interior of my lair. A head of the Dragon cut-off; and still there is much more to finish in this valley once paradise lost.

Chapter 15

Revival of Past Sins

*N*ow just weeks away from our first waypoint deployment operation and tensions remain high. Ricky Recon receives new orders to report to his original outfit somewhere in the lower Mekong. Sins he committed finally forgiven. We are all as much anxious to see him depart, as he is to go. I doubt he will share much of his experience here with his fellow Recons. Recons are well-conditioned killer bulldogs; a useful breed when kept in the same pen.

We get incoming on my birthday, but no one killed and little damage, except to Motor Transport. Thank God-- they miss the warehouse! Just before dawn the next day, a woman seeks refuge into the compound holding a baby. The line-duty soldier hyped on Obestitol (gook liquid speed) blows her and the baby to pieces with an air-cooled turret mounted M-60 machine gun. He claims not to have seen her, until the last moment, when she was only a few feet away. Automatically, he grabs the two handgrip triggers, empting half a belt before letting go, thinking a zapper swooping toward him. What he saw really is anyone's guess. Why the woman did such a foolish thing remains another mystery. Nevertheless, I stop taking Obestitol after this.

The departure of Ricky Recon means I find myself one man short. It often requires eight men to carry the larger boxes from the staging compound several hundred meters away to the loading dock, and at least two men to wheel it into the warehouse using the hand-pallet jack. Bush and Badwarrior take shifts working in the office, except upon occasions when need arises requiring necessity of extra brawn. I consider it unfair to be denied daily of the biggest and strongest men in my unit, just because of their secretarial skills. Nonetheless, we all have our MOS. Still I often think it personally taxing that I must be knowledgeable in operations and to be everywhere at once.

During transport of the heavier containers, it is prudent to always have one or two extra bodies present. Gunny Corell perceives my difficulty and places requisition for another hand. The request filled within 24 hours, presenting me with another washed-out grunt born and raised in a Porto Rican neighborhood of New York. The only thing I remember about this fellow now is his Big City gangland attitude. Something about the cold and defiant animal-squint of his eyes that makes me uncomfortable from the beginning. In Nam you cannot always choose what you get, so against my better judgment, I determine to use him.

The first day proceeds without complication, but the second day this man grows belligerent, threatening every few minutes to quit. He complains continuously: the day too hot, the food not fit for pigs; brags about being a hero and how he ought to have been shipped home with honors. I do my best to ignore him. After all, there are many discontented souls here. We are in the middle of moving a container weighing not less than four hundred pounds, which requires all our effort. Without warning, the Porto Rican releases his corner and begins swearing.

"Fuck this Marine Corps shit!"

Snapping orders to lower the container, I face the man.

"What's your problem, Marine?"

He mumbles something personally threatening, at the same time pulling a penknife from his pocket. Perhaps I should have been afraid, or at least cautious. Instead, I lunge into action, grabbing him by the throat with one hand and the wrist waving the knife with the other. I lift him physically, while simultaneously bashing him several times against the crate edge. He staggers senseless to his feet, the knife no longer in his hand. I next drag him kicking and screaming into the warehouse, making sure to slam him against a crate now and then, all the while maintaining a firm grip on the back of his collar. Once in the office, I throw him on the floor in front of Gunnery Correll's desk.

"I want this man out of my unit!" I demand, staring my superior dead in the eyes. "I want him gone today!"

I storm out, leaving the whimpering man bleeding on the floor. Before evening chow, he packs his gear with a new assignment to mess duty. Rumors soon begin to circulate that he plans to *"Frag"* me. *Fragging* is an expression used in Nam to connote assassination by throwing a grenade under the sleeping quarters of the intended victim. Usually, Officers and NCOs the most preferred targets of *fragging* often carried out by a disgruntled subordinate. The first time I hear about *fragging* is while stationed with Fox Company. Two Sergeants in charge of the Commissary, targeted because of unethical business practice, withholding the good stuff from the men to sell on the black market. Apparently higher ups also involved. Someone decides one night to put an end to the business operation by tossing a live grenade under the floor. One man dies, the other horribly mutilated. *Fragging* is the most serious of any rumor; but, like all rumors, there is no proof, until the event happens; nor any foreknowledge of when it might occur.

It is one thing to confront danger face to face; another to be the target of an assassin. The Marine Corps I serve and trust can offer no protection, no natural force that can convene on my behalf. Always a chance the threat just talk, or maybe this only another empty rumor started by my men to make me afraid. My choices limited. Either, I can strike first, in which case, I will become the murderer; or else try to devise some kind of defense against the unknown. I am too young, too noble to consider the first option. Therefore, I set about to secure my personal area. I sleep in an enclosed small porch attached to the rear of the warehouse with a single exit. The two large sliding doors of the front loading dock secured by heavy chains and locks, making entry this way impossible. I dig a foxhole to the left of the rear access. The attached partition has no window, notably vulnerable on the side facing rear. Using empty c-rations cans, I string them together on five lines made of bailing wire fifty feet in length. Attaching one end to the metal siding nearest my bed, I bury the cans in the sand following a zigzag pattern. The desired principle is that any rough movement of the wire will create vibration through the cans transferring the reverberation into the metal sheeting of the warehouse to act as a giant alarm. Often disturbed awake by a sudden gust of strong wind, I soon become accustomed to discern the difference between the pulse of natural force or a potential assault.

In retrospect, I do not know if really I was protected, but at least I felt protected. Days and nights pass, and nothing happens. By now, more convinced than ever the threat just another empty rumor. One night I remain awake later than my usual habit, choosing to stay in and eat a meal of c-rations, rather than go to chow. I even manage to pick-up a few minutes of Hanoi Hannah on a small shortwave radio. Once the North Vietnamese propaganda station degrades into garble, I shut off the radio and turn in for the night. At first, the metal shingles make the familiar taught sound by rising wind pressure; and then, a distinct rattle, not at all rhythmical-- my alarm sounding off as designed.

I stop breathing, listen with anxious anticipation. Perhaps it is just an unusually intense gust of air; perhaps a rodent burrowing in the sand.

Again, it chimes loud and clear, too large to be an animal that inhabits these dunes. Without further guessing, I grab my M-16, crack open the door, and roll into my prepared foxhole. The moon shines full, the dune landscape bright and perfected, disarmingly lovely. I remain absolutely still, surveying every detail, scrutinizing every possible would be shadow. Several feet away, I glimpse what appears to be a head rising over the crest of a crisp wind-swept dune. Clicking a round into the chamber, I release the safety and take careful aim. The man's animal instincts must have kicked-in, warning him of impending danger. I can barely make out the blur of something hunkered low, like an evasive football running-back fading into deepening shadows.

Without any doubt my assassin has paid me a visit. Leaving the security of my foxhole, I cautiously search the area. In the moonlight, everything takes on a surreal quality of perfection, the pale sand smooth and unblemished. Then I see it. The grenade half-buried near a depression where the would-be murderer had taken position, the retaining pin nearly removed.

The distinctive sound of a round clicked into the firing chamber enough to frighten him away just in time. Next morning, I present my evidence to Gunnery Corell. He takes the grenade and examines it thoroughly, as though looking for some reasonable explanation other than the obvious meaning of this deadly instrument.

"Good work… Corporal," he proclaims, looking a little shaken. "I'll handle this. I can't give you the morning off… but I'll make it up to you someday. Take it easy and don't worry, son."

I detect in his eyes that Gunny feels some responsibility, and also relief. I wish to think his reaction one of affection; and not just because he almost lost the only qualified supply personnel he has. It is hard to believe that something like this can happen, until it happens. Only by then, it is usually too late. I was lucky this time, but Gunnery Corell knows it even more. After we return stateside, this man of complex emotion will take me to Reno and make introduction to a delicious candy-land world of legal prostitution at the Mustang Ranch in Nevada. This is the closest Gunnery Sergeant Corell capable of bonding to another person; nevertheless, in his own way a man of strong conscience, always good to his promise. That future weekend of alcohol and women remains in my mind the summit of manly adventure. Unfortunately, Corell also gets a case of gonorrhea at the Mustang Ranch. Once again, I am lucky.

After noon meal the next day both our problems resolved by a gruesome event. The door to the kitchen flies suddenly open. Out staggers the Mess Sergeant, the Porto Rican scissor-locked on the larger man's waist, screaming unintelligibly. He keeps hacking him in the head and shoulders using a dull butcher knife. Reports by those who unarm the assailant say his eyes shined blood red, demonic, simultaneously crying and laughing. The Sergeant recovers with the loss of an ear, choosing to remain in his service. When asked what happened, his response jaded, as though he were reciting the daily menu.

"I assigned the Spic to soup detail, and the crazy SOB just jumped me from behind for no reason. I hope they bury him in a hole for this, along with his whole Spic family!"

No charges are laid for the grenade incident. It is my understanding this man returned home to receive a medical discharge. For a long time I think about what I might do if ever I see his face again. Now I no longer remember that face at all, as so many others that have receded into the shades of the past.

Our time grows shorter with every passing day. I am altogether in control now-- certain without any doubt of my unfaltering resolve! Even Watson only smiles sheepishly with genuine respect when we pass. They are all my men now-- willing to obey my orders without question. Yet, through this victory spawns emptiness, more complete than any I might have imagined. I eat alone, sleep in isolation, no one to talk to, no one to call friend. My Sergeant never arrives; by now clear he never will. The warehouse has become a congested staging area with nearly four hundred fresh new boxes, numbered and sealed, stacked two and three high ready for transport. Another rumor circulates that the carcass of a tank buried beneath the Chow Hall. It begins as a joke by a Corporal from Motor Transport serving his second tour of duty.

"There's a Patton buried right where you are sitting," he promises to one of his fellow NCOs one morning during chow.

"You mean a tank?" The other man laughs. "I guess there are two more hidden under the LZ."

"I don't know about that, but take my word, there's a lot of hardware buried around here going back to ten years ago."

He further makes egregious claim that a few amphibious crafts called Amtrak also buried in the dunes behind the warehouse, and several others scuttled in the shallow water just off shore. At first, it sounds fantastic, but soon rallies the attention of the base CO.

The one thing most disliked by the Colonel is to be in the dark about something to do with his command. He drills this soldier mercilessly, until finally convinced there might be some truth to the rumor after all. Using shovels and pickaxes, several men begin digging beneath the Chow Hall's foundation. On the evening of the third day, they strike something metal. The following morning confirms the corpse of an M48A3 Patton tank just as the Corporal promised.

The Marine Corps prides itself on the ability to survive on a shoestring budget. There is a saying: that what the army throws away, the Marine Corps makes better and more efficient than the original design. There is a lot of truth to this. We still have serviceable equipment dating back to the World War II era. By the time the Marine Corps throws something away, it truly is junk. This day a cardinal sin uncovered; the hidden bodies disinterred one by one, and soon the heads will fall. Ten days later, two Chinooks land near the beach carrying some officers, as well as a bunch of out-of-shape civilians. Those already acquainted congregate into small groups speaking in low tones. The morning after their arrival, two bulldozers trucked to the scene and start scooping out the dunes behind the warehouse. An hour later, the first of three Amtrak amphibious vehicles hauled out with cargo chains. The spectators somber, standing with heads bowed, as though attending a funeral. But really it is a resurrection. One of these rusting relics brimmed-full of fuel, and might have started with a little maintenance.

I have little knowledge of the true scope of meaning attached to these events. Because of military secrecy, I think all these witnesses here just to verify the recovery. Only much later do I learn that these civilians once the officers in charge of a military relocation during the early years of the war. The flaw in any organization is that the books must balance. If the numbers do not match with the inventory, then there is a problem, and vice-versa. All inventories must reflect an MOS number with a traceable history. When this particular unit pulled out, they discovered irreconcilable errors in the inventory, discrepancies of quantities and part numbers. If it happens to be a jeep motor, or a box of haversacks, you simply junk it. --But what do you do with a 45-ton tank and seven amphibious craft? A conspiracy of command decides it easier to make these discrepancies nonexistent by simply erasing them from the books. I honestly do not know what I would have done in their position and under the same conditions. Every sin exacts a pound of flesh; and it is certain these men paid dearly.

After the excavation, I walk down to the landing area near the beach and fraternize with helicopter crews. One of the pilots, named Herman (same name as my Great Grandfather on my mother's side), born and raised in Greer South Carolina just the other side of Paris Mountain

where I grew up. Our common view of the same mountains observed from opposite sides immediately makes us homeboys. We begin sharing a bottle of whisky Herman keeps stashed under his pilot's seat. Being several years older and more educated, this man possesses an experience of the world far exceeding anything that I might have dreamed. Although a gentleman and an officer stamped in the likeness of the base commander, Herman endowed with a demur less assuming, more kind, more human-
- the first man in whose presence I feel truly comfortable, and a person I learn to genuinely respect. Not just because of his superior rank or because Herman and I from the same locale. I will always remember the deepness of his expression, the tired visage of a human being that has seen too much; yet a gaze soothing to the souls of others. Humility bred of experience, making me feel that I, too, share importance in the web of this ambiguous war.

The rest of the helicopter crews gone for some cold beer, Herman and I retire to the cockpit of his Chinook, where he breaks-out a pint of whiskey stashed under his pilot's seat. Conversing for nearly an hour about the social geography of the same place, witnessed from different extremes, an unspoken bond begins to form. He then moves into the co-pilot seat, motions for me to take the other seat, and begins randomly flipping switches and turning dials. The mammoth twin blades of the Chinook slowly crank to life, turning counter rotation to each other, the powerful engines wheezing and whining, a beast awakened from an unnatural slumber. The green florescence of the instrument dial reflects surreally on his face, making Herman's eyes even greener; his long slender fingers moving naturally along the keyboard as though fine-tuning a musical instrument. The untamed mammoth lurches in anticipation, mixed with the alcohol burning in my veins.

"Okay Carolina boy-- you want to take her up?"

"Would I ever!" My youthful enthusiasm erupts.

Providing several minutes of instruction to explain the control of a floating arm he calls a "joystick", Herman engages a lever making the engines rev high, becoming deafening.

"Here we go!"

I must admit I am as much apprehensive as excited. This unexpected adventure boosts my confidence to new elevations, making me believe I can do anything-- be anything! In retrospect, I suppose the impulse of this unwise decision and total lack of military protocol could have ended very badly. But we are drunk, both Marines, both from the same mountains, and both bored in a foreign land. But more, we are a generation indoctrinated into the same never-ending conflict watched on TV since the days of early youth.

As the spinning propellers gain momentum, the vehicle shakes and hisses, vibrating erratically, seemingly shaking apart. Not willing to show how terrified I really am, I keep my hand steady on the floating control aware now that the slightest movement unbalances the propellers of this acrobatic machine. It is like being in the belly of a wrenching dragonfly in one of my great grandfather's stories told to me as a child. It also brings to mind a recurring nightmare dreamed as I got older of two antagonistic giants, one pink and one blue. These two enemies hate each other and always engage immediately in furious battle. During this violent embrace they fall, rolling over me, suffocating me beneath the press of their soft colored flesh. I first experience this dream, while feverish with the Mumps, unable to attend the funeral of an unknown relative. This nightmare dream continues into adolescence, and then vanishes without conscious reason. This moment I remember that dream vividly clear.

"Pull back easy on the stick!" Herman yells above the noise.

I follow his instructions, the dragonfly shoots back like a slingshot, the nose tilting down nearly forty-five degrees-- truly airborne at last! Now that the engines at increased throttle and hydraulics fully pressurized, the floating yoke responds to the slightest pressure.

"Easy," Herman yells again. "Bring it slow to the middle, and then ease forward slightly."

Fortunate for me my alert copilot controls the foot pedals, his fingers flipping toggles and adjusting levers, until the resonance steadies and the vehicle levels out.

"You are doing good," he yells again above engine roar, which helps to bolster my confidence. "Just relax; this baby was designed to fly itself."

By now we are high above the trees and headed out over the ocean. In truth, I do not know how much me actually doing the flying and how much Herman. Nevertheless, I feel in control, navigating this impressive bumblebee of engineering marvel with just a gentle touch of my fingers. This is the fulfillment of imagination since childhood to actually fly a machine of the air. I am Smiling Jack in the cockpit-- a true Captain of the skies! This benevolent man has made my dream a reality. I do not know why he did what he did. I will later give him a few cases of c-rations, but this hardly payment enough. At one point, he decides it time to take over, so I reluctantly relinquish the control.

"Don't worry," he says sympathetically; "if that's what you want to do someday, you'll make a fine pilot."

I thank him smiling; this being the first time I have smiled since many months, a genuine expression of innocent joy. Before returning back to base, he says he wants to show me something. Hovering in a stationary position, just beyond the shoreline, Herman instructs me to look down. Approximately twenty feet below the clear surface, parked side by side, lay four distinctive bodies bathed in green florescence. The South East Asian sun has nearly disappeared below the horizon of the China Sea, imparting a shimmer of eeriness to this graveyard of four Amphibious Craft scuttled nearly ten years in the past. Yet, testimony of these corpses has continued to survive long enough to convict those responsible.

The next morning, Herman and the two Chinooks lift into the air with their human payload of civilian and military passengers. Apprehensive that the Colonel might call me into account for my excursion, I make a point the next day to lay low. He seems to have eyes everywhere, but nothing is ever said. Helicopter pilots in Nam generally exercise their own authority, unless under strict orders. Herman violated no protocol by taking his machine up. Of course, if anyone knew that he allowed me to fly it, then there might be hell to pay. Since already in hell, what is a fire of a few degrees hotter? Fortunately, no harm done, and I doubt there ever a moment when he could not have salvaged the situation. This good soul has brought me something; something I need and have lacked my whole life: a real sense of self-confidence. Like so many others, I will never see him again. And this man from the skies remains an enigmatic part of me to this day.

We are only hours away from the official departure date. Everything prepared for operational deployment; the truck convoy waiting in line to be loaded. If only Charlie will let us go in peace. My name, along with two other men comes up on the duty roster for OP East, an observation tower located at the extreme end of our perimeter. The South China Sea borders to the left; to the front and to the right thick foliage of dense jungle separated by a barrier of coiled bobbed wire. This three men outpost vilified by a tragic slaughter several months earlier. According to an official investigation, the last watch fell asleep, allowing a Zapper to slip through the wire, cut the throats of the two men asleep below, and then slip back out without detection. The bloodied barbwire and a few bare footprints all testify to the assassin or assassins-- a wonder that no clamor set off. The only survivor swears to be awake the whole time, only the accumulated evidence damning.

OP East is the loneliest, most isolated of all lookout positions on the base. Twenty minutes by jeep, an hour by foot, it is the least protected of all the outposts, no more than a naked unfortified lookout tower in the middle of nowhere. Until recently, a direct line connected to the

Command Post; but a mortar barrage ruptured the underground wires, prompting a command decision that walkie-talkie phones sufficient, considering the shortness of our remaining time here.

I take the first watch lasting until midnight. The two relief soldiers each crawl into a separate small sleeping tube made of the same steel material used in the construction of military hangars, my warehouse, and Quonset Huts. This night is particularly magnificent: the stars as clusters of vivid jewels radiating in a black cashmere sky and dripping into a shimmering silvery sea. The full moon, already ascended high above the cancerous crest of black jungle, shining intensely, the light diffusing into a ghostly hue settling over sandy dunes strung with shadowy tentacles of barbwire. I ponder through imagination how a man might pass through the maze of these sharp strands and not be sliced to ribbons. Also, there is the challenge of buried claymores. -- But Zappers are more than mere men. They dope themselves with opium and Buddha rituals. Able to slip through the wire as quickly as a man running, wearing nothing but a tunic, they come prepared to die. Slipping as shadows within shadows, booby-trapped to explode if detected, wraiths only, armed with a knife razor sharp.

Just the thought of these demons make my hair stand-up, as I survey the surrounding area for any signs of movement. A standard magazine only holds a total of thirty rounds, so no one ever uses the much faster automatic fire, and less often semiautomatic. Still, it is comforting to know the potential of this companion weapon.

My base issue consists of a battery-operated walkie-talkie phone, a Star Light Scope, powered by a green isotope enabling night vision, and of course, my ever-present M-16 rifle capable of firing a semiautomatic burst of sixty rounds per minute. The phone is supposed to be used to check in once every hour, unless there is activity to report. The Star Light Scope, an amazing piece of equipment, able to change night into day. I possess only a base knowledge of its function learned during a few training exercises. In present situation, I discover this device more than a little comforting to have on this exposed perch stranded at the dark side of the moon.

Everything about this assignment adds to a heightened sense of isolation; a feeling of abandonment, wispily tethered to the living world by a thin dimensional string connected between heaven and hell, between light and shadow. To the west extends the dark appendage of Finger Lake, a narrow black tooth gouged into the delta. To the east opens the clear China Sea, adorned by a necklace of Vietnamese fishing boats just off the coast, the reflection of yellow twinkling lanterns strung together lighting a way to fishermen casting their nets. Crouched directly ahead is savage fuse of the jungle, predatory, and with eyes of death everywhere. The absolute darkness conjures within me every fearful nightmare experienced since earliest childhood. It is as a terrifying passage into realm of every unknown lurking within shadows. At least with the aid of my Star Light Scope, I will see first the devil's mask!

By midnight, I am still alert and wide awake, so I make the decision to continue through the next watch, confident that my sleeping companion below will welcome the relief. The moon climbs ever higher into the sky, visage of an oblivious consort displacing the myriad stars and shining full upon me as the flare of a spotlight. A stiff breeze, neither cold, nor warm blows from the sea, the shivering lanterns drifting farther from the shore. The night pleasant-- so pleasant I forget the element of time and of space-- I forget I am in a place of war!

As I said, the Star Light Scope is an amazing invention, bathing everything in a bright florescent hue. However, if one happens to see another Star Light Scope looking back, then it appears as an orange disk. At approximately 0200 hours, I see just this: an orange disk peering at me through the jungle foliage several hundred feet forward of my position. My heart begins racing; my mind grasping at every possibility. Even though the Chinese regulars equipped as well as us, it is unusual for them to be this far south... unless... they are planning an offensive. There has been speculation of this imminent possibility prior to our unit evacuation. On the other hand, it could also be a friendly, perhaps lost, perhaps awaiting orders. The disk appears again, disappears, clearly changing location, now closer. I radio in and report to the dispatcher my situation.

"Negative— there are no units in that sector." The dispatcher's voice crackles over the phone. "Report back with an update every half hour."

In theory, issued military equipment is failsafe. In reality, the M16 jams frequently, Starlight Scopes die, radios lose signal strength, and of course the unacknowledged reality of rampant drugs, as easy to acquire as the candy on the streets of New York. What I do not know at the time, but will later learn from an individual source, the radio dispatcher has been smoking opium all night, so high that he completely forgets about his duty and my communications.

Half an hour later, I radio in again, but only static. This means either the battery of my walkie-talkie too weak or the receiving equipment turned off. Then by ordinance of some maniacal intelligence, my Star Light Scope dies, leaving me alone, blind, and hopelessly exposed.

In panic, I try to rouse my sleeping companions. I yell loudly, the sound of my voice swept away by the rising tide of a stiff ocean breeze. My first impulse is to descend the high ladder and awaken the others. Only I will needlessly expose myself to a trained sniper with a mounted night scope. I crouch low behind the sandbag barrier, realizing how little this protection, noting the surrounding walls constructed of a few strips of corrugated steel, two sheets of plywood, and some sparsely placed sandbags along the bottom platform edge. The unfolding scenario reminds me of the futility felt as a child while hiding under my desk during school bomb-drills to survive a nuclear attack from Russia. This position offers little protection from my imagined sniper. Several times, I peek over the edge, my mind searching the blackened terrain for any movement— for anything suggestive of a target. Yes, as irrational as it may sound, I want to kill first— or at least to go down fighting! Not to be picked- off by a single shot I will not even hear; my brains splattered within the confines of this suspended cube poised at the end of the earth. Fear gives way to rage. I rage at the Marine Corps for not having better equipment! Rage against my nation for sending me here in the first place-- and against a trained and experienced Sergeant, who never arrives!

"Damn this junk– damn this war-- Damn you all! Go ahead— shoot!" I swear defiantly standing-up.

Only a deafening silence of wind, the heavens paused. By now the hysterical prankster of the full moon has ascended to zenith, appearing as a javelin of reflected light pierced into the heart of the universe and inviting the souls of men into a vortex of lost madness. I reverently remove my flack-jacket, carefully place my rifle against a wall, and step boldly out on the narrow outer ledge constructed along the face of my elevated perch.

"Dead men don't die— dead men fly!" I shout, laughing hysterically, hot tears streaming down my cheeks, my arms spread in acceptance of things inevitable. "I fly free with the dead!"

I see my body standing at the edge of a grand arena, an insignificant element of mortality fixed in time and space. My soul sucked suddenly into a bright eddy spinning around the hub of a paper moon. The jungle changed, becoming a spot of dark matter swirled into a basin filled with yellow eyes. I swoop over those jeweled fishing boats to observe the Vietnamese fishermen tugging on their swollen nets. I see mountain plateaus rising surrealistically from delta plains circled by screaming demons. I am immortally among them, lost, without flesh or purpose of will. Then I am ushered into the presence of a mind and a will spreading throughout the burning constellations, suns and galaxies of suns, mere firefly existences. Here I am conscious of another consciousness neither evil, nor good, the living soul of all that is, and all that will ever be in corporeal illusion. In the distance below, continents rise and fall as islands of sand born and erased in time. Great kingdoms that were, and kingdoms yet to rise-up, enslaved to a consciousness older than civilization. I circle these new suns at the beginning of ignition, sparked suddenly into fervent heat, then cool into fading light, soon extinguished into darkness eternal.

Upon imagining I have reached beyond the measure of all existence, I am back in the present, my knees weak upon realizing how near the edge of this precipice I stand.

Morning mist has already begun to rise out of the tangle of dense jungle, moving inland. It is as new flesh spun from ashes of the previous darkness, ushering another dawn in Vietnam. Something has happened this night, something I cannot explain. Something died and something born. Now that I am dead, what does it matter if I should die again? The dominion of terror now departed, and still I witness another day. Living fear will never again touch me the same.

Chapter 16

Taking of Hill 34

I never tell anyone about my experience at OP East. I now considerthat I really am mad, and only imagine that I might also be sane. Nevertheless, I will keep this madness to myself. At 0500 on Sundaymorning, another two trucks join the convoy, one carrying two RTFs, the other a mini-crane. The mini-crane hoists the big guns of 105's, stoves and cooking vats from the chow hall, along with anything elsetoo large for manual extraction. The CO determines not to make the same mistakes of his predecessors. There will not be one scrap left for Charlie to nibble on. By midday, the procedure halted because of a leaking hydraulic seal on the hand pallet jack. Even though we now have an RTF, it proves useless in the restricted confinement of the warehouse. The operators of these monstrous machines are more than a little contentto lie back and take a cigarette break.

Our only solution is to repair the floor jack. Gunny and I go to work. Retrieving the proper manual and cross-referencing the correct part numbers for the hydraulic seals, we dismantle the unit, working like surgeons performing a delicate procedure. We first remove the heavy control arm, and then loose the large hex nut on top of the reservoir tank by combining our strength using a pipe wrench. My job, as trusted assistant, to layout the components in the exact order removed. As simple as this device appears, the internal mechanics prove complex with an arrangement of small cylinders, valves, and oil rings, pressurized by a top and bottom main seal. Gunny knows from experience that a bottom seal the problem, and the more difficult to extract. An hour later, the operation a success, the unit topped with fluid, good as new.

By 2100 hours, the diesel motor convoy idles into formation and shuts down for the night. All loaded and ready for our scheduled dawn departure and we say our final goodbye to Marble Mountain. I decide to sleep in my old quarters again. A nostalgic experience causing me to remember my first days here, about Neider with his many books, those many first evenings we spent playing chess together. I think about how pleasant it had been in the beginning, compared to my time spent in the field. How good it was to be dry, without worrying about leeches and the slow leprosy of jungle rot. I think most about those I left behind in Fox Company, my respect for them greater than for these men in the next room. A strange sense of guilt prevails being spared the discomfort of field duty because of my MOS and orders of relocation that have perhaps saved my life and limbs. Another kind of guilt for not being able to forgive those that have forced my hand, making me something I did not want to become, and for destroying an illusion of comradeship that once I felt, and will never feel again. I resent the hardness in my heart, and wonder if I might still be capable of human emotion-- or if I will ever truly feel anything again?

After lights out, I step out and behold the dark presence of Marble

Mountain for the last time. A snaking mist rises on the back of a sullen breeze, sifting over the ghostly terrain, crawling through avenues of this soon to be abandoned compound, as the spirit of some ancient mind felt only by instinct. It is a primordial consciousness seated upon the thrown of a waning principality of greater magnitude; yet tormented by knowledge that all things mortal and immortal defeated in the errant course of time. Almost, I can sense demons in the air, hear the anguish of disembodied souls swept endlessly to and fro through this restricted realm, pulled irresistibly into the dark temple passages of this ancient edifice. It is as though a mind reaches out and touches my mind, a cold passionless intelligence seeking a space to invade. Feeling a chill not of flesh and blood, I retire inside and hide under the covers of my bed like an apprehensive child warned not to watch a late-night horror film.

This last night at China Beach, I slumber without dream, without anticipation of physical retribution; no longer concerned by what these men might do-- what more can they do? At first light, the convoy diesels cough to life, soon roaring with anticipation. Motor Transport takes the lead, all personnel pile into the convoy of tented trucks by companies. Before the morning sun crests the horizon, the first transport noses through the front gate. We are on our way to a new assignment in some unknown region of this exotic country. I am now just one of the guys again. Not a Corporal, not an Acting Sergeant, just a soldier crammed into the back of a troop truck. We travel nearly all day, often at a snail's pace through gutted passages, forced to take long detours, and cross makeshift pontoon bridges constructed by the Corps of Engineers. In some areas, the surrounding jungle so tight pressed that the larger trucks scrape away the outcropping foliage, leaving behind a bleeding greenish- yellow trail. At noon, the convoy stops fifteen minutes for reasons of obvious relief. Men have been pissing all morning over the back tailgate, not always with success. A man named Private Eddy, the equivalent of a school clown, even takes a needed crap by hanging his ass over the edge of the tailgate to the mortified disgust of the occupants in the truck behind us. Upon hitting a bump, Private Eddie slips and almost tumbles out backwards. After a round of tense laughter, Eddie takes his seat a little less enthusiastic. I can only imagine what it might have been like to write a condolence to the family.

"Dear Mr. and Mrs. Eddy, your son, Private Eddy, killed today after falling out the back of a moving truck white taking a shit. Nevertheless, he died bravely and with honors, etc., etc."

Yes, this is one letter I am glad I need not to write. For the first few hours expectations remain high of an enemy ambush. Surely the VC aware of our evacuation-- perhaps even sees this as an opportunity to strike. Then again, maybe Charlie just glad to see us go, being content to reclaim occupied territory. A local attachment of ARVINS left a week earlier to join stronger forces in the south near Ho Chi Ming City; and according to reliable reports, the Viet Cong move-in within hours of our departure, hoisting in the shadow of Marble Mountain a Red Chinese Communist flag. It still hurts my Marine Corps ego to think about this. Not a feeling of defeat, but because we gave away our position without even a battle. This again is not rational; nevertheless, it is the Marine Corps way of thinking, an indoctrination of pride I will retain for years to come. However, I remain in remembrance that wars are not won or lost by battles on the ground only, but agendas in high places. No one man wins or loses through mortal conflict alone.

We make our way south, then west, and turn south again. By late afternoon, we halt at a fork in the road. The Colonel summons his officers together and proclaims an in-transit R&R at South China Beach for all personnel. In unison, we shout our approval. Actually, this will prove a smart move by the Colonel. It exemplifies the gladiator spirit of reward in times of war. According to the rules of engagement, every soldier assigned to foreign combat duty is entitled to an unstated period of Rest and Relaxation. With the cessation of rotations, the R&R, also stopped, leaving the entire process in limbo. This brief detour proves the ideal solution, a way to resolve the command dilemma. So legal heads prevail-- and God knows we need a few hours of recreation!

The main equipment convoy continues south to Hill 34 with an armed escort, our new compound near the naval facility at *Qui Nhon*. The lighter troop trucks, along with a transport loaded with mess provisions, takes a detour due east toward the southern coastal extreme. This portion of China Beach forms a natural inlet, too calm for surfing, with virgin white sand beaches, palm trees, and turquoise water. It could have rivaled any resort area in the world. The trucks arrange in wagon train formation becoming our perimeter of protection. The grunts start digging foxholes assigned to rotating watches. Personnel from the Mess Hall busily begin preparing for the evening meal, making spits, building fires, and erecting makeshift tables. After a general warning, the rest of us rush into the warm currents of the China Sea. The water surprisingly shallow, only waist-deep for more than a hundred feet out. We release to the moment as playful children, loudly splashing around, no longer soldiers, no longer in a war zone-- just a bunch of young men having fun for the first time since many months.

An hour before sunset, a Huey flies in loaded with steaks and beer. An hour after this, most of us so drunk, we begin to eat the steaks raw, the blood dripping from our mouths and down along our bodies. As the sun dips into the western horizon, many, including myself, continue to wade in the shallow waters, oblivious to all. We are, after all, on R&R, drunk and happy, beyond the reach of any potential danger. Imperceptibly, the color of the water changes from turquoise to darker green, taking on the hue of new motor oil. The evening tide slips in calmly, unnoticed by all. There are fewer of us now, no more than twenty staggering bodies, but still enough noise to rouse the dead. I stand perhaps fifty feet from shore, a beer in hand, the nearest other soul not less than ten feet away, when suddenly I feel the water tugging from behind. The thick dark tide of a surging whirlpool begins to swirl around my waist. Regaining balance, I twist around to face a broad purplish-grey dorsal fin within arm's reach. The great shark continues past me toward shore, turns, and slips back toward open water gliding harmlessly between the easy pickings of an intoxicated herd. Perhaps, this prehistoric creature more curious than hungry; or perhaps a member of a less aggressive species such as a Whale or Blue Shark; whatever the reason, it departs as clandestine as it arrived.

Someone belatedly yells, "shark-shark", causing us all to stagger quickly back to shore, some terrified, some too intoxicated to understand what going on: all arriving unharmed back on dry land. This marks the official end of our water activities. We continue to drink, consume raw meat, and huddle well into the night around separate tribal campfires. Each tribe with its own particular brand of music produced by high frequency band radios or tape machines; and the all too familiar odor of Opium laced Marijuana, a lasting legacy of the Vietnam War. Remarkably, there are no fights, which is often the case when men and alcohol mix. I guess all decide to set aside differences-- at least for this night. Tomorrow the war will continue, but at least this night peace prevails. Even I find solace in the recorded melodies of Bob Dylan, huddled around a crackling pit with some grunts and a Mess Sergeant.

I know none of these men, nor do they know me. Soon the drowsiness of alcohol overshadows my mind, my body as dead stubble consumed in the dying flames. I look up into a stunning night sky laden with a myriad of distant suns, soon to burn out, soon nothing left, and imagine being in paradise at last far from the inescapable mechanism of war, free from the web of violence trapping us all. I see the distorted face of the rising moon ghastly, snared in a jungle camouflage, and sleep thinking only this.

Morning stabs brightly out of the brass China Sea, the sun a fire-breathing dragon dredging to life corpses with cruel hangovers. R & R over, we are again on duty. All hands pitch in to dismantle the camp. Every scrap of leftover food and litter gathered into a pit and consumed by incineration grenades. Marines leave nothing behind. By 0900 hours, the wagon train breaks apart, and our remaining convoy heads south toward the port city of *Qui Nhon*. By mid-afternoon, we are within three miles of the city limits, but swing west, along a bombed-out road, patched with loose rock and mortar. Thankfully, the Corps of Engineers have gone before us. Two hours later, we pass through the gates of our new facility.

Hill 34, a compound inherited from the U. S. Army, aesthetically as uninteresting as its name. It is literally a hill of red clay worn slick by abuse. At rest on the top of this hill is Chow Hall, a large square sagging edifice, leaning precariously to one side because of erosion. The Big Guns dig in about midway, then the grease bays of Motor Transport; and at the very bottom of this muddy knoll sags a another large edifice designated the new home of 2nd Battalion Supply. Strategically placed positions around the hub of Hill 34 is a concentric network of Grunt Divisions. The Commissary and the Command Post occupy center of the base. I think our commanding Colonel the only one to really consider these new accommodations better. Here he has a private recreation room with pool and tennis tables; and just outside his front door an LZ prepped with a private helicopter camouflaged in one corner.

There is little difference about the warehouse, except being much more spacious, but structurally less sound. We still have no RTF. Even though the requisition for one promised and approved, but like everything else on back order, it will never arrive. They could have given us one from the convoy once everything unloaded and staged in this new facility, only this would create too much paperwork. In the end, the two RTFs secured along with the mini-crane, and piggybacked away to another phase of operations. For us, it is business as usual.

The first week of our new occupation, the Colonel calls all hands together for a command speech. Swaggering onto the tarmac of his swept LZ dressed in faded washed camouflaged fatigues, spit-shined boots, and a matching soft cap with the familiar black eagle insignia of his rank pinned on the crest looking ready for combat. Normally, this eagle bright silver, except it might offer Charlie too tempting of a target. Another detail I should mention, one never salutes a superior in a combat zone. This is a sure give away to any sniper. Just the pomp and glory of this strutting officer marching back and forth bellowing loudly should be enough to tempt the squeeze of an itchy trigger-finger. But why should the enemy do us any favors?

"Men," he begins, clearing his throat, "you are standing on Gun Fighter Hill, one of the bloodiest offensives of the war. This will be your new home for the next nine weeks. Remember that zipper-heads still in the area and knows you are going home soon. So watch your backsides."

He goes on to talk about the pride of our accomplishments, how there is much more work ahead, and the possibility of rotating day passes to an in-country R&R facility at Tam Ky for those that deserve it-- more about this later. At the end, we snap to attention and summarily dismissed to the performance of our duties. As I said, no one salutes; but I am certain there are those that want to-- who would happily make this macho soldier a marked target.

It is much hotter here than at Marble Mountain, now absent the ocean breeze to push away the mosquito laden humidity. Here, also, a dreadful rat infestation reminiscent of something I read as a child describing medieval France during outbreak of the Bubonic Plague. Some of these vicious animals grow large as cats, with long sharp teeth, and slick crimson eyes that glare fearsomely out of shadows. Particularly menacing, these distasteful creatures often congregate in packs at night pillaging through the garbage bins near the Chow Hall. Often they can be heard hissing and gnashing over a scrap of food. Occasionally, these altercations turn deadly, leaving behind a large bleeding half-eaten carcass for us to find the next morning. This further supports evidence of a macabre urban legend circulated on Hill 34.

No one has ever seen Big Al— not really. There are those claiming to glimpse in a shadow something large and sluggish moving just inside the perimeter, a crippled red-eyed demon dragging its hind legs. Some say that Big Al shot by a gook-sniper after the Vietnamese army abandoned the position during the last assault and managed to crawl away, becoming a war-cripple like so many others. They say Big Al refuses to die and continues to haunt Hill 34 to this day. Although this tenacious creature once the same as any other rodent, scavenging crumbs to survive, turns ferocious, begins to think and hunt like a man. Big Al becomes King of the Rats, changed grotesque and growing unnaturally large by consuming the flesh of those dying and those dead during the terrible offensives and counter offenses that took place here in the early days of the Vietnam conflict. Hill 34 receives its name after the Viet Cong attack with a human wave assault altogether massacring the company of American soldiers that attempted to hold position here. After a brief occupation, the Cong chased out by a stronger opposition, the United States Marines claiming Hill 34 as its own.

So Big Al, King of Rats, continues to roam here unchallenged as a kind of mascot. This dark sovereign allowed eminence in the shadows of exhausted imagination to take our minds away from the invisible presence of the true enemy. Because this creature of shadows exists immortal, it imparts a fantasy of immortality to our existence. The legend of Big Al represents the antipathy of our final countdown in Vietnam. Remaining days and nights of this legend destined to remain obscure in memory, as do all sublime shadows born on the crest of a full moon.

I pick-up two more men at this new assignment: one named Ruppert, the other Timbrink. Neither man knows anything about Supply operations, but both eager to fit in. Ruppert, tall and blonde; Timbrink short and blonde: both men share marks of combat fatigue. Before their transfers, these two total strangers to each other, pulled from different in-country regions. However, one would think them brothers the way they stick together inseparable. I cannot help but be reminded of two characters from a Kipling story The Man Who Would Be King read from Rudy's baritone sounding lips so long ago. One named Daniel, the other Peachy, ex-soldiers in search of fortune and adventure. Their bond of friendship the same, a loyalty that eventually destroys them both.

Our first task at hand is to dismantle and destroy many of the crates containing field equipment, and then to reconstruct fresh new ones. This order particularly discouraging to all and seems unnecessarily redundant, since visual inspection confirms none of the containers compromised. Nevertheless, these rules of military protocol the new norm of warehouse operations in a facility nearly twice the size of the one left behind. Another change is that we must now all bunk together in the upper skeleton loft broken into several open partitions separated on ribs of wooden beams. These new sleeping arrangements, although not ideal, offer some protection from the enemy within. The NCO and Officer's quarters are separated on a second loft above the administration office in the center. Gunny and the Captain occupy two enclosed rooms with doors. My living space consists of a cot with a mattress on an eight-foot square platform surrounded by a frail wooden fence as one might see on farms. In many ways I feel like a guard dog stationed on a precarious perch and hope never to sleepwalk here. Again, I remain isolated, but comforted by the knowledge that behind a nearby closed allies rest.

Morning of the third day Gunny calls me into his office. As always, he looks grim. His face, hatchet-shaped, beginning at the sharp edge of a long narrow nose notched into the center of his forehead, and with slits for eyes that glare beneath the hood of iron-gray eyebrows painfully hacked into a countenance of serious discipline. I do not remember Gunny ever really smiling. I believe this ability perhaps the first fatality in the slow-motion train of unhappy events crashing into the tragedy of this man's unhappy life.

"Nine weeks, Corporal, we have only nine weeks to prepare our inventories— except this time we are responsible for a full battalion operational count. That means you will liaison with Sergeants from the other four Companies and oversee their preparations, as well as confirm the final count. We are the spearhead and you are the point of that spear. That particularly goes for weapons. Remember, you are responsible for the content and final count of every container— so make sure the count right before signing off on it."

"But Gunny, what happens after I leave. What's to prevent someone taking something out?"

I do not feel particularly comfortable with this added level of responsibility.

"Because," he says reaching under his desk; "you will lock every container and every piece of equipment with this."

In many ways, it looks like any other Crimping Tool used to band crates, except this particular one has a round flat emblem at the end about the size of a silver dollar. The principal simple: a special lead sleeve passes through the final metal band and then crimps it closed using a lead metal washer. This unique crimping instrument creates a seal embossed with the regiment code of Second Battalion Marines imprinted on the metal medallion. I do not know rather this special tool an invention by Gunny and the Captain, or if it belongs to the security of another article of military protocol. Nevertheless, the application ingenious, greatly enhancing our protective security. This tool kept under lock and key in a file cabinet behind Gunny's desk, requiring that I sign for it at each use. In addition to this, a strict separate manifest maintained secretly in the same location with an exact count corresponding to my paperwork and cross referenced with red numbers stencil-sprayed on each completed piece of logged inventory.

The first weeks spent breaking apart the specified containers, building new ones shipped fresh from the naval port; and then re-sanitize, transfer the inventory, and a final procedure of marking that container with an indelible number. After each inspection by the Transport Control Agents, I personally seal the final band using the special Crimping Tool. If Gunny and the Captain not impressed, they are most definitely pleased.

I must say that even I experience a sense of satisfied accomplishment. Of course, there is nothing fool-proof. Later, a container comes up one riflescope short. My signature appears on the inventory control slip, and I remember personally confirming the count twice before sealing the box. Closer inspection reveals that someone forced open the box from the bottom on one side, tearing through the lining paper, stealing a desired souvenir. Traces of dried blood indicate the perpetrator snagged a nail during this intrepid act. It had to be someone aware of the contents in this particular container; which only reinforces the idea that nothing is ever secure from the ingenuity of rats and thieves. Nevertheless, I cannot help but to admire the determination of the intrepid soul responsible.

Another detail about Hill 34, more somber and ranked closer to civilization, it possesses an air nearer to the definition of military protocol. It is a bit like the feeling one gets when walking through a VA Cemetery on a Sunday afternoon. Another feeling I will experience many years later at the Little Big Horn outside Billings Montana: a feeling that the ghost still present among the headstones of those fallen dead resurrected in pale light of the moon. I think that perhaps all battlefields are like this. It is my belief that honor, bravery, and violence do not dissolve away with the perishing of the flesh from generation to generation.

Vietnam sleeps as a serpent ready to strike at any moment, a moment when one least expects it. So peaceful here, we grow complacent, thinking now mostly of going home; the prospect more real than ever before. I even begin eating at the Chow Hall again like everyone else and sit in the NCO section among men many years my senior. By now, most know me only as the Supply Sergeant and greet me with the respect of my rank and position. At least I have earned respect, if not friends. Early each Monday morning a young attractive Vietnamese woman arrives on the back of a garbage truck to empty the dumpsters. This pretty girl speaks some English, having a lovely French accent, which I have remarked in times past. Often she exhibits particular fondness toward me, always smiling and making a point to wave hello and goodbye. This particular morning I am alone in my warehouse. She appears at the entrance of the large sliding door near the dumpster and approaches cautiously. My men assigned to tasks elsewhere, no other witnesses around. I have just completed logging in a confirmed count of several C-rations pallets staged for a helicopter lift, only vaguely aware of the garbage truck's arrival.

"You Marine in charge?" The woman enquires, stepping fully into the warehouse.

"You're not supposed to come in here," I say in my most authoritative voice.

I realize just how appealing she really is. Long black hair done in a ponytail and dark oval cat-eyes that smile playfully, the Asian woman appears seductive in all feminine glory. This particular day she is wearing a loose white blouse, allowing her breast free movement underneath. For some reason, I always imagined her older; but close like this, I judge her age less than thirty, her complexion smooth porcelain reflecting on high polished cheekbones. Many of the Vietnamese women have black teeth from habitually chewing betel leaves; but this woman an exception. Her front teeth straight and even, as white pearls, evidence of good dental hygiene practice. Only a few Vietnamese in the south can speak English, most limited to Vietnamese or colonial French. The fact that this womanable to articulate so well in my language means she has more than amoderate level of education.

"You give me C-rations for my children—I *sucki-fucki*!"

What she says, and the way she says it so direct that in the momentI find myself altogether speechless. She then grabs the front of my pants and pulls me between two pallets. As she fumbles with my fly, I look into her eyes. All I can see is the blank emptiness of necessity, a willingness to do anything for survival.

"Do you really want to do this?" I ask, touching the softness of her face.

"You give me box of C-rations— I do for you."

Again, there is that emptiness. In the moment I see in this woman my mother, my two sisters, the mothers and sisters of all who might find themselves desolate in a desolate time. Moved with compassion, I push her gently away.

"You don't need to do this...I will give you C-rations for free."

I reach to the top pallet and retrieve three cases, each containing twelve meal packets, and hand them to her.

"This is for your children."

"You good Marine— you good man," she articulates with tears in her eyes.

At least I know the tears real. She tosses the cases of food into the back of the truck and waves goodbye. Every week after this, I make a point to give her a couple of cases. I never knew this woman's name, and she never asks to know mine. Nevertheless, I always hope that her children had enough to eat, and that something might remain at the end of our evacuation once the Viet Cong military move in.

It is an extraordinarily beautiful night, first night of a new moon. Sleep a challenging skirmish against unbearable humidity infused with the constant whine of buzzing mosquitoes. Surrendering to the futility of restlessness, I step outside to smoke a cigarette in the hope of finding some relief. The stars weigh down heavily, as a bulging fish net billowed over the shadowy terrain of Hill 34. It is like standing on an alien planet, seeing constellations strung across the zenith never before witnessed. The myriad of stunning points of light, although feeble, provides comfort somehow, a sense of peace and good will to all men that behold the collective wonder of their presence.

It is little more than a wiz--an innocuous sound breaking through the heavens shot from somewhere in the dark. Charlie could not have hoped for a better shot. Like the time I make a perfect hoop from the middle of a basketball court, swooshing flawlessly through the net; and as then, no one to witness the perfectly timed event of a mortar shell tumbling through darkness and into the open door of an ammo bunker. The air suddenly empty, sucked into a vacuum, followed by a bright flash. A wave of intense heat rushes into my face, blinding my senses with a spark of searing white flame etched into night. I remain prostrate on the ground, realizing only now that I have been flung several feet backward. A plumage of fire consumes the stars in a sparkling mushroom rising overhead, as the hood of a serpent with many shining eyes. At first I hear no sound at all, my mind and body numb; then aware of a distant thundering of smaller explosions, continuing to ripple through a blacken shroud, present time begins again.

A smoldering crimson mound radiates into morning with the occasional crackle of exploding rounds. This single mortar finds its mark, leaving behind a smoldering crater. Fortunately, no other casualties, and even though my position more than two football fields from ground zero, the force of the explosion enough to lift me bodily, and tossing my corpse backward several feet like a GI Joe doll. My right knee dislocated, my leg pinned under the weight of my torso. The injury deemed superficial at the time. My knee swells to twice-normal size for a couple of weeks; however, after a quick examination by the Medic to confirm nothing broken and an unanticipated snap of relocation, I quickly recover. It will be many years before I realize the true extent of the damage. I now have my Achilles heel, only I do not know it.

Charlie scores one for the team this night; one the Colonel will not easily digest. Military minds immediately go to work planning a major counter offensive. Many will pay for this bold attack. As a result, at least two innocent lives destined for waste, two men under my command handpicked to face fangs of the serpent. Two lives sacrificed; never again the same. Venom in the dragon heads remaining has still deadly course to run.

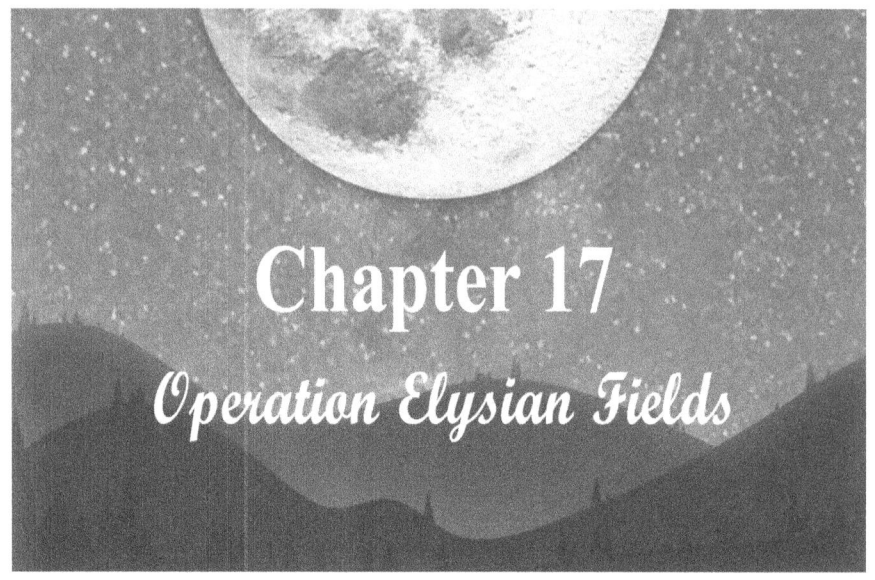

Chapter 17

Operation Elysian Fields

*S*econd Battalion, First Marine Corps Division conducts a decisive military offensive against the enemy of South Vietnam in early summer of that year code name Operation Elysian Fields. Reconnaissance has provided coordinates for a helicopter drop, mounting an assault not seen since the early days of the war. I volunteer to be part of this operation, being bored and eager for more action.

"Sorry, Corporal," Gunny says, refusing my request. "No key personnel are allowed. We can't afford to lose you, son."

"But I want to go. --You are going, why can't I?"

"If something happens to me, then the Captain will take over; but there is only one Supply Sergeant. You'll have to sit out this one."

I feel to resign then and there, except deep down I know he is right. I have become an indispensable component at a pivotal junction of a

Battalion operation. Still, it bothers me that Gunny allowed to volunteer and I cannot. However, an even grimmer task falls upon me. I must choose two men from my unit to accompany Gunny into combat. I first consider Sein and Badwarrior, but decide their combined efforts too valuable. I could have chosen Watson, only he probably would have refused. Besides, he and Bush are my best workers when relieved from office detail. In fact, all my men now important because of many months of on-the-job training experience. Unfortunately, this leaves only Ruppert and Timbrink.

"You two men pack your field gear, and report to Gunny Corail at 0500 tomorrow morning in back of the warehouse." I order reluctantly. "I'm sorry, but I think you are the most qualified."

"Why should it be us-- just because me and Timbrink are new that we don't count the same?" Ruppert makes protest.

Of course, this is the reason, but I make another excuse about them being combat seasoned. I can see in their eyes that they do not believe me. Next morning, I roust the two men from their sleep, and as good Marines, they march off to the LZ with Gunny to board a waiting helicopter. Ruppert looks for a moment back: his amber hair as the gold of summer wheat, his eyes glittering in the early morning twilight. He tiredly slings his M-16 over his shoulder and follows his comrades like condemned Prometheus. Unlike the morning star, he will never shine so beautiful again.

Altogether, operation Elysian Fields lasts only a few days. Each night I watch the Cobras spraying red tracers over some distant patch of jungle like Arachne of ancient Greek mythology weaving a wondrous tapestry of death. Thick black smoke of napalm drops billow apocalyptically over the morning horizon, followed by the crackling of fierce firefights in progress. It is though the poison of a raging battle infects my soul even from a distance. Bitterness and restlessness seems to permeate everything we do, everything we think. I might mention that a small attachment of

ARVINS move into the compound on the same day operation Elysian Fields begins. Some of these soldiers live with wives and girlfriends in a small village to the south, arriving to join their unit in the morning, and then returning home before the final securing of the gates. I confess that I share little affection for ARVINS, even if they are considered loyal allies. They have earned the unfortunate reputation of not being reliable; and sometimes of running away during a fight. I suppose this an American prejudice circulated second-hand by the grunts. Nevertheless, this perception persists, often clouding my judgment when it comes down to trusting my back to these allied soldiers.

On the sixth day it is my turn on the roster for the south gate watch. This is only one of three access points to Hill 34 considered vital: the front gate, the rear gate, and a desolate location to the south guarding a narrow dirt road bordering a strip of jungle marshland. The first thing I do upon arrival is to check for booby traps. A favorite pass time of the enemy is to plant a grenade somewhere along the metal frame in the anticipation that a careless soldier might swing open the barrier without proper inspection. Sometimes it works-- more often than anyone cares to admit. This morning, however, I examine every inch before unlocking the heavy hasp. I take my position in a sunken dugout bunker about twenty meters from the entrance protected in front by a barrier of stacked sandbags.

Gate duty, considered the longest watch assignment on the rosters, consists of six tedious hours with nothing to do except to watch and to wait. Every half hour I check-in my position with an 'all clear." Time here is a seethe of perspiration humidity that drips thick with pestilent mosquito, eventually dissolving into intense heat of another delta day. During the first hours, I scrutinize the tactical security of my position, only to realize once again, there is little. Venerable to an open assault, to Zapper attack, and to sniper fire, I reconcile to the possibility of expendability. The rows of bobbed wire that extend around

275

the compound on either side represents a daunting deterrent; this poorly defended aperture inviting assault, indefensible by one canary in a cage. purpose of this particular outpost becomes clear: failure to check in or radio silence means the outpost compromised necessitating deployment of reinforcements. This assessment only adds another nail of frustration to my growing list of military grievances.

By late afternoon, rice farmers begin straggling along the road on their way home after a long day's toil in nearby paddies. They look tired, desolately resigned to an existence of labor in fields of ancient rich black mud mired up to their knees, the sun burning as an oriental dragon on their backs, as mosquitoes cluster in the shade of their woven straw cone hats. They care to know nothing more than this. For these peasant farmers this war of nations only vaguely pertinent to the daily drudge of necessity; nevertheless, some might be snipers, were snipers in the past, or might become snipers. As I think about this, I remove the safety from my M-16, take careful aim at each passerby, and squeeze the trigger ever so slightly. I am in this moment judge and executioner. How easy they might be to kill…just a little more pressure, and one less potential enemy sniper. Then, as though waking from a bad dream, I flip back on the safety, toss my weapon aside. I feel shaken to the core of my being, not because of fear and anger; but because this moment I realize I am capable of indiscriminate murder. Perhaps, secretly they are snipers; or perhaps they are just exhausted farmers on their way home after a hard day's work. Realizing action only the tool of thought; the blood of innocence-- though not shed this day-- remains a stain in my conscience to now.

Less than an hour remaining, it seems certain Hill 34 secure for a little while longer. Then something grips my attention. I hear a familiar popping sound, the earth kicking-up, violently disturbed a few feet in front of my position. Other shots whiz in the air, one striking the wooden beam just above my head. I am being fired upon!

Immediately I grab my rifle, secure the strap on my helmet, and hunker low, carefully scrutinizing the swampy barrier, certain one of those farmers positionedin a nearby hollow. I am about to call in, when a stray round ricochets from an inner support post. The fire action not coming from outside,but from inside the compound!

Perhaps two hundred yards behind my location stands a caged enclosure, once used to retain prisoners of war, and later designated an ARVIN command post in the event of aVC assault. Two men, one an ARVIN regular, the other a Vietnamese civilian, stand within this rarely occupied facility making target practice aimed at an empty crate. The problem is that my outpost in direct line-of-fire of the container mounted against a chain-link fence.

This total lack of comprehension infuriates me. We are in a war zone, not a playground. In a fit of anger, I think to return fire, but quickly decide against this wisdom. I shout at them, but they remain absorbed in their game oblivious to everything else. Therefore, I devise a plan of retribution. Slipping out of the bunker, I secure the gate and crouch into a drainage ditch opposite the entrance and wait. An hour later, the two men saunter toward the exit, gibbering playfully in their native language. The ARVIN soldier swaggers nonchalantly with a carbine rifle strung over his shoulder, and shakes the secured gate in frustration. I jump up from behind, my M-16 locked and loaded. I motion for the carbine to be placed on the ground. The ARVIN makes protest and steps toward me. I knock him to the ground with the stock of my weapon, lower the muzzle to his head.

"So help me God— I'll blow your head off!" Hours of pent-up rage unleashed at last. "That goes for you, too!" I shout, motioning to the other man to get down on his knees, hands in the air.

I do not know to this day if they understood my words, but my intentions unmistakable. The civilian, barely a teenager, begins crying. The older and more experienced ARVIN snarls something terse to him and they both bow their heads in submission. I sling the Carbine over my shoulder and march the two captives back to the Command Post with hands behind their neck. I turn them over to base security and fill out a report. If nothing else, the two guilty of mischief, as well as the unauthorized discharge of a weapon on a U.S. military base. The Colonel is delighted. Like most everyone else, he has little affection for ARVINS.

"Surprised you didn't shoot the zipper heads!" He says with an approving nod after reading my report. "Soon, after we are gone, they'll have a whole shit-load of target practice!"

It is dark by the time I trudge up the barren hill, the ghostly warehouse shadowed iridescently by a quarter moon cutting darkly into a darker horizon. The dim light of the familiar building beckons to my tired body. It is not home; but it is as close to a home as I might hope for here. The ARVIN Captain steps from behind a bush with the stealth of an assassin. He is a husky older man, combat seasoned, with grey hair, and eyes dulled of emotion from too many years fighting an enemy whose victory inevitable.

"Why you arrest one of my men?" He demands, a hand clutching the handle of a .45 strapped at his side.

"Sir," I report, and snap to attention; the ARVIN officers deserving of the same respect as our own ranking officers.

"You hear me-- American soldier!" He puffs angrily: "My man in brig because of you!"

"Damn-Straight— those men fired inside a secured compound, and in direction of my outpost! I could have been wounded or killed. It's lucky that I only arrested them."

My anger reignited, an instant rage rising to the surface, an ever abiding presence residing just beneath the veneer of fragile composure.

"We allies— you stupid Marine!" His hand fidgets nervously the handle of his holstered pistol. "You think you better than us?"

I automatically raise the barrel of my M16 rifle; flip off the safety and stare unblinking into the small animal eyes of this man.

"If you have a complaint, Sir; then I think you'd better take it to the base commander. Your men broke protocol and endangered my life. They will be disciplined accordingly...Sir!"

I have butterflies in my stomach. This one not like the two captured earlier today. Instinctively, I sense that given the opportunity, this man capable of killing. In every respect, he is a combat soldier familiar with blood on his hands; his conscience long dead. Many years later, I will cross the path of a lone wolf in the wilds of the Yosemite Rockies and be reminded of the deadness in this man's eyes glimmering viciously in the pale moon light. We stand there silently facing each other for many tense moments.

Then he smiles, his blackened teeth painfully visible even in this dim reflection, turns, and scurries quickly into the night. I do not feel completely safe until reaching the lighted interior of the warehouse and securely bolt the door. A small detachment of ARVINS pull out the next morning, not to return. I suppose the Captain and the Colonel came to some kind of military understanding.

The next morning, Gunny, Timbrink, and Ruppert return from Operation Elysian Fields, dead tired and dirty; but at least are back in one piece-- or so it appears. The change not so noticeable in the beginning; the operation considered a success with only a few wounded. After a couple of days rest, Ruppert and Timbrink return to their usual jobs, without once complaining.

By now the full compression of Southeast Asian jungle heat has begun, melting everything under its influence. Even the large diesels cough spasmodically, almost suffocating in the rising humidity. Before mid-morning sun our Marine Corps green t-shirts soggy with sweat, clinging to our bodies throughout the day like a sticky extra skin. We work harder and more hours than ever before, our objective clear now. We are all going home soon.

Ruppert begins to wane most that month with the waning of the South East Asian moon. In just a few weeks, he changes from an Adonis weighing a hundred and seventy pounds of muscle, to an emaciated skeleton barely more than a hundred pounds. He often perches for hours on the edge of a sealed crate like a horrible Gargoyle, his face becoming sunken and crater-scarred, his eyes grey and lifeless. Timbrink also changes, but in a different way. He becomes inattentive to orders, nervously running around looking for things, only to forget what he is looking for in the first place. He gets confused easily, compulsively pulling his hair, his eyes rolling around like a mad man. I suspect he is in fact mad, a madness different from my own, yet madness nonetheless. All become mad here in one way or another.

Gunny perceives immediately the scope of the problem. He counsels both men, ordering me to stand-down and let him deal with the situation. I suppose that Gunny feels some obligation to these men, a sense of loyalty shared by soldiers, who have experienced combat together. He could have simply put them on report and had them shipped-out on a Section 18; instead, he takes them one by one into a locked room during the last weeks, and attends to the needs of each man as they undergo cold turkey. Gunny, himself, rarely sleeps, rarely eats during this gruesome period. At the end, he issues orders that every man in Second Battalion Supply keepers of our two Marine Corps brothers; expressing that it is the responsibility of us all to remain vigilant to insure Ruppert and Timbrink not find opportunity to relapse. However, Ruppert has a secret stash and turns into a zombie again after only a few days. Gunny does not utter a word of condemnation, but takes the man back into that room and repeats the cleansing process. Despite Gunny's many other failings as a man, I will always consider him a saint for this singular act of self-sacrifice. Of course, we will lose both Ruppert and Timbrink in Hong Kong. The local Hong Kong police eventually track them down a week after our departure. Both men arrive stateside ahead of us and receive a

General Discharge. Gunny and I will visit them in the brig and make pleas on their behalf.

I will always remember the sad look of defeat in Gunny's eyes, the eyes of a fallen angel, whose burden of guilt cannot be covered. I, too, share his bearing of responsibility. The mantle of command had rested on my shoulders as well; and I am the one to make the choice according to tactical logic. But all I could jealously think at the time is that my blood denied on the battlefield of Operation Elysian Fields.

Chapter 18
The Rain of Hanoi Hannah

Second Battalion First Marine Division positions to implement another notch in Marine Corps history. It seems everyone remembers the beachhead assaults, but so very few the first withdrawals. Second Battalion, designated to pull out of Vietnam intact, prepared in military readiness. This means every field platoon, every relay communication post, every helicopter, and every piece of artillery, even the transport vehicles: inventoried, tagged, and logged. Some of the larger equipment, such as tanks and Hueys, ship directly to Qui Nhon Harbor under heavy escort.

As in all operations of this magnitude, the best and the worse in men leech to the surface. Some of the baser types become dealers, distributors of dangerous substances to their comrades oblivious of the consequences. Black Market Exchange based on personal greed, representing an enormous challenge in the war against communism. The way it works deviously simple: so simple that only a few seem to notice. Soldiers have family members and friends send them cash hidden in personal letters or in care packages. These they trade to the local Vietnamese for MPC Military currency at a ratio of ten to one. These bills sophisticated counterfeits, nearly perfect in every detail, representing denominations from five cents, up to one dollar. Those participating entrepreneurs in turn buy a money order using the bogus bills and mail the certificate back home. Rumors circulate that enlisted men, as well as a few officers, accumulate thousands of dollars in this way. The U.S. Treasury wages its own war, even here in this distant battlefield. Every so often, andwithout warning, we receive instruction to bring all of our MPC bills to the Adjutants office to exchange them for a new generation of currency. I still have some worthless bills to this day because I failed to exchangethem within the prescribed period.

There are also scavengers of every rank. I learn to be diligent when it comes to protecting the integrity of my final count. I remember particularly well a hot afternoon when a Major from the armory drops by and begins rummaging through containers as though at a flea market. Everyone else at the chow hall having lunch, I decide to remain here and open a can of cold rations, taking opportunity to update some paperwork.

"Can I help you, Sir?" I ask politely.

"Looks like you boys are packed and ready to go," he states in a friendly Tennessee accent. "Yep, this war is coming to an end."

In one hand a field compass taken from an open container near the door as he walked in. I do not say anything, at least not immediately. He next steps to a box marked "classified." The top, although placed, has not yet been nailed shut and banded. Nonchalantly, he lifts the cover to peek at the contents. I forcefully stomp my boot on the lid, snapping it shut as he quickly pulls his fingers to safety.

"What the hell is your problem, Corporal? I want to see your warehouse Sergeant."

"I am the warehouse Sergeant, Sir!"

Judging by the smirk on his face, I know already what he is thinking. He arrogantly reaches down to raise the lid again, and again I apply pressure with my boot shifting all of my weight forward. We stare at each other eyeball to eyeball, like two gunfighters preparing for a duel.

"You will remove your g-damned boot and let me see what's in this box!" He commands firmly.

"Sir— this is classified inventory. It is my duty to inform the Major that his request cannot be fulfilled without special permission— Sir!"

"Corporal, I'm warning you. I am a ranking officer, and I'll see to it that you are busted down to private before the sun sets! Now, I am giving you an order— open that box!"

"I must respectfully decline the Major's order— Sir! If you like, the Captain and Gunny will be back in half an hour. You can make your request to them— Sir!"

"By God, you have been warned Corporal!"

As he turns to leave, I quickly grab his hand and remove the compass from his grasp.

"This is inventoried and secured property, Sir!" I say without politeness.

He stands there in shock, altogether dumbfounded. I have added injury to insult. I know he will take his complaint straight to the Colonel. I have refused a direct order from a superior, and therefore in violation of Marine Corps protocol. In fact, there are few infractions of greater consequence, other than stealing or desertion. However, I am the only ranking personnel in the warehouse on this day, recognizing my prime responsibility to protect my inventory, even against a scavenger of superior rank. How the Colonel might see things is an altogether another matter. When Gunny and the Captain return from noon chow, I provide a detailed report of the event.

"You snatched something out of a Major's hand— a Major?" The

Captain jumps up in defense of a fellow officer.

"He had no business being in our warehouse." Gunny defends. "You did good Corporal. I hope that jack-leg learned a lesson today!"

When it comes to military politics, Gunnery Sergeants have a lot of pull. Even though out-ranked by attending officers, very rarely their edits challenged.

"All I can say is good luck, Corporal…a Major…" The Captain turns and saunters into the lair of his office.

Just after evening chow, I receive the expected summons to the Colonel's office. There is the glimmer of a smile on the Captain's face; Gunny just looks down and shakes his head. Upon entering the lion's den, I see the Major seated in a chair across from the Colonel smokinga cigarette. Judging by the butts in the ashtray, I determine he has been here for some time presenting his case.

"Reporting as ordered, Sir," I state loudly, snapping to attention.

"Do you recognize this United States Marine Corps Major, Corporal?" The Colonel growls in his usual distemper.

"Yes sir," I reply, surveying the petty grimace of the officer, who hours earlier had invaded my warehouse.

"Did you disobey a direct order from this officer?"

"Yes, sir, but it was because-"

The Colonel leaps to his haunches like an enraged bulldog.

"No excuses, Corporal— you will apologize to the Major now— is that understood?"

"Yes, sir-- I apologize, Major, for disobeying a direct order, Sir!"

The Colonel then turns to the other officer.

"Okay Major, you have your apology. I will deal with this Marine myself. In future, you will stay out of the warehouse, and away from supply operations— dismissed."

The Major, although not completely happy with this arrangement, stands up and dismisses himself. He is after all only a Major. What can he say more to influence the decision of a full-bird Colonel? Once he is gone, the Colonel smiles approvingly.

"Good work, Corporal— that hyena has been under my skin since we have arrived here. –But by God, you put him in his place." With unprecedented gentleness, he pats me on the shoulder and shows me to the door. "You let me know personally if he comes within fifty feet of your warehouse."

My attitude toward the Colonel changes after this. I do not tell the Captain, or Gunny, or anyone else the events of that meeting. This night the Colonel and I reach an understanding of mutual respect, which will remain our profound secret.

Real R&R comes as a surprise to us all. The Captain calls Supply Company to fall in and reads a special bulletin issued from Battalion headquarters.

"Tomorrow at 0600 hours all Supply and Motor Transport personnel are to report to the tarmac and board a waiting transport for embarkation on a 12 hour R&R to Gun Fighter Hill-- courtesy of the Marine Corps!"

Gun Fighter Hill is a controlled area on the outskirts of a local village called Tam Ky in Quang Tin Province located a few miles south-east of our position. This area has been the entrenchment of an armored cavalry division of M113 Sheridan tanks ever since its liberation from VC control. A decisive battle inscribed in the history books demonstrating the most effective tank deployment in the Vietnam conflict. This American victory establishes dominate strategic presence, creating an ideal location for an in-country R & R. As in all battles, there are certain names, times, and dates describing actions and counter offensives leading up to the exchange of territories and shifting of power. In those early years, Hill 34 one a strategically vital area of occupied territory, lost once to the enemy in a terrible massacre, and then recaptured, with the province of *Quang Tin* spoil to the victor. To some *Tam Ky* and Gun Fighter Hill represents terrible reminders of human cost exacted on bloodied battlefields. It will become to me, a place of unexpected pleasant memories. Particularly unforgettable is the sequestered fantasy island of Tam Ky: a place of beautiful prostitutes, exotic foods, steam houses, and tropical wonders that remain rich tapestries of adventure like few experienced in my life since.

Next morning we board the waiting trucks clean, shaved, our hair slicked-- almost the appearance of being civilized men again. Less than an hour later, we pass under the arched main gate of Gun Fighter Hill, a checkpoint resembling the entrance to an arcade, with two larger than life rifles crisscrossing the familiar Marine Corps emblem. Less than an hour later we arrive at the guarded outskirts of *Tam Ky*; and from here escorted to a designated portion of the village cordoned off for our protection. We are provided just enough accessibility to create the allusion of actually roaming free through an exotic city, complete with shops and an economically thriving local population. From what I can see, Tam Ky village equivalent to any small town in the world, by definition not quite a city, yet more than the small poor farming districts surrounded by terraces of rice paddies.

The first activity on our agenda is to eat– compliments of the Colonel— authentically prepared Vietnamese dishes served inside the Commissary, a controlled restaurant that also serves alcoholic beverages. My southern pallet in the beginning not accustomed to this alien array of hot spiced food, I soon begin to appreciate the many unpronounceable courses with a wash of cold beer. I have little idea how even to pronounce the many culinary presentations, except that the serving waitresses lovely. Some of it taste like seafood— or at least I think it is seafood-- only I do not know if it even possible to find a restaurant using these same ingredients today. Nevertheless, I eat everything on my plate without question and no worse for the experience.

After our authentic in-country meal, all allowed to go our separate ways. I have yet to see Disney Land, and will later be reminded a similarity of experience. The primary objective of most is to find a bar and a whorehouse, activities both plentiful and usually under the same roof. I am one of the less fortunate. I have brought little money, thinking for some reason that everything would be free. Of course, these girls cheaper than one might find anywhere else; nevertheless, they remain out of my price range. I might have been able to afford one or two that even a keg of beer unable to make attractive. Even these would leave me penniless; therefore, I exorcise practical sense by avoiding personal temptation. I spend much of the day walking around, sucking down beers, and observing the local artisans weaving hats or making jewelry from crustacean shells. I enjoy watching the women, who I think not prostitutes, many wearing delicate white and black smocks that move nearly transparent when the wind blows just right. Conversation impossible, since none speak English-- or at least I do not believe they do.

Military Police escorts begin rounding us up at around 1700 hours. After returning to the Commissary for an all-American steak dinner, the officer in charge announces that we are going to a local bathhouse. At the time, this sounds little exciting to me. The idea of taking a hot bath, though appealing, not exactly the stuff of an R&R adventure, especially considering this is to be our last event before returning to base.

At 1900 hours, a troop truck arrives to carry us to a location in the secret heart of Tam Ky. The bathhouse, a large traditional pagoda-style building, as modern as any spa facility in a capitalist free society, makes all of us feel like we really are back in the civilized world. First on the agenda, a forty-minute Turkish sweat, followed by an ice-cold dunk in a cylinder-shaped pool, and lastly to run a gauntlet of pretty--- mostly young women possessing wooden switches-- who whip our backs and buttocks. Although, the swishes sting intensely, the pain quickly subsides, leaving the whole body pleasantly warm and relaxed. Lastly, I follow one of the women escorts into a massage room, where she instructs me to lie on an elevated bed. The lights dim, incense of perfumed flowers intoxicating the air, mixed with the scent of a lovely soft lady of Vietnam fills the chamber with exotic pleasure.

"Blow-job ten dollars, hand-job five dollars," she negotiates with practiced tenderness.

She has the most beautiful almond eyes, her black hair cascading delicately over a partially exposed left breast, leaving me with little desire to escape the delicacy of this temptation. Oh, how I desire to feel those painted luscious lips on my throbbing penis.

In the end, however, after a moment of fruitless coaxing, I settle for a hand-job , gladly expending the last five dollars in my pocket. The best five dollars I have ever spent. There is just something chemical about a woman's touch, something that a man simply cannot give himself. I do not remember anything after this wonderful orgasm, until harsh lights stab into my eyes. I am alone, rudely awakened by the bulldog bark of a Marine Corps Gunnery.

"R & R over, Marine— get dressed and report to your transport— ASAP!"

The dream over, I am back in the Marine Corps.

I will remember fondly these few hours spent in a small South Vietnamese village made prosperous by U.S. military presence. I cannot help but wonder what happened to it after we left. I wonder about that pretty young girl, which gave me a moment of pleasure in a room of exotic incense. And if the small town of Tam Ky changed for the better of for the worse after Gun Fighter Hill fell for the last time, Already that was so long ago... but still I wonder.

The following days prove to be the busiest since arriving in Nam. Word is that the LP9 Transport that will take us back stateside already arrived, docked securely in *Qui Nhon* harbor. This adds a new element of anticipation-- proof that we are really going home. However, unknown to any of us at the time, something unthinkable has already happened. An incident involving a USS Battleship, also moored in the harbor for needed repairs, armed with twelve lethal anti-personal nuclear projectiles. Two of these missiles are missing. It is my understanding that these controversial weapons exists as a defensive deterrent only, and considered a subject highly political. On record, therefore, they do not exist at all, and never did exist. How Charlie accomplished this act of espionage remains anyone's guess. We are-- after all-- playing in his backyard, the rules of the game his own.

Then one morning cinders of despair rain from the sky, dropped by a low-flying non-military airplane. The flyers read as follow:

*"Within 48 hours The Army of the Republic of Viet*nam (spelled according to the original designated name given to it by the Qing Emperor before invasion of foreign lands during the last imperial Dynasty that eventually becomes the present Republic of Communist China). *"In days to come the new Republic will launch two of your own nuclear devices completely destroying your position. Those who retreat now, go in peace, or else be consumed in a fire more intense than your rain of Napalms."*

Even *Hanoi Hanna* takes to the air spreading word, likening our position to that of *Hiroshima* and *Nagasaki*, laced with graphic adjectives and adverbs describing the worse kind of death. With the sincerity of a pleading mother, she urges us to heed these benevolent warnings from above and escape before it too late.

Of all the ways to die I might have considered, this by far the worse. But what if I should survive? I imaginethe script of every horror film I have ever seen. Men made monsters condemned to roam the shadows of the earth terrifying to all that inhabit the light. Even monsters have their tales of redemption. Years later, I will attend an evangelical event in Long Beach, California, and hear the personal testimony of a young man my age caught in hot phosphorous blast of anincineration grenade. He survives as a monster with human eyes, only to lose his wife, his family, and his friends. Nevertheless, by the grace of God, this man finds hope and peace through salvation. I remember thinking how this earth-bound visage could have been me had things happened differently.

Command loses no time. A detachment of armed military police posted at every gate; all souls accounted for by Company row call. Regular activities suspended until further notice. Summoned to the LZ, we wait for the Colonel to appear wearing his neatly pressed jungle camouflages, the bright silver bird of his rank stamped defiantly to the crown of his hat. The man has balls.

"Damn these Zipper-heads! They think we are a bunch of pussies— but by God we will show these Gook bastards that we are Marines— Devil Dogs! Don't you men worry-- Recon is on their asses like flies on deadmeat."

He pauses to clear his throat, eyeing each man like a vulture preparing to dine. This is when the Major of my recent encounter pipes in with a timid suggestion.

"Sir, maybe we should relocate all vehicles and key personnel to *Qui Nhon* until the crisis passes."

It is clear that he does not wish to gamble on the cat and mouse stealth of Reconnaissance. Like most of us, he just wants to get back home. We are leaving anyway, what difference might a few weeks make? Let Charlie burn the shit out of this rat-infested hill! It is just another piece of abandoned real estate once we evacuate.

"Major-- who in hell made your sorry chicken ass God? Marines do not abandon a position! You men will dig perimeter foxholes ten feet apart, and five feet deep. You will sleep, eat, and shit in those holes, until ordered differently-- dismissed!"

We are now clearly all prisoners to the moment. Without recourse, we do the only thing we can do. We dig the graves of our foxholes. That Major disappears after this public embarrassment by his superior. Probably, he finds a deep hole to his liking, making the decision to stay there until the shit settles or the Colonel dead. It is more likely that he has already prepared special arrangements for himself. Who can blame the selfish bastard? Nothing about this war makes much sense anymore.

The type of projectile in question is, in appearance, as any conventional small rocket, deployable from a stationary or mobile launcher, except that it contains a nuclear isotope less than the size of a pea with a fusion detonator. It has a lethal dispersion radius of more than 500 meters of incinerating nuclear reaction, and a fallout factor of more than threetimes this distance. It is minute compared to modern nuclear payloads with multiple warheads, each with enough fusion material capable of devastating several major metropolises. Nevertheless, nuclear is nuclear; Hill 34 the designated target.

In accordance with American Folklore, there is no greater honor given, than to those whose lives lost fighting for a noble cause. Since the battle of Chapultepec, when NCO's and Officers fought side by side to the last man, to remembering Calls at the Alamo, Custard's last stand, and the massacre here on Hill 34-- no call to honor rings out more proudly through the hallowed halls of history than these. However, personally I have little desire to join them this day or any day. We are on the threshold of going home-- what doa few less days make. This time I fundamentally agree with the Major. Why not just pack-up early and go? Perhaps, this sentiment represents the core reason we could not win the Vietnam conflict. The enemy, on the other hand, possessed with the willingness to send hundreds of unarmed men, women, and children in wave after wave, just to detonate the claymores and die in the coils of barbed wire so that regular soldiers might cross over their sacrificed bodies. I have heard horror stories— stories that continue to give me nightmares-- stories of American military outpost over-run by such a human wave assault. Perhaps their demons are greater-- or perhaps their willingness to die greater than their demons. Perhaps, because we are from another land armed with superior weaponry that we are unable to comprehend the desperate measures of a society with a history spanning dynasties; a population subject to gods many; divided principalities of warring spirits seated in high places. That lurking beneath the enchanted oriental veneer of this place reflects face of resolute determination to secure dominance over their own dominion, a reflection similar to our own revolutionary history, except for root ideological differences. Nevertheless, this is not our land; nor is it our history. We have little comprehension of what it means to be part of this distant mythical hemisphere. The roots of these mountains resting on a separate plate of tectonic movement; these rivers spawned from another source, representative of a linage older than the Roman Empire. We imagine ourselves liberators, but perceived by many as conquering invaders from an alien culture. What chance do we have against thebrainwash of hundreds of generations… and is it possible, we could have been wrong all along?

After this morning briefing, I find a spot on the perimeter nearest my warehouse and begin digging a hole six feet long, three feet wide, and five feet deep. I take with me the worn cover of a Holy Bible. I believe it once belonged to Neider. I must confess that I had never read the bible. I remember hearing about it through Grandmother Bessie, or in passing from a Jehovah Witness named Mrs. Stokes, who drops in to see mother from time to time, often leaving behind stacks of Watchtower literature mostly describing the Apocalyptic end of time. Mrs. Stokes, herself a stoic presence, never smiles; rarely speaks about anything beyond herreligious convictions; and always leaves Jean sad and doubtful. After one such meeting, Jean decides that Christmas a pagan tradition and that we will no longer celebrate it as a family. Of course, in retrospect, I agree with her reasoning. However, we were all pagan then, only did not realizejust how much. One Christmas we go without a tree or wrapped gifts, our collective reactions less than favorable. Here I am faced with the eminence of a real holocaust. If there is any meaning written in this book to save me, I wish desperately to find it now.

I spend an entire day and well past dark reading the book of Genesis and part of Exodus. However, I become hopelessly entangled by the laws of Moses. I keep seeing in my mind, an austere portrait of this patriarch holding the tablets of the Ten Commandments, as painted by Rudy during the early years of his marriage. Finally, in a fit of frustration, I fling the cryptic book far from me, and into the surrounding darkness.

"There is no God of salvation!" I proclaim angrily, and shake my fist at the appearing stars. "It's a lie— all of it just lies!"

What little faith I have, dies this night. I feel even greater emptiness than ever felt before; hopelessly lost and on the brink of eternal damnation-- the emptiness profound. It is one thing to consider the inevitability of death, another to contemplate total oblivion-- or worse! I remember the promise of Grandmother Betsy warning often of *"the consuming flames of fiery judgment to come!"* On the other hand, if there is no God, then there is no judgment. Then what more is there to fear or to hope for? This revelation marks the first day and the first night of my eternal damnation.

By early morning, tropical heat weighs down, forcing into the narrow crevice of my dug foxhole as a winepress, squeezing my mind of the little remaining sanity. Using my poncho blanket, I erect a makeshift canopy to shelter from the boiling sun. By mid-day, I begin to hallucinate, imagining the glint of a falling projectile, certain that I hear the whining sound of a rocket engine. I wait tensely for the explosion, but no explosion comes. I think I am not alone in this perception, seeing other men in the distance rising from their positions, their heads as emerging prairie dogs, looking about in anxious anticipation. I do not remember a more hellish day since arriving in Nam. Although the canopy protection from direct exposure to the sun, it only intensifies the heat and humidity. Even the mosquitoes refuse to venture more than a few inches above the black bottom of the pit, making them easy to kill— but you can never kill them all! I am a condemned man-- barely a man-- but condemned all the same. I feel worms in my stomach, eating me slowly from the inside.

"Maybe mom right after all--" I say to myself-- "maybe I am being consumed by the hunger of a Tape Worm!"

I neither eat, nor do I really sleep. Time becomes a physical presence unbearable, an invisible parasite draining my living soul of vital essence. I can see the crumpled Bible a few meters away, where still it lays as reminder of things lost in a past only vaguely remembered-- but no salvation there! Pride and anger prevent me from crawling out to retrieve it. I want to cry— to scream my indignity-- to curse a God I have never known. Now I am just an animal made to die! Only now constrained to another acceptance-- another kind of death—an impending death of the soul! Not only am I dead; all of Hill 34 now a camp condemned.

The Colonel remains hidden in his command bunker, along with a couple of higher-ranking officers, a fueled helicopter ready for immediate takeoff centered on the LZ. At least there is a chance someone might live to tell the tale. I begin to think about all the things I wanted to do in life, and all the things I will never do. I think about Rudy and Jean; about their sometimes peaceful existence on the Blue Ridge foothills. I think about my little brother and two sisters; and how I had taken them all for granted; and the complicity I might have continued to share with them. All those potential moments of life lost in confusion of a past nevermore!

In truth, I no longer even remember how or why I have ended-up here, or the original source of my discontent. In a daydream, I imagine I can see those blue hills off in the distance, an opal mist crawling up the slopes, slipping over the crest into a heavenly stream of a guardian moon. I wish to vanish with the vision, to become light as air and escape the purgatory of this tortuous waiting.

Waiting is the worse! The slow pulse of the universe approaching inevitably, as all of creation waits and waits in expectation of the unknown. It is night. I can tell because of the moistness that seeps from the depths of the earth cool on my back. I do not remember falling asleep, only now I lay at the bottom of this self-dug trench, a corpse in the grave acutely aware. Then I am somewhere else, somewhere in the past, somewhere in this moment just as real.

An inland bay rolls darkly below, like thick motor oil, reflecting sharply shards of broken light. I stand at the edge of an onyx precipice, surrounded by a host of planets and stars in some strange and distant galaxy. It is a place darkly beautiful just as it was then-- and what came before, only vaguely recalled. I have stepped through a portal in time and space: once again in the nod of my heroin trip. How can I be here? I know it must be a dream; but at least it is in this moment a pleasant escape. So I continue to linger just a little longer.

She appears beside me a queen beautiful in this realm of eternal night, a fluttering wraith etched in the shimmer of a full moon. Adorned in black chiffon, she is as the reflection of a lovely moth transformed.

I might only describe her as being familiar, the femme fatale of mydreams. She represents the source of my being; and it is through her I find strength of will, a creative purpose in the world of men. She is the sensual in my soul, that part of me transcending time, elevated above the animal groaning of my generation. Softly, she leans forward, her vermillion lips inviting me to passion. Then in an instance she changes.

Sharp fangs pierce deep into my neck, an insatiable hunger never satisfied. I struggle desperately to awaken from this nightmare. I am back in my foxhole— or so I think! The stench of death and decay continues to press into my nostrils, the walls seeping black blood. In the distance a wailing of human misery spanning every generation since the world first began. The thing still clings to my neck, a large bat-creature with red demon eyes, flopping sickeningly against the moist walls and putrid bottom. I try to scream, but no sound; my body petrified. In state of half-life consciousness, my mind of reason struggles against this demon spawned from terrifying dream! My heart races against the fury of battle drums in a jungle night. I feel as Faustus lost inside the gates of Hell-- trapped in a place of darkness at the edge of eternity from which there is no escape to the souls of men!

Now fully awake in a nightmare, I struggle to my feet. It is early morning, the stars fading into twilight, a sullen glow spreading disarmingly over the jungle. I will not sleep again, not this morning-- not ever again the same. This awful dream-- if it was truly just a dream-- continues to linger, as constant reminder of a dark realm that exists on the fringe of this worldcomprehended through light and shadow.

An hour after sunrise, a siren sounds shrilly. At first, we do not comprehend the meaning-- thinking perhaps the rockets inbound-- this the last audible cry of our humanity! Several minutes pass, and nothing. Then Gunny and the Captain appear, calmly approaching my position.

"Recon did it," Gunny pronounces with enthusiasm. "By God it was close— but they killed every one of those Sons-of-Bitches!"

The Captain orders a roundup of the men and for supply personnel report immediately to the warehouse. It is pointless to ask if any need a bath and a shave. After more than 48 hours in a fox hole, we all do; only daily rations remain short, until the water towers replenished and retreated with iodine. At 1300 hours, the Colonel calls all squads to the LZ. He gloats, as expected, praises the Recons as true Bull Dogs. He even makes special mention to our bravery, saying that it reflects the highest discipline of the Marine Corps. In truth we are just glad to be alive. One crisis has past, another more deadly still to come, as we prepare for another day in-country.

Chapter 19
Wind Called Mariah

*O*ur confidence bolstered after the recent victory, there seems nothing that might impede our scheduled departure. In the eyes of my men, I am now without question their Sergeant. Even Watson follows my every order precisely and without hesitation. There is more to being a United States Marine Corps Sergeant than discipline and respect only. There are times I must be a consoling mother, like the time Cong's girlfriend sent him a 'Dear John', shattering his force of will. After this letter, he sits in a corner alone and listens repeatedly to the lyrics of a song by The Doors. Finally, after weeks of seeing him like this, I know I must do something.

"We're all going home soon, Cong. You've survived hell, and that hell is in you now. When you get back, you will track down Jody, and get your girl back. Remember one of our Marine Corps marching songs:

Jody, Jody six feet four,

Jody never had his ass kicked before!

I'm gon'na take a three-day pass,

And really slap a beating on Jody's ass!"

I reach over and turn-off his tape machine.

"I need you here, Cong—I need you now. Jody will get his when your bad ass gets home."

Jody, a fictitious character, is the supreme nemesis of every Marine, and perhaps of every soldier in all the armed forces. He is the one who steals the wives and girlfriends of soldiers in training or while off fighting on foreign soils. He is the one that marches for peace with the women of our land, while the ground soldier engages communist forces in fierce battle. In short, Jody is anyone not military-- or at least even ex-military. He is the one that will pay for all our disillusioned dreams upon our return from hell.

I am already sounding like a true Marine Corps Sergeant. In the moment, there is uncertainty how this mountain of a man might react to my brash pep talk. As I have already said, Cong, the largest and strongest man under my command, with East European Baltic features reminiscent of descriptions ascribed to ancient Scythian warriors, matched by a primal emotional presence. He may just as easily have eaten me as an unfulfilling snack and spat-out the bones. Instead, the glimmer of an evil smile sparkles within his deep eyes, barely glimmering pools tucked beneatha matted hairy brow.

"You're right, Sergeant. I will find the son-of-a-bitch and make him pay!"

I did not wish to be Jody when this Sasquatch from the jungles of Nam arrives home. I always wonder if there might have been a better way to nurture this man's present pain. Nevertheless, Cong will continue to fight and survive, which is more than I can say for Ruppert and Timbrink. Not even a Gunnery Sergeant able to thwart their destinies. They are, after all, latecomers to the fold, and never can all be saved.

'Friendly Fire' is the most shamefully concealed incident in any military. It happens more often than anyone dares admit. An incorrect compass bearing a mistaken position-- friendly forces find themselves under a drop zone or in a firefight with each other. Sometimes, the event ends without casualty, sometime with tragic consequence. These mistakes often kept internal, rarely reaching the awareness of those back home. Then, there are errors of incompetence just as deadly.

Everyone is supposed to have a certain level of proficiency in their perspective MOS training. Lives are always at stake. We all have a job to do: Supply, Motor Transport, even the Mess Hall. Rarely anyone stops to consider the consequence if supply requisitions wrongly filled or the potential loss by the improper maintenance of combat vehicles. As long as the machine functions, then why should anyone question the mechanics? But something tragic happens, a terrible oversight by oneof our most trusted souls, costing many lives, and many more on the brink that nearly die.

We are a few short days from stateside redeployment, only we forget where we are, and that the serpent, a chameleon ready to strike when least expected. Several hours before evening chow, the monster Huey arrives, sent from a position further south, transporting cases of fresh frozen T-bones and vats of live lobster. This gift compliments of Second Battalion Command to give us all a sort of last supper commemorating this final week before our big departure. I have never eaten a lobster. My first impression is that it resembles a large red bug. Nevertheless, I am willing to try anything at least once. To my surprise, I like it, consuming several of the crustaceans. This will indeed be a culinary experience worth remembering. By 1900 hours, I feel an overwhelming tiredness and decide to turn-in for the night. I try to read, but experience a headache and difficulty to focus.

I dream I am falling uncontrollably into darkness. My eyes pop open, a strange crackling sound, the sensation of hot pokers searing my brain, I awake vomiting and shitting uncontrollably. Somehow managing to roll from my cot to the floor, I begin dragging myself to the wooden stairs. I try to rise, but too weak, and tumble down the steps to the bottom. After some moments, I manage to rise to my feet and stagger to the door. Without remembering how I got there I am outside. Pellets of rain have begun falling, striking my parched head like blows of a hammer. Lighting splits the heavens, gutting the belly of low black clouds. The tropical storm empties ferociously, a deluge that promises to drown the earth of all mortal uncleanness.

My immediate desire is to make it to the latrine, oblivious to the possibility I am dying and that my body fighting the effects of a deadly poison. A sudden tightness in my chest, my arms and legs heavy as led-- I collapse, vomiting green bile, paralyzed facedown into a puddle of rising water. I manage to turn my head just enough so my mouth and nose not submerged-- just enough to breath-- but not more than this. Flashes overhead reflect in the shallow puddle igniting the water into gold, changing to amber, and then to dark red. The water continues to rise around my lips ever so slowly, every breath painfully difficult.

I remain like this until morning, acutely aware of the surrounding dusk, as the storm retreats into the distance. By now, my breathing begins to come more easily. Somehow the animal of my being finds strength to roll over. The sun has just peaked over the horizon, the morning sky streaked with the magnificent arch of a bright rainbow; the hissing in my head finally beginning to subside. I lay like this for minutes or for hours—no longer does time have meaning. Finally able to stand, I make it to the latrine, but what I need most is a cold shower. At least I am one of the lucky ones still among the living.

Bush is med-e-vac out, along with many others. More than twenty souls died in total. The Mess Sergeant-- demoted and later Court Marshaled-- cries inconsolable over the carnage. I personally do not condemn him now. Not because he is guiltless-- but who really is innocent? He made a mistake, one that cost lives. As the Sergeant in charge, it is his responsibility to ensure all the bugs alive before being cooked. He should have trained his men better-- been more diligent to his position. However, no man judges him worse than he judges himself. Maybe it not altogether this man's fault. Those last days mark the beginning of the end of this war, and the end of American values, as we understood them then. The drug culture of the hippie generation has subtly infected all our minds, supplanting the idea that getting 'high' more important than duty; and spawning the idea that rebellion more important than tradition, than family, or friends. We are already a nation divided-- a nation that will value pleasure and material excess more than the integral actions of individuals. We are the last sons of perdition standing upon the threshold of the American Empire's imminent decline-- only we think ourselves crusading heroes.

A more somber presence prevails after this incident. I think often of Neider, as he counted-off his last day. I remember how happy he was that last morning when he climbed a jeep promising to transport him to a freedom bird. Will any of us really leave this purgatory alive? But finally we do leave.

On the first day of June 1971, a large convoy of trucks files through the main gate. By evening not even a tent pin left on Hill 34, not even a scrap for Charlie to munch on-- our evacuation complete. I look back one last time with some regret as we depart through the final checkpoint in a jeep shared by three other NCOs many years my senior. Instinctively, I know this day marks the end of an important era in my life. Never will I see things the same after this; never will I be the same again. Soon, all my experiences in this place called Vietnam will recede into distant memories, some rich and darkly beautiful, some better forgotten. My Vietnam, a geographical location of latitude and longitude pinned on a world atlas; yet remains more than just a place, more than just a history. The Vietnam I knew exists always in my mind and my soul, a place where I abandoned my innocence in a region of spiritual darkness. Some part of me lost; some part found. A part I think sometimes better resigned always to shadows of the past.

The LPD 10 sent to take us home dominates the improvised docks, a wooden lattice constructed of old and new, rebuilt by the Corps of Engineers to accommodate larger American military ships. It seems nothing they cannot accomplish. This transport naval vessel, painted a familiar light grey above the waterline and a darker grey below, is a towering goliath that dominates the small harbor. It is designed for one purpose only. The entire stern of the ship is a massive door a quarter the size of a football field that lowers to become a loading ramp, overlaying evenly with the specially reconstructed pier. A gaping grand cavern extends into blackness, an open belly of metal ribs with upper and lower decks supporting the integrity of this massive camel designed to cross the open sea fully loaded with an entire military compliment. Positioned a few meters behind the bow looms the dominant command bridge, a three-story grey building arrayed with sophisticated communication equipment: antennae's, radar, and sonar. The two upper decks strictly off limits to all except to the ship's officers with MPs posted at all the gangways. Heavy crane winches sprout idly from the aft portion like Flintstone dinosaurs ready to begin work.

I can barely contain my excited enthusiasm, as I stand in line along the gangplank, register my name, rank, along with my serial number, and receive a vanilla-colored envelope containing new orders. This steel goliath will be my new home for the next several weeks. The icy air-conditioned ship interior below deck provides instant relief, reminiscent of a luxury hotel lobby. However, the comparison ends here. The NCO quarters, a short narrow corridor near the bow with heavy metal doors at each end, remind me of scenes from submarine movies with men huddled in cramped quarters waiting for the next deadly depth charge. Ship life below decks is anything, but spacious. A row of retractable metal-framed bunks, slabs of heavy springs stacked four high like poker cards against one wall, spaced only inches apart when pulled down into a reclined position. By misfortune, my assigned bed is one on the very bottom, not so bad as long as the bunk above me remains open. Then a huge Corporal from Texas arrives from behind and takes occupancy of the one above. I never considered myself claustrophobic, but tight places always conjure up feelings of a dream I had as a child being smothered by those two wrestling giants. The unconscious mind of that child asks: Is this the prophetic fulfillment of that dream? Even though the man twice my weigh, the solid steel springs do not give a fraction. Nevertheless, it is a little disconcerting to imagine patties of human flesh stacked one on top of another, weighing only inches from my nose, and me on the very bottom. I suspect that the condition even worse for this robust Corporal, since he is one in the middle. The breath of this man's shoulders such that I doubt he could sleep in any other position than on his back. By good fortune, this giant finds another place to lodge, which means I can now leave the above bunk in a raised position. Still, something about sleeping in the steel belly of a ship makes me uneasy. I will repose restless the entire trip home, a slumber as one undead, trapped for all eternity in the blackness of a sealed coffin.

Those last days, the harbor of *Qui Nhon* turns a hive of activity, the LPD 10 a sleeping titan suddenly awake. Large stationary cranes jerk angrily to life, moving tirelessly from sunup to sunset. Forklifts buzz around with impressive coordination and skill. I offer my services as a lift operator, but rejected on the premise of dock procedures and protocol. I envy the precise accuracy of those at the controls of these impressive pieces of equipment, the heavy huffing machines ballet dancers agile to their touch, without wasting a single motion.

Docked opposite to the LPD 10 is a French cargo ship named the *La Salle*. The hull painted black, with yellow blotches where the skin has peeled from age and neglect, touched-up with the only available color to protect against further corrosion. Empty of its cargo, the bow rises several feet above the red water line, revealing cankers of bleeding rust seeping painfully through a canker of sea barnacles. Not a living soul above decks to indicate living occupancy; and except for the presence of a faint light inside the bridge, the spectral vessel seems a derelict from ages past. For some unexplained reason, this sagging artifact of the sea holds a certain fascination. I remain on deck after evening chow to watch the strange apparition fade obscurely into twilight in the hope of glimpsing even one soul aboard. As mysteriously, it is gone the next morning; this Dutchman vanished like a fable in my mind: a figment of imagination doomed to wander the open seas, until the end of eternity.

On the last day, we attend a USO show hosted by Bob Hope and entourage of skimpily clothed beautiful dancing Dixieland Chicks. Provided an abundance of beer and pretzels, we revert to howling animals ready to pounce on anything that gets our attention. A security of MPs stationed around the stage rudely shoves back any glassy-eyed spectator that approaches too near, diligent protectors of these taunting females. A brawl breaks out somewhere in the crowd, swiftly subdued by a second squad of MPs stationed in the rear and carrying batons. Ruppert and Timbrink ride on the wave of a mob in an attempt to storm the fixed barricade, only driven back by an impenetrable wall of trained sober Marines on active duty. In a way it is good to see them drunk and happy, free of the demon of their drug addiction.

This glittering show of American entertainment represents our inoculation back into stateside society, the tantalizing promise of how things were, and how they might be again. –But of course this, too, is only a lie.

The physical conflict of South East Asia now ended-- at least now ended for us. We feel it in every fiber of our beings. A natural element of uncertainty lingers still, inconspicuous, as a Monson night, when Charlie moves through shadows of a waking dream. Then one moonless evening the LPD 10 slips quietly unannounced out of Qui Nhon Harbor and into the open China Sea. The dark shore vanishes in the murky horizon a lost land already forgotten, a place, that in some odd way, I will miss for the rest of my life. We are returning warriors from a war of glorious defeat; only unaware of this in the moment. Our collective patriotism blinding us to the fact that America engaged in an unpopular conflict costing many lives on both sides, dividing loyalties, dividing families, and dividing politics. We think ourselves heroes of our fatherland, never once considering the shame of our orderly retreat. Too young at the time to know any difference; and even if I had, I think still I would have done things the same. Honor is preserved in the righteous heart of present challenge, not in the collective revision of history formulated through intellectual retrospect. The only thing known with any certainty is that I was there; my conscience clear. I survived, or at least some part of me has survived; and Second Battalion of First Marine Division returns to American soil intact.

Morning on the China Sea is a phenomenon of indescribable wonder. A grand golden dragon rises out of a purple horizon; wings spread magnificently, a spectacular beginning to a new day. I find those early days on the open ocean disconcerting in the beginning, to awaken with nothing to do, no accountability, no one to account to me. Navy chow, although superior to C-rations, little compares to the generous portions of Marine Corps chow. Most of the day, resident seagulls swarm around the ship, screaming belligerently above the constant rush of the warm Asian wind. We Marines linger idly in the sun on the promenade deck just rear of the bridge, while the sailors zealously perform their assigned duties. It surprises me how much effort required to maintain

a military vessel. Rudy served in the Navy for four years, telling stories on summer nights under the stars about people he knew and exotic adventures in foreign lands. I remember only vaguely the parts about scrubbing decks with brushes on hands and knees, or dangling over the side on roped planks to scrape barnacles and apply fresh paint.

The middle of an ocean landscape is a barren wasteland, nothing but empty sky and the constant pressure of a stiff breeze. The open expanse of water as a magnificent emerald cloth stretched from horizon to horizon. Escorted on occasion by herds of passing dolphins in pursuit of schools of flying fish floating beneath the safety net extending over starboard and port side, the LPD 10 makes steady headway loaded with an entire war Battalion. After a while, it starts to get to you, as the mind reaches into the grand depths below, dredging up secrets of lost and forgotten empires. Mounds of glittering treasure spilling along desolate mountain peaks higher than Mount Everest, and into subterranean valleys: sought wealth of lost kingdoms just lying on the floor of this grand promenade waiting to be scooped-up. If only one knew where to look.

On the open deck I feel one with the Pelican that glides astern in a sweet spot waiting for the next dump of our garbage; and later akin to the aerodynamically agile Albatross that takes up the position after the Pelican gone. Here I meet a Corporal from Admin named Fitzgerald. He reminds me a little of Neider, a bit of a nerd, quiet, with an unassuming intelligence. I like him immediately. It turns out that he also likes playing chess; only we are unable to locate a chessboard. Fitzgerald, a make-believe cowboy from Montana, is a dare devil at heart, whose fantasy to one-day ride bulls in a rodeo.

"Why would you want to do something like that?" I ask in amazement.

I have my own young macho dreams, but riding a 2000 pound angry bull not one of them-- maybe a horse-- but a bull! I imagine trying to lasso grandfather Hamby's old Billy Boy. No, this is not something I could ever see to do.

"It's like Daniel in the lion's den," he replies looking out into the zenith. "You look into those animal eyes, and you just know there's no turning back, and no force on earth that can save you if things go bad. It is just you, the bull...and God."

"Did you ever actually ride a bull?"

"No," he confesses; "but I have seen in their eyes. My father took us to the rodeo every time it came to town. He was a district manager for a national food chain, sent to Montana from Buffalo-- but he always wanted to be a cowboy! I'm going to do what he always wanted to do, but couldn't."

Honestly, Fitzgerald just does not look like a cowboy, and I find it difficult to imagine him riding the muscled back of an enraged bull, tossed violently like a rag-doll with one hand free, the other hanging desperately to a rope strap choked around the creature's thick neck. Nor does he look like a Marine with four years of service, a returning veteran from the Republic of Vietnam. I guess this another reason whyI like him. Neither of us looks the part.

On the third night out at sea, we watch the musical 'Paint Your Wagon' projected on a large screen erected against the back wall of the upper decks protected from the wind. It is a moonless night, the canopy of stars surrounding us magnificently, as a portal traveling through timeand space. A song in the film *"They Call the Wind Mariah"* written by Alan Lerner evokes a spontaneous reaction, and we all begin to sing orhum the lyrics, particularly at a certain place that goes:

They call the wind Mariah.
Out here they have a name
For rain wind and fire only
When you're lost and all alone
There ain't no name for lonely
I'm a lost and lonely man
Without a star to guide me
Mariah, blow my love to me,
I need my gal beside me
Mariah, Mariah

As though the host stars sympathetic to our collective nostalgia of home, these astral guardians begin to weep meteors, confetti of lights streaking through the night sky overhead. This altogether infuses us with exhilaration, lyrics of jubilation born into the vastness of an extraordinary universe of unification. This moment in time always remembered and easily forgotten. Inspired with emotion, I think of my lost childhood, asking these heavenly bodies for guidance back to a simpler time. This night I sleep more peaceful than recalled since a long time and dream of a *Wind Called Mariah.*

The next morning, I awaken to a peculiar quiet. Absent, too, the familiar vibration of the engine turbines. Particularly odd, the realization not another soul stirs within hearing. Have I slept so deeply, so long? I feel like Rip Van Winkle rising from a hundred year slumber, not knowing what to expect. Quickly dressing, I stagger along the metal staircase, four flights up to the common deck. My fellow Marines stand crowded against the railing in silent awe; their faces as young boys looking through the display window of a toy store. A stunning city sparkles at the base of a mountain. Chinese Junks, private yachts, taxi passenger boats litter a busy metropolitan harbor.

"Hong Kong," I hear someone whisper.

This grand city of dream and adventure spreads before us as an

Emperor's promise. Shangri-La left far behind, we now pass through the ark of a great middle kingdom. Words can only weakly express the astonishment of this first glimpse into the dragon's golden eye. Hong Kong, the great gateway into the true Far East, a pearl desired by two empires, the contract of a century's lease soon to run out. However, it is still a British colony now, custom-made to every young man's dream, a place of strange customs and of abandoned romances. Hong Kong, a worldly principality nestled at the feet of patient overlords, a possession of sand sifting through the fingers of all who try to grasp it. Bright in the morning sun, this city of Oz beckons to my young imagination with anticipation. A passenger jet slices overhead through a silver stream of smog and veers sharply toward the mountain. Discovery of this new land has just begun.

Signs from the East

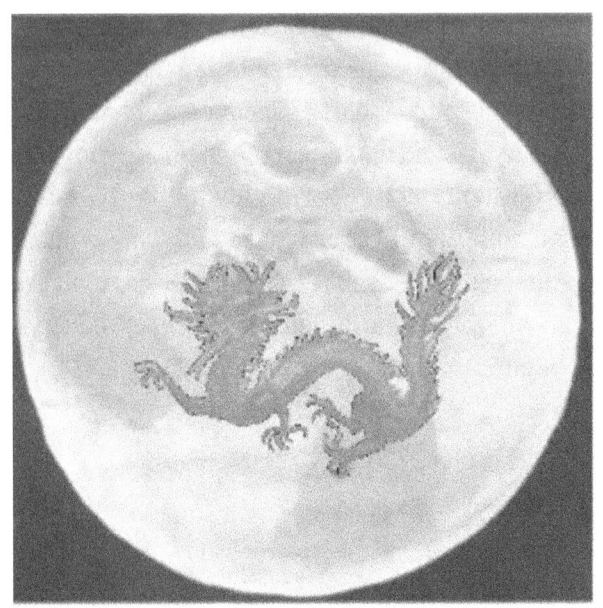

China Eyes

Her eyes his mother's eyes
Painted on a China doll
Before the world changed
Before the sun and the moon divided
On a tapestry of silver and of gold
Before an onyx pool filled the center
Of the room where once she loved
A place of solitude and belonging

The silent hours into eternity
All that remains slipping away
Into dark corners of past memories
When the son of war but an infant
Swaddled in the sleek oriental wood
Creviced in the embrace of ebony arms

Her eyes into his eyes
Through rich Eden of her thoughts
His shadow crouched in a garden
Touching the shadow of her soul
Until all the world changed to shadow
And all shadows to light

Her eyes the eyes of a doll
His mother's eyes deep and nurturing
Reflected far away to a place invisible
Where he is still a child
Watching secretly the tears flow
From her painted eyes
Eclipsed in a moon long ago

Chapter 20

Hong Kong Queen of the Orient

$\mathcal{T}$he LPD 10 drops anchor mid-harbor approximately two hundred yards from shore. Ninety-six-hour passes issued to everyone — everyone, of course, except on-duty sailors and the military detachment of MPs. Like policemen everywhere, these guys never seem to have fun.

At 0900, we receive a disbursement of several hundred dollars in U.S. greenbacks from accumulated back pay. During our tour of duty, each man receives an extra allotment every month of nearly one hundred dollars extra for combat pay. This stretches far to buy cigarettes, toiletries, and goods from the local commissary. Of course, a dedicated entrepreneur might grow that sum to any denomination. For the rest of us, it is the pay of toil and sometimes blood. Nevertheless, at the end of a year, time and grade, this combat pay grows into a rather hefty bankroll, amounting to a hefty wad of cash for a few extravagant days of real R & R.

Several small boats lowered alongside designated to transport us to and from the ship. At the bottom of the gangplank stands two armed guards and another two seated in each boat, one at the bow, the other aft. We receive instruction to salute upon disembarkation. There is little formality upon our return, considering most of us passed out or so pissed to care about Navy protocol.

Fitzgerald and I have become good friends by now. We giggle like schoolchildren, as the small craft bounces over the shallow waves and drops us off at the feet of Marco Polo's China. We have each exchange a few hundred dollars for a large chunk of predominately red-colored Hong Kong hundred dollar bills at a rate of five to one. Only in Hong Kong is a dollar a true dollar. I do not say this felicitously.

As early as 1842, Hong Kong has represented a major commercial trading port, ceded to English rule after the First Opium War that resulted in the Treaty of Nanking, and later the Kowloon Peninsula, after the Second Opium War in 1860. All foreign and domestic currencies converted to sterling weight controlled by foreign exchange banks to provide a balanced taxable commerce. It is during the Japanese invasion of World War II, the military Yen becomes the only legal tender at an exchange rate of 100 yen to the dollar. However, in 1945, the restored Hong Kong government, backed by British support, declares all yen notes void. The Mint on Sugar Street begins printing bills of the new currency backed against the stronger U.S. dollar exchange rate. Hong Kong dollars, therefore, stay in Hong Kong-- or at the least in China.Even as far back as 1868, the Japanese government owner of the HongKong mint on Sugar Street, and silver trade dollars declared the new currency from the USA, Great Britain, and Japan. Then in 1898, theSino-British Joint Declaration, negotiated between the UK and Guangxu, the then Emperor of China, leases Hong Kong to Great

Britain for a period of 99 years-- a devil's promise that by 1970 already nearing the end-- all printing operations now moved to the offices of Hong Kong Note Printing Unlimited. All this history aside, I find myself a military man on shore-leave with a bulging chunk of the local currency in my pocket, making me a Kingpin of the world!

The first thing Fitzgerald and I do is to have lunch at the Hong Kong Hyatt Regent Hotel. I order a hamburger, complete with lettuce, onion and tomatoes, fries, and a Coke. Fitzgerald chooses something a little more cultured to the setting accompanied by an American brand beer. My plate arrives first. I take a bite, and immediately realize there is no mustard.

"Mustard, please," I say to the oriental waiter.

At first, he does not seem to understand my request; then his face brightens. He rushes away and returns moments later with a small tub filled with something pale yellow. Although not the bright yellow condiment I know, it will do. I might add here that I have always liked mustard on my hamburgers, more than ketchup or mayonnaise. The waiter continues to eye me politely, as I spread several spoons on my bun. With flavored anticipation, I open my mouth wide and bite again into my long awaited sandwich. My eyes begin to water, a suffocating burning rush coursing through my nasal passage and into my head.

"Those are the hottest onions I ever tasted,' I say out loud, my next bite no less tolerable than the first. "I think there is too much pepper."

"No pepper," the waiter replies innocently. "You no like Chinese mustard?"

He then bows, smiles obsequiously, and leaves. By now, Fitzgerald's order has arrived. We sit across from each other and eat our meals in silence. Upon completion of my burger, I heave a deep breath in nauseous relief. My companion begins to smile and then breaks-out in full laughter.

"I can't believe you ate the whole thing!" He laughs embarrassingly loud. "The mustard-- that's what he meant— Chinese mustard is made with horseradish, and you put enough on there to kill a horse."

At first, I do not see the humor. However, after a few moments of reflection, I, too, begin to laugh. I had sat there for 20 minutes, taking bite after bite, without even once considering the cause of my long-anticipated dream   burger's damnation something other than the onions or sprinkle of unseen pepper. We both spontaneously break into loud laughter, so robust that several restaurant employees, including our waiter crowd around us and join-in. The joke on me-- and it feels good to laugh again, even at the expense of my own ignorance.

We next visit a local bar, down more than a few drinks, and then continue our odyssey from one den to another. Hong Kong City is like all large cities, networked by a jumble of congested intersections, towering skyscrapers, and hundreds of shops. As in every metropolis, it also has its alley ways: small meandering lanes littered with discarded waste and faceless ghost haunting the shadows lost to the world of light. As evening settles, we take what we think a shortcut between boulevards, only to find ourselves lost in a twisting maze off the beating path. Several tiers of freshly laundered clothes hang overhead, fluttering in a breeze, colorful flags of urban poverty. Also discovered here, the oasis of an underground bar recognizable by a flashing red neon sign of a dancing Japanese Geisha and guarded by a slobbering patron nearly passed-out beside the entrance. Judging by his appearance, this unfortunate soul European, perhaps German, crumpled as a fresh handkerchief soiled from use.

"This looks like a good place to score!" Fitzgerald says, dragging me into the dimly lit lair.

The interior looks like any bar; smells like any bar. As my vision begins to adjust, I discern the shadows of several patrons slouched against a long obelisk littered with glasses of beer and exotic drinks attended by two observant bartenders. In dark corners shadows congregate around small tables, men and women speaking in low mumbled tones in a language altogether alien.

"I don't think I like it here," I whisper.

Fitzgerald only nudges me toward a table where three women sit like china dolls with large beautiful eyes. Instantly, one of the bartenders abandons his post and rushes over smiling ghoulishly.

"American G.I.s sit here– Girls no mind— you sit!" The man insists, pointing to chairs for Fitzgerald and me.

It takes a couple of hard drinks in this new establishment before we find the courage to speak to these exotic creatures. They giggle every time we awkwardly say anything. The girl in the middle possesses a striking presence, very pretty, but too young to be in a bar. One of the older women perceives my interest and changes places with her so that we might sit side by side. She says her name is Ning, a soothing tranquil name, lovely to hear spoken sweetly from her lips. Ning speaks some English, at least enough to negotiate. After consulting with the older woman, who had swapped positions with her, a brassy business arrangement reached, necessitating I pay the matron a hundred Hong Kong dollars. Afterwards, Ning and I depart together to her nearby apartment. Fitzgerald gives me a sly wink at the door, his sights set on one of the other women, who seems spiritedly interested in him buying her drinks. He will later tell me how they end up drinking nearly all night, and the only thing he remembers clearly is waking up in another strange alley completely broke.

In retrospect, I believe Ning even younger than she looks, still a child, not more than sixteen years old. A cute round China-doll face, with eyes slanted like those of a newborn kitten, so innocent that I reluctantly begin to develop thoughts of my younger sisters. My mind rebels against this familiar association, unwilling to accept that I could have sexual desire for a little girl still playing with Barbie Dolls back home. As we meander through the maze of a secret labyrinth, our paths cross a Chinaman selling large inflatable animals. Somehow, I end up buying an orange and yellow rabbit nearly as tall as my escort, which her small arms clutch securely, until we reach a modest apartment she calls home.

Led into a small sparsely decorated room furnished with a properly made single bed, Ning instructs me to lie down, disappears into the toilet. I look around, realizing this not the home of a prostitute. On the dresser is a silver framed picture of man and a woman holding a readily recognizable baby girl. Beside it is a vase of fresh peacock feathers and a mother of pearl handled princess hairbrush. Everything about this room so clean and neatly arranged, my very presence here somehow feels unclean. At this moment, the child-lady comes tiptoeing out of the bathroom wearing only a small white cotton negligee imprinted with lilac-colored flower blossoms, and slips beside me under the covers. After a few moments of hesitation, I clumsily remove my t-shirt and snuggle beside her.

I can feel her small heart beating rapidly, sighs of frightened anticipation in her breathing. She closes her eyes tightly, tears seething between the slits. Something comes over me; something I cannot explain exactly. My desire changes to compassion. I feel in my own body the anguish of this young woman, not yet a woman. I just lay there, holding a child in my arms. I know nothing of the circumstances that lured this adolescent girl to that bar; nor the relationship she has with the older woman. I believe this her first time with a man; and hope it to be her last under this kind of circumstance. All I really know in the moment is this frightened girl in my arms. It is up to me to be stronger than my lust. To do anything else will mean violation to my honor and a dishonor to an innocent.

Early morning light streams through an open curtain. We have fallen asleep in each other's arms, and dreamed I know not. Ning continues to sleep deeply as children do. Quietly rising, I dress, kiss her on the forehead. I then count out the equivalent of twenty dollars U. S. in Hong Kong bills and place it on the dresser beside the photograph of a family like families everywhere.

And still to this day memory of that larger than life orange and yellow rabbit stands beside the doorway of a child's room, a grand guardian spirit to keep away the darkness: a forgotten shade from that night fading into twilight never to return.

The next day, Fitzgerald and I hook-up again. We both a little wiser, a little poorer— but what the hell-- it is only Hong Kong money! We start drinking earlier than usual. At this period of time in my life, beer nothing more than a cold beverage; the real stuff to begin a day is Vodka and Seagram's whiskey. By midafternoon, everything as unreal as it gets-- both of us lost in this strange city at the end of the world. By chance, we stumble into an exotic bar somewhere near the downtown core. We might have left immediately, both of us sensing that we lack the class for such an elegant establishment. This place bares the sophistication only seen in the movies. Richly decorated with polished antiques, renaissance paintings of English country sides, garnished with portraits and sculptures created by hands of masters gathered from many past worldly estates, it is a grand as any English castle. Plush Chinese hand-loomed rugs flow as oriental ponds on the floor, depicting legendary dynasties of greatness, unknown to other residents of the globe. Even the counter glistens brilliantly, a mahogany edifice supported on the back of an intricately carved fire-breathing dragon with Ruby eyes and bright burning brass claws. Stoically positioned behind this imposing barrier is the presence of a well-dressed gentleman, who merely arches his eyebrows. We are just about to leave, when another man appears behind us adorned in a fine silk suit accentuated with a black bow tie.

"Welcome," he says stoically; "may I seat you?"

Dumbfounded, we merely nod our heads. Once behind the safe

confines of an ornate table, we feel less obtuse-- not that we now belong-- but less conspicuous. The exquisite surface of our table so meticulously polished that I can actually see my reflection in the dark wood. I think to myself how much Rudy would appreciate the finery of this workmanship-- how much might Jean wish to possess even one of these wonderful heirlooms to edify her home.

The waiter takes our order and returns moments later with the selected drinks poured into the finest crystal from which I have ever drunk. Even Fitzgerald, whose mother born into an elite family, and therefore familiar with the finer things of life, remains speechless as his eyes devour every detail of these rich surroundings.

Our server remains fixed as we take the first sips of our common beverage choice embellished in uncommon vessels. Once satisfied with our expectations, he clears his throat and discreetly asks:

"Have you gentlemen come for an escort?"

Fitzgerald and I only look at each other. I always thought of an escort as a chaperone guide; the description of one whose purpose to maintain a certain sobriety. Why would I want that? I am on R & R returning from a war zone—it is my right to be wild and uncivilized! Fitzgerald, however, is quick tounderstand the meaning.

"That's exactly what we are here for!" He blurts out, giving me a sly wink.

I know from this wink his wonderful imaginative mind at work, and so I say nothing, only nodding my head. The waiter disappears into a back room, returning several minutes later followed by a parade of exotic ladies. They blend elegantly with the surrounding decor; each uniquely dressed, as one might observe at a fairytale ball. Fitzgerald is immediately entranced, reminding me of a little boy with money to spend, as he surveys the many inviting choices in a candy store. Strangely, as lovely as these women are, none captures my interest enough to spend seven hundred Hong Kong dollars for three days and nights of companion service. Despite Fitzgerald's urgings, I remain resolute, determined to keep my money for other things. My friend has already made his choice, a mature woman dressed in a blue silk dress, who giggles shrilly each time he speaks. Although I find this irritating, she seems right for him.

"Chinese lady no good for you," the waiter says, scratching the side of his smooth-shaven face.

"No, I'm not interested," I reply.

He then excuses himself, goes speaks to the man behind the bar. The two seem briefly to be at odds, but apparently reach an agreement satisfactory to both. The bartender promptly makes a phone call.

"You wait— I have special girl for you," the waiter implores obsequiously upon returning to our table.

I really have no further interest to purchase a chaperone, regardless of the price. I still feel unsettled by my encounter with Ning. Although lovely, oriental women strike me as being too much child-like, fragile, and easy to break like my mother's Japanese dolls received as a gift from my Uncle Junior. Nevertheless, for Fitzgerald's sake I wait and say nothing.

Nearly an hour passes. We are preparing to leave when in walks a young pretty girl with long auburn hair past the shoulders, and large sensual eyes flashing brilliantly in the dim light of the bar. Her front teeth protrude slightly, making her young lips even more interesting, more sensual.

"I am Lin," she introduces herself speaking perfect English, her voice as a mountain brook slipping over the familiar contour of smooth stones.

Like a moth lured senseless into a burning light, I just sit there speechless, altogether mesmerized by the enticing splendor of this fascinating creature from the east. I later learn that in Chinese her name means "beautiful jade", a name accentuated by the unusual piercing dark hazel of her eyes-- a name that continues to haunt me with regret to this day. It turns out that Lin the same age as me, but the similarity ends here.

This particular evening, she is wearing a mini-skirt and a sexy white top that reveals the mature fullness of her breast, an animal in prime that disturbs the animal within me.

"You like girl— yes--" the waiter announces, craftily arching his eye.

He knows from experience that I desire this pearl of pearls at any cost. I gladly pay-- not seven hundred-- but eight hundred Hong Kong dollars for the company of this wonderful presence. Yes, I am truly in

love for the first time in my life, or else infatuated, as never before.

That first night is vague in my mind. We eat in some expensive hotel restaurant chosen by Fitzgerald's companion. My taste buds so deadened by alcohol that what we eat leaves little impression. Rather good or bad, it was expensive. We end up taking a room with two double beds in the same hotel. Lin and I sleep in one bed, Fitzgerald and his lady in the other. I want nothing more than to make love with this most extraordinary woman, only I am too drunk and too shy to try. I will later learn that her father a Frenchman from Paris, who had an affair with Lin's mother while visiting Hong Kong on business. This is the reason for her exotic beauty, a Eurasian mixture of east and west. Such unions are common throughout the commercial history of Hong Kong, creating a blend of Chinese tradition and continental fashion. Lin is an oriental pearl of special acquisition worth any price. A prize I selfishly wish in the moment to always keep.

The next day we go shopping in the downtown core. As a metropolis, Hong Kong is not that much different from any other commerce district in the civilized world. Square honking British-made taxies race aggressively along modern boulevards packed with anxious passengers. Lumbering city buses and a variety of single passenger vehicles compete for the same narrow right of way. Daredevil pedestrians scurry between the idling beasts stalled in traffic as opportunity allows, every man and woman for themselves. Signaling lights seem no more than a formality, mostly ignored by all. Traffic cops wearing white gloves conduct the flow with better precision at the hubs of the more congested intersections. It is nothing like the small-town America where I grew up. I will later observe this same disregard to the rules of the road in other countries as well. Particularly in Spain, Italy, and most especially in Mexico, Islands of the Caribbean, although not the most offensive, are most aggravatingly slow, places where motor vehicles appear out of place within context of architecture and roadways. Hong Kong not like any of these, but is representative of every metropolitan of commerce in the world buzzingwith economic potential.

I am dizzy by the time we arrive at the entrance to a swank Hong Kong clothing store and ushered in by the Doorman dressed in a gold tuxedo. Unsurprisingly, Lin is well acquainted with some of the floor Salesmen and speaks to them authoritatively in Chinese. With sweet professionalism, she introduces me as an American customer ready to invest. Immediately, the parade of penguins begins. Tape measures whip-out from their pockets, as they start measuring me from head to toe. Suit jackets, expensive slacks, and silk shirts appear from all directions. Shown to a changing room, I strip from my Marine Corps dress green uniform, and don the worldly fashions of the early 1970's. Transformed within the hour, I step out a prince wearing a sharkskin grey suit, a black silk shirt, and white tie. I place an order for an additional three suits sent to my home address. However, they never arrive.

Later in the day, I pay anotherfifty Hong Kong dollars to a reputable merchant Lin also knows for an ivory globe containing smaller globes, each carved inside the other, and an additional forty for an ivory bridge with intricate Chinese carvings depicting some ancient history of a dynastical change unknown to me. These relics also lost in the mail, stolen, or else never sent.

Interestingly, the one purchase that will make it back home, not from the counter of any downtown commerce center. The next day we take a cab to the city outskirts north of the main harbor, a small cove not even on the map, a dwelling place of the less fortunate residents of this grand metropolis. Lin and I are alone; and my escort wishes to introduce me to her favorite uncle, a person of meager means, whom she says struggles from day to day in poverty. We arrive at the home of a simple artisan living in a shanty shack supported on weathered wooden stilts far from the modern wharfs. Her relative, as do many others, spends each day carving intricate ivory and exotic wood pieces from raw inventory provided by merchants; and paid mere pennies for many painstaking hours of creative effort. It fascinates me that a simple poor man capable of creating such exquisite artworks of beauty.

The family resemblance is undeniable. Although Lin many years younger, I can see something familiar in the eyes, the same cheekbones, the same jester in the way this man moves his head, even the structure of the hands similar. Except for the difference of age and gender, they are as much alike as any father and daughter. The kind warmth expressed when he looks at his niece makes me realize that this uncle an important part of Lin's life while growing up.

Greeting us with polite warmness, the man insists we sit for a cup of tea, spreading before us a platter of sweet cakes made with fish and rice meal. I hesitate, feeling guilty to take of his meager sustenance. A sharp stare from Lin makes me realize that not to eat would be an insult. After consuming the few offerings, her uncle proudly shows us his latest creation. Sixteen beautifully carved white ivory chess pieces approximately three and a half centimeters in height. Each represents the royal hierarchy of warlords of a dynasty that existed during the ancient writings of Sun Tzu, depicting an emperor and his empress clad in armor, two warrior knights on galloping horses, two stoic bishops, and two slender pinnacled towers. Besides these, eight smaller pawns to complete this faction of opposition.

"They are beautiful," I say, handling one of the masterfully carved pieces.

"You like— I sell you," Lin interprets.

I agree to the purchase without any coaxing from Lin. He promises to complete the remaining sixteen pieces in less than a week and place them in a handcrafted wooden chessboard box. He shows me a sample ivory piece stained a light tealeaf brown to indicate how the remaining sixteen pieces will look. Without further negotiation, I pay cash money of more than two hundred Hong Kong dollars to a man I just met and who probably makes less than this amount over a period of many weeks. In retrospect, it was perhaps a foolish investment. Why trust the integrity of one so poor? Nevertheless, I will learn something of importance through these experiences: the sincere promise of a simple good man worth more than the many guarantees of greedy elite. I give an extra thirty Hong Kong for shipping, scribbling my mother's address on a piece of napkin. A month later, Jean receives in the mail a most extraordinary wooden box inlaid with mother of pearl containing thirty-two delicately carved ivory pieces, each as unique as the imaginative skill of their creator.

The next day our two escorts decide to take Fitzgerald and me to Kowloon. Kowloon, a small town situated on a peninsula opposite side of the harbor, branded officially off limits to all American soldiers, considered a buffer zone between the British leased Hong Kong City and greater China. It shares many of the benefits and commercial luxuries enjoyed by its neighboring island-- except that according to the territorial lease agreement-- Kowloon remains a communist territory. There are no laws explicitly prohibiting us from going; therefore, with youthful fearlessness our ally, we ignore the restrictions, dressing in our newly purchased civilian clothes, pretending that no one might notice our distinct jarhead haircuts.

I find Kowloon City more pleasant and peaceful than the capitalist bedlam on the opposite side of the busy harbor. Narrow walkways meander through village streets lined with neat little shops, a few bars, and several restaurants. A large cultivated recreation park begins at the docks of Victoria Bay, the start of a serpentine walkway winding through sculpted gardens laced around mystic hills and fusing into even greener passages beyond.

The first thing we do upon disembarkation from our water taxi is find a local bar. To the disappointment of Fitzgerald, who comes from a long line of liquor connoisseurs, absent are the customary traditional American spirits his pallet used to. My motto being, *'if it has alcohol and can be swallowed, it cannot be all that bad'*. Here we discover an assortment of Chinese beer, Chinese wines, and several bottles of light and dark liquors behind the bar stamped with name logos altogether alien.

"What the hell," Fitzgerald remarks; "when in Rome drink as do the Romans, or in this case as the Chinese."

Indiscriminately, we begin to experiment the foreign elixirs by their color: some thick and syrupy, much too sweet and with high alcohol content, others enough bitter to make one gag. Lin suggests I try something called *Baijiu*, a clear alcohol distilled from sorghum, or in some regions made from glutinous rice, which tastes a lot like Russian vodka, except milder. So deceptively mild, in fact, that Lin and I down several of these in less than an hour.

Chinese beer has a unique history all its own. Germans were the first to brew beer in China. In 1903, a German-British brewing company established locally to produce German style beer for Westerners. From 1915 to 1945, the Japanese take over the brewery by confiscating the German share and buying out the remaining English shares after World War I. When Japan defeated at the end of the Second World War, the brewery reverts to property of the Chinese Nationalist government. This originally western enterprise nationalized into state-owned when the People's Republic of China usurps dominion, but continues to this day producing the finest beer in China.

We finish our drunken spree by quickly downing a Qingdao beer, with a loud toast from Fitzgerald that *"the Marines have arrived!* Deciding our alcohol saturated bodies need food, Lin directs the group to a quaint, clean restaurant, a Chinese *'mom and pop'* establishment stagnant with tradition. Imagine us drunk and pie-faced and not a fork or spoon in sight.

"You eat Chinese way," Lin instructs sweetly, attempting to train my fingers as to the proper grasp for holding chopsticks. "It is like the first time you eat as baby. First, you hold food, and then you move food to mouth."

Fitzgerald catches on quickly, having eaten at Chinese restaurants as a child. The closest for me growing up is Chow Mein Noodles from a package. Nevertheless, I practice the basics before our food arrives.

It seems Chinese people like eating above every activity. The two major categories are Cantonese from the south and Szechuan from the southwest. Of course, there are other styles less continental such as *Hunan*, *Shandoug*, Zhejiang, *Jiangu*, *Fujian*, and *Anhui*. Because China geographically immense and spread out through so many regions, each with a unique history, one ends with a variety of choice. Cantonese from the South, Cantonese from North, from the East and from the West, with further influence by contamination of bordering customs. This is also true for all the other styles of preparation, each as different as the different provinces, and even down to the denomination of family personal history.

My principal order consists of Spring Roll appetizers, followed by a main course of Cantonese Duck with rice. Lin commands a common plate, the name of which I do not remember. The Spring Rolls appear first. As an indoctrinated American, I am not in the habit of sharing my food. Once something touches the domain of my plate, it is mine, and mine alone, with an unspoken protocol of first come first served. I quickly realize this not the way it works here. The next plate to arrive is a mountain of fried rice laced with colorful vegetables (and God knows what else) placed in the center of the table. Fitzgerald and I only look at each other bewildered. The girls, however, begin immediately picking at the mound and encourage us to do the same. As I awkwardly probe the mélange with the tip of my chopsticks, I realize something still alive and moving like withering worms sprinkled on the surface.

"What the hell!"

Lin delicately captures one of the writhing creatures between her two sticks and brings it toward my mouth.

"Just baby Octopus," she coaxes soothingly. "It is a delicacy, rare to find so fresh. Open-- you taste it is good!"

It continues to move in my mouth, but stops moving when I bite down. Realizing Lin right, the thing is delicious, with a light vinegary taste, tantalizing to the pallet, invigorated with the freshness of the sea. This is one of those preparations, whose origins remain vague. The tentacles of live baby Octopus are skillfully chopped-off, then garnished over the principal plate. Just before serving, a sprinkle of rice vinegar causes the legs to convulse similar to the way fresh frog legs react to the heat of a hot frying pan. Without further encouragement, I wolf down as many of the writhing tentacles I can find, using my trusted fingers as reliable backup to the inefficient chopsticks.

I am a little surprised that my soup arrives before the main course of my Cantonese Duck. Served in a large oval bowl filled with a white tasteless partridge, I find the dish a little bland. However, a little salt makes it palatable. The matronly server eyes me with curious detachment, as though she expects me to do something. Not wishing to offend her, I immediately engage in shoveling down soupspoon after soupspoon of the tasteless mash. I have consumed nearly half of this white glutinous pottage, when Lin reaches into my bowl with her infallible chow sticks and retrieves the half carcass of a small duck.

"That is only to keep duck warm and tender," Lin smiles superiorly and places the cooked fowl on an accompanying plate.

"Yes— but I like the soup, too." I insist unapologetic and continue to eat the rest of the starchy paste.

I might be in China, but I am also an American in China. Besides, by now I have grown accustom to the flavor of this white substance, deciding that with the addition of enough salt and pepper it similar in flavor to my mother's Dumplings eaten as a child. The Waitress politely lowers her head and departs into the kitchen. To this day, I cannot remember the flavor of that duck, but the bowl of mash I will fondly never forget. After lunch, we wander aimlessly around town. We still have six hours left in the company of our paid escorts. Somewhere in the park stands a modern pagoda temple that Lin and her friend both wish to visit.

"I'm not exactly a Buddhist," she explains. "My mother converted to Christianity when I was very young, but it always makes me feel peaceful to visit these shrines. They are a part of my culture— a part of me!"

Inside, it is like churches anywhere in the world. There are pews, lighted candles, and burning incense. Instead of a cross, a Star of David, or symbol of the sun, a giant gilded Buddha sits at the altar with a brilliant sapphire stone between vacant painted blue eyes. Lin reverently lights a scented stick and places it in an ornate vase containing other smoking ovations. I do not say anything. I think the sincere devotion of this young woman touches me in a way I little understand in the moment. My impression of our meeting represents many things in my mind, a haunting that will never completely go away. I recall her body made beautiful in season and how seductively deep her eyes. Even though we share the same chronological age, her experience of human nature far exceeds my own. This lovely girl of Eurasian descent serves as guide through a strange and exotic principality that ultimately expands my vision of the world. Perhaps a spiritual quality as well, something she knows within herself, something that evades my consciousness then. Here in this Buddha Shrine Lin perceives more than artifacts of stone and bronze, this building representing more than an edifice of religious hope to shelter the naked existence of human kind.

You always hear about how many people there are in China; but you never imagine a quiet open space devoted as a place of leisure. This park in Kowloon is one of the largest and loveliest I have ever seen, divided into several gardens and walkways through sprawling Chinese Banyans and Stone Wall trees. Once the site of a British military battery named Whitfield Camp, Kowloon Park now a garden that flourishes with enchanting ancient beauty. Many varieties of birds flutter through tree branches or light on queerly sculpted shrubs, colonies of frogs mounted on large floating lilies even in the daytime; and families of white swans swimming boldly on the dark green surface of a clean unpolluted lake canal more like a river with currents. We collectively decide to rent a rowboat and explore with daring intrepidity. Provided two oars, we receive terse warning not to venture beyond a certain point and to remain on the Kowloon side. In Marine Corps fashion, Fitzgerald and I man positions bow and aft of the small boat, with the two girls seated in the center. It takes us some moments to get a rhythm, but finally effectively combine our collective efforts.

After several minutes following an upstream course, we allow inertia to glide us to the bank on the opposite shore. I perceive a mottled monster with large globular eyes pass under the bow that must be at least four feet long.

"What from hell is that?" Fitzgerald shouts, seeing it also.

"I don't know! Maybe it is something from the ocean-- or maybe even prehistoric!"

"Whatever it is-- looks hungry to me."

We both pull toward the center of the craft, both apprehensive of this monster-size fish, and wonder if these fresh water ways of China hatches a breed of man-eaters unknown to us westerners. Cautiously, my companion begins probing unseen depths with his oar. Lin and the other woman spontaneously break out in loud laughter.

"Chinese gold fish," cries one of the girls.

The two women cover their faces, continuing to giggle. Fitzgerald only looks at me and shrugs his shoulders. Neither of us really know what we will do should it return. I sincerely doubt either of us possessed with desire to catch it. We decide to do a little exploring on this side of the lake. Leaving our lady companions here to watch the boat, we hike to the top of a steep hill to get a better view from this side. Upon reaching the top of the ridge, we see something altogether unexpected.

The opposite side of this hill tapers into a plateau, with a narrow winding road just a few feet away. However, what we observe makes the blood in our veins run cold with fear. Two Chinese Army Military trucks are barreling toward us loaded with armed soldiers. How could they possibly have known? Without hesitation, we race back down the hill, shouting "Get in the boat the Chinese have arrived!"

Upon reaching our craft, we shove it into the river and begin rowing frantically. This moment even our two escorts remain uncharacteristically silent. They sense our tension, sense that we are truly scared. Adrenaline pumping still, we unceremoniously ground the boat on a pebble shore near the place we rented it. Each grab a girl by the hand and start running toward the dock. Without wasting any time, all pile into the first available water taxi. We look at each other and begin laughing, feeling now safe, as thesmall craft struggles against choppy waves headed toward the familiar safe haven of Hong Kong.

In reality, I do not know if it a mere coincidence, our conscience creating a specter of events; or if the Chinese Red Army really after us. Nevertheless, we are both relieved upon reaching the firm ground sanctioned by the protection of western capitalism. I will never forget those few hours spent on the Kowloon peninsula, gateway into the enemy fortress of greater China. In my generation the specter of Communism real, indoctrinated with belief that China an enemy of war, a place that holds harnessed a sleeping fire-breathing dragon.

This is the evening we say goodbye to our escort companions. I wish to say to Lin that I am sorry we met in these circumstances; and that I think more highly of her than just a paid escort. When I look into her large oval glittering eyes, I say nothing at all, nothing that can even begin to speak the longing I feel now. I embrace her instead; the warm perfect fit of her body against mine saying what no words can express.

"Do you like James Bond?" Lin turns and asks as she walks away.

"Do I ever!"

"Sunday, I go with my cousin to see 'You Only Live Twice'. Would you like to go with us?"

I do of course-- and of course, she knows I will. We arrange a meeting place in a square near the movie theatre. The day of the rendezvous, a late afternoon sprinkle blanketed the streets of Hong Kong, adding a slick sheen to my new sharkskin suit. I easily spot the two girls standing at the designated spot, both eating something bought from a street food vendor. Lin's cousin is a pleasant girl about the same age, but shy and more reserved, dressed in a pale green jumpsuit having a chubby round-faced demur one might expect of any traditional Chinese girl. In comparison, Lin a beautiful untamed stallion. She wears a pleated mini-skirt, a matching air force blue dress jacket, studded with silver buttons, and a pale blue chiffon scarf. It is not just what she wears, but how she wears it, making her in my eyes a fashion statement. Yet, there is something innocent and vulnerable about her, which makes me feel a present source of strength she lacks alone.

Lin holds my hand tightly through most of the action scenes, making me feel I am protector of her feminine softness through imagined moments of intimacy portrayed ona larger-than-life screen.

I enjoy the film, except that the vocal recording in Chinese with English subtitles flashed quickly across the screen. It makes me feel like when I was a child pretending to read a book just by looking at the pictures. However, the movie less engaging in the moment, than Lin's sensual presence beside me. After the spy thriller, we go to a restaurant known by Lin's cousin that actually serves American style hamburgers, fries, and real Coke Cola. I later learn that the hamburger meat actually fifty percent composed of something called tofu, which explains the oddness in flavor. In retrospect, it is not the worst I have ever eaten. After this teenage meal imported from Western culture, Lin's cousin turns to me and articulates in English.

"Watch your heart 007. Good Chinese girl not easy to find in Hong Kong."

The two women hug each other goodbye and she disappears into the crowd, leaving Lin and I alone at last. I must admit that although I enjoyed this other girl's company, I am glad to see her go at last, feeling her presence more as a chaperon invited to ensure chastity. In reality, it is I, who interfered with their plans of the day; only I could not see it at the time. At least now I selfishly have Lin all to myself. After her cousin gone, we begin walking aimlessly about, saying very little to one another. Then Lyn takes my hand, smiles impishly, and states something in practiced English that altogether takes me pleasantly by surprise.

"Would you like to come to my home for tea?"

Lin inhabits a top floor apartment located in a maze of buildings at the foot of Victoria Peak near the infamous noisy *Kai Tak* airport. From here, one can actually see in detail underbellies of large jetliners as they align toward the line up with the mountain, and then turn sharply for the runway. After having a cup of Chinese Green Tea, we move out to the balcony and embrace. At this precise moment a new 747 floats overhead like a lumbering giant bumblebee, falters slightly, and dips away into a final approach,

"No need to worry, "she assures me, feeling my apprehension. "They never fall down."

This one night together, we join as men and women join everywhere in lust and in love. Lin a woman after all-- not some iconic creature assembled out of a package and marketed on a street corner. She is flesh and blood to my flesh and blood, a woman in every sense to make me complete and with purpose. We spend the night and the next day together, believing we are in love, believing that nothing can ever separate us. It is as young love should be; as only it can be to the young.

That evening, I return to my ship intending the next day to go to the U.S. Consulate and formalize paperwork of our commitment to be married. According to the 'War Brides Act', any military personnel engaged in a romantic relationship might declare the consummation to the local Consulate Office and file for immigration papers. Lin plans to meet me on the docks at 0900 with her identification papers. We have decided to get married immediately. The rest just a matter of details and of waiting, this wonderful oriental jade will be forever mine.

I awake at 0700 to the vibration of a peculiar hum I have not heard since a long time. Quickly dressing, I rush on deck. To my horror, the anchors weighed out of the water, the ship in motion. I run in panic to the stern of the vessel. I must get off— they must let me off! Two MPs stand guard near the railing. They eye me suspiciously, knowing already what is in my mind. However, it is by now already too late. That grand oriental city shrunk to a twinkling trinket at the foot of a diminished mountain separated by miles of ocean.

Later in the day, I find Fitzgerald-- or rather, he finds me moping at the poop deck still gazing eastward--both MPs gone, now that land no longer visible.

"I lost her," I moan near tears. "She was the best woman I have ever known, and I've lost her forever."

"Don't take it so hard." Fitzgerald says in an attempt to be consoling.

"Look at it on the positive side. She was just a prostitute, and a babe that cute probably would have dumped you the first time someone came along with real bucks. If you ask me you've been saved a lot of grief."

I never thought of it quite this way; and strangely enough, Fitzgerald's jaded insight makes me feel better somehow.

"Want to go get some chow," he coaxes, giving me a friendly nudge.

Looking back one last time, I see vanished upon horizon of the China Sea a mythical land vaguely remembered, a place in time made of China dolls and dragon boats, a grand city of the world I will always remember as Hong Kong.

Nor will I ever forget Lin, a girl nearly my own age, made beautiful in season, a jewel of the orient that I might have married. Yet, there is still a world far greater to know; and time the great healer of all that is lost. I have never stopped thinking about her completely, never stopped wondering how things might have been... but this is end of a love story from long ago. A story I will always keep special in my heart.

Chapter 21
Star of Providence

J had lost more than my heart in Hong Kong. Ruppert
and Timbrink also vanished, only to turn-up two days after our
departure. The local police arrest both inside an Opium Den, and
transfer custody to the Military Police. Because of Gunny's
encouragement, I make a written plea on their behalf for leniency,
but never see either man again. Word is that they flew back, making
it stateside a week before our ship arrives. Both men will receive
summary discharges, as is the case of so many others. We stop over
in Honolulu for less than two days, ordered to stand at attention and
salute the Arizona as we pass by the erected white monument
marking the tomb of this vessel sunk in Pearl Harbor. No one allowed
shore leave for reasons not completely clear. I personally do not care. I
have had my fill of R & R.

Strange, so few to greet us upon arrival at San Diego Harbor a week later. Those that do are mostly local family members of Navy men. Now that the war winding to an end, we think there will be jubilation for the first Marine Corps Battalion to return stateside intact. But quickly learn we are not the returning heroes of wars past. However, a waiting convoy is waiting to transport us to our newhome Camp Pendleton. I cram into a Jeep with six other E-5 NCOs. By now I am officially promoted to Sergeant, the completed paperwork processed during the voyage. On the way, we decide to break away fromthe main group and stop at a western style bar with two stagecoach wheels at either side of the entrance that also serves fast food. Seating ourselves at one of several tables, we ask the waitress—a not so pretty overweight blonde— for a pitcher of beer.

"We don't serve baby killers here," she replies disdainfully.

You can imagine our dismay. We may have been a lot of things— but not baby killers. One of the older Sergeants looks coldly at her, and says in measured tone.

"A pitcher of beer-- and we want it now!"

"You heard the Missies," rumbles a voice from one of the back tables occupied by six large ranch fed cowboys. "You boys best get the hell out of here while the getting good!"

We leap up in unison, our chairs flying backwards to the floor. There will be a fight, but there is no doubt of the winner. If necessary, we will kill them all. I suddenly feel like an enraged wild animal unleashed. I have already considered what I will do— all of it deadly. The cowboys also on their feet, a violent showdown at this stagecoach saloon poised imminent. After several tense moments, the senior Sergeant, who had requested the beer, coolly states to all concerned.

"Okay men— let's get out of here. It's not worth our careers."

After some protest, we leave, backing out cautiously like reluctant gunfighters forced to back down. This is my first experience with the new prejudice that has infected America. It will not be my last. The flags no longer wave in our honor— no longer are we defenders against the specter of communism. We owe our thanks in part to Lieutenant Calley at *My Lai*, the drug culture revelations of Timothy Leary, songs about tuning war into sounds of peace chanted by rock star mania, and the changing will of political agendas. Vietnam has become a dirty word in everyone's mouths. Were they right? And perhaps they are right within context of the season. Everyone tired of hearing about funerals, tired of receiving their sons home maimed and mutilated or delivered in a box because of carnage by modern weaponry-- tired of the anger that lasted and lasted... and continues to last still!

Were they wrong to condemn us? Yes— they were wrong. We did not cause the Vietnam conflict. Ours not the brainwash policy of a national idealism instilled in us since children. War is always the will of doctrines and complex ideologies designed by powers of influence. The common man–as the soldier on the ground--is but a pawn in a strategy beyond simple comprehension in a game played by forces with greater design. We were not Nazis fulfilling the evil dictates of a genocidal policy. We were United States Marines decorated in the colors of our country, many of our brothers wearing those colors for the last time. Nevertheless, there remains a dark soul from Vietnam, a soul that continues to infect us all in one way or another— but only a few that prophetically fulfill their homicidal fear. We had left our native soil young and gallant, only to return marked sons of perdition. However, we who continue to survive, determine not to sweep easily under the carpet of collective shame. If military training has taught us anything, it is that we remain a unit and we were there-- which must count for something!

Camp Pendleton still remains the same, even after a lifetime. Over 200 square miles of dry California desert hills, extending along the Pacific Coast from the small town of Ocean Side in the south, to San Clemente in the north, also the location of President Nixon's resort home. Second

Battalion, First Marine Division redeployed to an arid remote region in the interior, thirty miles from anywhere. This is to be our new home and my first stateside command as a promoted Sergeant. But not beforea long deserved three-week pass to go back home to see my family and find peace left behind. Or so I hope. As I wait for the bus to take me to San Diego, I begin shivering with cold even though it is late June and the temperature hovering in the 80s. My body acclimated to the tropical heat of South East Asia, a physical reminder that will not go away. Like everything else, it will take me some while to adjust.

I fly from San Diego to Atlanta on Military Standby. A rickety old single-prop Cherokee hops the last hundred miles to Greenville. I am home. First on the agenda is to take possession of my new car. I had requested that Rudy find me a Cameo, preferable a blue convertible. He has bought me a 1966 red Fairlane instead. Now I have nothing against Fords— but a Fairlane! Had it been a Mustang, I would have been only mildly disappointed. Nevertheless, I am assured that it is an extraordinary deal for a thousand dollars, a one-owner car, clean and mechanically sound, once belonging to Chef Massey, a friend of the family that works for the Poinsett Hotel chain. I must admit that in retrospect it turns out to be an excellent vehicle, reliable, with a powerful 301 engine requiring very little maintenance during the years I own it. It just not what I wanted

"Thanks dad," is all I can say.

I pretend to like the boxy automatic that reminds me of the caboose of a train, accepting that this is my stepfather's idea of a better investment. In time I will even grow to respect its performance-- but will never really like it.

That first night we sit as a family in mom's impeccable living room and talk about events of the last year. Rudy junior has taken over my old paper route, Penny has a boyfriend, and Cindy shows exceptional drawing skills. Mom talks about her garden, Rudy about how great Chef

Massey's marinated steaks on the barbecue the last weekend, and how he is considered the most famous hotel cook on the southern seaboard. But no one expresses much interest in my ordeals of the last year. How mightI blame them? Was it even possible then to really express all the pent-up emotions-- the anger-- the fear-- the death of my last innocence in one, or in many conversation? Yet, I desperately wanted them to listen-- if only to the silence of my suffering. A cry from the wilderness they cannot hear, and I cannot speak.

"This is bullshit!" I curse abruptly in mid conversation and unceremoniously walk out.

I then jump into my new car and spin down the driveway. I do not know why I feel so angry. My anger not at them, really; rather, it is a deep seething anger closer to irrational rage. I just had to get out of there. This moment I realize the person I once was truly dead. The person I am now dangerous and unpredictable. I do not particularly like this changed self; but it is me, the person I have become, and the foundation of the personI will be in the future.

I drive around a bit, as though searching for something I have lost— only I cannot remember what that something is. I race the familiar road that skirts the ridges of Paris Mountain, only to realize that the suspension of my Fairlane too soft to navigate at the daredevil speeds achieved by Ronnie's supped-up Falcon. Next, I go to the Poinsett drive-in, then into town along Main Street. Someone in particular I am looking for; someone I have a score to settle. A neighborhood bully I fought once and got my ass kicked because I was too drunk to properly defend myself. Only I cannot find the Irish bastard. Just as well, since I am in a killing mood.

I end up at the houseof my cousins, Ike and Kit. They still live with their parents, recently moved into an upper-class condominium development on the east side of town in the midst of having a party. I drink a couple of beers, talkabout nothing, and leave less settled than when I arrive. As I back out of the parking space and put the lever in forward, the back wheels spin slightly in a bed of gravel spread along an adjacent walkway. A car pulls directly in front of me, blocking the exit. Two men dressed in uniforms leap out of the other car carrying guns. I calmly get out of my car and demand to know the problem.

"Put your hands on the roof of the car," commands one of the men impatiently, coming toward me pointing a .38 revolver.

I only momentarily consider the possibility of resistance. By now the second man, short and lean, has foolishly circled around from behind and is fumbling with a set of handcuffs. I do not like the idea of being handcuffed for no reason--and certainly not by paid security guards. In an instant, I know instinctively what to do next. Spinning around, I grab the smaller man by the jugular, using him as a shield.

"What in hell is this about?" I roar as a Marine Sergeant ready to do battle to the death.

These weekend cops stand paralyzed. They are, after all, only over jealous employees looking to put a feather in their cap, neither ready to die. For me, on the other hand, I am not only ready to die, but ready to take as many as possible with me. I explain that I am here visiting my cousins and have done nothing wrong. Both men appear lost as what to do next.

Just then a local police cruiser pulls into the entrance. Out of the passenger door steps an officer of the law brandishing a single barrel shotgun. As a Marine conditioned to accept real authority, I release my hostage and submit to this recognizable enforcer of law. Handcuffed and transported to the city jail, I spend the night angrily defiant. Next morning, Rudy arrives looking, as always, ashamed. I do not even bother trying to explain the details of what happened. I know it will not make any difference. Released without even a fine, my car returned without penalty or charge, the police actually apologize, saying that they did not know I was a war veteran on leave. But all that Rudy can see is the embarrassment of me in trouble again, forcing him to drive down town in early traffic to get me out of jail. An all familiar ritual he has performed before.

Other than polite cordialities, none of us talk much after this. I think that maybe my family now afraid of me— not of me exactly, but of what I might do. I know they are all glad to see me; however, also that they want me to go back. It is only my third day, with more than twenty days of post-combat leave remaining. The next afternoon, I drop by to see Linda, the girl I met before going overseas, which ends in a near disaster. There is nothing about home that is home anymore. I feel alien, awakened in a strange land found only in the Twilight Zone. Deep down, I know I will never belong here again.

Less than two weeks into my extended leave, I pack my recently acquired Ford Fairlane and begin the long road trip back to California. Rudy expresses concern that the car might not make it, worrying about the oil, the transmission, the breaks, and how long the journey. I am determined to go back with my car, regardless of the risk. In truth, I have never driven more than a hundred miles in my life-- so what is another thirty-two hundred miles?

This time I feel greater sadness in departure than ever felt before. Sad because I did not find the peace I so desperately need. Sad because in my gut I know something lost that can never be again. Filled with anticipation and great expectations, I follow a carefully outlined map given to me by Rudy. In his mind, this route the only direct way across America: the way that existed, as a young sailor boy, when he hitched across country back to his Navy base. It is the only way he knows, as though he is the last of a species soon extinct, remembering the passage of his younger days by herd instinct, wishing to impart this knowledge to me.

"Remember to check the air pressure on your tires—and don't forget the oil! –Damn, son, that's a long drive-- be sure to rest."

"And don't you dare get anything to drink!" Jean adds stiffly, tears in her eyes.

I promise them both and depart, a young man off to engage in another war. Only this war rages within me. As I back the Ford Fairlane down the hill, I see my family and the place of my childhood differently, more distant than ever seen before. It is a place in my mind forever stationary in time. My mother and father standing side by side, a couple as couples everywhere, in every generation, who chose to build their nest in these Blue Ridge hills, a place I once called home. Two angels standing guard over a garden of paradise lost-- a forbidden principality I will never find entry into again.

It is already mid-afternoon by the time I reach Atlanta, taking here a detour into Alabama. It makes more sense at the time to skip onto the Interstate 20, but I know nothing about road navigation. Fearing the unknown, I decide to stick to the carefully outlined directions so thoughtfully provided. Although I will eventually take many trips across the continent, this the only time I will really see the backbone of America. I travel zigzag, sticking mostly to rural avenues and less traveled lanes, which crisscross more expedient throughways. These long winding roads of isolation and poor maintenance, dotted with small towns across the American east that melt into the more barren western frontier. Many of these towns destined to vanish, some to become grand cities. Traversing desolate asphalt and concrete roads, often no more than dusty lanes, I become aware only at the end the historic nature of this route. The famous Old Route 66, made legendary by Steinbeck's novel, The Grapes of Wrath. Of course, I do not even know who Steinbeck is at this time, and even less about the history of my own land. What I know even less about is how to properly read a road map, a lesson thoroughly learned before this journey's end.

Several years later, I will take the fabulous Sunset Route train excursion, spending three days and two nights crossing empty desert plains, through gradually greening hills from New Mexico to the Texas Gulf; and into the mosquito-infested bayous of the economically impoverished Louisiana. On that trip, I will have opportunity to spend a day and a night in the enchanted French Quarter of New Orleans. It will prove a tedious, but luxurious journey, discovering America in the comfort of an observation car balanced on a thin strip of track, particularly unsettling when crossing the empty expanse of the great Mississippi River with miles of water on either side. However, this is another adventure written in stars of the future.

I plan to take Rudy's advice and find a motel upon reaching the Louisiana border, but instead stop at a Crystal Burger outside of Jackson, Mississippi, to grab a bite to eat and ask a local for directions. Instructed here that the Interstate 20 the best route to take, making me realize that my many hours of detour a waste of time. After this, I decide in future to study the map for myself. I also find something else at the Crystal Burger Takeout altogether unexpected: twenty hamburgers for two dollars and coffee at ten cents a cup. I order twenty hamburgers and ten cups of coffee to go. Although small compared to a regular hamburger, they prove tasty and filling, and will last me all night and into the next day. I place the Styrofoam cups of coffee in a line across the dash, gulping down one after the other in secession while driving. Stimulated by too much caffeine, I drive through the night, stopping only for gas, and crossing into Texas a little after sunrise.

There is nothing longer than a Texas mile. Empty open ranges extending into an empty horizon farther the eye can see with the exception of an occasional grain silo marking the dynastic presence of a ranch. A hundred miles away great puffs of clouds hove r as flying saucers, shadowed underneath by grey trails of falling rain, and pierced through with radiant white laser beams of sunlight. I welcome even one of these vagabonds of relief to blow my way; but none do, always remaining tauntingly in the distance, as though this strip of highway I travel marks the unremitting boundary of purgatory.

There are few towns, all with names reminiscing cowboy mythology, and just as few gas stations. Outside of Dallas, I stop at a truck stop and eat a Texas steak. It proves tough as cowhide and tastes of old grease. I also buy some over the counter caffeine pills before filling up with gas.

"Supposed to be heavy wind tonight," the gas attendant warns, shooting out a glob of tobacco spit. "If I was you, boy, I'd settle down here 'til morning."

"I'm not afraid of a little wind."

I pay for the gas and drive into the red eye of the western setting sun. By midnight, I begin to hallucinate, as a result of fatigue and too much caffeine. I hear voices in the back seat of someone talking, but no one there. Once I think to see someone sitting in the passenger seat. Beyond the beam of my headlamps, large lumbering shadows begin to move across the road. As my mind tries to come to terms with these disembodied apparitions, the steering suddenly becomes difficult to handle, the vehicle shuddering violently. Instantly, everything changes black.

I have passed into the dark mouth of a sandstorm. Slowing down to a crawl, I creep the swaying vehicle to what I hope is the softer shoulder. As I perform this dangerous maneuver, I expect any moment the impact of a Simi-Truck passed a few miles back. Fortunately, nothing happens and I come to a full stop. Buffeted furiously by the storm, the Fairlane shakes and sways like a foundering ship in a storm at sea, the wind howling demons; and a smell of dry parched earth like the odor of brimstone seeping into the cabin. With nothing else to do, I lie across the front seat and sleep in the belly of this hell.

Awakened rudely by piercing light of morning; the storm now passed, the barren Texas landscape stretching into an endless brown horizon. My car rests several yards from the highway, a few more feet, and I would have driven into a dry gully. However, this is not the worst of it. The sandstorm has left its evil mark! Tiny swirls mare the hood and windshield, particularly visible in direct sunlight. These handprints of nature will remain for as long as I keep the car. No one to blame; I accept the decision mine, having been fairly warned. At least I am alive, ready to hit the solid pavement again.

Finding a truck stop cafe fifty miles down the road, I stop, eat a tasteless non-breakfast, and drive some more. I pick up two hitchhikers near Odessa, a man and a woman, whose names are Joseph and Mary. Judging by their dirty worn-out clothes, they are hippies. Both many years older, exhausted from years of excess drug use, and are exhausted and penniless. We talk a little, but the conversation soon becomes disjointed. The man keeps repeating an agitated monologue about an unpleasant experience in Houston that got them both locked-up for three days.

"They was filled with pure hate!" The woman interjects more than once, as though this singular feeling the sum of their collective experience.

She is not very pretty, with rotting front teeth and tangled matted hair, more suitable to the mange of an unkempt Collie. Nevertheless, I pity them both. I am glad when they finally shut up and drift into needed slumber. I really do not know why I have picked them up. I am not a hippie sympathizer, nor have any interest to explore further the drug culture. Maybe it is just loneliness after driving so many hours; or maybe it just bothers me to pass two human beings stranded in the middle of this hell called Texas.

By now, I am altogether exhausted. I see a sign for El Paso and make the decision to find the nearest motel. I actually think at the time that I have unwittingly passed into Mexico, judging by the pueblo-style of architecture and signs for the Mexican city Ciudad Jureaz, just on the other side of the Rio Grande River. In Spanish it is spelled *Rio Grande*

Del Norte, a blooming oasis on both sides of the river, slicing through the Chihuahuas Desert, separating two historically divisive countries. In 1881, the Southern Texas and Pacific rail lines join the Atchison Topeka and Santa Fe railroad lines to make El Paso famous overnight, becoming a place of attraction to many. Because of its ideal climate and fertile earth, the population booms with a constant stream of newcomers. This influx population fed over time by businessmen, Chinese railroad workers, gamblers, prostitutes, thieves, and of course gunfighters baptized in old west lawlessness. After the loss of five sheriffs in less than a year, it seems El Paso will never be tamed or safe, with the unsavory reputation as the Six Shooter Capital of America. Then comes along a man named Dallas Stoudenmire hired the position of town Marshall. Stoudenmire quickly gains respect by shooting first and asking questions after. Fast on the draw and deadly accurate with his pistols, Dallas Stoudenmire also becomes famous in the *"Four Dead in Five Seconds Gunfight"*, where he survives victorious against uneven odds on April 14, 1881. El Paso now has a promising future after all, as did the west overall. Later the battle at the OK Corral in Tombstone, Arizona, and many other such showdowns, allows law and order to prevail, civilizing the uncivilized men that once roamed these open plains.

I pay for a single room with a single bed. Without ceremony, I rip next off the top mattress and throw it on the floor for my guest to sleep on. I lay down on the hard box spring and am out immediately. I suppose they could have robbed me, even murdered me as I slept, and taken everything. Instead, they sit quietly in a corner the next morning, like two haggard mice, lost and hungry, waiting patiently for me, their new Moses to awaken.

The first thing we do is have a Mexican breakfast-- my compliments— in a Spanish style restaurant overlooking an early morning dessert prairie-- beans, steak, and peppers-- served with a view that could have been taken from the pages of a novel written by the famous western novelist Louis L'Amour, whose books I adored as a child. I desire to linger here in this nostalgic legend for a little while longer. The sun climbs over the horizon unveiling the dry burnt hills of a hostile no man's land. It is now time to hit the dust trail again.

I drive all day and into the night, through New Mexico, and into Arizona, staying on Interstate 10. However somewhere along the line, I end up on the Interstate 8, also known as the 'desert highway'. Seeing a sign for a town somewhere outside of Yuma, I hope to find here lodging for the night, along with something to eat. However, the town is gone, the road dead-ending into shifting dunes. Low on gas, too exhausted to drive another mile, I decide to rest here until morning and curl up on the front seat. My two travel companions are already passed-out in the back, just content not to be sleeping in the open.

Early morning in a dessert is eerily beautiful, as one might imagine the terrain of another planet. The horizon changes from dark purple, to lavender, then vermillion. The zenith becomes pure cobalt blue, not a cloud in sight. My new acquaintances continue to sleep, so I let them rest for a little longer. Exiting the car to take a piss, I decide to explore a little, curious to how an entire town could just disappear. Climbing up a smooth white sand dune, the answer to my question rests in a shallow valley on the other side. The town is not gone, rather buried. Several oxidized rooftops made of tin protrude through the sand. A weathered grey wooden porch appears in tack with windows and a door like those seen in western movies. I peer through one of the opaque windows, but can see nothing. Excited, I brush away the sand from around the entrance and push hard against the door. It opens after only a little resistance. Once upon a time, this had been a place of commerce: perhaps a feed and supplies store, a saddle shop, or maybe even a tailor. An adjoining room in the back blocked by a flow of creeping sand that has found access through a broken window or some other opening, filling steadily the vacant space. Except for a few broken bottles and a busted rough hewn table, the place empty. It reminds me of the hulk of a sunken ship, a ghostly Dutchman raised momentarily from the deep, soon to be covered below this ocean of shifting sand again. I shiver and get out of there as quickly as possible, not wishing to be buried with it. In the future I will see other ghost towns in Death Valley abandoned after the gold rush days, but none will leave me with a more profound sense of haunting than this one. I always planned to come back here one day, but never find it again. It makes me wonder how many other secrets roam a lost generation drowned in these tides of ever-changing sand.

The couple are awake and standing outside by the time I return. Snapping orders that its time to leave, they scamper into the back seat without so much as a whimper of complaint. Already they are getting use to military life. An hour later, we reach the outskirts of Yuma and pull into a truck stop for another breakfast. I can see in faces of thesehitchhikers that something troubling them.

"We're almost there," I say, examining the crumpled roadmap and sipping down the last of my coffee.

"Almost for you," interjects Mary sourly. "We still got over 500 milesto go after you drop us off near your base."

"She gets like this sometimes ever since she became pregnant. Don't pay her no attention." Joseph says, expressing gratefulness to me, while attempting to quiet Mary.

I do not say anything, but continue to study the map. As it turns out, I have arrived early with almost a week of leave time remaining. By now the highway my own-- no longer am I that timid son, who began this journey across the grand American continent. I cannot exactly say I have grown to like these hippies, but in this moment a strange sense of compassion comes over me. Without revealing my intentions, I fill up with gas; take the 95 north, and fifty miles later jump on the 10 west toward Blyth. I have determined to get these people at least as far as Los Angeles.

A desert mile is a desert mile and without shortcuts. As the late morning sun blazes across this barren landscape, I become mesmerized by the lack of change, my mind grasping any aspect to make a familiar shape or contour in the harsh absence of tangible dimension. Every sound made by the cracked pavement, even the distinctive hum of the V8 301 engine, a familiar longing matched by the pulse of my beating heart. This is the land explored by Louis L'Amour in search of detail for his next western adventure. Too young and too bold to be afraid, I launch into this arid no-man's land unaware of a thousand things that might have gone wrong.

Blythe, California, "Gateway to the Golden State" is a blooming oasis fed by the Colorado River, and from here east stretches more desert to the east. The terrain changes gradually to shades of brown, becoming dry and hilly. Within a few hours, I see a sign that reads San Bernardino County. Many miles later I drop onto the cloverleaf of the Hollywood freeway, instantly in the thick of a NASCAR race: automobiles accelerating in excess of seventy miles per hour, slipping between lanes, and jockeying for position. Exhausted as I am, I manage to merge into traffic by sheer luck. I can see through the rear view mirror the terrified looks on faces of my passengers, they have abandoned themselves to angels of providence. This is the fast lane of Los Angeles County, the land of glittering promise rising between a desolate dessert and the blue infinity of the Pacific Ocean. Perched high on a hill sits the Hollywood sign welcoming all to this entertainment kingdom of the world. We have arrived at the psychedelic foothills of California stardom.

I cannot remember the miracle of how I found the Greyhound bus station; only that along with the aid of a few helpful directions the distinctive logo with a grey running dog appears through a maze of streets somewhere near Hollywood and Vine. I purchase two one-way tickets to San Francisco for about twenty dollars each.

"Make a good life for your kid," I say, placing the tickets firmly in the pregnant woman's dry heat-withered hands.

She only smiles, tears in her eyes. Although Joseph remains silent, I can see the gratitude in his face. They are still strangers to me; but we have shared many miles of road together. This makes us almost family... the first of many I will come to know in the course of my life.

"God bless you," Mary calls after me. "We won't never forget you."

It is dark by the time I arrive at the gate of Camp Pendleton on the San Clemente side. I am beyond tired and look forward to a few days of rest before checking in for duty. That night I dream I am still driving a long and endless road, the blistering hot sun surrounded by heavenly hosts in a sky of perpetual twilight: a way endless, without beginning and without end. And the chance meeting of a couple guided by providence now boarded on a bus in search of a star glimmering in future distance.

Chapter 22
Sins of Wander Lust

J have become one poisoned, dying slowly. Except for Gunny Corell and Badwarrior, no one else remains, all transferred to their perspective MOS stations, and still not a true supply man left among them. I feel strangely isolated. I had grown accustomed to those familiar faces, even if they were masks of discontent and seething rebellion. Then the replacements arrive, all fresh boot camp green, young, and anxious to please. With less than twenty-six months service, I have already become an old soldier. Now a Marine Corps Sergeant at the beginning of a promising career. A Corporal is assigned to me, a man three years my senior, yet unquestionably resigns to the chain of command, willingly follows my orders with unwaveringly commitment.

Gunny Corell fulfills a promise made to me while in Nam with a weekend treat at a whorehouse in Nevada called The Mustang Ranch. We leave the base after evening chow and drive nearly all night staying over in Reno to rest up. Gunny wants to play the slots before going the last eight miles east to Storey County. We do not talk much during the more than 600-mile drive. Corell takes on the demur of a younger man behind the wheel of his tequila sunrise yellow 1966 Malibu SS convertible, wearing easy-rider sunglasses, a scarlet bandana tied around his head, and a bottle of dark whiskey discreetly wrapped in a brown paper bag. Every now and then, he passes the concealed bottle to me, insisting I take a swig. It tastes like gut-rot, strong enough to remove fresh paint, with a potent backwash that gnaws bitterly in the throat long after the first gulp. In this context Gunny is a real cowboy born to the open range, driving into the western sunset, our voices howling tunes of screaming radio music. Man and machine one, he follows instinctively the desert highway toward his favorite watering hole. This is probably as close to being married as this Gunnery Sergeant will ever allow himself.

"Wait until you see the babes!" He says when we drive through a friendly arched gate bearing the black insignia of a wild stallion and down a long lane flanked by smooth white rocks.

The house simple, resembles a horseshoe wrapped around the driveway with a main entrance in the center. Gunny knows just where to park his car, giving a familiar salute to several employees that wave back with delighted recognition. He is home at last and looks forward to a few hours of pleasure surrounded in the arms of a strange woman.

The interior resembles every brothel, dimly lit, shadowed by several drunken patrons slumped around tables in dark corners. We are happily received by a bosomed blond, who robustly escorts us into an adjoining chamber.Here the ambience more ornate, tastefully decorated by plush couches and chairs, tiffany lamps on small antique tables clustered with beer bottles. Glasses of colorfully mixed concoctions held leisurely by men and women lounging together in content repose.

"It's been so long!" The blond winks to Gunny, indicating he is a special client of many years. "You and your young friend sit over there on the sofa, and I'll see to it that you are well taken care of."

Gunny smiles slyly and licks his lips, a proverbial drooling hungry wolf. We do as instructed, receive a complimentary drink, and wait for the parade to begin. It is like being in the Valley of the Dolls. There are no women lovelier than found at the Mustang Ranch. Tall and short, thin and graceful, pleasingly plump, snow queen white to almond brown: all scantily dressed to evoke the imagination of any man. Gunny knows exactly which one he wants. It takes me longer to decide, like being in the fruit section of a supermarket wanting to test each one before making a purchase. I remember thinking to myself: this one too ripe with age; that one too innocent: one too light, another too dark. I finally settle for a raven-haired beauty with Irish green eyes, perfect, except for a crooked front tooth, only noticeable when she grins. Like all these ladies, she is a professional, studied in how to immediately make me feel important.

Life is all about validation and feeling of purpose in the moment. I will later become aware of what a woman experiences in the face of unrealistic expectations of a clientele conditioned to fantasy excursions. Even this oldest occupation designed in world history has its fiscal drawbacks.

Her hair and body smells of fresh flowers; the tips of her fingers and toes as cherry-coated candies made to eat. The only way to describe her is forbidden fruit so sweet in the mouth; a fantasy desert to empty the emptiness of the soul. We make sex, rest a while in the parlor, have a few drinks, and then return back to her room, where we indulge in another round of sex. There is something particularly fanciful about the unreal. This is the magic of a brothel. A man's Disney World to tantalize the futility of desires created through worldly aspirations inspired by things believed unobtainable. Dreams not his own, corrupted in emptiness made in the end even more empty.

I never knew how much Gunny Corell paid for us both that day. It is already dark by the time we return to Reno and park outside an all-night gambling casino. Gunny stays up the whole night drinking and playing the Slots. I curl up to dreamless slumber in the back of his Malibu, until rudely awakened by the morning desert. We are already a hundred miles outside of Los Angeles, Gunny now dressed in his Marine Corps fatigues and wearing his starched jungle cap. He is less human again: a son of duty and military protocol. We never speak about this weekend, as though it never happened. I will one day pity this man trapped in a web of fantasy, an emaciated insect slowly drained of essence by creatures born of fantasy. But even more disturbing, I see in him a glimmer of my future self, the ultimate promised reward to all sons of valor.

The following week an unfortunate showdown occurs, which will change everything. I have become unpleasant even to myself, bitter, and with a chip on my shoulder. What had been an asset to Gunny in Nam is now a liability. He saw it coming; I saw nothing at all.

It is past 2100 hours, all working overtime to bring 2nd Battalion Supply back to full operational status. My new crew arrives zealous to the task at hand, an added benefit of having young recruits. The welcomed addition of an experienced Corporal trained in Supply operations a personal relief. We still have morethan a hundred boxes to open and add to inventory. The process slow and time consuming to meet regulatory mandates imposed by various government departments regarding treatment of cargos exposed to tropical condition. Also, I am still understaffed, having only half the necessary compliment.

I operate the forklift, snapping orders from my perch. I have just wheeled into the bay a large container I know contains items of security. It is my intention to finish this box before calling it a night. Only Gunny disagrees, having other plans.

"Everyone dismissed until tomorrow morning," he shouts above the whine of the forklift.

"After we finish this box," I snap back.

"I said dismissed, Sergeant!"

I swing off the machine and face him with deadly intent, as I had faced so many others in the past. My rage changes instantly to shame. I can see the hurt and disappointment in his eyes, but it is already too late. I wish this moment to be something else, not the thing I have become. But this is now my nature. He knows it; and so do I. He again orders everyone dismissed and instructs me to come into his office.

"You are a good Marine, son; but you need to learn more self-discipline;" the tone of his voice tolerant, yet firm. "I'm transferring you to Amtrak Division. They need a Supply Sergeant, and I think you will be better off there."

Pride prevents me from saying I am sorry. Not that it would have made any difference; nevertheless, I should have said it. I truly respected this Gunny, but forgot my position in the scheme of things; forgot that this man had been more to me than just my superior. Deep down I know he is right to get rid of me— the only way to save me. Therefore, Gunny Corell sends me among those he knows as poisoned as I am.

The next morning, I receive my new orders, pack my Sea Bag, and drive to the most southern extreme of Camp Pendleton. Amtrak Division, located near the beach just outside of Oceanside, is a much more modern facility, the supply depot comparatively twice the size of 2nd Battalion. My new assignment consists of three subordinate Corporals and thirty-six supply men, all with the right MOS, most being seasoned veterans. I am still youngest of the NCOs, only now a top dog.

The officer in charge is a black First Lieutenant from Mississippi namedJackson, slick and polished; the Gunny crumpled and sloppy, like a junk yard dog looking for scraps from the master's table. As different as they are, these two men somehow share an affinity of thought transmission with just a mere glance. I immediately trust neither of them; a feeling that will later prove justified.

Without knowing it, I have entered into one of the darker passages of my life. Nothing gives me pleasure; no pain too great; numb to every sensation. Long weekend-passes take me wandering from the Tijuana border in the south, to regions inhabited by the stars north, and west of Los Angeles. Sometimes I take a buddy along. More often I make these excursions alone. On one such empty highway north of Simi Valley during one of these nowhere excursions, a wood-paneled Ford station wagon with a set of steer horns mounted on the hood races past on my left. At the wheel seated a hefty cowboy wearing a broad tan colored hat. It is the legendary Dan Blocker, actor that portrays Hoss Cartwright in Rudy's favorite TV western Bonanza. I would love to get an autograph to send home, so I begin honking my horn, waving foolishly. He only tips his hat and floats away into the desolate horizon at more than eighty-miles an hour. My immediate thought is that perhaps I am somewhere near the iconic Ponderosa Ranch. Years later, I will learn that Dan Blocker never even lived on the famous make-believe location, which is in reality located near Reno Nevada. But at least on this day I feel near to something loved by my Dad, which makes me feel somehow more near to him; pleasant reminder that somewhere in this world expanse, I might still have a family.

Another time, a Lance Corporal buddy named Dex, whose family emigrated from France after the Second World War, pleas for us to go to Mission Hills in search of the rich and famous. Dex is a Hollywood star gazer, versed in details about tabloid lives of nearly all the cinema 'vedettes'. He is particularly enthralled by the singer-actress Dinah Shore, able to rehearse each of her failed relationship, to her favorite color, even knowing the perfume she wears. We park the car on a deserted road far from the front manor and sneak onto the golf course estate by climbing a steep hill leading onto the green of the eighteenth hole. Evening has begun to descend over the manicured landscape, bathing the surrounding grounds in a most distinctive red hue unique to a Southern California sunset resulting from massive smog vapor. Dex and I saunter casually along the fairway and from green to green trying to act natural, as though we somehow belong. Suddenly my companion's eyes glisten and he charges excitedly in the direction of an elderly lady wearing a white golfer's cap prepared to make a putting shot.

"M- Mrs. S-Shore," he stammers just above a whisper.

The woman does not even flinch, but aligns herself against the irregular green and makes a perfect cup from four meters away. She then turns around and faces us, the golf club raised slightly over her right shoulder, poised as an angel armed.

"You boys are pretty far from home," she says dryly. "I would say, judging by your appearance, you are Marines on weekend leave."

"Yes, Mam— I have been hoping to meet you. Ever since I was a grasshopper in the field you have been a lovely flower to me. *Tous les jours Je pense t'es tres belle!*"

Dex then hangs his head shyly, grinning like a small boy in the presence of a royal queen. I must admit that I am impressed Dexter actually speaks another language, plus with the charm of French accent. I think Dinah Shore also impressed.

"I'm not as fresh as I used to be. But it is sure nice to know that someone still thinks of me in that way."

Her voice changes softer, more familiar to the Dinah Shore we know and remember on the big screen in the heyday of her career. Now she is an older lady with burnt leathery skin, her once lovely face wrinkled almost beyond recognition. Dex seems not to notice, or else this fact unimportant to him. They end up talking for several minutes like star-crossed friends laughing happily at memories both remembered from different sides of the television set. Abruptly, this conversation ends, a finite moment of reality arrived.

"You best go back the way you came," the older lady concludes, shouldering her golf bag. Then adds sweetly: "This is, after all, private property, so I don't want to see you back here again."

"Can I at least have your autograph?" Dex implores, producing from his shirt pocket a pen and crinkled photograph of the actress of when still young.

She writes "To Dex, a charming young man at the beginning from one near the end— Merci," signed *Dinah Shore.*

Dex is giggly as a school child during the long drive back to Camp Pendleton. He talks about how he has seen all of this in his dreams, and how many other stars he still wants to meet in person. As for me, I feel relief just to have gotten away without being charged with trespassing-- or worse-- for this kind of stunt. Thankfully, Dinah Shore a good person and a patriot, who found it in her heart to overlook our youthful imputableness to presume upon her privacy. This is the only, and last time I take Dex along, deciding that California just too small for a man with the magnitude of his star treks.

On one memorable weekend, I stumble upon an outdoor concert hosted by an unknown, particularly weird looking singer named Alice Cooper. I think the music okay under the influence of beer and teen-mania. I almost end up having sex with a rich pretty debutant, except she gets sick and vomits on the front seat of my car. I practically push her out the door, as I attempt to clean the upholstery. She calls me a selfish bastard and staggers back into the concert hall. I decide that perhaps she is right and drive back to my base.

One of the more interesting weekend excursions is with a Corporal named Wilkes from Fresno County, located in the center of the fertile San Joaquin Valley. This farming community, three hours north of Los Angeles, is also a Mecca to the California Cowboy. An hour and a half from Bakersfield, it nestles between the central coast mountain ranges and the prominent winter ski resort of Mount Whitney rising dominant over the Sierra Nevada to the east. Weekend rodeos are common place here, as are horse ranches and sprawling orchards separated by miles and miles of open range. But what really makes Fresno special is the abundance of Wild West Shows. Fresno will eventually gain the reputation as being one of the most prosperous communities in Central California. To Corporal Wilkes it is just a place he calls home.

I first meet Wilkes during our semi-annual physical proficiency test required of all NCOs; both a little out of shape, huffing and puffing like clogged-up diesels after a three-mile morning run. We barely manage to beat the clock, with only seconds to spare. We also both take a vow to drink a little less in the future. A promise we will also both break. Wilkes is average in size, and speaks with a distinctive western drawl. I had supposed him to be from somewhere in the mid-west, like Arizona or Colorado. I am surprised when he tells me Central California.

"I'm from where the sun always shines, and a place most people don't know nothing about. We're as cowboy as you get— not like those Hollywood slickers with them designer boots. My Dad spent his whole life breaking horses for other folks. Then one day he got broke real bad by an Appaloosa. I was just fifteen at the time, and we couldn't afford no funeral. I still remember the day me and my brother carried him up into the back country wrapped in bed sheets. We buried Dad in a cowboy grave on his own land near our house. I hike up there sometimes and make sure the rocks stay placed proper. I reckon the military will take care of this cowboy, but we all ain't so lucky."

Wilkes invites me to an October Festival held in Fresno on every weekend of Halloween. We split the gas, arriving at his mother's home on Friday night at around 9:30 P. M. civilian time. The house looks like something out of the movie 'Hud', a two-story structure sagging to one side, a slightly tilted front porch with a broken swing once occupied by romantic couples, now abandoned like the house through many years of neglect. In the light of day, flaking paint and patches of rotten wood appear, as further evidence of abject poverty, and perhaps a little laziness. Rudy never would have allowed his estate to dilapidate into such condition as this. Nevertheless, it is home to Wilkes and his family, or at least until it collapses on their heads.

The mother, a haggardly woman, closer in age to my grandmother, is nearly blind, and smokes hand-rolled foul-smelling cigars. I get impression that Wilkes represents her last fruitful conception, an undesired miracle during a moment of poor judgment. She takes a shot of straight Bourbon from time to time, saying it does wonders for her arthritis. An older brother and sister, both named Jesse (spelled Jessie for the sister), also live in the house with their six children from two previous marriages. Both freshly divorced again, and neither with any regular source of employment, sit looking at each other contemptibly while watching reruns on a late-model color TV. These are indeed the poor in spirit; lost souls of the American heartland left over after the Grapes of Wrath, wishing only escape from the disillusioned reality of their lives. Wilkes introduces each of them without even a hint of embarrassment. This is his family after all-- regardless of shame-- and besides they happily share their roof with us without asking anything in return. I suppose that in the end shelter from the elements trumps all other considerations.

The next morning, Wilkes and I rise early, pile into the cab of a 1960 Chevrolet pickup and accompany Jesse into Fresno City. Jesse, wearing scuffed cowboy boots with worn-down heels and a sweat-stained Stetson-styled hat, is as typical a cowboy as I have ever seen. He does not say much, and when he does speak, the words so garbled that I need to ask Wilkes to translate. Our first stop is a liquor store. Here we each buy a pint for the road. It soon becomes evident that Jesse is jealous of his younger brother for escaping the family pattern of ignorance and poverty by joining the Marines. He is doubly jealous of me, one who represents to him an authority figure. In fact, it eats in his crawl all day, seething out on occasions in the pattern of a disrespectful remark, or an outright insult. In the beginning, I just laugh it off. However, by the time our bottles grow half-empty, so does my patience also begin to grow shallow.

"You sound like a dumb southern hick," he remarks when I comment that Fresno a much larger town than I expected.

"At least I'm not a make-believe cowboy still living at home with my mother," I jab back. "Where I come from men hold their whiskey and learn to shut up about things they know nothing about!"

Wilkes seated in the truck seat between us is mortified by the scene unfolding. He knows only too well his brother; and also fears I might kill the ignorant bastard if necessary. He makes a plea for peace, saying to his brother that I am a respected guest. Jesse hears none of this. Guest or no guest, he is determined to do me harm. Pulling the pickup over on the side, he jumps out ready to do battle. I swing out the other side and meet him in front of the vehicle. Wilkes is wrong about me killing his brother. I have known tin-men like Jesse before, and know there is only one-way to relieve his pain. I had seen the frustration in his eyes the night we arrived. He is the embodiment of every man harboring bitter resentment to a lifetime of repression. Because of lack of education and the xenophobic terror of a changing world existing beyond the familiar confines of his nativity, Jesse lashes out in rage against a father that beat him down, against the suffocating insecurities of an alcoholic mother and sister. But what grinds in Jesse's gut most is the betrayal of a young wife that takes-off to parts unknown with their two children in the first five years of marriage. All adds up to a life of defeat. Jesse sees in me every authority figure that has ever lorded over him; mistakenly believes this an opportunity to win at last.

Jesse is a tall lanky man, sinewy tough by ranch-hand work. He could have been a challenging opponent, except he never learned how to really fight. He charges immediately like an enraged bull bellowing threatening obscenities, his upper body extended slightly forward. At the last possible moment, I step to one side, grab his hair and slam him into the truck front grill. I then pounce over him ready to finish the job.

362

Jesse just lays there whimpering, blood dribbling from his mouth. Once again, he is a man defeated.

"Please— Sergeant," Wilkes pleads on behalf of his brother.

Wilkes is without a driver's license, so I end up driving us back to his mother's house. Upon arriving, Jesse begins mumbling threats about going inside and getting his father's Winchester if I did not clear out. I grab him by the throat; look him coldly in the eyes.

"You pull a weapon on me be damn sure you kill my ass with the first shot-- because you won't have time for a second."

Jesse leaves again humiliated; nor will he return home for the rest of the weekend. Wilkes makes a weak effort to apologize for the actions of his brother. I only half believe his apology. Jesse is, after all, Wilkes' blood brother, and I only a stranger. Nevertheless, we both pretend that nothing has happened.

Jessie, the sister, has observed everything through an upstairs window. She does not particularly like the brother of her name-sake, and is glad to see him reduced down a peg. It turns out that Jesse a bully when drunk to all those that know him, including his mother and sister. Later in the evening, I will see Jesse at the barn dance, but he makes an effort to avoid me. We both know the dead seriousness of the situation. Both know that he is a drunkard loudmouth, lacking the stomach for a fight to the finish. But, also, I should have figured him for a coward and better prepared myself.

The festival begins with a country-style potluck banquet: pork ribs, chicken, hamburgers, and hotdogs. Including tubs of mash potatoes, fresh corn, western baked beans, and as much keg-beer one can drink for just five dollars a head. Determined to get my money's worth, I eat for an hour, drink for an hour, and then eat and drink even more. Jessie introduces me to one of her friends, a woman named Annie, who I consider to be in the neighborhood of thirty-five years old with rich red hair tied back in a ponytail by a yellow ribbon. Tonight she is wearing a suede and denim cowgirl outfit, her lovely feet adorned by sexy sandals not at all western. She tries to teach me how to square dance. By now I amdrunk enough to believe I am becoming good at the two stepped *do-si-do*. Excusing myself, I slip out back to find a dark corner of relief fromall the beer I have been guzzling.

Upon returning, I am intercepted by two men that step from behind a shed, both carrying baseball bats. I recall seeing them earlier sitting on a haystack talking with Jesse-- an association now clear. I prepare myselffor battle to the death. I am certain that even as drunk as I am I can take at least one-- but both, and without a weapon? Nevertheless, I am determined to go down fighting.

"Jacob— what are you boys up to?" A stern female voice enquires from behind.

It is Annie. When I did not return, she has come looking for me. "Get back inside," growls the larger of the two. "This ain't no concern of yours."

Annie then produces a silver derringer from under her suede vest.

"Alright then, put down the bats and face him one at a time." She demands coolly. "Don't think I don't know how to use this, Jacob." She next turns and aims at the other man; "and that goes for you, too."

After a moment of hesitation the would-be assailants back away, disappearing intothe night. Nor will I see them or Jesse again for the rest of the evening. Saved by the loveliness of a woman and her peashooter, I thank Annie,boasting I could have taken them both.

"I'm sure you could have, darling, but I don't get out much, and this is a special night just to have fun. I prefer my men fresh— not fresh from battle."

We continue to dance, drink, and have fun until past midnight. The next morning I awaken in the attic room provided to me by Wilkes's mother. Annie is by my side, her mouth wide opened, and snoring loudly. In the bright morning light, she looks older than the night before, her skin dried and cracked with deep lines around her eyes and mouth made by a life of hard work and disappointment in this harsh sunbaked valley. Like everyone else, she is divorced, raising two children alone, her youth and beauty fluttering whimsically, as a colorful butterfly in the last days of August. One uneventful morning, Annie will wake-up suddenly old, and will just fade away like a tapestry in a counterpane of richness of yesterday gone by.

We spend most of that Sunday just driving through the countryside along isolated roads through alleys of cultivated fields belonging to wealthy stewards of these rich farmlands. After eating an early dinner, I drop Annie off at a dilapidated house, where her two children are waiting.

"Come back and see me sometime, Sugar," she teases, giving me a last hug and a kiss.

I promise I might, but never do see Annie again. Wilkes and I drive back to base, arriving early enough to get a good night of sleep. This is one of the few weekend excursions, I remember truly enjoyable. Wilkes, on the other hand, has his fill of home and family for a long time to come. This is the last weekend pass we will share. Not that I blame Wilkes or his family. They represent the salt of this other earth that still remains to me alien. I am grateful to have had the adventure to share some of the pleasures and the hardships of their existence. And I always will appreciate a night spent with Annie of the old west.

As unbearable as the routine of everyday life, on base, it is the routine that helps me get from day to day. I become tyrannical in my duty as Sergeant in charge of the Third Platoon Barracks. Each morning I hold an inspection and read out the orders of the day. On occasion, someone new expresses unruliness or out right out belligerence. Or sometimes I just did not like a man's attitude. I would single out this individual; tell him to report inside the barracks, and to wait for me. Then leaving a Corporal in charge, I follow the man inside and invite him into the privacy of my sleeping cubical. I then turn into a demon, slamming him against a wall, making clear that our difference in rank now suspended.

"It's you and me now, Marine!" I rage. "I don't want any shit in my ranks— is that clear? If you think you can take me, then now is the time."

Sometimes the man might take a swing; usually too shocked to do anything at all. For those that accept the challenge, I unleash fury almost superhuman. I have become indestructible, numb to pain, and much stronger than revealed by my stature. After a while, I even begin to sadistically look forward to these violent encounters. Of course, I am taking a risk. There are rules governing actions considered unbecoming of an NCO. But those rules enforceable only if someone should see. Nevertheless, Vietnam has taught me one thing well. Power and respect of command is in the man, not in his rank. I never order anyone to do something myself not willing to do— but by God he will follow my orders without question!

My most harrowing experience is the time I drive my car to Tijuana with a couple of drinking buddies. One crosses into Mexico at *San Ysidro*, California about twenty miles south of San Diego. It is a beautiful sunny late Friday afternoon. We have just received our monthly paychecks and are thinking what most young men usually think most about.

As we pass through the border station into the city, a feeling of wonder and adventure intoxicates us all. There is just something exhilarating about travelling into another country, even if it is a close neighbor. Traffic a snarling nightmare, based more on the law of opportunity, than flow regulators of traffic signals. Each time I stop on a red, the vehicle behind continues to nudge me forward, as do the vehicles behind him. Whereas, a green light means anything goes-- or not at all, a red light means cross if you dare. I quickly learn that rules of the road here more of a guideline and less a legal requirement. Even the police appear to turn a blind eye, and all I can do is just following the flow.

By late afternoon, we park in an alley below 3rd Street and find a hole-in-the-wall that serves us cheap Nachos and beer. After consuming more than prudently wise, we wander on foot from bar to bar, drinking and eating, meandering aimlessly from avenue to avenue. Somewhere along the line, we pick up a middle-aged whore, who agrees to show us around as long as we feed her drinks. At nearly midnight, she takes us to a private club with live entertainment.

Upon entry to this seedy environment, I suspect immediately that this will not be the usual kind of entertainment. A naked woman is strapped to the top of a narrow table in the center of the stage. No sooner do we arrive, the show begins. A mule led in by two men straddles the table and the woman, its penis hanging between her spread legs. With practiced ease, she begins stroking the large organ until hard, and allows the beast to penetrate her. At first curious silence invades the crowd of mostly men, followed by nervous laughter, and then delirious applauds sweep through the arena of excited spectators. I am altogether dumbfounded, a sentiment of shock shared by my two companions.

We decide not to stay long; this kind of performance a bit raw for our still tender moralities. The whore remains behind, finding a more interested customer with richer taste. We spend the next hour trying to locate my vehicle. Fortunately, I remember a faded billboard advertising *Tecate Beer.* I suppose there could have been many such signs in Tijuana. Fortunately for us this landmark proves accurate; my distinctively red Ford only a few streets below parked on a curve.

Believing myself completely sober, I light-up a Marlborough, and start the reliable 301. Just as I pull out of the parking space, another vehicle appears out of nowhere, headlights off, and rams into the driver's door. The three of us pile out of the passenger side, since the driver's door side mangled and sealed shut. I circle around the back, grab the

Mexican driver of the other car before he can escape, pinning him firmly to the ground. He is drenched in Tequila, two empty bottles in the front seat. This individual so drunk he can barely stand, and keeps mumbling something in Spanish that sounds like *"sin Policia."*

"Come on Sgt— let's get the hell out of here before the Mexican police come!" One of my companions urges me.

I should have listened, but for me I am clearly not at fault. The position of the two cars, the fact that the offending driver too drunk to stand, and smells of Tequila-- makes me over-confident that there can be only one possible interpretation of the accident. Realizing there is no persuading me, my fellow Marines desert toward the border on foot, abandoning me to my own foolishness. It takes half an hour for the police to arrive. By this time, my captive has begun to sober.

"Gringo tonto-- Gringo tonto," he shouts repeatedly.

These are the only coherent words in his vocabulary, so I decide it just his way of hurling insults, or else a plea of release. Judging by the amount of damage to my car, it is unlikely I will catch and release. I dutifully surrender my prisoner to the first arriving officers, along with a detailed report of the event. They make notation of how the two automobiles positioned, examine the empty bottles in the offending vehicle, and commence to handcuff me.

"I'm not the one guilty," I protest.

They look at each other, say something in Spanish, and then handcuff the other man as well. Shoved together in the backseat of the police cruiser, my fellow prisoner begins vehemently screaming at me.

"Gringo tonto!"

He then spits in my face, swearing incoherently. Although handcuffed from behind, I give the fellow a violent head-butt, knocking the Mexican senseless. I am unaware at the time that he has been calling me "a stupid English-speaking American." Although this might be true within context, I still dislike that this SOB spit on me. The two cops only glance back at us and start laughing ghoulishly. I should have known this only the beginning of a very long night. Driven into the heart of downtown Tijuana, we are placed together into a common cell and remain handcuffed.

Mexican justice is an endurance of waiting with only an expectation of real justice. I suppose it like this in many places of the world. My Spanish nemesis, now sober, cowers in a corner, his bruised head buried between his knees. After some time, two different policemen enter our cell, handcuff us together, and herd us into the back of an enclosed truck. The engine starts and carbon monoxide fumes bellow into the cabin. I bang on the walls of the moving vehicle to no avail. After what seems an eternity, the vehicle comes to a stop, the door opens, and we are dragged disoriented into the fresh night air. As my head begins to clear, I realize I am in a hospital examination room. Someone I think is a doctor dressed in scrubs enters, takes one look at me, and signs a form attached to a clipboard. Herded back into the same truck, we are transported back to the precinct station by a more direct route.

Only now do I begin to comprehend the true gravity of my position. My Spanish speaking cellmate has altogether vanished. An appointed Mexican lawyer informs me he has been released on the bases he is penniless. Turns out he is not even the registered owner of the other vehicle. In Mexico a high volume of cars are purchased on a gray market to unlicensed drivers having neither registration nor proof of ownership. These cars are impounded and recycled into a system lacking legal oversight. I, on the other hand, have over three hundred dollars in my pocket--and someone-- anyone with money-- must be the one to pay!

"It looks very bad, Senor," my legal representative informs me next morning. "You have been in an automobile accident in Mexico, and have been charged with drunk driving."

"What do you mean?" I protest. "The accident was not my fault. It was the other driver who was drunk, not me."

"I am sorry, but according to the official doctors report you were intoxicated when brought into the hospital. I am afraid the law is clear on drinking and driving. You have only two choices, either pay the fines or prison."

I become irate. I rave about the gas fumes, about the fault of the other driver-- all to no avail! Returned to my cell and instructed to consider the consequences, I sit alone in silence, realizing completely the futility of my situation. An hour later, I call the jail keeper. I am ready to pay. It ends up costing me almost to the penny what I have in my wallet. Charitably, they leave me with ten dollars. Fortunately, I have another twenty stuffed into the toe of my shoes just in case. The police adjutant hands me a document along with directions to certain locations. I must go to each in specific order and get a paid seal stamped on the release form. Once this accomplished, I will be provided the secret location of my car. I spend the entire morning, traveling from one end of Tijuana to the other. Each place I must pay a small fee: anywhere from one dollar to three dollars. I arrive at the last building just after noon. A short little man, with the appearance of bureaucrats everywhere, has just hung a closed sign.

"*Estoy cerrada por el dia.*" Dryly says the teller putting on a sweat-stained jacket.

I plea for him to place the final stamp on my document, but he only shakes his head and slams shut the window of receipts. It is Saturday afternoon, which means the office closed until the following Monday. I next go to the U.S. Consulate building demanding justice and the return of my property.

"I'm sorry, son. Most likely, you will never see your car again. This kind of thing happens all the time. People forget Mexico is another country with its own laws. You should have taken out Mexican insurance at the border. There is nothing I, or the United States government can do for you."

Discouraged beyond words, I walk across the border back into the U.S.A., and catch a bus to San Diego less than 20 miles away. While waiting for the next morning bus to take me back to Oceanside, I stop in a Christian Serviceman's Center sponsored by the U.S.O., eat something, and fall asleep on a couch in the recreation room. No one bothers me-- and God knows I need the rest. The next morning, I return to base rested and broken.

The first thing I do Monday morning is contact the insurance company to assess my coverage. I still believe there is a chance to recover my car and only make inquiry about the accident deductible amount. The agent specifies that liability for theft is not covered in my policy. My next challenge is the most difficult of all. I call Rudy long distance.

"Dad," I implore embarrassed; "I need to borrow three hundred dollars."

I then proceed to explain to him the situation. I have calculated that with the repairs I need at least this much. I swear to repay him as soon as I can. There is a long silence. Rudy does not like to loan money; nor do we have the best history between us. With a deep sigh of promise, he agrees in his simple honest way to wire me the money by Western Union. This will be the only time I borrow money from him. It is also the first time I hold genuine respect for this man of stoic principals, without the specter antagonism of my childhood fear. I guess this moment he sees in me a little of himself while in the Navy. Maybe my experience helps him relive his younger days when he was free. Only Rudy's father never helped him; not even when he almost dies in an automobile accident. Because of this I feel sorry for my stepfather, feel sorry that everythingRudy did, he always had to do alone.

True to his word, the money arrives by Western Union on Wednesday. Next morning I put in for a 96-hour pass beginning on Friday in order to have two extra days beyond the normal weekend pass.

A fellow Sergeant gives me a ride as far as the border of *San Ysidro*. I arrive at the government office building with time to spare and get the final stamp of release. Here I receive directions to a junkyard located on the southern outskirts of the city. Why is my car in a junkyard?

"A junkyard," I repeat with dubious realization.

My worst fears are starting to play-out, a specter of acceptance that I might never again see my red Fairlane. Presenting my completed paper at the salvage yard entrance, the gate keeper returns my Marine Corps duffle bag stuffed with the contents of my glove compartment and trunk along with my Bowie Knife, but minus an expensive Marine issue diving watch I thought well hidden inthe spare wheel well.

"Where is my red Fairlane?" I demand sickly.

"I'm sorry Senor; no car like that here. Maybe you should ask the police."

I know this greasy Mexican is lying.

After several minutes of arguing the logic of having my bag returned, but not my car, I pretend to give-up and walk in the direction of the police station. Once out of sight, I circle around to the back and scale a wall with strings of bobbed-wire coiled along the top. A few scratches later and a rip in my pants, I am on the other side. Fortunately, I have brought along a spare key hidden in my base locker just in case.

Mountains of scavenged cars pile in every direction, many newer models, some in almost factory condition, gutted and stripped to the bare frames. Surely, my car somewhere among them, already decimated, or else gone, already sold to an interested buyer somewhere in deeper Mexico. Careful to avoid detection, I move stealthily through dark corridors of stacked automobiles. Half an hour later, I feel altogether discouraged. It is certain I will never set eyes on my Fairlane again.

Then I see it! Parked in a deeper shadow of a narrow alley hidden between two teetering stacks of wrecks, protrudes the distinctive front grill facing out. The driver side door and rear quarter panel badly smashed, but other than this, it is exactly as I remember. To my grander surprise, the keys still hang from the ignition. The engine turns-over easily, and I slip shift lever into drive, and nose the hood noses into sunlight.

The great escape begins! I begin navigating frantically through the maze of automobile carcasses in search of an exit. Emerging finally into a clearing, I spot the only entrance and exit of this place. Several Mexicans appear from behind junk piles carrying pipes and chains. The fat entrance attendant steps out and takes a position in the way holding a shotgun.

"By God— I'll take every one of you sons-of-bitches with me!" I howl in bulldog fashion.

Stomping hard on the gas pedal, the 301 Ford leaps forward, raising a fishtail cloud of red dust mixed with mud. I take deadly aim at the armed bandits. They scatter without a fight. The gate keeper, however, stands firm, with weapon raised. I am determined not to surrender my vehicle again. It is either him or me. He pulls the trigger, but I suppose the round a dud. As he fumbles to reload, I accelerate into passing gear with every intention of running down the fat bastard. In panic, he throws his shotgun, hitting the front bumper of my car and dives behind the safety of a tree.

I never slow down, taking the most direct route toward the border crossing. Judging by my recent experiences, I have little faith in the justice of this country. For all I know they might try to arrest me again for stealing back my own car.

To my relief, the border guard waves me through without incident. I immediately find a local body shop near a motel in San Diego. Dropping off my damaged car, I am guaranteed completion of repairs by Monday after noon. The owner of the shop is ex-Navy and understands the importance of military schedule. He is three hours late because of difficulty finding another door; nevertheless, I arrive back on base with time to spare. I could have gotten it done cheaper and faster in Mexico-- a chance not worth taking! I rest peacefully that night for the first time since more than a week. I dream I am in a firefight surrounded by Mexicans. It is a good dream; and by morning light, I have slaughtered them all.

Chapter 23
Beacon in the Night

a Supply Sergeant enjoys certain rank privileges. For one thing I rarely need to report to someone else, unless to confirm the completion of some important mandate. This freedom allows me to disappear for hours at a time, sometimes to nap in my car or listen to favorite hits on my new 8-track stereo. The best quirk of all is the day we receive a container of high-tech equipment that includes sniper riflescopes, Mark 2 Ka Bar combat knifes, and night vision binoculars. I quickly learn that Gunny and the Lieutenant thieves with expectations I join their syndicate.

"Look at it this way, Sergeant," the Lieutenant says, handing me one of several elegantly designed cobalt-grey hand weapons; "who's going to miss three pieces, so long as all our inventories match. It's not really stealing if we three agree, and we deserve something for our efforts. You are one of us now. If we don't stand together, then who else will?"

I can tell by his tone that I have little choice. Gunny eyes me like an old hound licking his lips in anticipation of his next morsel. I am either with them, or against them. I convince myself there is no harm in joining the conspiracy. Gunny and the Lieutenant are, after all, my superiors. As long as the three of us agree it is right, then it is right. At the time I never considered that they both live off base, and can easily stash their booty; whereas, my treasure trove remains in the trunk of my Fairlane. I am already destined for a fall, only never see it coming.

The last week of November, we begin practicing maneuvers off shore. An LP, smaller than the one that brought me back from Nam, takes us to a position about two miles from the beachhead loaded with several Amtrak vehicles. Each Amtrak contains a platoon of men packed like sardines in a tin can, which drives off the back of the extended platform, and sinks into the ocean depths. Several terrifying moments later, the vehicle only partially emerges just inches above the water line and begins dieseling toward the shore in military formation as a herd of belching hypos. It is particularly frightening to be inside one of these barely floating bricks. Especially disconcerting moments of total blackout, as these heavy armor-plated canisters descend into silence of the deep. Then a red florescence fills the narrow confined space glistening with sweat, the metal plates groaning with fatigue, the pressure building critically inside our ears. Finally, the pressure subsides, followed by instant relief of engines engaging and powering through the lull of ocean waves sloshing against and over the outer shell. The natural mind says that something this heavy cannot possibly float, but it does float by a calculated formula of volume displacement. Nevertheless, I cannot say I ever fully embrace the experience and often imagine myself trapped in a doomed submarine plummeting into an ocean grave. I am glad when this week of training finally ends.

I become increasingly bored with the passage of time. There is no more challenge; nowhere I wish to go, nothing I wish to do. I begin drinking more frequently and in greater quantities. I do not drink because of pain, or even because of habit. I drink because I feel nothing. And at least drunkenness feels like something forgotten. Everything everywhere begins to look the same to me. North, south, desert mountains, the blue passage of the Pacific Ocean— all elements existential of a world mixed together and infected with a parasite called humanity. I am only one of many; yet I am alone. I feel like a creature on the outside, becoming more isolated, more a monster each day. Occasionally, I pick up a whore if I am lucky, or buy a prostitute at a topless dancing bar in Oceanside whenever I feel rich enough. Nothing I do fulfilling for long. One Friday night I rent a motel room in San Clemente, buy a couple bottles of Seagram's Whiskey, and settle in for the weekend. I just need to get off the base, get away from everyone and everything. After a few beers at a local bar, I return to my room around 2300 hours. While lying on the bed watching TV, I notice another door adjacent to the bathroom. Thinking it another clothes closet, I open it.

Behind this door is another door, which to my surprise opens into another room similar to my own. Immediately, my eye catches a woman's black slip hanging on the edge of the closet door. Embarrassed, I quickly close the access, and go back to watching television. After a struggle of several minutes, curiosity gets the better of me. What could be the harm of doing a little exploring since no one home? In truth I feel a strange obsession for that glimpsed black garment, the vaguely remembered whisper of a Siren latent in darkest imagination. What I do next beyond explanation, beyond the rational of my manhood. I take the inviting article of clothing into my room and put it on. A feeling sweeps over me reminiscent of when I was a child first entering puberty. I masturbate several times, each orgasm less intense than the last. I cannot say it good, exactly, only different, a feeling of no longer being me!

Early next morning, I hear voices of a man and woman next-door. Those absent occupants of the attached room arrived. Jumping out of bed in panic, I round up all my things, including the soiled black slip, and skulk stealthily to my car.

The chill California morning, bright and clear, stings my conscience with full knowledge of my secret act. I feel altogether ashamed and perverted. I am a reprobate criminal with all eyes watching. I try to blame it on the alcohol, but I know it not just the alcohol. Something unexpected has happened, something that threatens to collapse the pretense of my entire existence. The burning question in my mind: *What am I?*

That entire day I drive up and down the coast with the body of my sin hidden in the trunk. I must get rid of the evidence. At sunset, I find myself parked in front of an isolated shore in North San Clemente at foot of a high cliff supporting a small vacant beach mansion reportedly owned by President Nixon. As red ball of the sun descends into the zenith where sea and sky mix together, I sadly lift the black carcass from the crypt of my car-trunk, remove my socks and shoes, and step into the relaxed surf at low tide. The garment floats momentarily, then flutters, disappearing into the graying depths as an animated shadow reborn. Another strange impulse overwhelms me. I feel suddenly to embrace her in this keep of solitude and peace, feel an irresistible desire to swim off into the red warmth of this sunset and to be free at last. The water reaches chest-high, the shock of a cold current impelling me with knowledge that my next step will be my last. I turn to survey the shore of men one last time.

In the dying embers of light, I vividly see something unexpected, something that shocks me back into the living moment. It is an image clear and unmistakable, radiant against the spreading twilight. A man hangs against the cliff face several feet from the top, wedged between rock crevices with arms out-stretched, appearing snared in helpless agony.

My first thought is this man has fallen, although miraculously saved, dangling injured and needing assistance. Without thinking, I exit the water and race toward position of this unfortunate victim.

Upon reaching the base of the cliff, last rays of light vanish below the horizon; only unrecognizable clumps of shadows remain. I continue to shout, straining against the darkness, but hear no reply; nor can I see anything that even resembles the crucified man seen so clearly from a distance. I would have reported the incident to the police, except that my conscience fears someone might identify me as a suspect entering a private motel room and stealing a woman's undergarment. Also, by now I am no longer certain if what I saw real or product of imagination.

I go back to my base that night, but return early next morning. The man is gone. Nor is there any semblance of the previous night's apparition so clearly witnessed. I come back to the same place at sunset, and still nothing. Over the next several days I check the San Clemente local paper for any mention of a rescue or a fatality, but finding nothing.

In time, I forget about the crucified man; forget about my indiscretion with an anomalous woman's slip. My sin buried in a watery grave; the evidence bound forever in the everlasting embrace of the deep. One of the Lance Corporals, named Harrison, is a self-proclaimed Buddhist of Japanese descent on his mother's side. He tells me that Buddhism more a discipline of philosophy, than a religion. I like Harrison because he has a calm intelligence that reminds me of Neider. The idea that this man professes a belief in something more than physical existence impresses me little. By now even Rudy's agnosticism seems a concept requiring greater faith than possible for me to consider. Nevertheless, I remember while in Nam that there were times in the still of night that something reached out and touched me; a thing strange and tangible: something that was there and yet not there. Also I remember voices of torment in the air, and the coldness that remained after. This is as close to things inexplicable as I wish to conjure. Still, there is a down to earth sincerity about Harrison that raises my curiosity. This man's rank less important to me than his perceived knowledge, a knowledge I wish to explore further.

One day he asks if I believe in spirits, so I share with him the time I floated disembodied among the stars; and how that some part of me did not wish to return. Then for some anomalous reason I share with him the recent phenomenon of the man crucified on the cliff face. How real it seemed, even though I could find no evidence of the event.

"It sounds as though very powerful demons have been trying to communicate through you," he replies reflectively.

"Demons," I chock in horror.

"We Buddhist believe there are good and bad demons all around us. Through alliance with these powerful entities, mortals can achieve great success, or commit great evil. It is important that one learns discipline and chooses wisely. True Samurai Warriors of the past embraced the importance of these alliances. The most important part of their training is to learn control, become one with their demon, and resist influence of other invaders. Or else, a more powerful demon will make the choice for you."

This talk about demons makes me uncomfortable. Suggestive of questions even more frightening! How to recognize or fight something unseen-- something that might be inside you? How might one bond with an entity old and immortal that exists beyond boundary of light and shadow?

The following weekend I accept to accompany Harrison to his Aunt's house in Laguna Beach. She works as a manicurist; her husband a gardener. Both their families incarcerated during the Second World War, as were many Japanese-Americans at the time. They lost everything; forced to start from scratch after end of the conflict. They live in a small lovely home in a part of town considered poor; and yet, by magic of tasteful design and skilled horticulture, an exotic garden blossoms behind their simple dwelling. Terraced walls support a forest of miniature flowering Bonsai Trees planted along a winding path and through a maze of connecting ponds stocked with behemoth gold fish carp that meander lazily just below the surface. A Japanese rock garden carefully placed along sandy furrows, a design steeped with significance to a culture I knew little about at the time.

Positioned in center of this Eden is a black lacquered box with two dove-shaped doors about thirty inches tall and twenty inches wide, which houses a calligraphy written scroll. On a pedestal placed in front of this miniature temple robustly sits the familiar idol of a gilded Buddha.

"This is our *Gohonzon*," the woman says with reverence, guiding us unerringly to the spot. "Here we chant the Mandala of Nichiren. This is the seat of a very powerful Buddha giving luck to those who chant believing."

I little comprehend the meaning, except that Harrison, his Aunt and Uncle, along with other invited acquaintances join here every Saturday to practice a customary ritual by chanting a rehearsed script in front of this significant shrine. The participants range in age, as well as demographics, each devoted to quests for riches and success. They believe that by chanting repetitiously *"Nam Myoho Renge Kyo"* in front of this *Gohonzon,* each has been blessed with supernatural prosperity. One claims a timely check appears mysteriously in the mail, while another becomes the recipient of an unexpected inheritance. Harrison's Aunt proclaims that a rush hour traffic jam evacuated before her eyes, or at least while her eyes closed during chanting. New cars, romantic encounters, even positions of success— all attributed to inspired moments of chanting in reverence to this *Mandala of Nichiren.*

Privately, I consider the whole idea silly; but upon listening to the severaltestimonies of those present, I begin to have a more open mind.

"What can be the harm in giving it a try?" I say to Harrison, assuming a position facing the effigy.

sitting Buddha-fashion with legs crossed, arms supported on our thighs palms-up, all begin chanting with eyes closed: "*Nam Myoho Renge Kyo*"over, and over in unison.

Harrison's Uncle rhythmically chimes a brass bell with each chant, creating a repetitive monotony at first irritating, but then lulls into a kind of relaxing rhythm. I do not receive the expected vision of some secret material desire, but do experience a most incredible lightness of being, as everything around me changes electric, endowed with energyever-present and omnipotent to my comprehension.

Here the source of another consciousness touching my consciousness since earliest memory. Here a worldly luminescence, darkly beautiful: a presence part of every particle contained within the matrix of existential reality. This is the defining force of Nirvana, the touch of a familiar spiritual being touching my spirit. My demon inspired with new understanding and determined purpose. This moment I embrace the seductive enticement of astral experience: atemptation to slip the bounds of mortal existence and meld into the mind of a powerful consciousness ancient as the universe. I perceive hierarchy's of force, principalities with destined purpose rising and falling into the ebb of a singularity from end to beginning. This immense mind of the universe trapped into cycle of entropy, destined to inevitable extinction, as all energy through thermodynamic dissipation. As majestic this revelation, I feel apprehensive to the greater meaning glimpsed through mortal present.

An infinite spark awakens suddenly in my being—something that has laid dormant in primal memory. I am that little child again transfixed by the infinite wonder of the stars cognitive for the first time: aware now of my demon and that demon aware of me.

Without consciously knowing it, this represents an initiation of mortal and immortal conflict. Waged in the balance is future of my immortal soul. Never again will I return to this garden of discovery, nor receive any of the trinkets so vigorously sought by these children of present hunger. Nor will that light so blinding in the moment remain light, but will change into darkness indescribable, becoming a collapsing void compressed into a dark center, grinding slowly the last of my humanity to dust.

"Did you receive anything?" Harrison enquires, as we drive back to base.

"More than I ever expected," I reply reflectively; "I think I saw my demon, and many others. Who knows— I might become a Buddhist one day."

Harrison only smiles, bobbing his head wisely, as any emissary sent on an important mission.

Chapter 24
The Color of Marine Green

I transfer Harrison to another barracks, deciding it better this way. I try chanting a few times, but riches never come, nor any more revelations. Becoming a loner, I have now entered a void, a place of spiritual dryness. Except now I am fully aware of just how dry it is. The Marine Corps wants to keep me. At Nineteen, I am the youngest Marine to make Sergeant E-5 in recent Corps history; and already on the list to make Staff Sergeant within three years, assuring a prosperous military career. Where else did I have to go? Home is now a dream of paradise lost; the future atlas written in distant clouds; but none of these dreams really my own.

"The Marine Corps needs good men like you," says the Adjutant, a well-seasoned Warrant Officer with flushed cheeks seated comfortably behind the perch of his desk, reminding me of a smiling corpulent bird heartily fedon insects in the peak of summer.

"Sign-up on the six year plan you will get five thousand dollars, the assignment of your choice, and theCorps will even make you an officer one day... if that's what you want."

He adds this with a hint of disdain in his voice. Warrant Officers are a breed of enlisted Privates, who have worked up through the ranks, some as high as Master Gunnery Sergeant, becoming a specialized rank between NCO and commissioned Officer. They are usually called Gunners, a term of maverick endearment. No Warrant Officer has less than eight years, time and grade, some much more. This most elevated "Gunny", respected on both sides of the isles, willfully shuns privilege of becoming an officer, empowered to say anything to anyone regardless of the other's rank. Considered experts in their field, capable of filling any chosen post, they go where most needed in the moment. All those that I have had privilege to meet lack a sense of humor.

History of the very first Warrant Officers were technically proficient career-men chosen from enlisted ranks because of their experience to serve as advisers and instructors to newly commissioned offices lacking field experience. Although appointed by the same process as commissioned officers, they remain a breed unto themselves, a unique phoenix born of military protocol. In civilian terms, these seasoned men in uniform considered as company executives. An unspoken mutual code of acceptance exists between higher-ranking officers and these mustangs of the military, demanding they be given the same courtesy and respectby lower ranking officers, as to any other superior. It is a fact that a W-3is the only rank in the service, who can tell Captains to go jump in a lake with impunity, and not even a Full Bird will challenge him openly. I am more than a little awed that a W-1 personally proposes I re-enlist, as though I stand in the honored presence of a General. Nevertheless, I still have not fully decided. The question: not if I will reenlist, but rather for how long and where to go? Six years seem like a long time. In reality, nine years counting the three inactive I still have left. Then again, how can I turn down this kind of money, as well as a promising career in an elite organization I have grown to love?

"Thank you, sir," I say with humble admiration, "I just want to make the right choice."

"Of course, Sergeant-- take all the time in the world! The Marine Corps is the best of the services, patient in choice, and looking only for the few and the proud."

I leave this meeting more gung-ho than ever, feeling truly honored in the presence of this old soldier, and all the soldiers like him, some fallen, all engraved with the immortal merit of loyal duty. It is like comprehending for the first time the meaning in Tennyson's poem Charge of the Light Brigade" that goes:

Cannon to right of them,
Cannon to left of them,
Cannon in front of them
Volley'd & thunder'd;
Storm'd at with shot and shell,
Boldly they rode and well,
Into the jaws of Death,
Into the mouth of Hell
Rode the six hundred"

However, an incident occurs a short time later that will cast a shadow of doubt on my future plans. By this time I deem Marine Corps protocol of discipline as a supreme doctrine. In my book, all men are Marine Corps green, all subject to the same rules. Vietnam had been a chaotic exception; stateside military a safe haven of hierarchal order distinctively restored. The events that happen next unthinkable and without justification to the proud few; especially those who have lived and died in the true spirit of *"Semper Fidalis."*

It is Friday night like any other Friday night. Men hurrying around the barracks, either preparing for a relaxing weekend on base or an off-base adventure, as each prepares for time they can call their own. As for me, I plan to go to an Oceanside topless dancing bar where I know an older woman named Katherine for whom I have a crush. I am just walking out of the shower, when one of the men intercepts me complaining that the music coming from the cubical areas too loud. It is loud, so loud that it completely drowns out all other ambient noise.

"You men turn down the blaster," I order the three black men dressed in white Mess uniforms.

There is a nod of compliance, as one of the three lowers the volume. I retire into my quarters, make a quick change into civilian clothes, splash my face with aftershave, and feel like a nickel in the sun. Five white men are waiting outside my quarters looking distrait.

"Sgt you gotta do something about that music," pleads the tallest one.

I immediately comprehend his meaning. The same inconsiderate music dominates the environment, defiantly blasting a Hendrix tune.

"I told you men to lower the music," I command, stepping to the opposite side of a sleeping rack where the three brothers gather.

They jump up in unison. One of them shoves the metal framed bunk bed sleeping rack, violently striking me in the forehead. I realize immediately my rank provides no immunity, as these three men nearly twice my size swarm around me. I take a defensive stance in preparation for deadly battle. With the palm of my hand, I strike the mouth of the first in range, sending him down with blood streaming down his face.

Another, I kick in the ribs, and then in the groin. I would have finished him were it not for the third, who grabs me around the neck from behind. The other two recover and lunge viciously at me. Somehow, I manage to twist free and grab a heavy electric floor sweeper abandoned during evening cleanup. The heaviest part makes contact with one of my attackers, sound of a loud crack, shattering his arm below the bicep, putting this one permanently out of commission. This provides opportunity for the other two to regroup. Again, I am in a choke hold from the rear, as another assailant lifts my feet off the floor by the front.

I see my fellow marines forming an arena of spectators, passively watching the kill, not one wishing to intervene. An all familiar scenario witnessed before. Just then, three hard-hat MPs with nightsticks break through the crowd-- my rescue just in time.

Except for a little blood and a few bruises, I am unharmed-- my Marine Corps pride suffering most. I report to the MPs the events leading up to the attack and am provided the proper paperwork to 'write-up' these thugs in uniform. For me the case is clear and simple: three privates   have disobeyed a direct order and assaulted a superior. My expectationis that Marine Corps justice will prevail.

These are the beginning days of the nineteen-seventies, a revolt of racial division redefining America's new post-war identity. The Beatles are now re-branded with a crisp new green Apple Records logo, the flower children already wilting along with the disgrace of defeat. The lyrical guitar of Jimmy Hendrix is now the new definition of electric rock. And unknown to me, it is also the new era of Black Power, as millions of subjugated Americans break oppressive shackles of past prejudice. I do not say that racism did not exist in the service. However, in my limited experience, it was rare and not systemically tolerated when the ugly head reared. Nevertheless, something has begun to change in my nation, something poisoning even to the integrity of the Marine Corps. I never considered possibility that this military I knew and served loyally for nearly three years might be rotten at the core. This night beginning revelation of the new reality.

Race related incidents start being reported weekly. A white man found stabbed to death in the alley between two barracks; a black man hanged from a flagpole. The divides continue to escalate, becoming a clearly identifiable race war between segregated tribes of black and white. The media has gotten wind of the growing violence, every incident considered news of contention, demanding full disclosure. But it really becomes a gut reality one morning just prior to morning reverie. I awaken to the presence of several shadows hovering over my bunk.

"We Brothers take care of our own," someone wearing a mask whispers gruffly. "We are going to warn you only once. Drop the charges, or you will never testify at the Court Martial."

I comprehend my imminent peril. Somehow, these men have gotten past the barrack's watch and into my private chambers. Or maybe the barrack's watch compromised, a mystery I will never know for sure.

"Get the fuck out of my chambers, Marines!" I shout defiantly, angered by this violation.

A sudden swooshing of air followed by something heavy impacting the pillow just beside my head; it is sound of a weighted heavy steel padlock inside a woolen sock.

"I said to get the fuck out of my barracks!" I command coolly and roll over on my side, pretending not to care.

Maybe in this moment, I really do not care. Or maybe I realize that the advantage not in my favor this time, left with very few options. I wait tensely for what might follow, calculating my next moves when the attack comes. Not exactly a brave action, certainly not even smart; but I really did not know what else to do, deciding a bluff my best recourse. Fortunately the bluff works, as one by one these assassins leave. Maybe they conclude that since I cannot be intimidated, their only other choice to kill me— and I might take at least one down with me. Or maybe just enough Marine Corps discipline remains in memory of their training to psychologically deter against a cowardly attack on one of their Sergeants.

This early morning incident only makes me all the more determined. The tensions continue to increase daily, representing a silent crisis eating from the inside. The Civil Rights Movement, which had begun peacefully with Martin Luther King, now ended by the brutal slaying of this man of higher values. His vision of peace meant to reunite America by restoration of dignity to a people forgotten in the rush to build a better and more prosperous nation. This man's assassination ignites fumes of oppression bottled-up through generations of oppression. Everyone else in America just tired of paying the price of an unending commercial war. I find myself at the butt end of these many changing values and restructuring of loyalties now sweeping across the United States continent. At the time, how could I possibly have known whatwas really happening in my nation of shielded politics?

"Sergeant," the Battalion Full Bird begins gravely, after an urgent summons to his office, "in times like these one must consider what's best for the Corps. I have seen your record, son. You need to put your personal feelings aside." Then eyeing me steadfastly, "you do understand my meaning, son?"

"No sir," I reply honestly perplexed.

"I am referring to the attack in your barracks last weekend. You ruffed-up those boys pretty bad."

"Sir, those men disobeyed an order and assaulted me without reason. I was only protecting myself."

"Of course you were. But you have to think about how the media might perceive things. One of those men is still in the hospital, and all three were black-- and you obviously being from a southern state."

I cannot believe what I am hearing. Three privates the size of gorillas assail an NCO-- my tactics of defense questioned because of my place of nativity, and because of how the media might perceive the event!

"Sir, those men attacked me knowing that I am their NCO; and I have been threatened with physical violence since then. This has nothing to do with race, and everything to do with the honor of the Marine Corps. Those men deserve discipline, and I will not back down from my duty to see that justice carried out."

After a long silence, the Colonel takes a sealed folder sitting on his desk and drops it into the wastebasket.

"I'm sorry Sergeant, but in the present interest of the Marine Corps, this event never took place. One day you will understand— dismissed Sergeant."

Just like that, all testimony of the incident erased from the records. Maybe a part of me did want revenge; but the more sober part demanding Marine Corps justice. Once again, I feel isolated through the bearing of my position, betrayed by a flawed hierarchy, realizing once again that military protocol more a convenience, than statue of guaranteed.

I make a visit to the NCO club that evening and allow myself to get really pissed. I also understand something else for the first time: the real reason why military men end up drinking away their frustrations and their lives of sold conscription. This only a beginning descent into valleys of deep soul-searching!

Chapter 25
Messengers Sent from Beyond

*E*ven Lieutenant Jackson begins having an attitude. It is not so much what he says, but how he says it.

"Been ruffling-up any more brothers, Sergeant?" He asks nonchalantly one morning as I enter the warehouse.

I know what he means, and so does Gunny, only he prefers to remain neutral. His only loyalty his stomach, and cares about nothing so long as he gets fed. Gunny has been married more than ten years to a Mexican whore he met on the streets of Tijuana. According to rumor, she was less than faithful during the first few years of their union, until she became pregnant with twins and forced to settle down. Even according to Gunny the woman fat and discontented, defiantly reconciled to raise their two children in a cramped trailer located just outside the front gate. Nor does Gunny know for certain if he is truly the father. I also think it little matters to him as long as he finds his wife home at the end of every duty shift. Gunny is not a bad person, just lacks self-dignity, too easily contented, looking toward the day of his pending retirement and the salad days to come.

I feel more alienated than ever before. I have lost respect for the one abiding principal that defines meaning to my existence. The Marine Corps has become as a father and a mother to me; I the coronate son of promise. Now I am aware to the Machiavellian reality of politics, my personal honor sacrificed on the altar of public opinion. I still plan to reenlist. Only now, I will do it just for the money.

I drink more than ever before. Not because I like the feeling of drunkenness more; rather, I like that alcohol makes the bitterness taste sweeter. Southern California becomes as a familiar stomping ground. I wander up and down the coast, exploring every bar in every little town between San Diego and Los Angeles. I prefer San Diego more than L. A., mostly because of its nearer proximity. Also, it feels somehow safer and more familiar. Perhaps, the maze of one-way streets that travel crisscross for miles provides the greatest comfort, knowing that here I can never get lost. I am worse than lost-- only I do not know it.

One Saturday around midnight, I find myself in a district of San Diego city new to me. Parking my car near a square just off El Cajon Boulevard, I discover a restaurant named The Philadelphia Deli and order a highly recommended famous Michigan sandwich. Although exotic sounding, it is nothing more than a stale subway roll drowned in greasy meatball sauce. Fortunately, I have the stomach of a teenager. After the wash of a couple of beers I could just as easily have finished a prime steak dinner.

Opposite the square, an all-night movie theatre with the new release of a film starring Tom Laughlin called Billy Jack. A typical macho testosterone tale about one man's determined stand against injustice, I think the billing to be appealing. As a military man on the prowl, you learn a few things. For example, an all-night theater is a great place to sleep-off a hangover, or just to sleep. I pay my ticket price, find a seat near the middle, and settle in for the night. At around three a.m., I awaken to find a young pretty girl beside me wearing a pink miniskirt.

"I must have fallen asleep," I mumble shyly, righting myself.

This is when I realize that she has her hand on the crotch of my pants. She only looks at me, her eyes cool and unwavering. After a few uncomfortable moments, I lean forward and kiss this unexpected seraph. I know even then that there is something different about her, something familiar that I cannot quite discern with the intellect.

"Will you give me five dollars if I make you feel good?" She asks matter-of-factly in a voice that does not altogether match her demure.

Five dollars is all I have left, but in the moment I can little imagine spending it on anything better. I will not say that I did not know what she was. I knew, even if my mind refuses to accept it at the time. We end up making out on the carpeted floor littered with the garbage of spent chewing gum, empty containers, and used condoms behind the back bleachers. All the while Billy Jack continues to exact angry revenge on thosedeserving punishment, as he has done all night.

Because she does not wish for me to venture under her tight skirt, I end up having an orgasm by rubbing against her taunt body. It is one of the best encounters I have had since a long time, satisfying to an immediate hunger. But also, I feel emptier, as though a little of my soul drained away through the experience: an anomalous act of selfishness, being only about lust in the moment, disconnected and bestial.

At some point, I must have fallen asleep again, because when I open my eyes she is gone like an unreal spirit in a dream. In a way I wish it had been a dream; yet deep down I know it is not, and that the sin real. The bright Southern California sunrise burns painfully into my eyes upon exiting the darkened interior of the movie theatre. It is Sunday morning, the coolest time of the day, an incandescent mist that clings heavily to everything. Also, this is the coolest time of the day, when all made pure, cleansed of imperfection, a city of seeming light glittering in the sun.

It is another weekend like so many others. A Corporal from my unit named Emmet accompanies me on a trek of discovery. Saturday night we both meet girls at a popular dancing bar in San Diego. They promise to get us into a swanky club near the downtown core. Their scheme is to volunteer Emmet and me to take part in a magician's act. Ushered into a large room located behind the stage along with several other volunteers, a tall well- dressed man holding a gilded pocket watch proclaims that he intends to hypnotize us all.

"I will strip you of the layers you think to be, and discover what you really are below consciousness of the flesh," the Magician promises in a labored German accent. "More importantly I will take you back— back to a time before. Yes, you will regress to a time before time itself. Perhaps some of you perished in bloody battlefields of wars lost in history. Some of you inhabited the chambers of Kings and Queens; some sexy movie stars; some tyrants and monsters unspeakable. Look— look deeply into my watch, and see your hidden worlds through time revealed!"

I think the idea of being hypnotized tantalizing, as I imagine being anyone else except me: perhaps a beautiful bombshell, an intelligent leading gentleman, a hero warrior of strength, or a damsel in distress. He begins walking through the audience, speaking softly, his voice becoming a soothing unintelligible drone. He stops, stares into the eyes of a portly man and makes a command.

"You are a Chicken."

Immediately the man leaps from his seat and starts clucking loudly. To someone else with a full beard, he says:

"You are my lovely assistant, and will do anything I wish you to do."

Like the other, this person changes altogether different, begins touching his breast provocatively and starts prancing giddily around the Magician, like a not so pretty assistant.

He next approaches me, speaking in a tone that I do not quite understand.

"Excuse me," I say, "could you repeat that?"

He looks into my eyes for several seconds, and then continues his sweep through the crowd. After choosing five hypnotized men for his show, the rest dismissed. As promised, Emmet and I receive the reward of free tickets for us and our dates. I later ask Emmet if I was hypnotized and if I did something I do not perhaps remember.

"I don't think so Sgt." He replies hesitantly. "But just for a moment you did look strange, like he was speaking to you with his eyes. But I guess you didn't hear so well, because he shivered a little, stepped back, and moved on."

Once inside the club, we altogether lose our dates. They have what they wanted; entry into this swanky aquarium of sharks and barracudas, immediately attacked as fresh tuna. We, on the other hand, are undesirable guppies in a tank of dangerous underwater predators. Fortunately, neither of us is on any one's specific diet. Although this reprieve little comforts us in the moment, we probably were saved from jaws of things less pleasant, only ignorant at the time of aquarium habitats during feeding.

The main attraction of the Magician's show is a dramatic stage repeat of what we had already seen, involving the preselected five candidates. I think we both think the show rather boring, or maybe just too drunk by now to appreciate it. We end the evening by crashing on a couch at a Christian halfway house for servicemen on Adams Boulevard, and begin Sunday morning with a breakfast of eggs and a Bloody Mary. Later in the day, we go to the original San Diego SeaWorld, considering it more civilized than the cesspool of scavengers attended the night before. The communities of Seals are particularly engaging, which displays playful innocence I find enviable. Something I have so completely lost by now. It is past 1700 hours by the time we arrive back in Oceanside tired, hung-over, and penniless. Yet, neither of us wishes a return to base just yet. We go to a Christian Coffee House near the main, hoping to fill our empty stomachs and pass a few relaxing hours. Unfortunately the establishment altogether out of food and coffee, which also explains why only two soles there. As we prepare to depart, an older man engages me and begins quoting Bible scripture.

"The next day, as they went on their journey and drew near the city, Peter went up on the housetop to pray, about the sixth hour. Then he became very hungry and wanted to eat; but while they made ready, he fell into a trance and saw heaven opened and an object like a great sheet bound at the four corners, descending to him and let down to the earth. In it were all kinds of four-footed animals of the earth, wild beasts, creeping things, and birds of the air. And a voice came to him, "Rise, Peter; kill and eat."

Of course, I have no idea what he is saying or why he is even saying it.

"You have no cake or coffee, and you talk to me about food?" I chide hysterically, and then motion to Emmet it time we get out of here.

We go down the stairs and cross to the other side of the street with intention of catching a military bus back to the solitude of our barracks. Upon reaching the opposite curb, a frail elderly woman clutches my arm and implores I come into the adjacent building to hear choir music.

"Why should I want to do that, Grandma?" I demand sarcastically. She says, smiling shrewdly into my eyes.

"Because there is coffee and cake inside, and I know you boys are looking for something."

Once inside, we take a front row seat oblivious of what is to come. In all honesty, I thought the half dozen or so offerings from many local churches an etiquette lacking true value of entertainment. The sound of their many voices irritating to my military conditioning, as within I stoically label the noise of their singing a pious annoyance of squawking birds standing between me and a banquet table. Perhaps, my soul is lost; but my flesh also hungry. By will of Marine Corps discipline, I will hold my position with determined fortitude to eat my heart's desire of the clean and the unclean prepared at the end of this serenade.

Still a little hung-over from the night before, Emmet and I are less than respectful, neither of us having much church experience. Most of these choir members are young and clean-cut, as one might imagine religious members to be. Still under the influence of a weekend alcohol splurge, we make total fools of ourselves, taunting the young men, and making impolite jesters toward the girls.

Last to sing is a Christian Rock quartet calling themselves *The Choinia*, a group from a non-denominational gathering in north Long Beach. Two of three young men have hippie-style long hair, popular since the music revolution beginning in the mid-sixties; the third a cowboy picking skillfully an acoustic guitar. The lead singer is a lovely tall blonde girl resembling a flower child from the days of Woodstock, an Ophelia with blossoms sprouting from her summer hair and with eyes of glittering topaz. I am entranced by pureness of her presence from moment the music begins, unable to avert my gaze, transfixed by spark of living light ignited out of a churning void swirled from another space. The melody not of this world; but is a chorus of spirits indwelling the mortal voices of these unorthodox latecomers. A peculiar peace ebbs into my soul, an indefinable light permeating everything around us. This phenomenon touches me profoundly. Even Emmet, who rarely expresses any emotion at all, grows quiet and teary-eyed.

"It's beautiful," I say transfixed.

"Beautiful," Emmet mumbles from far away.

By end of this heavenly performance, Emmet and I feel as naughty schoolboys, ashamed of our former transgressions. The prepared feast in an adjacent room now small reward compared to the phenomenon of this celestial vision, an earthly repast greatly diminished in shadow of greater substance.

"My name is Karen. Did you like our singing?"

It is the voice of an angel, soft and feminine, a voice as pure as any I have ever heard, instantly filling the void of my emptiness. Upon turning around and facing this lovely apparition, my heart melts instantly into the clear blue of her eyes, making me feel somehow ashamed without really knowing why.

"The best music I have ever heard."

"It is given by inspiration of the Holy Spirit. We are all only instruments of God's will, even if always we don't know it."

Of course, I have no idea what she is saying-- at least not through the logic of my mind. We talk for several minutes, the words less important than the meaning. Before leaving with her companions, Karen hands to me a piece of paper with a Long Beach address scribbled on it.

"This is the location of our congregation. I hope you and your friend will attend the eleven o'clock service next Sunday morning."

I thank her and stuff the note into my shirt pocket. At this particular moment, I think to myself that I might actually go. After eating our fill, Emmet and I return to base broke, but contented, both reflective to meaning in recent events. This night I take a walk beneath wonder of a California desert sky. It is a night particularly extraordinary, night of a full moon coursing through corridor of the Milky Way. This not the first time I see stars fixed in a hemisphere so wondrous. There also slithers shadow of the dragon slipping surreptitiously through dark places in my mind with eyes smoldering: eyes that have haunted specter of my thoughts always, reminder of things past, and fear of an enemy not dead.

I toss the piece of paper on top shelf of my locker and forget all about it. This has become my way after every weekend excursion. The way clouded in oblivious forgetfulness and blotted-out before rising of the sun. However, this night I dream of a glittering angel singing beyond shroud of another dragon night and sleep for a change more peaceful.

www.ingramcontent.com/pod-product-compliance
Lightning Source LLC
Chambersburg PA
CBHW060853120626
46553CB00001B/67